Gun Digest PRESENTS

CARTRIDGES OF THE AR-15

A COMPLETE GUIDE TO AR-15 AND AR-10 AMMO

PATRICK SWEENEY

Published by

Gun Digest® Books, an imprint of Caribou Media Group, LLC

Gun Digest Media
5600 W. Grande Market Drive, Suite 100
Appleton, WI 54913
www.gundigest.com

To order books or other products call 920.471.4522
or visit us online at www.gundigeststore.com

CAUTION: Technical data presented here, particularly technical data on handloading and on firearms adjustment and alteration, inevitably reflects individual experience with particular equipment and components under specific circumstances the reader cannot duplicate exactly. Such data presentations therefore should be used for guidance only and with caution. Caribou Media accepts no responsibility for results obtained using these data.

ISBN-13: 978-1-9462-6785-6

Edited by Chuck Smock
Cover and Interior Design by Dave Hauser
Cover Photo by Yamil Sued

Printed in the United States of America

10 9 8 7 6 5 4 3 2 1

contents

INTRODUCTION

Author Patrick Sweeney began shooting under the sharp eye of his father, a combat vet of Europe. In the course of a varied career, he ended up competing in IPSC and bowling-pin matches, and formed and shot on two gold-medal winning U.S. revolver teams at the IPSC World Shoot, in 2005 and 2011. In bowling-pin competition, he quickly joined the small cadre of competitors who earned Master Blaster status in both handguns and long guns, and added Trivia Master Blaster, one of three people so honored. While doing all that, he learned gunsmithing, and in the space of a couple decades spent that time both fixing customers' guns and building his own competition guns needed to win matches. He also became a law-enforcement instructor and armorer, as well as setting out on the path of gun writer. In the course of writing 30-plus books, more than 1,000 articles, competing in four World Shoots, over two dozen national championships, and attending over two dozen LE firearms courses, he has achieved a pair of millions: one million rounds fired, and one million words written.

The AR-15, in all its guises, is now America's Rifle. There have been other American Rifles in the past. The list is long. The American gun-buying public is not fickle, but is more than willing to adjust to new technologies and needs.

At the founding, the rifle was the Kentucky rifle. With a long barrel (both for longer powder burn in the bore and longer sight radius) and slender lines, it was both elegant and effective. No, we didn't win the American War of Independence with them, that came about because we found the men willing to shoulder smoothbore muskets, and slug it out with British regulars. But rifles sure helped.

Then, when we expanded past the Appalachian Mountains, we found the smallbore Kentucky rifles, at only .38 to .45 calibers, were too small for the game there. That lead to the Hawken, a shorter, heavier and bigger-bore rifle, meant for work on big game like bison.

The next change came when cartridges came along. There was a split between the high volume and low power (relatively speaking) of repeaters, and the power of single shots. The exemplars there were the Henry rifle, with its short .44, later the 1866 Winchester, with centerfire cartridges, and the .45-70 in the form of the "Trapdoor" Springfield.

Inventors worked hard to marry the capacity of repeaters with the power of the .45-70, and the result were rifles like the Winchester 1886 and the Marlin 1895. These were lever actions, and they reigned supreme for many decades. From the end of the Civil War, to the end of the Great War, lever-action rifles were America's Rifle.

The experience of doughboys with the Winchester 1917 and the Springfield '03, brought bolt actions to the fore. This was not because lever actions got old. No, they still served as well as they had all along, the big change that required a bolt-action rifle was the change in bullet design. As long as bullets were designed for black-powder rifles, or derived from those designs, bolt actions had only a small advantage.

Spitzer bullets changed that. A lighter, but still heavy enough, bullet in a spitzer design, would have a flatter trajectory than the same caliber bullet of the full weight and round-nose design.

The example here is the cartridge that became the .30-06. Originally the .30-03, it featured a 220-grain, round-nosed, full-metal-jacket bullet at an optimistic 2,200 fps. It probably only did 2,100 fps, and at that it was heck on bores. The fast-burning rifle powders of the time were rough on rifling. Had the Army wanted to, it could have kept the new cartridge down at the ballistics of the previous cartridge, the .30-40 Krag. But where's the fun in that?

The British had already been down that road, their Cordite powder was even harsher on bores, and they had to deal with that and not make their new Lee-Metford rifles a thousand-round-use tool. No kidding, essentially accuracy could be gone that quickly.

The development of the spitzer bullet, the pointed-nose bullet, made round-nose bullets obsolete overnight. Changing the .30-03 to the .30-06, and the bullet from a 220-grain round nose at 2,100 fps to 173-grain spitzers at 2,700 fps, meant a soldier could count on a hit out past 300 yards, without changing his sights.

Lever-action rifles can't use spitzer bullets, at least not until Hornady developed the LEVERevolution bullet a century later. The points, in a tubular magazine, could and will detonate the primer of the cartridge ahead. Bolt-action rifles, using the magazine system designed by Peter Paul Mauser, make bullet shape only a matter of reliable feeding.

Bolt-action rifles ruled the roost for hunting and competition for decades afterward.

Right after World War II, there was an increase in autoloading rifles, but it was limited. In competition, bolt actions held on quite well for some time. Mainly due to their much better accuracy over autoloaders. Once the armorers figured out how to make an M1 Garand or M14 as accurate as a bolt action (or at least, hold 10 ring and X ring) the match organizers had to separate the two types, else all the medals would go to the autoloaders.

In the hunting fields, autoloading rifles had a following, but they never elbowed the bolt and lever guns out of the picture completely during the 20th century. The Remington 740, then 742, 7400 and so-on, gained more and more popularity, but they were part of the hunting, not claiming most of it. That was due in part to power. Deer hunters felt then, and many still do, that the .30-30 is the minimum caliber that gets the job done, and the only way to go smaller is to go up a good deal in velocity. That gets you to the .243 Winchester. With a five-shot maximum magazine capacity, and such a high threshold of power needed, autoloading rifles were going to be relatively large and heavy. A Remington 742, bare and unloaded, tips the scales at 7.5 pounds. But deer hunters would rarely use a rifle lacking a scope and sling; and by the time you get it loaded and equipped for hunting, the weight was closer to 10 pounds.

A lever-action .30-30, or a bolt-action rifle, could easily be made two pounds lighter. More than three pounds lighter in the case of the .30-30, if the shooter used iron sights. A not unreasonable choice, given the accuracy expected of a .30-30, and the anticipated engagement distances.

A couple things changed that.

First, the seemingly endless waves of gun-control efforts, aimed to a greater and greater degree at the AR-15. Starting back in the historical (now) era of the 1980s, revving up to the Gun Control Act of 1994, the AR was vilified. The more it was damned, the more people wanted it.

Then, when the act sunset (a rarity in legislation) in 2004, the doors were flung open and the flood began.

It has been calculated that in the years from 2008 to 2016, some nine million AR-15 or AR like rifles were manufactured and sold. The interest and demand have caused a sea change.

I talked with my friend and fellow gun writer Dave Fortier about this some years ago. He lives in Kansas, and, at an industry get-together, I made an offhand comment about lever guns in truck rear windows. He told me he hardly ever saw a lever-action rifle in a truck window anymore because, "all the kids had ARs." And a lot of the older drivers, also. If you were keeping a rifle in the truck, in case you saw a coyote that needed shooting (basically, any/all of them) then an AR was a better tool for the task than a lever action.

More women have started hunting in recent years, and for most women the classic Remington 742, chambered in .30-06, is too much. More than they need on deer, and more than they want to shoot. It is not condescending to point out that the average women in America, at just under five-feet, four-inches, and weighing 164 pounds, is not going to like shooting a .30-06. (And yes, 164 pounds is the best average I could find in statistics searches. In 1960, the average woman weighed under 140 pounds. I blame Big Sugar.)

But, hunting regs in most jurisdictions do not allow ".22 caliber rifles" for hunting. This dates back to the Depression, and efforts to control poaching. The idea was to keep people from shooting deer with .22 Long Rifle cartridges, which were (and are) marginal at best for the job, and a miserable end for a deer-so-shot and not immediately killed.

This, and prohibitions against full-metal-jacket ammo (again, in the best interests of humanely bagging deer) meant the AR, and its .223 cartridge, were off-limits.

That, however, acted as an impetus to cartridge designers and firearms experimenters, to see what DNR-approved cartridges they could wrestle into the AR-15 platform. In due time, with the expansion of the wild hog problem, even bigger cartridges came about, because hog hunting isn't hunting, it is pest control.

And as a result, we have cartridges, from the biggest to the smallest, in the AR-15 like we have not seen since the post-WWII days of wildcatting.

OK, here's a test. How many cartridges can you think of, off the top of your head, that the AR-15 can be purchased in? How many, with a good riflesmith, can be made to fit? Got a number? You're likely wrong. Some probably are at no more than half of the actual total. And there probably will be more between the time I send this to my editor, and it comes off the printing press.

What we're doing here is listing them, their history, their uses and the modifications, if any, needed to make an AR-15 you are building, re-building or modifying. You might be surprised. I was. You might even be amazed at the ingenuity of some approaches.

The ground rules are simple: It has to be an AR-15, or started life as, or be recognized as, an AR-15. And it has to be a real, actual cartridge you can buy ammo for or make. A lot of them are right there in the catalog or were for a time. A few you have to do yourself, but hey, that can be fun.

Hang on and stick with us. This is going to be a fun ride.

DEDICATION

This book is dedicated to all those we wish to protect, who depend on us and who are secure in the knowledge that we will do all within our abilities to keep them safe.

For some, it is the populace they serve. For others, it is the country. For me, it is family and friends.

That those who protect us, and we who protect ourselves, often select (or are issued) an AR-15 or something like it, makes the AR the modern tool; the 21st century equivalent of the Roman Gladius.

All of us owe a tip of the hat to the experimenters and researchers who have improved the AR-15 since its inception. I have said, and love to repeat, that the Army has been trying to replace it with something "better" since before it was forced to adopt the M16. That it has failed is due in part to the cleverness of Stoner and Sullivan, but also the persistence of the improvers.

In particular, I dedicate this to Felicia and the poodle pack, now down to one, but a very smart, very devoted one he is.

— Patrick Sweeney
January 2020

1

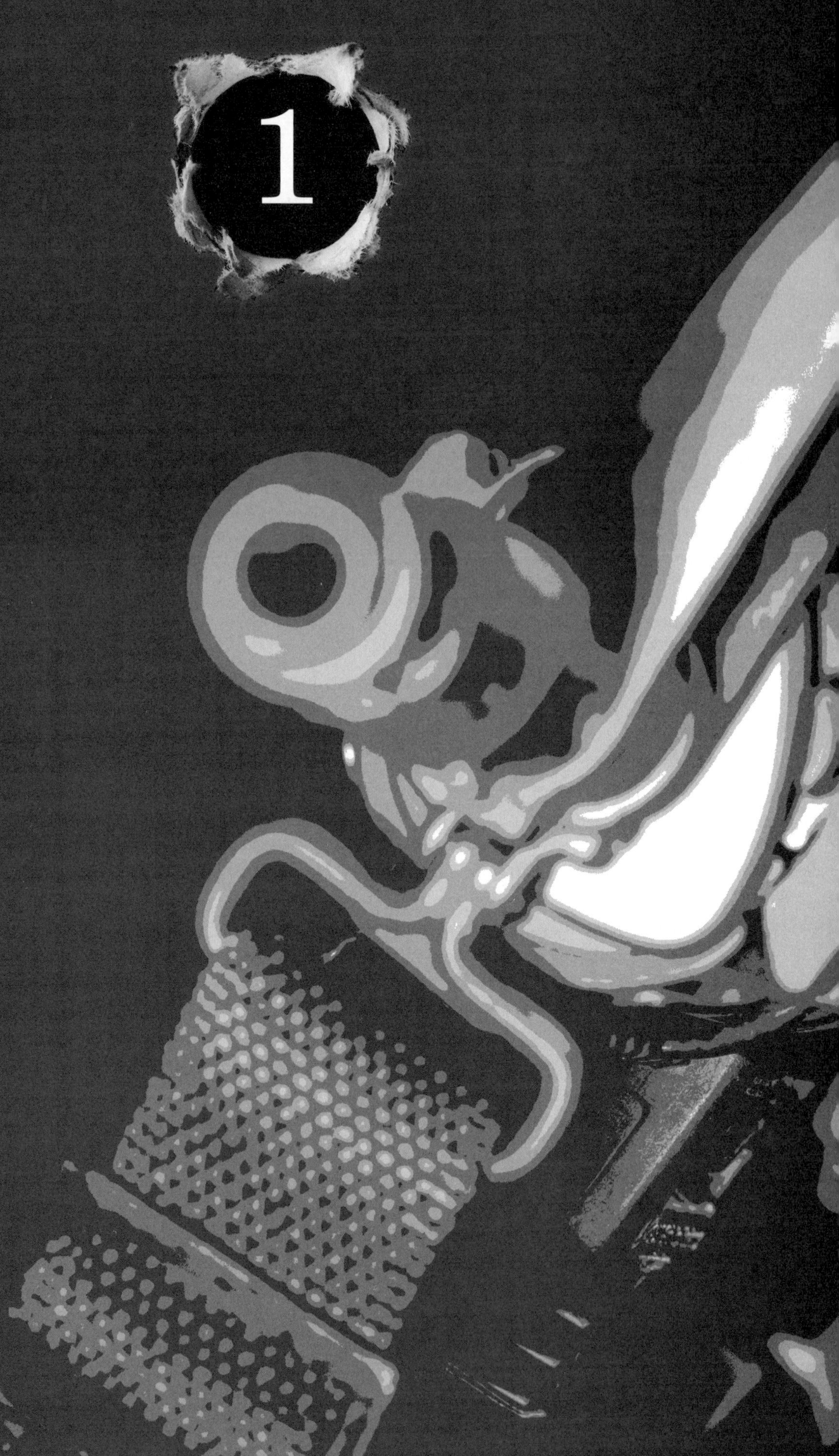

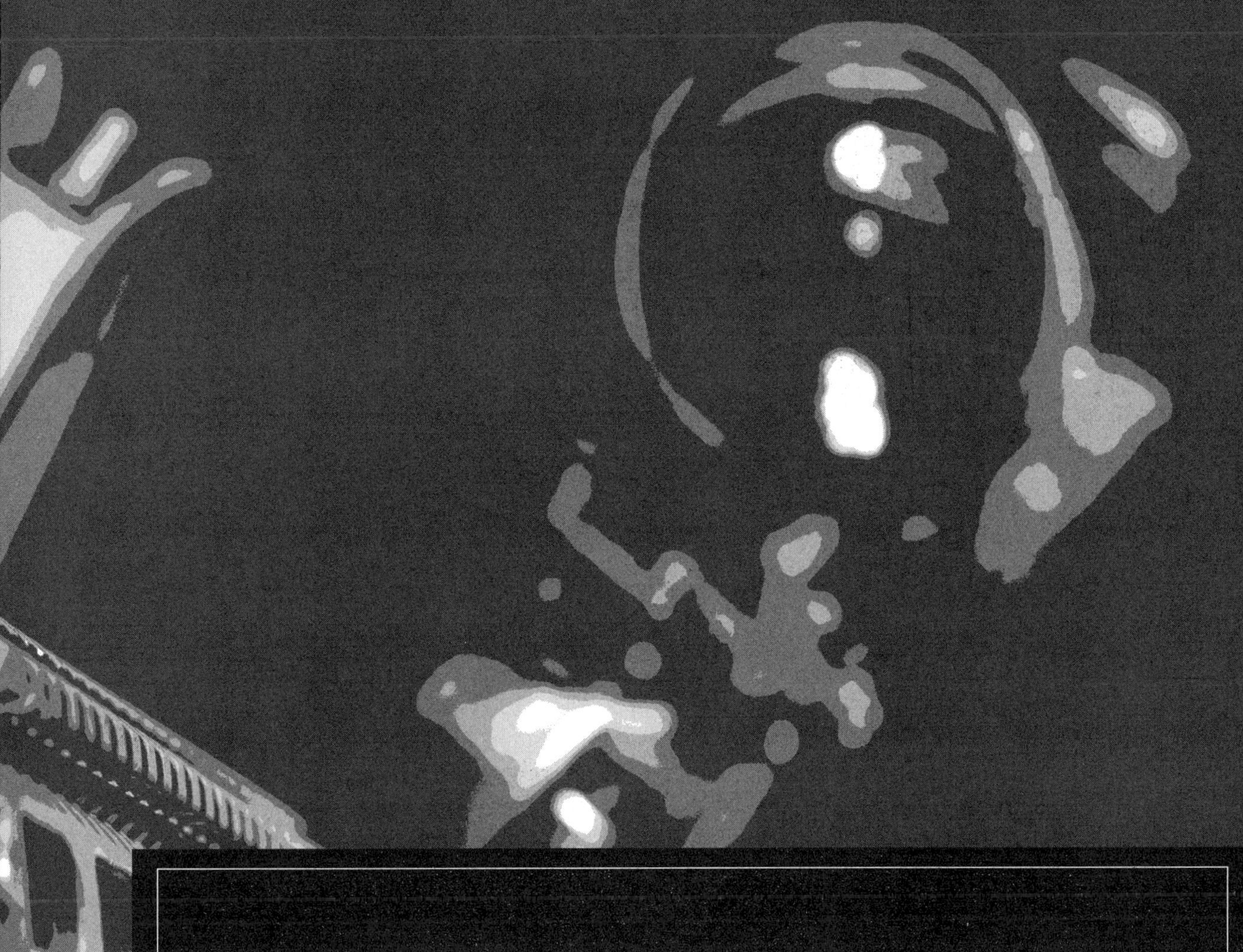

WHY THE AR-15?

The flippant answer would be "Why not?" But the technical answer is a bit more involved. It comes down to a combination of industrial design and "because I can."

Unlike earlier firearms, the AR-15 was designed to be an industrial product. Let's take as an example, the Springfield '03 rifle. Lots of people "sporterized" them back in the day. (And have long since incurred the wrath of collectors, who wish the rifles had been left alone.)

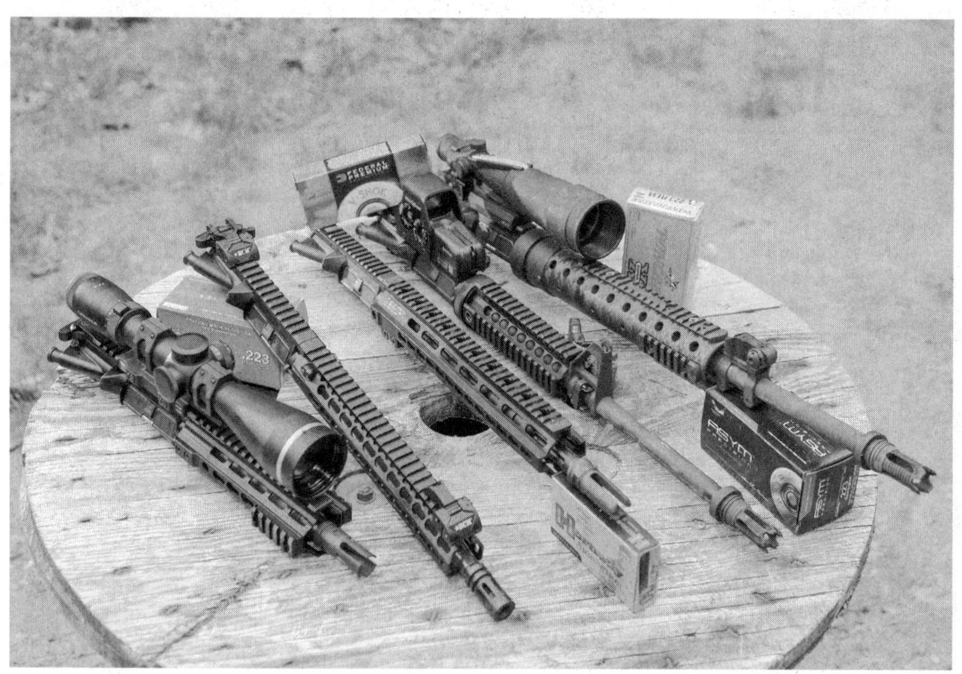

Changing calibers on an AR-15 can be as easy as simply swapping complete uppers.

Sporterizing a rifle involved taking off the excess metal, such as the bayonet lug and other hardware, the upper wooden handguard, even cutting the forearm back, trimming the stock, all to make it a bit lighter, sleeker and handier. After all, a hunter isn't going to be dealing with a bayonet-wielding opponent. (Or at least, one hopes not.)

The barrel might have been shortened, and the metal polished and re-blued. The safety could have been changed, and the trigger replaced. But those are relatively easy changes, something that could be done in a home workshop. None of them had the barrel replaced. This was due in part because the cartridge they were chambered for (in the case of the '03, .30-06) was entirely up to the task of hunting, but, also, barrel replacement was a technical, gunsmith-only operation, in part due to the high torque levels needed to unscrew the barrel. Another barrel-changing problem for the '03 was the extractor slot in the barrel. The breech end of the barrel has to have a slot milled in it, so the extractor can reach the case rim. The barrel has to have the threads carefully timed to tighten up with the slot just right.

Other rifles, like the Mauser 98 were less of a problem in those regards. But still, not easy.

But the '03 and the 98 have an additional problem: headspace. Installing a new barrel required juggling the dimensions of two different shoulders, the stop points, in the barrel and receiver. The distance, from the locking lugs to the chamber shoulder where the cartridge stops, depends on no fewer than four dimensions, with two more for safety considerations.

The manufacture of bolts, receivers, barrels and stocks were all specialized. To forge a receiver, then machine it to the final dimensions needed was just the start. Then it had to have a bolt fitted, a barrel installed, and all the dimensions tracked and kept within the acceptable range. A surplus military rifle had to have the barrel and receiver set matched with the bolt it left the factory with, or you couldn't really be sure it was safe to shoot.

Now, the AR-15. It was designed to have as many of its parts be available from common stocking manufacturers. And the specialty ones aren't so special. Let's take a vanilla-plain set of parts as an example: the pistol grip. The grip is a common synthetic, and there is no-doubt a host of formulations, pages of them, that would serve as well as the one the government specifies. It is held on by a common screw and a star washer. The plunger it holds, to activate the selector, can be supplied by any of hundreds of machine tool companies across the country. Ditto the spring that goes with it.

If you wanted to buy AR-15 pistol grips by weight, you'd have no lack of suppliers who could accommodate you.

And so on with almost all the pins, springs and screws on the AR-15. They can all be sourced, via competitive bid, from hundreds of suppliers across the country.

There are specialty parts, but they assemble easily. The barrel is a precision part, and the receiver it goes into is as well. The nut that locks the barrel on is unlike anything else, but you could practically wring the nut tightly enough with your bare hands to assemble the set. The barrel holds the locking lugs, unlike the receivers of the Springfield and Mauser. The chamber and locking lug dimensions have been held so tightly to spec that any equally well-made bolt will fit. Any.

Bolts and barrels are now so well-made that a lot of guys (and gals) who assemble ARs for fun don't even bother with headspace gauges any more. They know the barrels and bolts they buy will work, always.

The stock is a molded plastic part, held on by a standard screw. At least, the fixed stocks are. The tele-stocks differ, but they come as parts kits, and assembling a new stock on the back end of a receiver is almost as straightforward as installing a barrel on the front.

So, if you want to swap barrels on an AR, the task is easy. You could be doing it because you've worn out the one that is there. Or you want a better one. Or one in a different caliber. Remove the handguards, of whatever type you have there. Remove the gas tube. Unscrew the barrel nut, pull out the old barrel, plug in the new, and tighten the barrel nut.

The rest are just details. Compared to the AR, re-barreling a Springfield or a Mauser practically *is* rocket science.

So, if you are planning on having rifles in various calibers, you can buy a slew of bolt-action rifles, or

How accepted are AR-15 rifles? Enough so that it is not at all uncommon to see them in police cars these days. The old shotguns are now often loaded with "less lethal" ammunition. Police ranges are packed with officers learning or relearning the AR-15.

Another big advantage of the AR-15 is that magazines are plentiful, easy to modify, and if they become unreliable, not heart-breaking to ditch.

you can rebuild your AR or ARs. You could have a slew of ARs, as well.

The other reason is partly changing tastes. The bolt action or lever action of earlier eras just don't cut it for a lot of newer shooters. The AR-15 is also a broad canvas. If you want to paint or otherwise decorate your rifle (you only have to look at cell phones to see what some people's tastes are like) the AR-15 offers you more opportunity. It is, after all, aluminum and plastic. If you find you don't like the paint job you did as much as you anticipated, you can paint over it. Or clean it off and start over.

Also, this decoration is in the context of "If they say I can't have it, then I really do want one now."

The more some politicians beat the drum of "eeeevil assault weapons" and "nasty black rifle" the more people wanted them. Not to get into the politics, but it is just human nature. Some people (and a lot of them, in some areas) want something more when told that it is bad, or too much for them, or it is just not allowed.

A quip I read sums it up well: "In America, anything not specifically prohibited is allowed. In Germany, anything not specifically allowed is prohibited." As soon as someone says they want to move the line of what is prohibited, a lot of people want to get one "while the getting's good."

So, we have the easy to assemble AR-15, jokingly referred to by some as "Barbies for men" and the desire of others to take them away, or at the very least make them really difficult to acquire, and the result is going to be that people are going to line up to buy them. Which they did, do and will.

It has gotten to the point where you can go into a gun shop these days and have to look around and past the AR-15s racked behind the counter, to see the bolt-action and lever-action rifles. And there, those might well be represented more by the long-range competition shooters and the cowboy-action shooters, respectively. Hunting bolt guns? Hunting lever actions? It seems like everyone in America already has one of each of those at home in the closet, for when they go "up north" to hunt. But what do they take to the gun clubs? The ARs or the competition guns.

What do they keep in the truck or car, as a "truck gun"? An AR-15.

That's why the AR-15. And that's why this book.

(above) Even Colt got in on the "What caliber can I make today?" option. When there was consideration of a new NATO cartridge, Colt made test rifles chambered for it. No, the 4.32mm cartridge didn't go anywhere, but Colt could still test it, due to the adaptability of the AR-15.

For the ultimate truck gun, an SBR in 5.56, or one of the .300s, or 6.8, it is hard to beat a really compact AR-15. This is the LWRCI PDW, a personal defense weapon, and boy is it handy.

2

CALIBERS AND OTHER CONSIDERATIONS

What do we mean by "caliber," and what isn't included? And what is an AR?

OK, the idea of the caliber of a cartridge is sometimes a bit confusing. In part because marketing people sometimes get a say on what a cartridge is called.

Let's take an oldie but a goodie, the .30-40 Krag, a cartridge that isn't chambered in the AR, so we can write about it without anyone getting upset because their favorite is being "dissed." This was known back when it was new as the .30-40 Krag, but also as the .30 Army. In Europe, it is known (by those pedants who know it, it isn't exactly a big deal there) as the 7.62x59R. That is, a .30 caliber bullet, in a case 59 millimeters long, with a rim on it. But, there are other cartridges close to that, such as the 7.62x54R, the Russian cartridge; the .303 British, which in European parlance would be the 7.62x56R; and any British proprietary cartridge meant to be used in a single-shot or double rifle, with a .308-inch, or so, diameter bullet.

In the American use, we have the .30-30, the .300 Savage, the .307 Winchester, the .308 Marlin Express and the .30 TC, which all use .308-inch-diameter bullets. A step larger, we have the .32-20 and the .32 Winchester Special, but there, the .32-20 uses bullets of .312-inch diameter, while the .32 Special uses bullets of .321-inch diameter. And the .32-40 cartridge? It uses bullets of .320 of an inch and the .32 Winchester Self-Loading uses bullets of .321 of an inch, but not the same ones the .3

Granted, none of those are AR cartridges, and a lot of them are obsolete or nearly so.

So, let's look at the .300 Blackout, the .30 Remington AR, the .300 Whisper and 7.62x39. They can all use some of the same bullets, all .308 inches in diameter. The cases they are mated with will fit in an AR magazine. They range in power from pistol-range to solidly deer-hunting horsepower. And with the possible exception of the Blackout and Whisper, they are not interchangeable.

So, we have to consider the variables of a cartridge. They are: base or rim diameter, body diameter, length to shoulder, shoulder angle and location, neck length and cartridge overall length.

The last one is of great importance. You see, if a given cartridge doesn't fit into an AR-15 or AR-10 magazine, then it is for all intents and purposes useless for our consideration. (I'm overlooking the long-action AR rifles out there, just for this chapter.) It may well be the best cartridge ever designed, but if you can't fit it into an AR, then you can't.

So, we'll try to cover all the names of a given cartridge, but we might overlook a name or two. Also, a bit of history about that cartridge, and what all is involved in reloading the cartridge, if that is even possible. What we will do is tell you the dimensions, the uses of the cartridge, what kind of ammunition is available for it, and what is involved in converting an AR-15 to that caliber. It might be as simple as a new barrel. It might be more, like barrel, bolt and magazine. And in extreme instances, there is no conversion possible. You can only buy it in the given caliber from the manufacturer who makes it that way.

Oh, and until a given cartridge name is frozen in time, it can have multiple names. The two-fer known as the .300 Whisper and .300 Blackout are a perfect example. If you go back in time and look for it, you can find a cartridge known as the .30-221 Fireball. This was simply the .221 Fireball, necked up to take a .308-inch-diameter bullet. The .221 was itself a

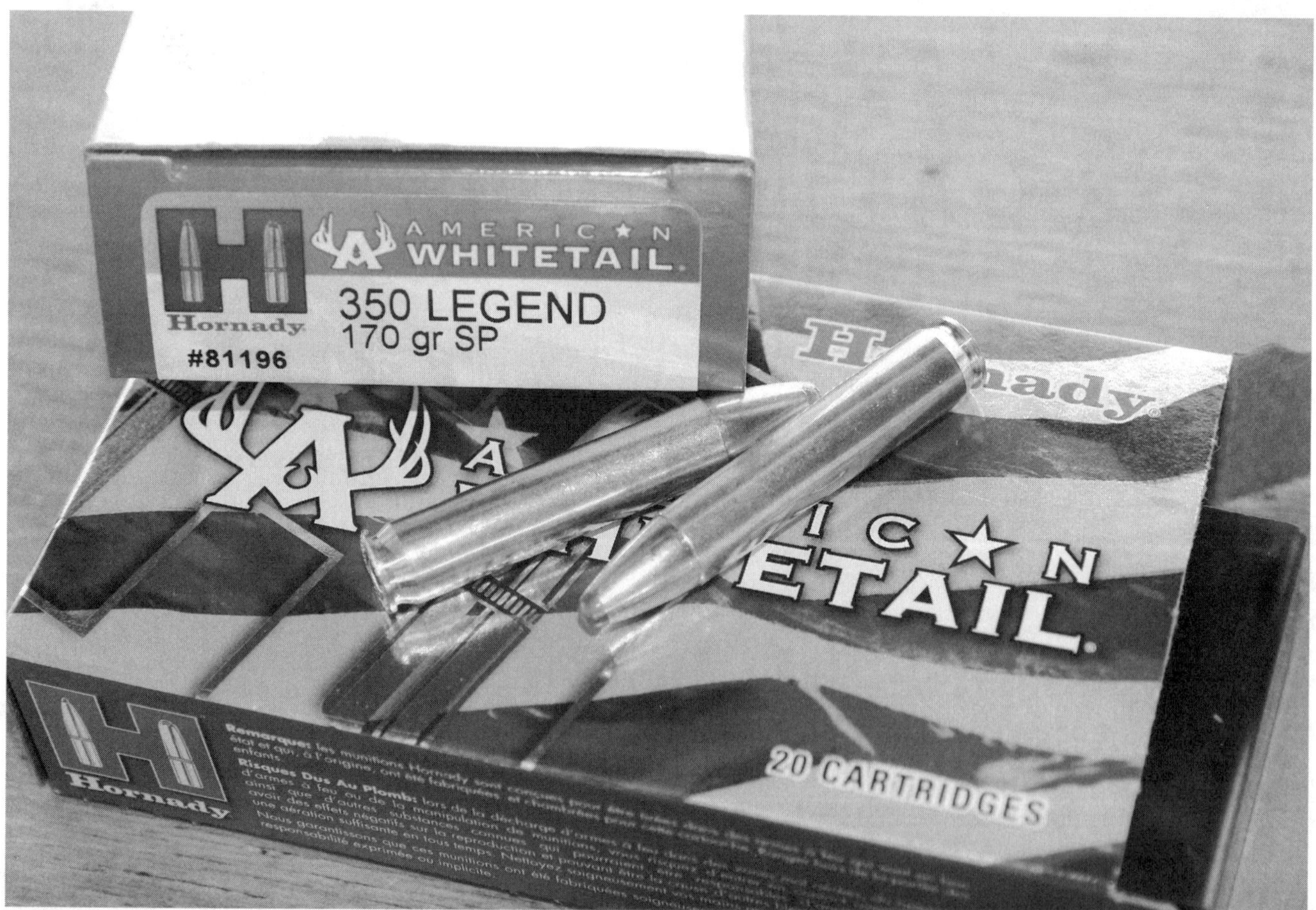

The cartridge originator gets to name it, once it is type-approved by SAAMI. Hence, the .350 Legend.

shortened .222 Remington, developed after WWII for use as a varmint and benchrest competition cartridge.

Depending on which experimenter bench it was, the general name of .30-221 Fireball could have a neck length that was different from other designs, a shoulder location, case taper, pretty much any of the variable could be different.

It isn't until it gains official adoption that the dimensions get set in stone. In the case of the .300 Whisper, it came with CIP acceptance. CIP is the European agency that determines cartridge dimensions and performance. In the U.S., that is done by the Sporting Arms and Ammunition Manufacturers' Institute (SAAMI). Who can offer up a design is a matter of membership. If you aren't a member of SAAMI, then you can't send them a cartridge drawing and ask for acceptance.

The .300 Blackout was offered by a company that could, and was accepted. The dimensional differences between the .300 Whisper and .300 Blackout are pretty much too small to argue over. And no, AAC didn't steal the idea, design or dimensions from J.D. Jones, who developed the .300 Whisper. But that will be covered in Chapter 10.

Cartridges that are being made, for firearms being made to accept them, that have not received official (CIP or SAAMI) approval, are referred to by two descriptors: wildcats or proprietary.

A wildcat is a cartridge that is pretty much a small-time or home-grown project. If you have a great idea for the .30-06 case, and you want it necked up (or down) to a particular bullet, with a shoulder location determined by you, you can have that. The chamber reamer makers, and the reloading die makers, can follow your dimensions. They will most likely have suggestions, or even be able to offer you the reamer that someone else designed last year, last decade or last century. (There are a lot of things that are not new under the sun.)

You build your rifle, you ream the chamber, you load your own ammo, that is a wildcat.

If you have a company, or a corporation, and you make rifles in that chambering, and you sell ammo that has been pressure-tested, and loaded by an ammo-making company, that is a proprietary cartridge.

A brief aside: SAAMI does not, and will not, confer its approval on any cartridge that is a wildcat, proprietary, or trademarked. Them's the rules.

It takes a lot of work to develop a new cartridge; a lot of work that has to be done before SAAMI ever gets involved. This is an accuracy-testing setup.

WHAT IS AN AR?

Let's start with the original: a rifle that is more carbine-like, with a 20-inch barrel, and a gas system that ports the gas back into the receiver. This is known as the Direct Impingement system, or DI. Next, we have the carbine, where we have (for us, for the moment) a 16-inch barrel, and the gas tube is shorter. The shorter barrel needs to have the gas port moved back so there is enough dwell time to drive the system. Dwell time is the time the bullet is still in the bore, having passed the gas port, so the bore can pressurize the gas tube and drive the system.

There is an in-between location, known as mid-length. Here, the gas port is farther forward, but not as far forward as that of the rifle. The idea is to gain the benefits of smoother (less jolting) gas flow from the rifle, but not have a barrel as long as that of the rifle. This started as a competition option, and has been accepted in some circles for tactical, duty and defensive rifles, due to the smoother action than that of the carbine-length gas system.

Shorter barrels than the 16 inches of the carbine are known colloquially as "SBRs." Short-barreled

The original AR-15 was a "full-sized" rifle, but one that was shorter and lighter than the then-current .30-caliber battle rifles. They are still in service, and still useful to those of us not in service. Photo By: Army Sgt. James Garvin

rifles. They are covered under the National Firearms Act of 1934, and are controlled like machine guns. NFA law requires a stricter background check, and a $200 transfer tax on each one you buy.

SBRs maintain the carbine-length gas system, and have the gas port diameter changed to fit with the barrel length and caliber. There is one more gas-system length, however, and it comes about because of the .300 Whisper and .300 Blackout.

The AR pistol gas system is the shortest of all. When AR barrels get under 10 inches in length, there's no place for the gas port, so it had to be moved back. This is also because of the .300 Blackout, in particular, because of subsonic ammunition.

A .300 Blackout, pushing a 200-grain bullet (more or less, it can be as light as 180 grains and as heavy as 240 grains) at less than the speed of sound, does not generate enough gas volume to pressurize a carbine-length gas system. The SBR in that situation won't cycle. So, by moving the gas port back, where there is still enough pressure, the designers can create a system that self-loads.

This gas port location and design is known as a pistol-length gas system.

This, of course, means that when you load supersonic ammunition (110- to 115-grain bullets, at a generous step over 2,000 fps) the pistol gas system has too much pressure. The SBR will cycle more harshly. There, unlike many other situations, you have a choice: build an AR in .300 Blackout that cycles smoothly and softly with supersonic ammo, and it won't be a self-loading rifle when fed subsonic ammo, or build it to work with subsonics, and have harsher recoil with supersonics.

This is America, you get to choose.

AR PISTOLS

If the AR is a rifle or a carbine, then what is an AR pistol? Basically, it is an SBR without a stock. Since it doesn't have a stock, it isn't a rifle, and that makes it, ta-daaaa, a pistol. A handgun.

OK, the law here is sharp, if not always clear. You have to have an AR lower (that is the part that is the actual, serial-numbered firearm) that was made as a pistol, or has never had a stock on it. So, you can buy a bare, un-built lower receiver, and build it up as a pistol.

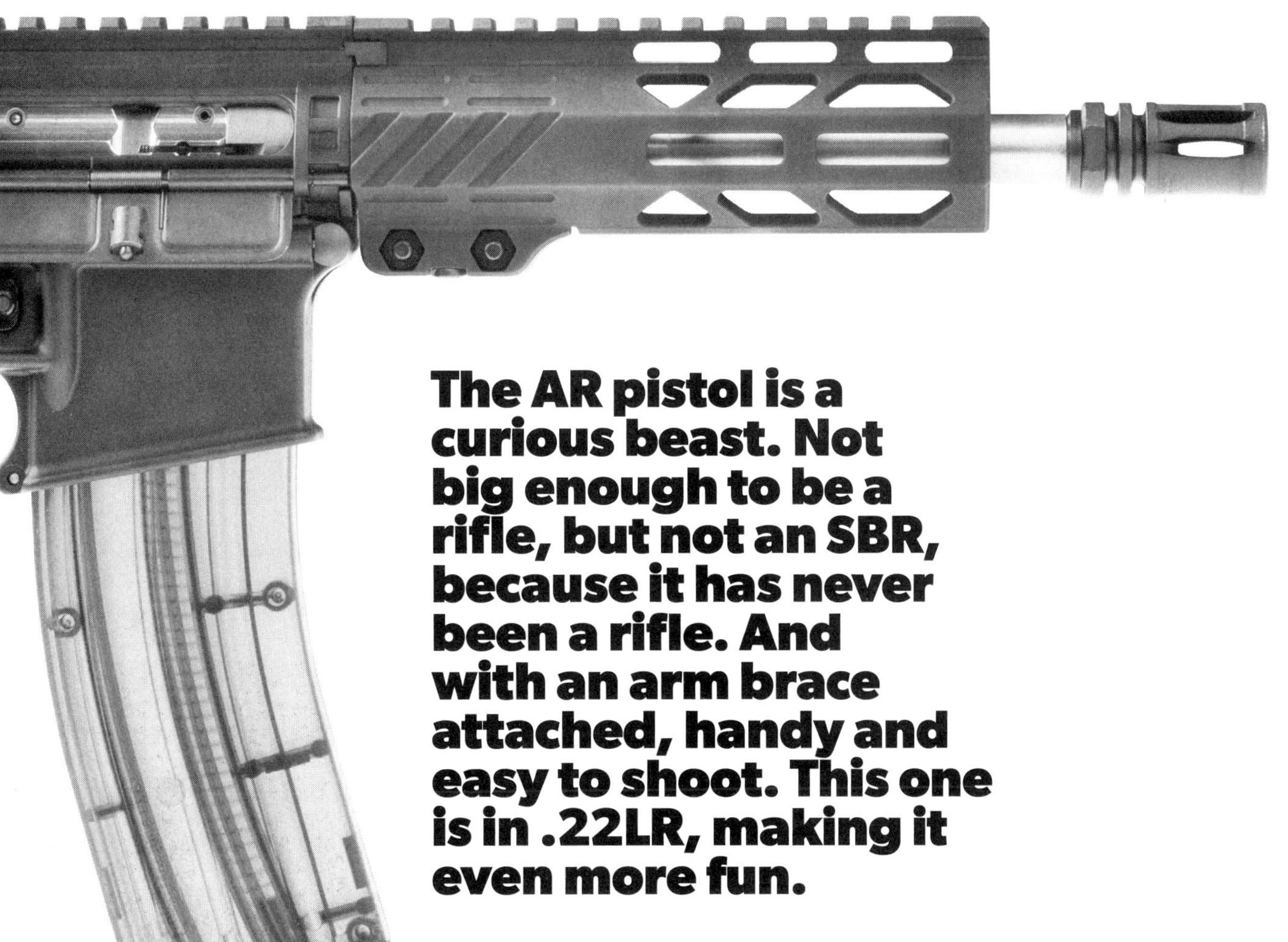

The AR pistol is a curious beast. Not big enough to be a rifle, but not an SBR, because it has never been a rifle. And with an arm brace attached, handy and easy to shoot. This one is in .22LR, making it even more fun.

As with all things, local laws apply. Just because the Feds say something is OK, if your local laws don't approve, you can't do it. In this, the Feds do not trump local laws.

This means an AR pistol can be an SBR in all things except the stock.

When we were first figuring this out, you needed a special buffer tube. (We'll go into the buffer-tube situation in detail in a little bit.) AR pistol buffer tubes were plain cylinders. Then, SB Tactical and Sig Sauer got together, and offered arm braces for AR pistols. The idea was simple: to allow disabled veterans who did not have use of both arms to shoot ARs. Shooting an AR one-handed wasn't easy. (Still isn't.) The arm brace made it easier to shoot an AR pistol one-handed.

Once accepted (it was accepted, then denied, then accepted again) SB Tactical and others expanded their designs, and made arm braces that fit onto standard carbine buffer tubes. Those are the ones that are not just plain cylinders, but have the dorsal rib to keep a stock aligned.

Now, the fact that you can use a standard carbine buffer tube (with some designs, not all) does not mean you can rebuild a carbine into a handgun.

You still must start with either an AR pistol, or an AR lower that has never had a stock on it.

The next question is simple: Can you shoulder an AR pistol?

The original opinion, and the one the ATF came back to after it was required to revisit the issue, is this: Simply changing the way a device is used does not change its definition. An example is a traditional handgun. Yes, they were designed to be fired with one hand. And in a lot of competitions, you are still required to hold them one-handed only. Holding a traditional handgun with two hands does not change its definition. It does not suddenly become a rifle, because you have more than one hand on it.

Similarly, an AR pistol is designed to be fired with one hand. Or, with two hands, however you can manage it. If you, however, hold it with both hands, and while aiming it, incidentally have the back end of the arm brace come into contact with your body, it does not change the definition; it was built as an AR pistol.

Now, this might change. Between the time I write this, and when it goes to press, or you read it, the definition could have been changed. I don't know how that can happen from the ATF. They have pretty thoroughly defined it, and discussed it. Changing now would be the regulatory equivalent of saying "We previously found that two plus two equals four. We now find that two plus two equals five."

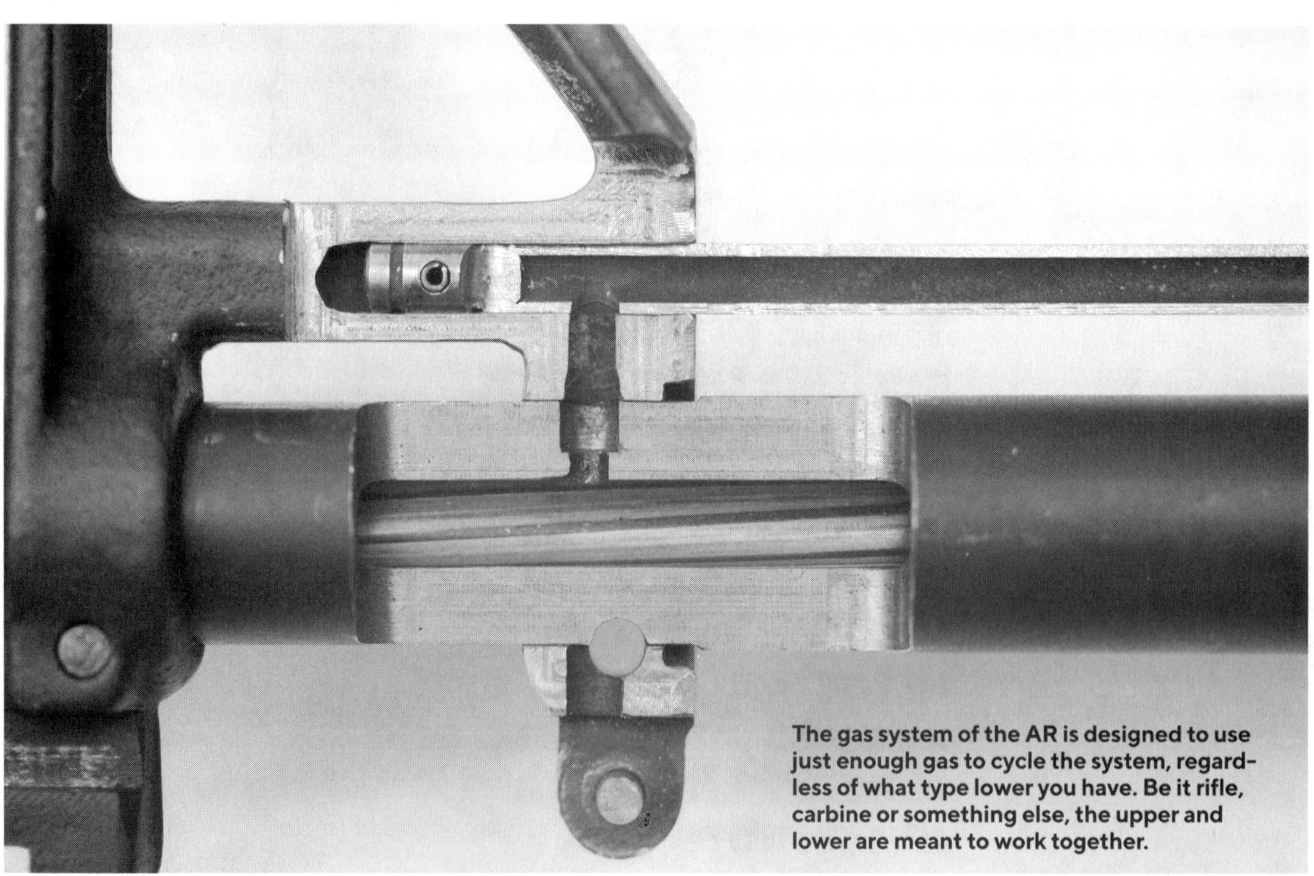

The gas system of the AR is designed to use just enough gas to cycle the system, regardless of what type lower you have. Be it rifle, carbine or something else, the upper and lower are meant to work together.

However, legislatively, the change can happen. If members of Congress decide an arm brace makes an AR pistol (or any pistol) a rifle, then they can so declare. And yes, I am making the comparison to Congress declaring that, by law, two-plus two equals five. They've done worse. When that happens, it goes to the courts, after someone gets arrested and charged, and convicted of such an offense.

Until then, putting the arm brace on your AR pistol up against your shoulder is not against the law. If you feel that doing so is just aggravating the opposition, might I remind you that there is nothing you can do that the far end of the political spectrum from us won't find offensive, short of not owning guns.

AR LOWERS AND BUFFERS

OK, the upper can be anything from a 7-inch barreled pistol in some moderate cartridge, to a 24-inch rifle chambered in something very robust. Do we have to have a buffer system to match? Basically, no.

The gas system of the rifle, carbine, SBR or pistol is throttled in such a way that the standard buffer weight and spring can handle it. However, the rifle and the carbine/SBR/pistol systems are not the same. The weights differ in mass and shape, and the springs differ. But you can build yours with either and have it work.

Now, some barrels will be "over-gassed." That is, to ensure ultra-reliable function, even with low-powered, inexpensive ammo, some makers will have the gas port drilled one size larger. This delivers extra gas to the system, and ensures it cycles and doesn't short-stroke.

In such a case, it is common to go to a heavier buffer weight in the carbine system; rifle systems don't need it. These carbine weights are either plain, or marked on their front face with an "H": "H1" "H2" "H3" in ascending order of mass.

Basically, use the heaviest weight buffer that will still reliably cycle your carbine or pistol.

PISTONS

Before the AR, rifles used pistons. There were some that didn't, but they were not common. The piston system is simple: at the gas port on the barrel, instead of a tube to channel gas, there is a rod. The gas pushes the rod. The rod either bangs against the bolt or bolt carrier or is attached to the carrier. The difference is simple. The gas gets vented out of the system at the gas block or gas port, and is not channeled into the receiver, as in the DI system.

Advocates say this makes the piston system more reliable than the DI system. Also, it is easier to dial the system (depending on the details of a particular design) to adjust for ammunition power or the use of suppressors.

To quote Kurt Vonnegut: "In this world, you get what you pay for." Sweeney's corollary is: "You pay for what you get."

The piston system does vent gas out of the action away from the receiver. But it still vents it. This makes the gas block just as hot as it would be, maybe hotter, than in the DI system. It also makes it tough to hold a rifle, depending on where the piston vents gas. As a last problem up front, the vented gas is at a higher pressure than it is back in the action, and this makes using a suppressor more difficult. The snap of the vented gas is greater at the block, where it is 17,000 PSI, than back in the receiver, where it is 1,500 PSI.

In the receiver, we have additional problems. The AR carrier blows off of the bolt exactly like a paper wrapper for a straw. Piston systems push on the carrier up above the centerline, and this creates carrier tilt. The tilting carrier has to be controlled, or else it will chew up the buffer tube or lower receiver. The usual changes made are to put anti-tilt pads on the bottom of the back of the carrier, to keep it from impacting with momentum. And, to increase the length of the buffer tube inside the receiver, where the tilt happens, to also reduce impact.

As a last bit of indignity to the beautiful idea of a piston, piston systems add weight to the AR. Also, by attaching more parts to the barrel, it becomes more difficult to maintain the gilt-edged accuracy that the AR can deliver. Accuracy can be kept, but it isn't always easy.

Piston advocates will always promote their favorite system. It can have advantages. But it isn't a cure-all.

PISTOL CALIBER CARBINES

Not pistols as in AR pistols, although they can be, but ARs chambered in pistol calibers. Typically, these would be 9mm, 40 and .45 caliber, but there are others. The progenitor here is the Colt SMG, a 9mm submachine gun built on the AR-15 receiver set. Since the pistols do not have much powder, or pressure, the Colt was made as a straightforward blowback design. Simply put, the mass of the bolt, and the spring driving it, are the only things that keep the action closed when fired. The bullet goes out the front, and the empty case, bolt and spring go to the rear.

The 9mm ARs were seen as an oddity for a long

A piston system doesn't make heat go away, it just dumps it someplace besides the upper receiver of your basic Direct Impingement system. It adds parts, weight and things contacting the barrel.

The AR can be converted to fire pistol cartridges, and you then use SMG magazines of one kind or another. Or pistol magazines.

time, but a few things caused a change. One is winter. Shooting for practice, or competition, outdoors in the winter can be brutal. Indoors, an AR in .223/5.56 is brutal. But, a 9mm, indoors, is just another handgun, even when it is a carbine.

Second is competition. My club was one of the first to allow it, and using a 9mm carbine on a USPSA/IPSC handgun course is wicked fun. We called it a "Pistol Caliber Carbine" or PCC.

It is now so popular that it has its own national championships in the USPSA schedule.

One approach to crafting the 9mm AR was to pin some blocks into the lower (Colt did this) to make it possible for a 9mm magazine to fit and feed. They used modified Uzi magazines for this. Later makers constructed single blocks that you didn't have to pin in place, and simply slipped into the lower down from the top when the receivers were hinged open.

ARs either have to have the lower receiver modified, or have adapters fitted, to use pistol magazines or SMG magazines.

The latest approach is to make modified lower receivers. These use Glock magazines (or other common hi-cap magazines) and the two PCCs are not compatible.

That is, if you have a Colt-type 9mm, and a Glock-mag-fed one, you cannot swap any parts from one to the next except the trigger components and the buffer systems. The uppers, lowers, bolts and barrels are all proprietary to their systems.

As a further divergence, but one we're still going to call an AR, is the Sig PCC, called the MPX. The MPX uses a piston system, not blowback, and it uses its own receiver set and magazines, but it is obviously AR-derived, so I'm going to keep it in the family.

WHEN?

First of all, the AR was positioned in time to be the firearm for this process. It is rather like the 1898 Mauser in that regard. When millions of GIs came home from the war, they found that the firearms companies were not always as responsive to their

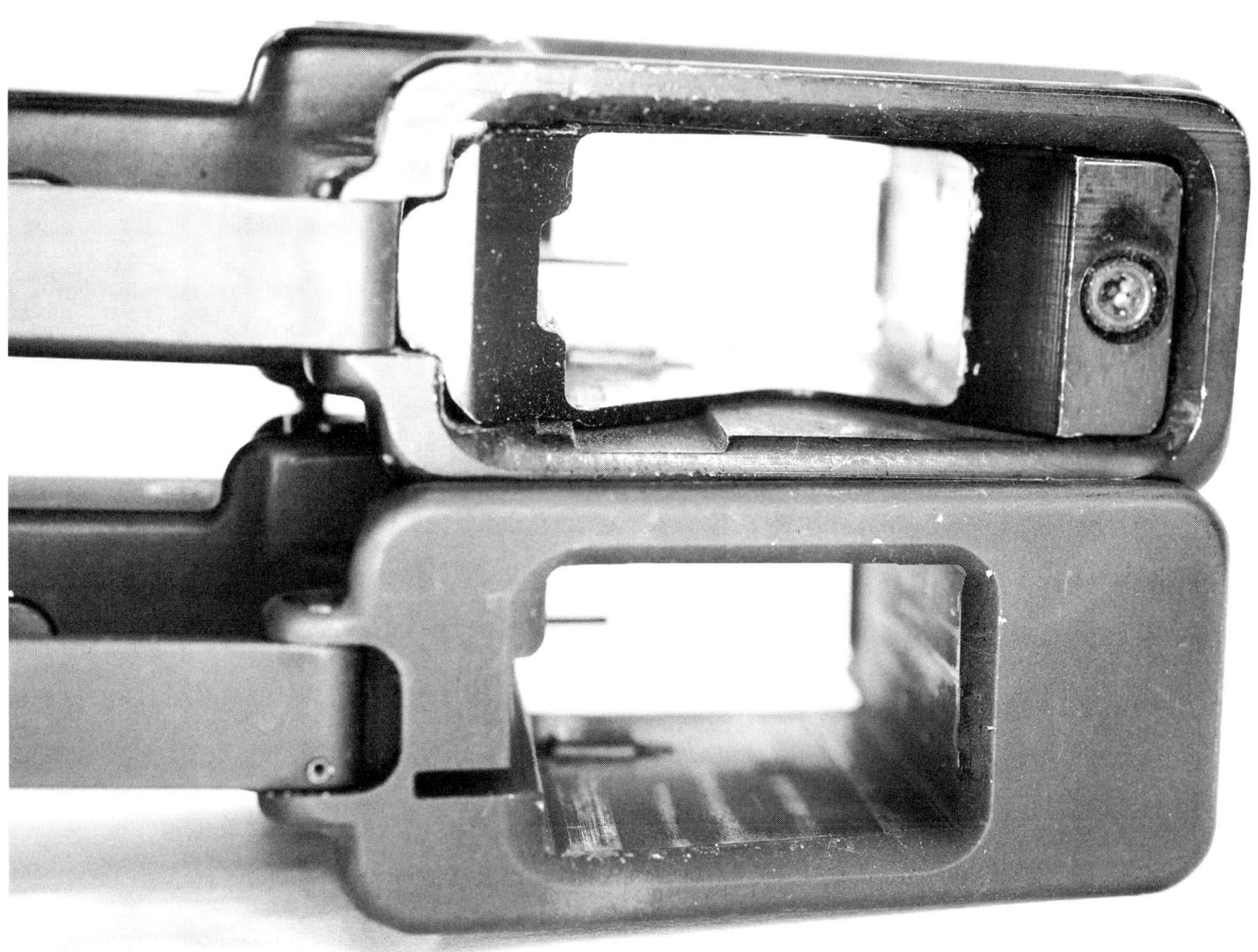

perceived needs as they might have liked. If Remington, Winchester and the others weren't willing to offer a rifle in the new super caliber, why then you could simply make one out of any of the bazillions of surplus Mausers to be had.

When a modern hunting rifle from "Remchester" might cost a working stiff $50, a surplus Mauser at the local gun shop, for all of $15 would do. With the excess wood chopped off, it was handy enough.

Then, changing barrels became common as a gunsmithing operation, and we were off to the races.

It took a number of decades, but the surplus Mauser supply actually started to dry up. By then, the collectors were hard at work keeping rarities or even not-exactly-common variants from being scrapped and mangled. But the advent of CNC machining made the problem not a problem. If you could design and make a new, exact-to-dimensions rifle receiver, for less cost and with less work than "blueprinting" a Mauser, then the Mauser is safe as a historical piece.

The AR-15 came along just as the supply of Mausers was starting to wane, driving up the prices of those rifles. Also, newer generations of shooters had come along, and they already knew about "those old rifles" and wanted something new. In a bout of irony, it was the very act of trying to remove them from the marketplace that caused the surge of interest. In the 1980s, the first wave of gun control aimed at AR-15s and other "assault rifles" began. The more some decried them, the more others took an interest in them. So much so that people scoured gun shows and surplus establishments, looking for the parts needed to assemble a rifle, and then acquire a bare lower receiver (the actual firearm, by law) and make their own.

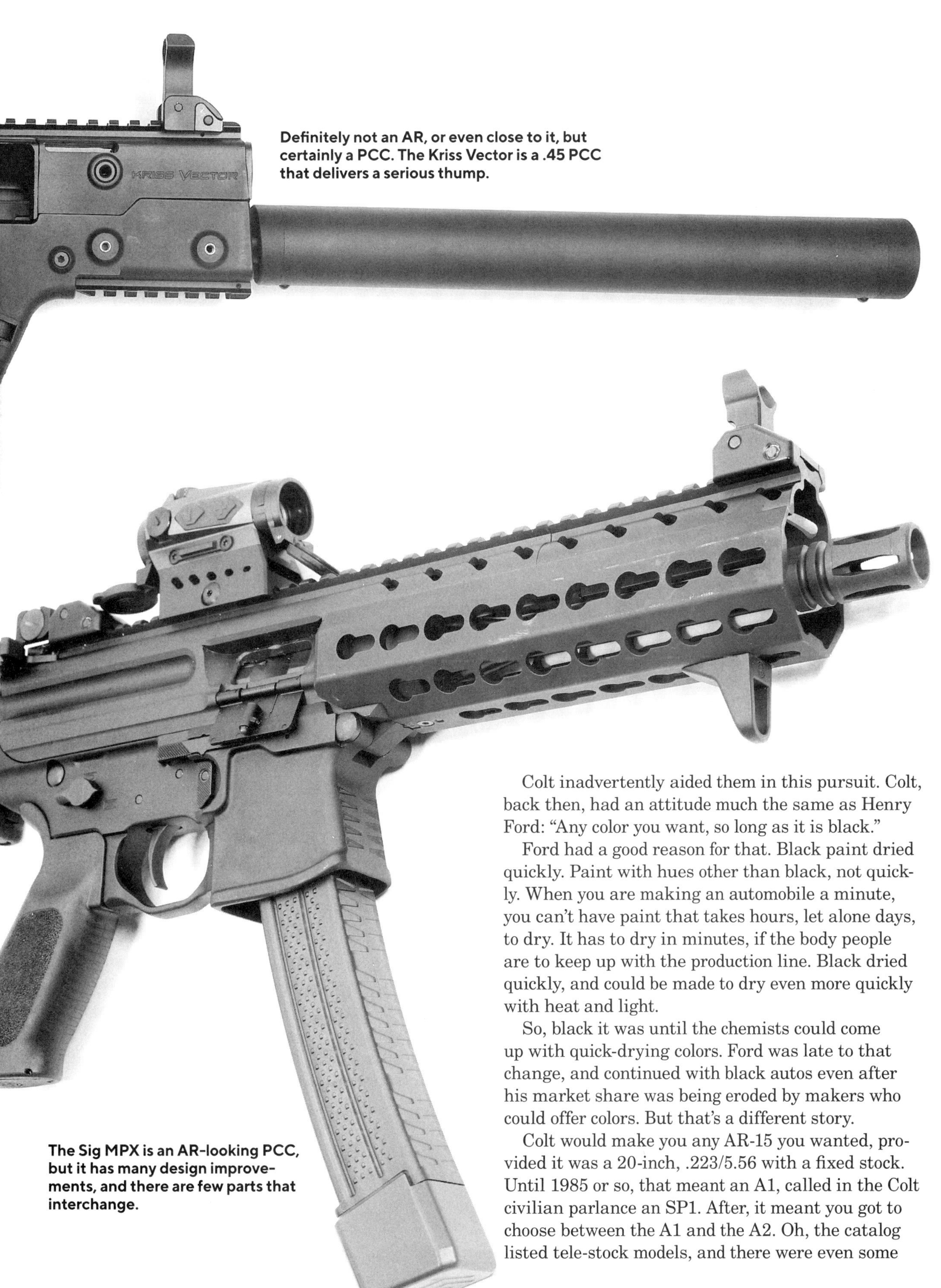

Definitely not an AR, or even close to it, but certainly a PCC. The Kriss Vector is a .45 PCC that delivers a serious thump.

The Sig MPX is an AR-looking PCC, but it has many design improvements, and there are few parts that interchange.

Colt inadvertently aided them in this pursuit. Colt, back then, had an attitude much the same as Henry Ford: "Any color you want, so long as it is black."

Ford had a good reason for that. Black paint dried quickly. Paint with hues other than black, not quickly. When you are making an automobile a minute, you can't have paint that takes hours, let alone days, to dry. It has to dry in minutes, if the body people are to keep up with the production line. Black dried quickly, and could be made to dry even more quickly with heat and light.

So, black it was until the chemists could come up with quick-drying colors. Ford was late to that change, and continued with black autos even after his market share was being eroded by makers who could offer colors. But that's a different story.

Colt would make you any AR-15 you wanted, provided it was a 20-inch, .223/5.56 with a fixed stock. Until 1985 or so, that meant an A1, called in the Colt civilian parlance an SP1. After, it meant you got to choose between the A1 and the A2. Oh, the catalog listed tele-stock models, and there were even some

The Mauser has gone from military arm, to surplus, to custom firearm. This Mauser, built by a European gunsmith, is an example. It is not just "blueprinted" but once built it was engraved, has been color case-hardened, and given gold inlays. Cost? If you have to ask, you can't afford it.

16-inch carbines made in the late 1980s and early 1990s that had fixed stocks, but good luck finding one.

So, since Colt wouldn't make a tele-stock version, shooters would find the stocks themselves, and tear down an A2 and rebuild it with a tele-stock. Once you start down that road, there's not much stopping you. All the surplus parts available could be used, modified, fitted and other parts made from scratch.

Then 3-gun competition began, followed by more gun-control efforts, an even more interest developed in making what was called "bad." As the surplus parts dried up, parts makers stepped in. After all, if you are a subcontractor, making [fill in the blank] parts for the maker of government firearms, you have to do something between contracts, right? As long as you aren't making receivers and firearms, you just make parts and send them off to the distributors.

I saw this happen in the late 1980s. The surplus parts I had been using, to fix customers' guns and modify ARs for competition, were gradually replaced with "surplus" parts that were clearly brand-new production.

The early days of 3-gun competition happened while we were still fixated on "real" rifles. Even with a scoring system slanted to advantage .30-caliber rifles, the smaller calibers were winning. My light-bulb moment happened when I shot our club's "Light Rifle Pop and Flop" match one year. This involved running downrange and setting 15 bowling pins on stands, running back, loading and shooting them off the stands. Time didn't start until you were back, but there was a limit. Run slowly, and time just might start without you.

I was using a match-conditioned Garand, and I dropped my 15 pins with 16 shots. And placed third. Second was won with an AR-15, and first place was won by a shooter using an absolutely wretched rifle. It was a Universal carbine, in .30 carbine, with the wire paratrooper stock, a 2X scope mounted in a side rail, and a pair of 30-round magazines clamped in a "jungle" clip. He had to reload, and he still beat me.

I went out and bought an AR-15 after that.

Then, the USGI "surplus" parts were replaced with parts that had been improved, upgraded or even altered from mil-spec, to make them stronger, or perform a function the government had no conception of. One example: Today, the idea of a free-float handguard is so common that anything else falls into the category of "retro." I built an AR carbine for competition in 1990 that had a free-float handguard. And I did not have to make the handguard from scratch, it was a readily available part by then.

HOW?

How is it that the AR-15 is so versatile? Two reasons, and two parts. The parts are the upper and lower. The lower readily can be assembled from parts by anyone who can avoid hurting themselves with a screwdriver. There is no bedding done, no stock shaping, no mysterious glass-bedding to be done. Just pick the parts you want and bolt them onto the lower receiver. And the lower is the firearm.

The second part is the upper, which can readily be swapped from one to another. You can have one lower and many uppers to ride on it in turn. And the gas systems of the uppers are all built to work properly with a properly set up lower receiver.

The two reasons are intertwined with the parts.

Reason one: Because the upper is not serialized, you can make it anything you want, as long as it isn't an NFA part. (Translation: no short barrels on rifles or carbines, only on pistols.) New shooters often go with a basic rifle or carbine to start. Then they add another upper, one suited for 3-gun, varmint hunting, whatever. Then they add another, and once they hit three uppers, they have this brainstorm: "Why don't I just get another lower, one suited to the XYZ upper, with a better trigger, while I'm at it?"

At that point, they have two ARs with three uppers, and are familiar with AR building. From there on out becomes "Barbie for men" and they add, accessorize, adapt and build.

Welcome to the club.

Colt would not make the tele-stock carbine back in the old days, or wouldn't make nearly enough for the market's desires. So, we had to make our own. Now, the standard AR-15 seems to be the semi-auto-only version of the military, also known in civilian hands as the M4gery. This is the real deal. Photo By: Mark C. Olsen, New Jersey National Guard

BARRELS AND ACCURACY

Barrel length has nothing to do with accuracy. A premium barrel, made as an SBR, will be an accurate rifle. A long barrel, made by a no-name barrel producer, might or might not be accurate.

The big advantage the AR-15 has over other rifle designs is the ease with which we can make it a free-float barrel setup.

When you fire a rifle, the barrel rings like a bell. The muzzle whips around, vibrating as an impressive rpm. Anything that contacts the barrel can change the frequency of the barrel vibrations. Changes in harmonics are bad for accuracy.

Originally, barrels were "bedded." That is, the wooden stock was made so it pressed against the barrel at certain points, with a given amount of pressure. This was to control the harmonics. Compressing three-quarters of a century of mechanical engineering, research, testing and competition, as barrels got better, it was found they needed less bedding. And once they got good enough, letting them simply wave in the open air was most accurate of all.

The AR-15 shoots best when the barrel has nothing touching it except for the gas block, and maybe a sight housing. The best barrels, with the best ammo, will shoot sub-MOA. That is, under a minute of angle, which is roughly one inch at 100 yards.

Some people feel a sub-MOA rifle is their due as an American. They want it as an over-the-counter purchase, with any ammo they choose, and the scope they happen to have on hand. Well, that's not real life.

Realistically, many shooters are not sub-MOA shooters. Most ammo isn't. A lot of optics are not up to the task. And, one group does not a sub-MOA rifle make.

And just to make thigs interesting, the advances in QC, CNC machining and design now have the current crop of vanilla-plain bolt-action hunting rifles out of the box as serious sub-MOA contenders.

Yep, you can buy a $500 hunting rifle that shoots like the sniper rifles of old.

COSTS

The big deal about the AR-15, unlike many other designs, is that for those willing to invest in a small cost for tooling, and learn a few basic skills, the whole rifle is user-serviceable.

For almost all the other designs, there are specialized tools needed to do pretty much anything, and the threshold for skills is much higher. Let's take as an example: a pair of big-bore battle rifles, the

The ease with which an AR-15 upper can be re-barreled is superb. Either because you've worn out the old one, or the caliber it is in has worn out its welcome.

AR-15 barrels can easily be changed, and they come ready to go with the correct (more or less, most of the time) gas port drilled.

M14/M1A and the FAL. To swap a barrel, you need a receiver wrench, a barrel clamp, a bench that will stand up to the torque limits of the work you are doing, and headspace gauges or reamers. For the AR, you need a regular bench vise, on a regular bench. You need a reaction rod and a barrel nut wrench.

The relative costs of those parts? For the M14/M1A, the wrench and clamp run $124 for the wrench, and $60 for the block. Plus, you will need a gas cylinder wrench ($26) and a receiver/barrel timing gauge ($80). Add in a chamber reamer ($100) and headspace gauges ($31) and you are spending almost as much on the tools as on the barrel, or $421 for the tools.

The FAL will run the same, with one proviso: The torque limits on the FAL barrel installation are almost absurd. The M1A calls for 85 ft-lbs max, while the FAL requires 100 ft-lbs to torque up. And then you get the extra bad news: The headspacing on the FAL is accomplished by means of a replaceable locking shoulder that fits into the receiver. You could, if the new barrel headspaced short, ream the chamber to make it work. But the proper method is to press out the old locking shoulder, using a gauge made for the task, and determine what size locking shoulder to replace the old one with. Then install it and lock it in place.

That's old-school.

The AR-15 needs a few tools. First, the reaction rod, to hold the receiver and barrel. This is a $99 part you can borrow from someone at the gun club, or go in on and buy, split between you and your friends so all can use it when needed. The barrel nut wrench runs you as little as $5.

Headspace gauges? "Where we're going, we don't need headspace gauges." (Bonus points if you know the reference.) And a standard bench vise, on a standard bench will do, because you only need 30 ft-lbs at the minimum, and once you get to 80, you stop. Most will snug up and align properly well below 80 ft-lbs.

As a result, swapping barrels on an AR-15 is easy. While the M1A and FAL have to have their gas systems (op rod and piston, respectively) precisely in line with the receiver, the AR-15 pretty much doesn't care. As long as you can weasel the gas tube past the barrel nut spikes, and get it in line with the gas key on the carrier, it is fine. Oh, the precision-oriented shooters will complain that you've given up a few fractions of an MOA in accuracy, but for most shooters, that doesn't matter.

Let's be realistic. Most shooters are two MOA shooters, at best. I'm not being disparaging here. Most of us can't run a 100-yard/meter dash in less than 15 seconds. That's just life. Why is it an insult to say most of us aren't better than two MOA? After all, at 300 yards, that's still a six-inch circle, and if you can place your shots inside of a six-inch circle at 300 yards, you will get the job done almost all the time.

So, quibbling over a few fractions of an MOA is silly. And as long as the barrel nut is tight enough to stay put, and the gas tube and key are happy, what's the problem?

There is also the matter of handguards. The M1A requires proper bedding of the stock in order to shoot well. If you match-condition it, (bed the stock in a detailed and precise manner) it will shoot as well as a vanilla-plain AR-15. There's no way to free-float the barrel of an FAL.

So, the potential is there for you to have a really precision-accuracy AR-15, if you build it properly. And, as with the barrel swap, that building of the AR-15 is a lot easier than it is with other rifles.

BARREL LIFE

How long does an AR-15 barrel last? That depends. It depends on what kind of ammo you use, what kind of firing schedule you have, and what kind of accuracy you expect.

The military has a basic yardstick of 7,500 rounds. But, soldiers have a much different problem than

Sometimes, a cartridge will have several names. And sometimes those names mean different cartridges. The .223 vs. 5.56 one is a case in point, especially for us. They are not the same. More on that in the next chapter.

The erosion gage is supposed to stop with the rod almost half a foot out of the receiver, not four inches into it. The erosion gage has traveled a foot farther into the bore than is expected.

the rest of us. They are using hot ammo, the M855, or the new, egregious and awful M855A1. This is throttle-to-the-wall 5.56 ammo, and they expect the rifles and carbines firing it to be used hard. They will be used wet, dry, hot and cold, with generous dollops of full-auto or burst fire thrown in. The end-users are expected to try and keep them lubed and clean, but that won't always be possible. The services expect most shooters, rifles and ammo to be shooting maybe three to five MOA. The high-end users will demand more, and usually get it, but they will often be happy with the same three to five MOA, because how much accuracy do you really need at CQB distances?

The varmint shooter has different expectations. First of all, sub-MOA is the starting point. Anything that wears to the point of shooting over one MOA is no longer a useful varmint rifle. At the same 300 yards, a one-MOA rifle delivers a three-inch group, and that's wide enough to miss a ground squirrel. However, varmint shooters have no full-auto or burst fire in their daily routines. They can stop and let the rifle cool, and scrub the bore any time they want. They often have two rifles, to use one while the other is cooling off. They will also be likely to have started with a premium, accuracy-delivering barrel. As a result, despite the more-demanding accuracy level, varmint shooters can often get many more rounds downrange than 7,500 before they consider a barrel "shot out."

A friend of mine is a combination service shooter and varmint shooter. He is a very accomplished shooter, but he teaches patrol rifle to law enforcement. He also competes. He regularly gets only 5,000 rounds out of a barrel before he finds it giving him problems. But, you have to keep things in perspective. He can, when his barrel is in good shape (he routinely swaps out barrels as they wear), shoot a group, on demand, at 100 yards, that you can cover with a quarter.

A few more examples before I leave you with a problem to be solved on your own time.

I once used up a plain, no-name A2 barrel, with a 1/7 twist, in a few seasons of high-volume practice and competition. I had one of the club members approach me, looking for a barrel to build a rifle he was going to give to his father. He wanted something that worked, was reasonably accurate, and since his father wasn't going to do more than plink once or twice a year, it didn't have to have a lifetime of use left in it. Since the barrel I had in that rifle was just starting to shoot over one MOA, I figured, "why not?" That barrel had just over 15,000 rounds through it by then.

On a recent patrol rifle class, we had an officer who was trying to check his rifle's zero. His patrol rifle was a full-sized A2, fixed stock, which he had been using for his entire career. His too was a no-name barrel (wish I could find the source of these excellent barrels lacking a name), but it wouldn't settle down and shoot a solid group at 25 yards. We always start classes with a zero session and accuracy check.

So, we checked his rifle, carefully, looking for all the usual suspects. Finally, I figured "Heck I'll check erosion." An erosion gage is meant to stop an inch or so short of the witness line, and when the witness line finally reaches the back end of the receiver (its data point) the barrel is considered eroded and past life. I thought the erosion gage was going to fall out of the muzzle. The aluminum plate on it stopped it from going in all the way. Once I un-tangled the plate, the gage went two-thirds of the way down the bore. That barrel had long been "shot out" and yet he had still passed the department's qualification course with it just a few months before this class. It still retained "minute of felon" accuracy at the length of a Buick.

Finally, a friend of mine does the maintenance and overhaul of carbines at a nuclear power plant. The security detail runs SBRs, with 11.5-inch barrels, and they are suppressed. He finds there are bolts broken on a regular basis, but he rarely has to change a barrel.

So, when is your barrel used up? When you can't shoot up to your usual standards would be one rule of thumb. Another would be to keep a log book, and a round count, and decide on a figure: 5,000, 7,500, 10,000 rounds, whatever. At the current cost of ammo, 5,000 rounds comes to a minimum of $900. After that much ammo, a new barrel (we're talking .223 here) for $200 is not a big expense. Which leads us to bolts.

BOLT LIFE

The AR-15 bolt leads a hard life. The original standard it was built to was the .223 Remington, which is a high-pressure, but not abusive, load. If you shoot only .223, or reloads that equal it, with a maximum pressure of only 50,000 PSI, then bolts last a long time. Especially if you do not do full-auto shooting (not a problem for most of us) and no suppressed shooting.

The hard work on bolts comes with the following, in a more-or-less order of increasing abuse:

- Carbine
- SBR
- Suppressed Carbine
- Suppressed SBR
- Full Auto

Each of those will be a shorter period than otherwise, if the ammunition is a steady diet of 5.56 as op-

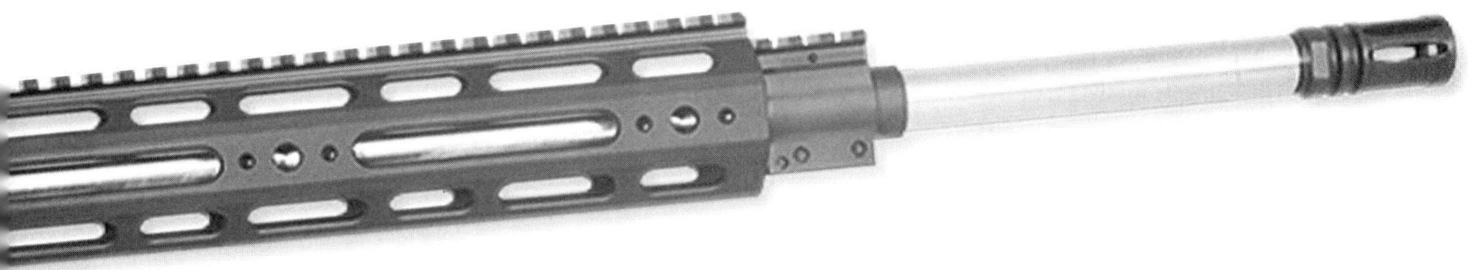

posed to .223, and if the firearm is not lubed properly.

The barrel that lasted over 15,000 rounds? That was a full-sized rifle. The bolt from that rifle is still in it, and on its third barrel. But it has never been subjected to full-auto fire, it has never run in a carbine, and none of the three barrels has ever been suppressed.

Now, I would not go depending on that rifle in a defensive situation, had I a choice. That bolt has had something on the order of 30,000 rounds through it (can rounds be "through" a bolt?) and if there is any bolt in my rifle rack that is destined to break, it has to be that one. But until it does, I'll keep using it.

How short a life can a bolt have? Let's pile up all the stressors: a suppressed SBR, subjected to bursts of full-auto fire. I'd be surprised if any bolt lasted more than 5,000 rounds of that. Since select-fire firearms are absurdly expensive, the vast majority of us will not have to face that problem. However, a semi-auto-only SBR, suppressed, is still going to have a shorter than typical bolt life, especially if you run it hard in practice or training. So, call it the military spec of 7,500 rounds.

At the current cost of .223 ammo at $180 per thousand rounds, that's $1,350 in ammo costs. An acceptable replacement bolt from Brownells currently runs $50. So, after $1,350 in ammo costs, a bolt adds $50 to the cost of a new barrel, which runs you $200. So, your ammo costs for practice, if we add in the replacement of the bolt and barrel once you get to the end of their life, is $213.30 per thousand rounds. Put it another way: if you take two years to "burn out" that barrel, and have to replace it, then your ammo and replacement costs have run you $800 a year. That's a little over $15 a week, which is less than what some people spend on flavored coffee beverages.

This is not an expensive diversion or entertainment, even if all you do is chalk it up as entertainment.

AMMO ASIDE

Now, these calculations have been made on the lowest-cost ammo, and the most common: .223. Where you can (at this writing) find .223 for $180 per thousand plus shipping, bigger calibers cost more. The current cost on .308/7.62 NATO is $320 per thousand, almost twice as much. On the flip side, you are not (trust me, you aren't) going to be shooting your AR-10 at anything like the rate you'll be shooting your AR-15. The barrel might not last any longer in terms of rounds down the tube, 7,500, but you won't be shooting that much ammo in two years. The simple cost of recoil is going to make it a lot more like work to shoot large volumes.

A range day where you put 200 rounds of .223 into the berm is a good day. A day spent putting 200 rounds of .308 into the berm is work, and you will be likely to be building bad habits, not good ones, by the end of the day.

My current project rifle is one in 6.5 Creedmoor, and there the ammo costs can get terrifying. The vanilla-plain ammo runs $640 per thousand rounds. Barrel life might even be shorter than the 7,500 yardstick we're using, simply because you go to the 6.5 for greater precision. When that falls off, there's not so much impetus to be using the really expensive rifle.

It is not difficult to find calibers that cost you more than a dollar per shot. A quick search turns up the .450 Bushmaster, .458 SOCOM and .50 Beowulf as costing more than a dollar a shot, and that's for the plain, blasting-ammo stuff. There are a bunch of others.

RECEIVERS

How long do receivers last? While the question might be asked, the answer is unclear. More receivers are lost through mishap, accident, abuse, neglect or just being dropped, than wear out. The wear points on the AR-15 upper and lower receiver set are few: the takedown-pin holes, the fire-control-pin holes, the barrel-nut threads and the lower-receiver hoop for the buffer tube.

The takedown-pin holes wear from the obvious:

steel pins sliding in and out, with friction created by a tight fit. The more you take it apart and put it back together the more they wear. Lubricant helps slow that process. However, it takes a lot of use to wear them out. As in, years and years of use.

The fire-control-pin holes are subject to both rotational wear and lateral stress. The rotational wear comes from the rotation of the trigger and the hammer. No, they don't turn much, but they can turn on each shot. The lateral stress comes from the hammer and trigger being moved and loaded. Each time the hammer is cocked by the carrier, the force of the carrier coming back both rotates the hammer and jolts it backward on the pin. The trigger is loaded to the rear on its pin each time it engages the sear hook of the cocked hammer.

These are not large forces at work, but they do happen thousands of times, once on each shot, and to lesser degree each time you cycle the action, to load, unload, check to make sure it is unloaded, etc.

To combat this, a company by the name of KNS makes anti-rotation pins. They are screwed in place with small round-head Allen-socket screws on the pins. The pin pairs have external straps that the pins are held by, and the assembly then forms a rigid box, with the straps outside the receiver, and the pins passing through, and none of it turns or rotates. A lot of shooters use these, but I never have, never having had a problem with pin rotation, or pin holes wearing. One of these days I might.

In any case, the lower pin holes are most likely good for tens of thousands of rounds of use before there might be a problem.

The upper receiver barrel nut threads are pretty sturdy. They can withstand a lot of on-and-off barrel work. I've swapped barrels on some receivers half a dozen times, and can't see any wear. Let's suppose you get only 10 barrel swaps before the threads start to punk out on you. That's 10 times the 7,500 rounds, and $1,600 in ammo and barrel and bolt combos. You've put a grand total of $16,000 of ammo, barrels and bolt through that upper. Replacing it for (current cost, again) $70 is hardly going to break the bank. In fact, using a brand-new upper for each barrel is not exactly an onerous cost, either. Which is what some people do, because they use epoxy to secure the barrel into the receiver, in order to wring as much accuracy out of the fitting as possible.

LAST OPTION

OK, one more choice you have to make, if the bug just won't let go. Let's say you have dreamed up a

cartridge that no-one else has. No one makes a barrel for it. So, what can you do?

Here's the path: The cartridge has to be a parent case that exists. It has to have a bolt face that exists. There has to be a magazine option to feed it. And it has to have a bore size that exists.

Let's call this theoretical cartridge the 7mm223.

OK, first thing is easy. Bolts will be standard AR-15 bolts.

The bullet choice will be limited. Most 7mm bullets will be long for the .223 case, so you will be stuck with something like a 120-grain V-Max from Hornady. You will have to neck-expand cases, and also shorten them, because the 7mm bullet is not going to work with a full-length .223 case.

Then there is the magazine problem. The fatter

7mm bullets will bind against the internal ribs of the .223 magazine. You'll have to be using something like (or the identical one) the Lancer mag that Wilson Combat uses for its 7.62x40 WT and .300 HAM'R.

That is all easy, or at least things you can do. Next comes the hard part: a barrel.

No one makes a 7mm223 barrel. You will have to find a gunsmith who does barrel work. He will have to acquire a barrel extension for the AR-15, and thread a 7mm barrel blank to fit the extension. He will have to profile the barrel, so it is the correct diameter where the gas port is supposed to be.

You will have to pay the freight to have a custom chamber-reamer set made. You will have to send the drawings in to someone like Dave Manson, and he will advise you on the pitfalls of your choices. Take his advice.

Then the gunsmith will ream the chamber for your barrel.

You can fit it to a receiver and do the rest of the assembly yourself. But there is still one more problem: gas port.

Have the gunsmith drill the gas port in the correct location (carbine, mid-length or rifle) and to the smallest diameter that is common for that length, in a normal .223/5.56 application. Then develop your loads, and when you find what you want, then and only then, re-drill the gas port so your ammunition cycles your rifle properly.

3

.223/ 5.56 AS THE BASELINE

The vast majority of AR-15s are chambered in .223 or 5.56. I will attempt to cover them only in this chapter, and except for one detail: What is the difference between those two calibers? The rest of this chapter I'll be reporting details relevant to the AR-15, using the .223/5.56 as the baseline.

In a nutshell, the .223 is the Remington design it offered up to SAAMI for adoption in 1963. It was the result of the testing the Army had been doing on small-bore, high-velocity projectiles for potential service use. The idea was simple: Armies probably didn't need a .308-inch bullet of full weight, one that could deal a mortal wound at 1,000 yards or more, when most infantry combat happened well inside 300 yards. In fact, the majority of it was inside less than half that.

they move, the space in which the powder can burn increases in volume. This slows, or dials down, if you will, the peak of the pressure curve.

When the bullet strikes the rifling, it (the bullet) slows down, and the pressure builds again. The powder is still burning, there is continued combustion. If the cartridge, the case, chamber and rifling are all designed properly, this secondary pressure spike is not usually as high as the initial one, and if so, the mechanism is not strained past design limits.

The bullet gets back up to speed and accelerates with the pressure of the gases behind it. Pressure then drops as the volume increases more, and the process is done for now.

OK, let's take that process, and try to increase it. We add more powder. This quickly causes the maximum pressure, that first spike, to exceed design limits. It exceeds limits even more if the bullet has not moved far enough forward to take some of the steam out of the initial pressure peak, and now when the bullet slams into the rifling, the peak gets added to by the secondary spike.

Here's an idea: We move the start of the rifling forward and make the angle it begins less steep. The bullet goes farther forward before it stalls, the stalling is not so great, and this really takes the steam out of the initial peak.

Now that we have some more headroom in the pressure curve, we add powder. We can even make it a slower-burning powder as well. We get back up to the allowed maximum pressure, but we have more powder, and thus we have more acceleration down the bore as the slower-burning powder keeps pushing.

That's the difference between the .223 and the 5.56. The 5.56 has its leade, the gap between the case mouth and the rifling, the gap the bullet has to jump, longer than that of the .223. The 5.56 does not run at a higher pressure, it just has a different way of controlling that pressure.

This is all well and good. But what happens if we take some 5.56 ammunition, constructed to burn in a chamber with a long leade, and we put it into a .223 chamber, with a shorter leade? Now we get pressure.

The ammo companies know the difference, and they do not mark their boxes capriciously. You should check your chamber leade before using ammunition marked as "5.56" and stick with .223 until you know for sure.

The first Armalite, the AR-15, was built in that cartridge. When it came time to have the Army actually adopt the rifle, the Army Ordnance department kept moving the goalposts. The "We're OK as long as it penetrates a helmet at 200 meters, wait, no, 300 meters," became 400, then 500 meters. In order to perform that task, the cartridge developers had to increase velocity. They did not, as some might assume, do so by simply increasing pressure. At least, not that simply.

OK, a brief seminar on how ammo works. When the firing pin strikes the primer, the primer goes off and ignites the powder. In handguns, pretty much all the powder has burned before the bullet leaves the case. In some instances, it has all burned before the bullet even begins to move. Rifles aren't like that.

Depending on the cartridge, the powder charge, bullet caliber and weight and powder burn rate, the bullet, and even the column of powder, can begin moving forward before all the powder has burned. The bullet begins to move forward out of the case neck, and then when it strikes the beginning of the rifling, it slows down. It has to. It takes a certain amount of time and energy to engrave the rifling shape into the bullet. Until that is done, the bullet will be traveling slower than it would otherwise be.

When the powder burns, the pressure builds until the bullet and unburnt powder begin to move. As

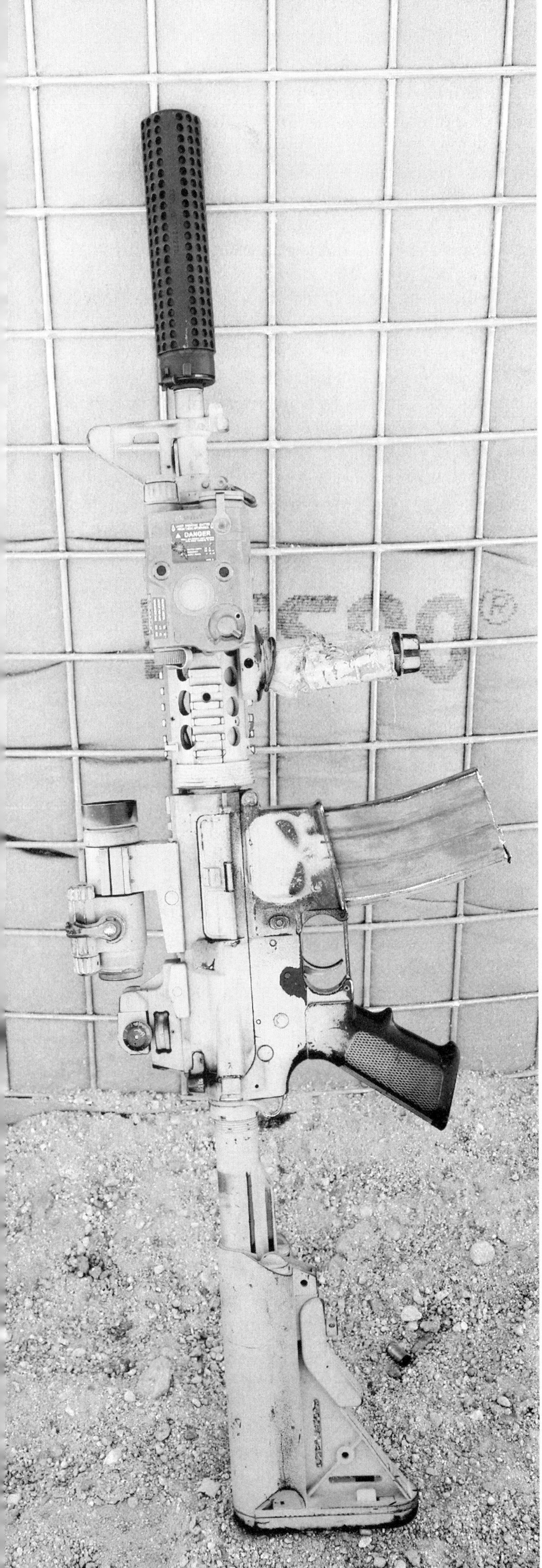

The military uses a lengthened leade to both drop pressure and gain performance. This is a legacy of a half-century ago, when it didn't want the AR-15.

The nominal maximum chamber pressure for both the .223 and the 5.56 is 55,000 PSI. Just as an aside, adding to the confusion of the chamber pressures, the American measuring method of pressure measures pressure at a different point than that used by the Europeans. So, if someone tells you "military and European ammo is 60,000, while commercial is 55,000," yes, that is true. But if you take the 60K European ammo, and you measure it according to the American methodology, it will kick up a 55K reading.

Oh, and most ammo does not run at the max. I have had various .223 and 5.56 ammunition lots pressure-tested, and I've gotten readings as low as 48,000 PSI. (In the appropriate test barrel for that caliber.) The 55K PSI might be the allowable max, but if ammo makers can get the expected velocity out of the ammo, and do so at 48K instead of 55K, they'd be stupid not to.

So, what happens if you put 5.56 ammo in a .223 pressure barrel, and take a reading? Bad things. I've seen, and heard other reports of, pressure readings of 70,000 to 75,000 PSI, when 5.56 ammo is fired in .223 pressure barrel chambers. The high-water mark, if you will, was a reported 76,250 PSI, with honest-to-goodness 5.56 ammo fired in a .223 test barrel. For those who don't have a calculator handy, that is a 38 percent increase over the book ceiling for a .223 or 5.56 with a proper chamber.

"But, I've shot lots of 5.56 through my rifle, and have had no problems." Certainly. And you might even have a 5.56 chamber. But you might not. That your rifle has held together, and worked just fine, is a testament to the safety margin built in. It is also abuse.

"My rifle has a 5.56 chamber; it passes the headspace check my gunsmith did."

Headspace tells you nothing.

Headspace is the measurement of the distance between the front of the bolt face and the shoulder in the chamber that stops the cartridge. For all intents and purposes, the distance that is allowed is the same for both .223 Remington and 5.56x45 NATO. There are those who will obsess over the thousandths difference between this or that standard, but the overlap is so great, relatively, that there is no difference. Leade matters, not headspace.

My barrel is marked 5.56, so I'm fine.

Markings might not matter.

Some manufacturers can be counted on to produce 5.56 leades in rifles marked 5.56. Colt is one, Daniel Defense is another, FN most certainly does. I'm sure there are others. But not all barrels marked "5.56" actually have a 5.56 leade. At an LE Patrol rifle class, to test this, we used a leade gauge (more on this to follow) on all of the students' rifles. Four had .223 leades. Three of the four were marked "5.56," the fourth was completely unmarked.

What happens if you take a rifle with a .223 leade, and shoot a steady diet of 5.56 ammo through it? A phenomenon known as "popped primers." The primers don't actually pop out, but the extra pressure expands the case head, sometimes too much, and then primers can fall out. When they fall out of the case, but stay in the action, they can get in the way of the moving parts and cause problems.

As a secondary problem, if you reload ammo, and pick up cases that have been expanded and lost their primers, you might not be able to make the primer stay in place in your reloaded case. Then, the primer might fall out before you can load and shoot it, and the firing pin hits nothing. Or it falls out as it is being fed, and the primer wedges in place, someplace not good.

There is a difference in the leade (the only place there is a difference) and it matters. Here you can see the difference, in sample chambers, split for photography.

So, we have a problem with chambers (actually leades, but "chamber" covers it well enough when you know the difference) and the markings don't help. What can we do?

We use a gauge to see if the leade is .223 or 5.56, and if it is the former, we ream it to the latter.

The gauge and reamer come to us from M-Guns, Ned Christiansen. The gauge tells you if the leade is .223 by sticking in place or being difficult to turn once inserted. The reamer reams the leade, and only the leade, to 5.56. It does not change headspace, it can't.

Now, some barrels are chrome-plated. Oh well, your choice here is a chrome-plated .223, or a 5.56 leade with the chrome reamed off right at the leade. Shooting your rifle is going to blast the chrome off the .223 leade in short order anyway, so the choice should be easy.

Last are the barrels that are treated with Melonite. This is a surface-hardening process, and the reamer won't cut it. In fact, you'll dull the reamer if you try.

With the leade reamed to 5.56, you now will not have the pressure spikes you'd had before. Life is good.

Yes, but reaming your chamber, even if it is the leade, has to have some effect on accuracy, doesn't it? Maybe it does, maybe it doesn't. One way would be to find or build a tack-driving accurate AR-15 in .223, then ream the leade and check accuracy again. What I do know is if there is an accuracy difference, it has been so small in the rifles and carbines I've reamed, as to not be noticeable in classes or competition. Someone who can shoot well enough to tell, like an NRA High Master in High Power, or a first-class benchrest shooter (competitive, not just the best guy at your club) might be able to parse out the change, if there is one.

I do know I have not seen a change in accuracy, nor a change in zero, in the rifles I've done. I have no hesitation in solving the pressure problem, with little or no risk of an accuracy loss.

As a cross-check, I wrote an article for which I took a bolt-action rifle in .223 and did this to it. Actually, the manufacturer was on the ball, and it arrived with a 5.56 leade. I had to pull the barrel, set the shoulder and barrel face back, then ream to .223 leade, and reinstall the barrel. I then chronographed it and shot it for accuracy. (And it was accurate.) I then reamed the leade to 5.56. Velocity dropped a bit, if you care, 50 fps or so. Accuracy? Untouched.

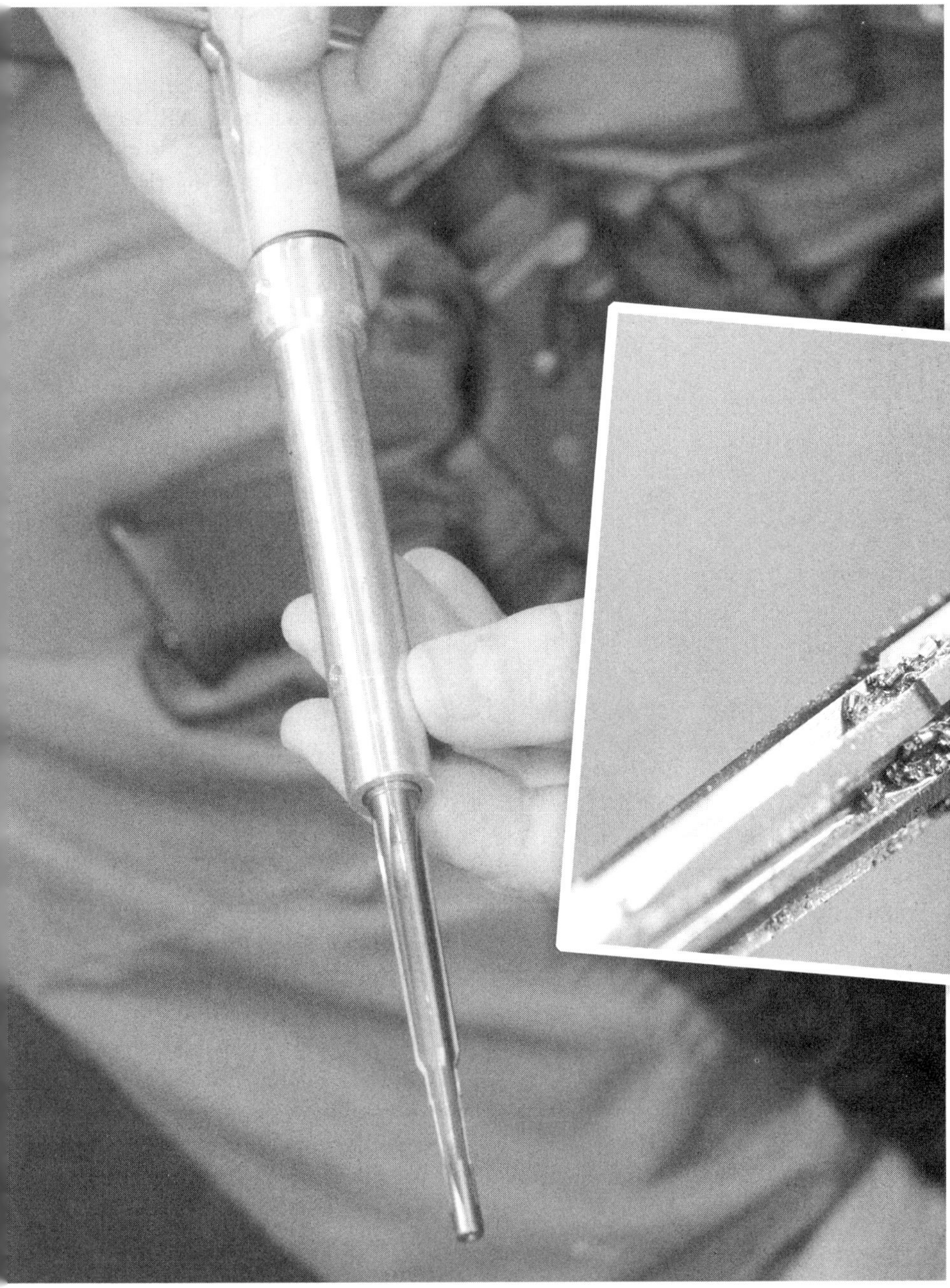

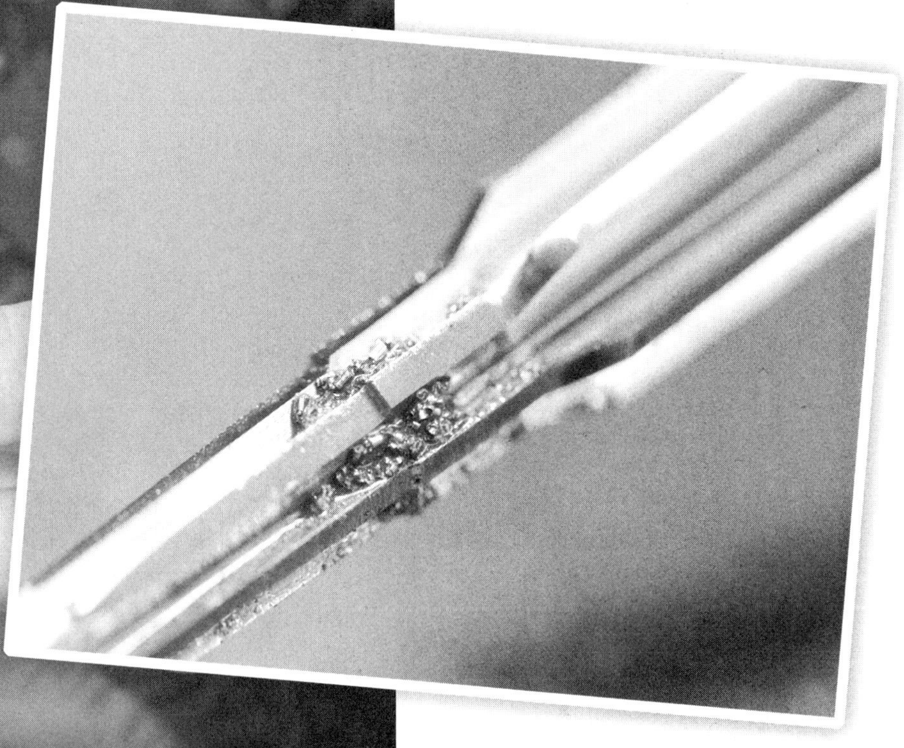

(above) This shows where the M-Guns reamer cuts. Just in the leade, and some in the neck if the neck is too tight. The shoulder does not cut at all.

(left) The reamer, assembled into its handle, ready to ream a .223 leade to 5.56.

(bottom) The M-Guns reamer lengthens the leade and adjusts the rifling angle. That's all.

It was a shame to send it back, knowing they were going to pull that barrel and scrap it, replace it, and send the rifle onward.

To put it into context, the common-as-dirt, one-MOA AR-15 isn't. Most ARs would be hard-pressed to demonstrate consistent one-MOA accuracy, even with match ammo. Most shooters, even with a one-MOA AR, could not consistently shoot groups that size. If you then add in the group-increasing ammo choice most of us make, that is, what is not expensive, then one MOA is a dream.

No, really.

I don't mean to be insulting when I say that I'd be willing to slap a $100 bill down on the shooting bench, for anyone at the gun club with their AR, who can shoot three sub-MOA groups in a row to take. And know I'd be taking it home with me. Even three that averaged one MOA.

So, let's assume that reaming the leade increases group size by a whopping .25 MOA. Who's going to notice? And yes, .25 MOA is whopping. You can't win a serious benchrest match with an aggregate that large, and yet in the AR-verse it is an increase not to be noticed.

Life is like that.

So, save the hassle, save the wear and tear on your rifle, and get the leade checked. Like the carrier key staking tool Ned makes, there's probably someone at your gun club who has the tool and gauge, get it done.

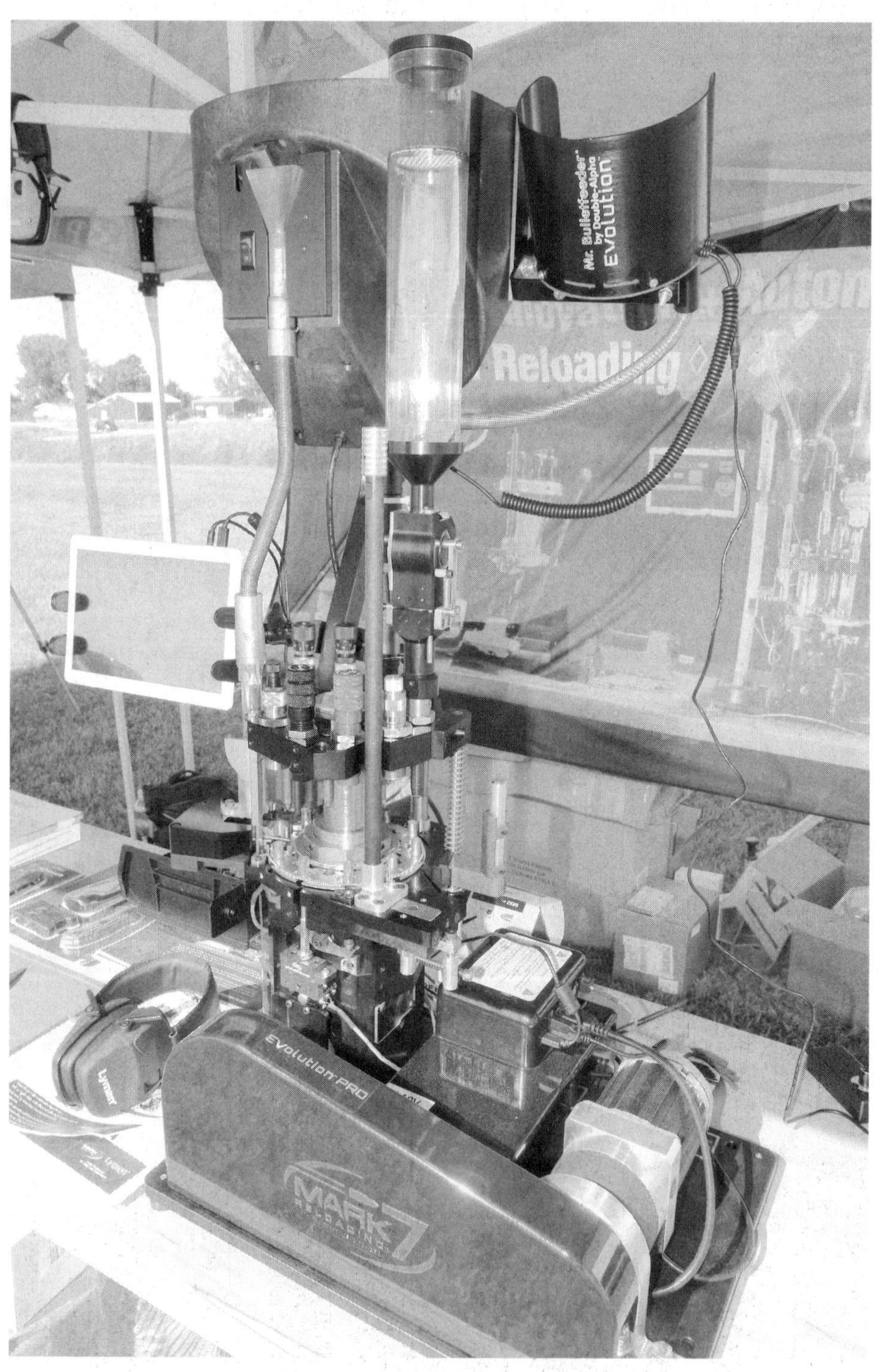

This Mark 7, a new acquisition by Lyman, will allow you to load .223 (or other AR calibers) in impressive volume. It is self-powered, so you set the cyclic rate. Just keep all the feed hoppers filled, and check ammo quality, and you will have hundreds of rounds an hour.

RELOADING FOR THE AR SYSTEM

When it comes to loading ammo for the various AR platforms, there is the old advice, and the new advice. I was talking with a fellow old-school loader, shooter and competitor, and he also vaguely remembered this: We were advised back in the day, that if we wanted our rifles to work reliably, we had to use small-base sizing dies.

Time to do a bit of history. A small-base die is one where the sizing dimension that contacts the rifle case down as low as it can, is dimensioned to bring the case to below standard specs. That is, if a rifle case was intended to have a diameter at the head (just to pick a number) of .400 of an inch as its factory maximum, most cases would be manufactured to be in the .396- to .398-inch range. Yes, a bit small, but the .400 dimension was actually spec'd, if you checked, to be .400-.004 for reliable function.

A standard sizing dies would bring the case back to .399 or .398, so the spring-back after sizing would leave it no larger than the maximum of .400. Are you still with me? OK. The small-base sizing dies were intended to squeeze the case head down to the minimum or less, so it would (in this instance) size it down to .395 or so.

This allegedly allowed the autoloading rifle to properly chamber the case.

This was considered gospel for the AR-15, because "it needed it." Why it needed it, and other autoloading rifles didn't, was never fully explained.

Those of us who had ARs, and were working on making them reliable, didn't bother with overworking our brass, and simply dealt with the other problems of reliable function, and didn't have a problem.

So, when you read advice to invest in a small-base sizing die, ignore it. Unless your rifle is the anomalous one, the real, actual, at the small end of chamber specs rifle, you don't need a small-base sizing die. What does matter is shoulder location, and I'll go into excruciating detail at the appropriate point.

So, what do you have to do, to have reliable ammunitions for your reliable AR-15 or AR-10? The broad strokes of your reloading process are these: Inspect, Clean, Size, Load, Inspect. Each step has as many steps as your situation, or your level of OCD, requires.

Mine is somewhat involved, but it suits me, and it makes it possible to load gallons of reliable ammo, so I'll lay it out for you.

CLEAN

Your AR brass gets smoked by the chamber pressure and gas blowback, and then hurled to the ground. If you are shooting suppressed, then the smoke is worse, and some ranges are worse on the ground than others. If you shoot unsuppressed, and the range floor (yes, the flat part of an outdoor range is called the "floor") is composed of pea gravel or distressed granite, then your brass is pretty clean.

In such instances, you get to go right through inspection, to tumbling.

My range is silt and sand, with a bit of loamy mud

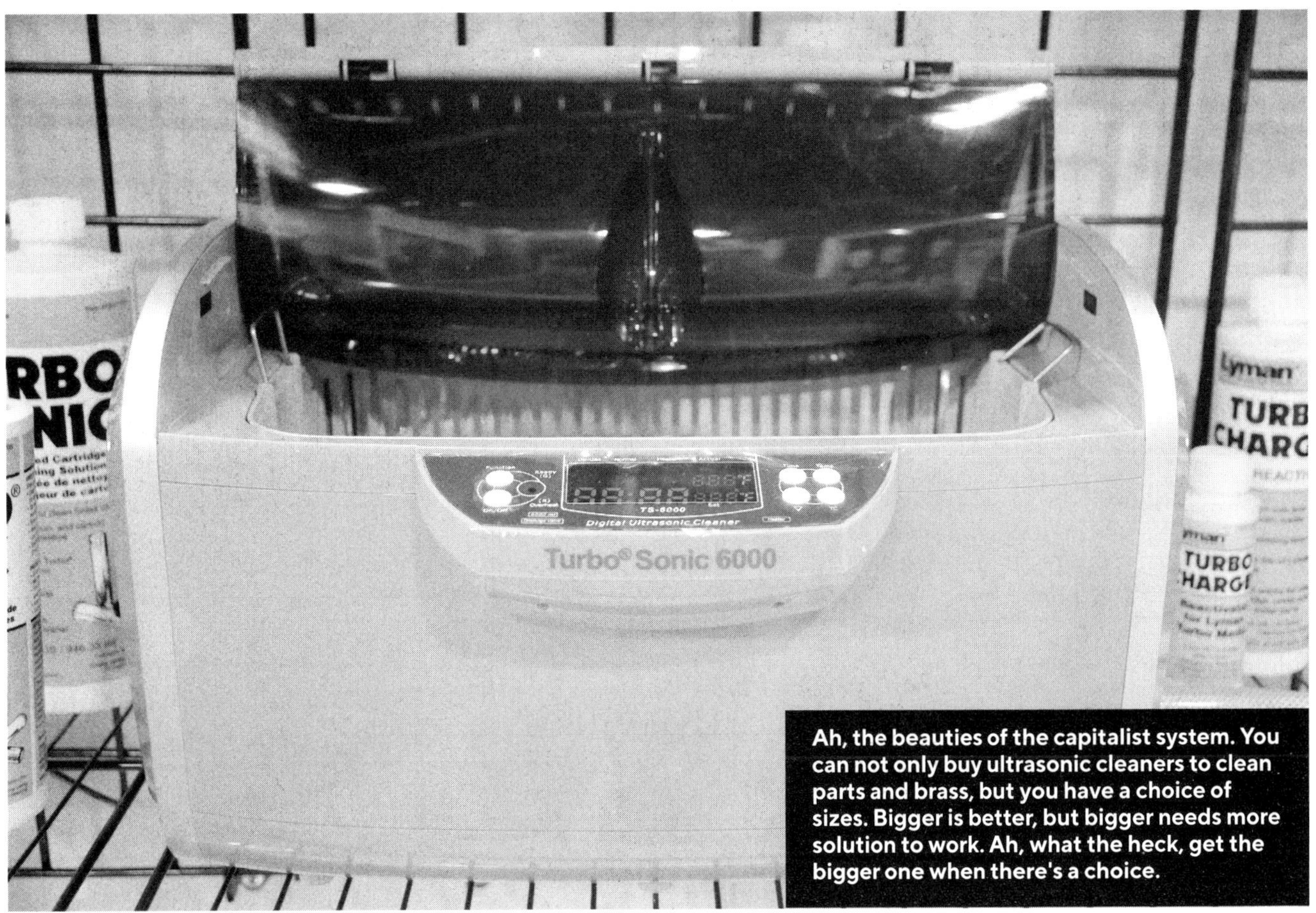

Ah, the beauties of the capitalist system. You can not only buy ultrasonic cleaners to clean parts and brass, but you have a choice of sizes. Bigger is better, but bigger needs more solution to work. Ah, what the heck, get the bigger one when there's a choice.

thrown in. If it has rained recently, the mud gets to be sticky. In any case, if the brass has been down there for more than a day, it starts to get kind of chocolate-y in color.

So, my cleaning process works like this:

First, I pick up all the brass that's there, mine and whatever is left in the appropriate caliber. My gun club is a "You left it; it belongs to whoever picks it up" range. So, I vacuum all the rifle calibers there, and sort them out.

When I have enough to process, I heat a pot of water, with its strainer. I don't get the water boiling, that temperature would be hazardous. Just hot enough to evaporate quickly, but not up to boiling.

I also mix up my chemical cleaner. I still use a leftover supply of Lyman concentrate, but when that runs out, I'll have to whip up one using citric acid and dish detergent.

The process is simple, if involved. I inspect to make sure the brass is all the same caliber and that there is no steel in it. (A magnet works wonders here.) I dip a wire basket of the cases into the hot water, then dump them out and drain the water. I then dump them into the cleaning solution to soak for 15 minutes or so. Once soaked, I decant the cleaning solution (save it, it works for a bunch of soaks) and run the brass back into the hot water, to rinse off the citric acid.

Back in the old days I'd do this in the summer months and let the now-clean (more or less) brass sun-dry on an old towel. These days, I simply put it into the Lyman case dryer, and finish drying. The hot water evaporates a lot off the cases, but drying doesn't hurt, and

(top) Clean, but wet, brass will spot, tarnish if left to air-dry in its own good time. To dry them faster, pour your brass into the Lyman dryer and let the marvel of electricity do your drying.

(left) The Hornady Lock-N-Load Sonic Cleaner will get parts, and brass, clean. Just use the correct solution for each.

it keeps them from being water-spotted.

Then, they would go into the tumbler, or vibratory cleaner. There, I'd let the corncob medium scour the rest of the tarnish off of them. This would complete the first clean. I'd either bag up the brass, or put it into plastic storage containers, and shelve them.

ULTRASONICS

Since the advent of inexpensive ultrasonic cleaners, a lot of shooters just dump their brass into the "sonic" with the correct solution, turn it on and let the timer tell them when it is done. That works, too. Also, there has been a lot of crossover from rock polishing to brass cleaning, and there are a bunch of shooters who use chemical solutions and stainless steel pins to clean their brass. Those all work.

I have my legacy system, and it works for me. Should I have to move someplace someday, and have to set up again, I would give the other methods a good, long look, because they are used by people with success. Basically, if it works, great.

If you don't need to load hundreds of rounds an hour, or can't swing the cost of a self-powered press, then this turret press from Lyman will be sufficient.

SIZE

The trick with sizing brass is to understand what it goes through when you fire it. The case head does not expand significantly when you fire, unless you are using off-the-charts loads. But the case body does expand, and the case shoulder bangs forward until it is stopped by the chamber shoulder. It also expands a small amount past that, due to the expansion of headspace caused by the pressure.

What you need to do is resize your case body back down to normal specs and bump the shoulder back to the minimum called for in the drawings. This used to be a lot more difficult in the old days, but now the die makers have it figured out.

The trick is in your setup. You want to install your sizing die in your press so that when you raise the ram (this fitting comes even before you start loading) it cams over just a bit at the end. The process is simple: Install your shell plate or case holder in the die; run the die up all the way and leave it there; then screw in the sizing die until it stops hard against the shell plate or case holder.

Now lower your ram, and give the sizing die an extra quarter turn. The die maker will give you the exact amount it wants it turned. This pushes the shoulder back to the drawing minimum and allows for reliable feeding and chambering.

Your secondary check is with a case gauge. This is a section of chamber that has been reamed in a cylinder, and the back end of it has two steps. Or a groove machined down the middle. The upper shelf of the step or groove is the maximum length the case can be from the shoulder. The lower one is the minimum.

When you are setting up your press, you adjust the die as above, and use the lock ring to hold it in place. You then lubricate and size one empty. Wipe it clean, and then insert it in the case gauge. If the case head is lower than the upper shelf, and higher than the lower shelf, you are fine. Higher than the upper means the shoulder is too far forward, and you will have chambering problems. Lower than the lower shelf means your shoulder has been set back too far, and your cases will have a short life.

Each time you shoot, the case stretches, and the shoulder moves forward. Sizing it pushes the shoulder back, but does not displace the brass that has flowed. That requires trimming.

There are two schools of thought here. One is to measure, and trim those that need it. The other is to trim them all. I am of the "trim them all" school.

I set up my trimming process to trim cases back to the minimum case length. I then run them all through it. If they don't need trimming, then the cutter never reaches the case. Fine. If it does, it gets cut.

Why trim? The chamber is only so long. If the neck of the case is too long, it will either stop the bolt from closing, or more likely, still close, but the extra brass gets squeezed down onto the bullet. This raises pressure.

So, once the sizing die is set up, you lube all the cases and size them. If you are using a progressive, you lube them all, and size and trim to length. Sizing also decaps the primers, because that's what sizing dies do.

You have a bucket full of sized, trimmed, lubed brass.

What I do is a cleaning step again, but just with hot water and a vibratory cleaner. No need for the chemical cleaning here, you just want to get the lubricant off the cases.

LOAD

The loading process uses a sizing die (I load on progressives, no single-stage loading for me) at the first station. However, since the cases do not have lube on them, nor do they need resizing at this stage, I use a separate sizing die, but one that has been backed out a turn. (More, depending on the caliber.) I keep the

decapping pin installed, and the purpose of this die is two-fold. One, it uniforms case necks that might have gotten dented in the cleaning, and the pouring from one bucket or box or bag, to another. Two, the decapping pin clears the flash hole of any tumbling media that might have gotten wedged in there.

Loading is straightforward. Seat the primer, drop the powder, seat the bullet, and crimp the case neck.

All ammo that goes into an AR gets a crimp. The recoil of jostling back and forth in the magazine, then the trip up the feed ramp, means bullets have to be secure in the case. So, I crimp.

INSPECT

I look each one over to make sure the bullet looks

If you have any feeding issues at all with your AR, and you do not crimp into a cannelure on the bullet, you will see problems like this. Good neck tension is needed, but you should always crimp if there's a cannelure to crimp into. And most bullets for the AR have a cannelure.

right, the case appears correct, and that the primer is in there properly. A moment's glance at each end tells you if things are right. Now, if you want to be as OCD as it takes, you could load ammunition up to anyone's performance. You want defensive ammo that you've loaded? I don't recommend it, but hey, it's a free country. Then you can. Long-range target ammo gets as much inspection, and fussing.

I view reloads as practice, training and drill-conduction ammunition. If I have a malfunction (and they are rare, indeed, because I am careful) then it is part of the training.

Once inspected, it goes into volume storage. Back when I was competing in 3-gun and bowling pins, my common storage bins were the fiberboard containers that eight pounds of powder came in. I had a lot of them, empty, to work with. (In my competition years, I routinely went through 35,000 rounds a year, and I was not at the top of the list of ammo-consumers. That takes a bunch of powder.)

The plastic ammo boxes from MTM will serve you well and hold enough ammo for a good day's practice.

POWDER SELECTION

Not all powders are the same. You must use the correct powder for your gas-operated system. The exemplar here is the M1 Garand, which is particularly sensitive to powder selection. The gas port of the Garand is at the muzzle, almost two feet from the primer. Once the bullet passes the gas port, the gas can flow into the system only until the bullet leaves the muzzle, called the gas dwell time. On the Garand, that is less than an inch.

On the AR-15, barrel length can make a huge difference in dwell time. On a rifle, the gas port to muzzle distance is 8.5 inches. On the non-NFA carbine, the distance is 7 inches. Ever wonder why the M4 has a 14.5-inch barrel? Answer: So the bayonet of the rifle would fit. As a result, the dwell time distance of the M4 is the same as that of the full-sized rifle, but the gas port diameters will differ.

On the shorties, the SBRs, it can be less than an inch, as with the 10.3-inch barrel on the MK18.

All of these have to deliver a jolt of gas to the gas key, and drive the system, regardless of barrel length or port location. As a result, they will have different gas port diameters. What the port diameters are is not the important detail here. What is important is that the system does not have a self-correcting feature.

One detail of the M14 was that the piston had a gas slot in it. Once the slot traveled past the gas port location of the barrel, it stopped being pressurized. As a result, it was somewhat self-regulating. So much so that many years ago, at The Steel Challenge, when it was in the Worker's Paradise of California, I entered the five-gun championships. Handgun, pump and auto shotgun, .30 and .223 rifle. For my .30 rifle, I used my M1A. I pulled the bullets from 150-grain factory ammo, and substituted 110-grain spire-points. The rifle shot them reliably, and more than accurately enough. The targets were 18- by 24-inch steel plates, out to 200 yards. I shot well enough to win a firearm.

The AR-15 can't do that. If you stray too far from the suggested powders (and there are plenty) you will find the gas pressure at the gas port too high or too low. Use recommended powders.

Also, use the correct amount. You gain nothing by exceeding book loads. The ammunition, powder and reloading companies are not stealing fps from your ammo by posting prudent loading data.

PRIMERS, REMOVING

Back in the good old days (which they weren't, mostly), we didn't have to worry too much about crimped primers. Most brass wasn't made with crimped primers, and so the problem arose only rarely in loading. Ever since 9/11, a lot of ammo has been made with crimped primers. Military production, military overruns, and ammo "made to military specs" all have crimped primers. This is to prevent primers from falling out in hard-use rifles, carbines and belt-fed machine guns.

Getting spent primers out of crimped-primer brass isn't too difficult. Most primer decapping pins handle them with little or no fuss. It is in getting the new ones in that the trouble begins. As in, they won't.

The crimped portion has to be swaged or cut away. Now, when I started reloading, the manuals that were available dated from just before to just after WWII. (I know, I'm old.) Some even suggested using a penknife to cut the crimp out of the primer pocket.

Even if you know what a penknife is, doing that with a bucket of brass is madness. They were thinking in terms of reloaders who were loading up once-fired .30-06 brass, for use in bolt-action hunting rifles. You might not need more than 20 to 40 rounds a year. (I know, that's just crazy talk, isn't it?)

So, you need a volume method of dealing with crimped primer pockets. One is to go with a Dillon 1050. Now the Dillon Super 1050, it offers volume. There are six die locations on the toolhead, and one of them is the location where the primer pocket swaging is done. As you run the brass through the press, the primer is expelled as the case is sized, and then the primer pocket is swaged to remove the crimp.

Back when I was loading on a 1050 (before they became Super) we used two toolheads. One was set up to do nothing but size, deprime, swage primer pockets and trim. With the automated case feeder, the press could almost keep up with a quick handle cycling. You simply used a measured cycle, so the case feeder could keep up, and your clean cases would be processed.

The reason for this: lubricant. Clean cases had to be lubed to be sized. Lubed cases could not be loaded.

So, once through the 1050 for processing, every single case to be had.

Then, pull off the processing toolhead, scrub the case feeder and set up the loading toolhead. Meanwhile, the processed cases would be cleaned of their lubricant.

Then, into the press for loading.

Now, the Super 1050 costs $1,800. A toolhead runs $205. Add the case trimmer at $338, the case feeder at $295, and you have a machine investment of $2,638, and that doesn't include dies, scale, etc.

Loading in volume requires an investment. But, with the full-on setup, including the case feeder, you can load .223 in volume, and load it at a throughput rate of 500 rounds an hour.

If your practice session at the range requires 250 rounds (and that's a lot of shooting) then it is a half-hour investment of time to load that practice ammo. Money savings? At the current prices, reloaded .223, assuming you are not buying brass (you pick that up pretty much for free around here) does not save you any money. I did a quick search for ammo for sale. I came up with a bunch that were just under or just at $200 per 1,000 rounds. Which is what the bullets, powder and primers will cost you for 1,000 rounds.

Now, other calibers will be different. And the .223 is most likely the anomaly. Its sheer volume means loaded ammo prices are almost at loss-leader margins for ammo makers and sellers.

If you are loading, say, 6.5 Creedmoor, then the equation is different. But it will take some time, and a bunch of shooting, to recoup the investment in a Super 1050.

Not that you shouldn't, but you should know what

The newest type of crimp is not a ring but a quartet of chiseled stabs. This is stronger (keeping primers in) and easier to apply.

you are getting yourself in to.

The lower-cost way to swage primer pockets is slower, I'll admit, but it doesn't gobble up two or three mortgage payments. And that is the Dillon Super Swage 600. It is a one-at-a-time press you bolt to your bench, but it does handle brass fairly quickly, for being one at a time.

PRIMERS, REPLACING

You need primers to load ammo. Primers come in two sizes, small rifle and large rifle, and two types, standard and magnum. (One could argue that they also come in leaded and unleaded varieties, but that's not the current option for many.)

Small is small, and large is large. That's easy. Standard and magnum? Some powders, particularly the slower-burning varieties of the ball-powder types, can be a bit difficult to ignite. Ball powder is just that, the powder is produced as small spheres, or further treated to be flattened spheres. The magnum primers are hotter, and thus are better for igniting the otherwise recalcitrant ball powders.

You use the size the case calls for. For almost all, this is not a problem. For the 6.8 Remington SPC, which can be had in one of each, you have to sort brass. There is no advantage to using magnum primers when the loading data calls for standard. In fact, you can cause problems. The hotter primer can boost pressure a bit. If you are already loading at the max level, adding in the boost of the uncalled-for magnum primer might be too much of a good thing.

You will read advice that you should be using "mil-spec" primers. These are known as No. 34 for large, and No. 41 for small primers from CCI. Before we cover why you might want to use them, we need to understand what is going on.

The primer, any primer, should be seated a few thousandths of an inch below flush with the case head. This protects it from inadvertent ignition from being hit by something while being handled or chambered. High primers are a problem that changing primer type won't solve. If your primers are coming off the press not fully seated, you need to solve that problem, not switch primers.

Primers are sensitive. I had a fellow competition shooter send me the evidence of an accidental discharge. Now, most of the time we use "AD" as a kind way of saying "Son, you screwed up." But this was an accident. The shooter was on an indoor range, with a tray of loaded ammo on the bench, out of its box. An empty, ricocheting around the booth, landed on the ammo, and set off one round. Once all the parts were collected, there was a clear impression on the fired case primer of the rim of a case. And the bullet showed no rifling marks.

Accident? You bet. One in a million? Probably much higher odds. But it illustrates that primers are sensitive.

Firing pins in rifles are not all spring-loaded. In pistols we have all of them spring-loaded, with the exception of the striker-fired designs, but they are mechanically held back from the breechface.

The AR-15 design does not have a firing pin retracting spring. When you close the bolt, the firing pin is free to jounce back and forth inside the bolt. If you have ever extracted a chambered but unfired round, you might have seen a tiny dent in the center. That is caused from the firing pin bumping the primer on closing. When the Army tested the M16 back in the early 1960s, the design had a heavier firing pin. The Army calculated that it would cause an accidental discharge once each 100,000 chamberings. Big deal, you say? A few years later we had 500,000 soldiers hard at work in a place called Vietnam. One AD each 100,000 chamberings would work out to a handful or more each day in-country.

After a lot of work and testing, the easiest solution was to make the firing pin as lightweight as possible and still be durable. This reduces the likelihood of a closing AD to one in millions of chamberings.

Now, if your primers are seated too high, you are going to have problems, and it isn't because of the inherent design of the AR-15.

The CCI No. 34 and No. 41 primers are for those who want some extra insurance in their loading. The primers are not as readily set off by a firing pin, but still 100-percent reliable, and thus increase the odds from one in millions to one in millions and millions.

In addition to the AR, there are a bunch of other rifles that do not have spring-loaded firing pins. Just off the top of my head I can think of the M1 Garand, the M14/M1A, and the SKS.

TESTING

In the old days, reloaders were looking to both improve accuracy and improve performance. There's a firm belief in some quarters that the ammunition manufacturers are holding back. They are, in effect, stealing fps from our ammo. BS.

So, reloaders would try to use a slower-burning powder, and more of it, to gain velocity, and they would do this while looking for "pressure signs." Before we go any further, let me reiterate: You can't use slower powders in the AR-15/AR-10, the gas system is acutely sensitive to burn rate.

Those experimenters would look for primers that were abused; flattened, cratered, pressed to sharp edges in the primer pocket. Or, they would measure the base of the case, to determine how much expansion had happened in the "pressure ring" of the case. All BS.

Quite simply put, by the time you see any "pressure signs" you are well past the safe margins of chamber pressure. Except for the occasional lost primer in a case, you are not going to see pressure signs in 5.56, fired in a .223 chamber, and developing 75,000 PSI. By the time you get there you are past safe. So, don't do that. Stick with published data, and don't try to develop your own "5.56 Magnum" that will "work just fine" in your AR-15.

HISTORY

It is not as well-known as it should be, the American idea of a voluntary professional standards organization.

What? Huh?

Let me explain. When I visited Germany a few years back, I had a chance to visit Walther, and also to see the Proof House at Ulm.

Now, whenever a firearm is manufactured in Europe, it has to go to the Proof House for proofing. There, the inspectors measure all the relevant dimensions. I happened to have a chance to inspect a gauge set for a given caliber. The gauge set was not just the GO and NO-GO headpsace gauges, but also pass and fail gauges for things like the groove diameter and bore diameter of the rifle at the muzzle. There were throat diameter and length gauges, and more.

Part of this is that gunsmiths in Europe might have actually made the barrel from a bar of steel, but that is something we'll cover when we discuss the American side of things.

The firearm is inspected, test-fired and stamped with the passing mark, the „proof mark" showing that it passed.

The Proof House is a government or government-controlled organization. You cannot offer a firearm for commercial sale unless it has been proofed and stamped. Even American firearms, when sold overseas, have to be proofed and stamped. I saw a few of these back in the gun shops when I was working retail, and gunsmithing. A GI would come back from his/her (mostly his) rotation to Europe, and sell a firearm acquired over there. It was just a bit strange seeing a, for example, S&W revolver, with German or British proof marks on it. I'm sure some collector would be happy to add such a beast to his or her colleciton.

There are no Proof Houses in America. Each manufacturer does its own proofing, and makes its firearms to the relevant dimensions because there are accepted standards.

And that's where SAAMI comes in.

Formed in 1926, SAAMI the Small Arms and Ammunition Manufacturing Institute, publishes the standards for each cartridge. Those standards will be the allowed size of the case in all its external dimensions, the chamber, and how much those dimensions can „wander" in manufacturing. Wander? OK, let's make a bullet for a .30-06. The accepted dimension for the bullet is a diameter of .308 of an inch, but you can't make each and every one of them exactly .308. To be precise, you can't make them, each and every one of them, exactly .3080 in diameter. Well, you could, but they would be fabulously expensive, and no one could afford to shoot them.

So, you then have to decide: How much can I let it vary from .3080? How about .3081, is that OK? Or .3082? The dimensions you are looking for are the „plus and minus" measure. So, the form will look something like this: .308±.0005. What that means, and it is vocalized as „three-oh-eight plus or minus five ten-thousandths" is that any bullet you make that measures between .3075 and .3085, inclusive, is an acceptable one. You can also do just plus or just minus. The former would be .3075 plus .001, and the latter would be .3085 minus .001.

Good bullet makers will do much better, and they will have as their in-house standard something like .308±.0001. They will also charge more for their bullets.

Accepted standards change over time, while the printed ones still stand. For instance, if/when there is a war on, the full spread of .3075 to .3085 is just fine. But in peacetime, and when better equipment like CNC machines and automated inspection are invented, the .3079 to .3081 spread becomes the norm.

But where do these dimensions come from? From the industry. From SAAMI.

SAAMI is a committee, composed of SAAMI members. They have technical geeks who report to them, but those on the commitee are experienced enough to have a handle on things. Not like aides reporting to senators or representatives, where the elected don't have a clue about much of anything. But I digress.

The dimensions of cartridges were hammered out over time. It isn't like they had to define every cartridge in existence in an afternoon in 1977. The makers of, for example, .30-06 knew back in 1926 with the formation of SAAMI what dimensions they were making them to. And the government also knew what it expected from .30-06 ammo, since that was

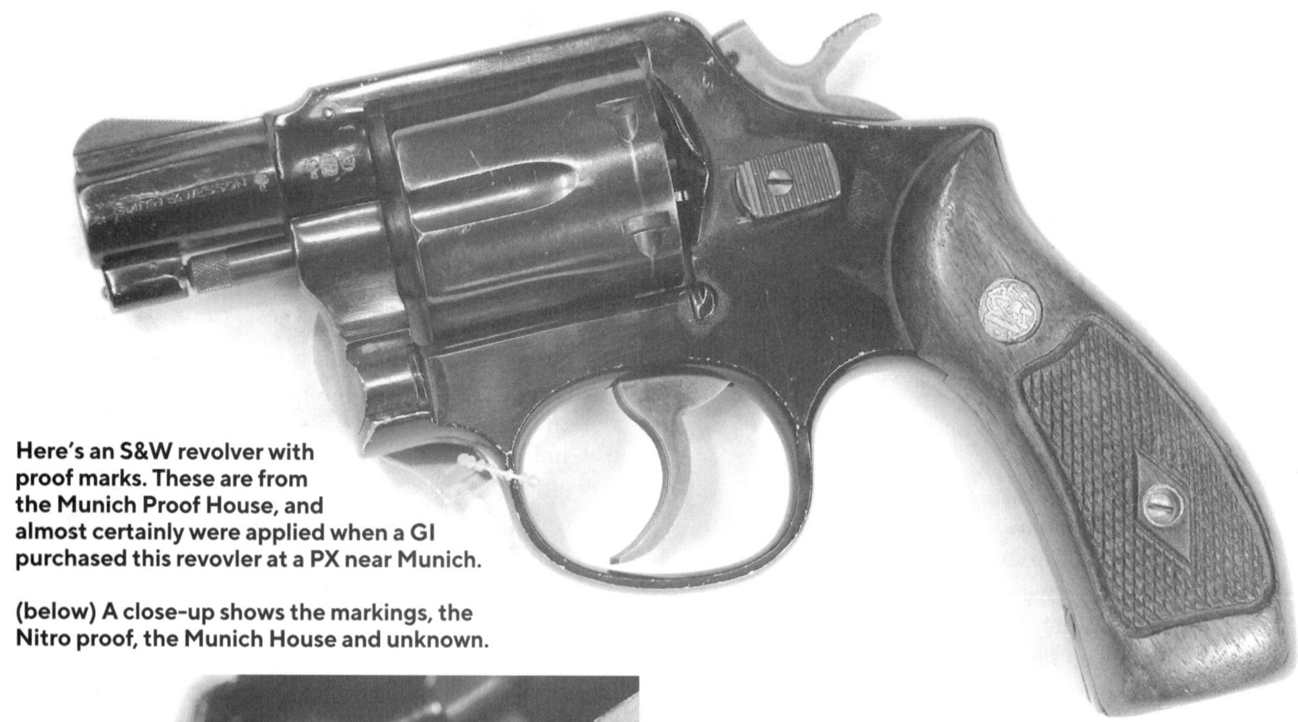

Here's an S&W revolver with proof marks. These are from the Munich Proof House, and almost certainly were applied when a GI purchased this revovler at a PX near Munich.

(below) A close-up shows the markings, the Nitro proof, the Munich House and unknown.

the rifle and machine-gun cartridge the government was using at the time.

So, in 1925, before SAAMI, Winchester makes the .270 Winchester. Since it is already in production when SAAMI is formed, Winchester just tells all SAAMI members what the dimensions are. Ditto the .300 Savage, made by Savage.

After 1926, then began the sticky problem of dimensions and standards. The solution was simple: Only SAAMI members could propose a new cartridge, and the SAAMI experts studied the dimensions, and the committee members voted on it.

This leads to a sore spot among some shooters: Only SAAMI members can propose a new cartridge be added. If you aren't a member, and you have a great new cartridge, how do you get it adopted? By being good. If enough people want your cartridge, some ammo makers (who are members of SAAMI) will look it over, suggest it be adopted, and convince the committee.

Europe has much the same sort of arrangement, called CIP, *Commission internationale permanente pour l'épreuve des armes à feu portatives* ("Permanent International Commission for the Proof of Small Arms"). Yes, French. The use of French as an official language for things European dates back to the several King Louis of France. It continues. CIP, unlike SAAMI, has as its members the governments of the members of CIP of Europe.

This is America, and you don't need the permission of SAAMI to offer a cartridge. (You do need a good insurance policy, however.) Cartridges that are in production, but not SAAMI-approved, are known as proprietary cartridges. Experimental ones that guys craft in their loading rooms or workshops are called wildcats. You can make a wildcat in your home workshop. Neck a case up or down, move the shoulder, have a chambering reamer made, and viola, you have a wildcat. If you then form a corporation, get insurance, and start producing that ammo for commercial sale, it is a proprietary cartridge.

Once you get SAAMI approval, then you've hit the big time.

The SAAMI technical mavens determine and approve of the appropriate dimensions, the dimensional spread, the operating pressure and so-on.

There are times when the world at large presents SAAMI with a problem that can't be solved, or that no one wants to walk into the middle of.

One such conundrum is the .223 Remington and 5.56x45 situation.

PRESSURE

I get asked a question, phrased something like this: "What are the SAAMI specs for 5.56?" Answer: There aren't any. The loading we know of as 5.56x45 is not SAAMI-approved, and the organization has nothing to say about it. The 5.56 is a military cartridge, and as such is under the purview of the Department of Defense. Asking what SAAMI has to say about it is kind of like asking what SAAMI has to say about an AT-4 anti-tank rocket. Not a subject it works on.

There is also the matter of how chamber pressures are determined, and how they are measured. The question comes up here as "SAAMI says the .223 chamber pressure is X, and CIP says the chamber pressure is Y. Is European ammo hotter?"

Yes and no.

The problem is how and where the measurement happens.

The U.S. process is to use what is called a "conformal transducer." OK, if you take a piezoelectric crystal, and run an electrical charge through it, you will be able to measure a certain resistance. Here's the trick: If you stress the crystal, the measured resistance changes. A compressed crystal will have a different resistance than an uncompressed one, and the difference is repeatable, consistent and measurable.

The "conformal" part means that the base of the transducer, the part that rests against the case, is curved to match the case shape.

Doing this means you can simply load a round into a test barrel (a very expensive barrel, not used for anything but pressure testing) fire it and read the pressure curve from the computer file you saved.

Where pressure is measured matters. If you measure in a different location, you will come up with a different number. This cutaway shows how a transducer is fitted to a pressure barrel.

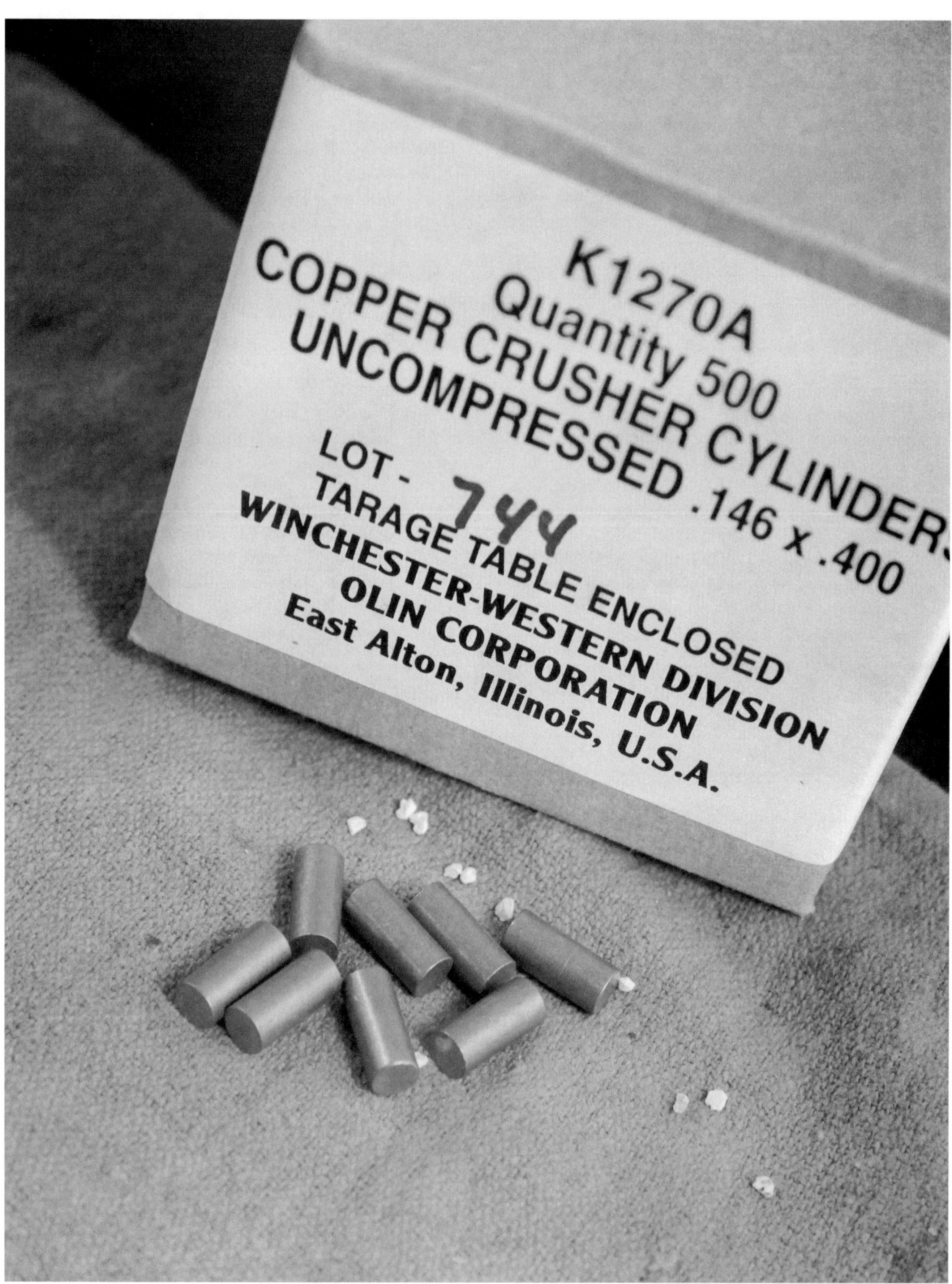

Here is a historical artifact: a box of copper crushers. Note that the label tells the user the lot number, and that the tarage table is enclosed. Use only that table with that lot.

There is one nagging detail: brass strength. We all know brass expands to the limits of the chamber walls, right? But, how much pressure does it take to start that?

Let's grab an example out of thin air, just because we need numbers. Let's say it takes 7,000 psi to expand a given case to the chamber walls. Another brand might need only 5,000, while a third requires 10,000. Houston, we have a problem. The solution is grunt work. The load being tested is fired in a separate barrel, to produce fired empties. Then, each is compressed to size, and expanded to chamber limits. That gives the ballistician a base number that is added to the recorded pressure number.

That way he knows the first brass gets 7,000 psi added to the test number, the second brass 5,000, and the third 10,000. If he doesn't, not only will the recorded pressures be lower than real, but they will differ depending on the brass used. That's not science.

So, when I send in ammunition to be pressure-tested, I have to send in a dozen fired cases of that load. And, I can't load up my test ammo (if they are reloads) using mixed brass.

In work this precise, this delicate, details matter. So, where do you place the transducer? Each cartridge listed by SAAMI will have the location of the

Let's grab an example out of thin air, just because we need numbers. Let's say it takes 7,000 psi to expand a given case to the chamber walls. Another brand might need only 5,000, while a third requires 10,000. Houston, we have a problem. The solution is grunt work. The load being tested is fired in a separate barrel, to produce fired empties.

A lineup of pressure barrels.

transducer specified, within the limits they have found matter. If you change the location, you change the recorded pressure. Let me re-phrase that. The pressure is what the pressure is, but if you were able to move the transducer around at will, you would get different recordings, based on where you were.

CIP uses a different method, and measures at a different location.

You simply cannot convert from metric to imperial and expect the numbers to be comparable.

Which leads to another bit of confusion: time. Back in the old days, before the digital revolution, pressure was measured by tiny copper cylinders. These cylinders, called crushers, were placed between the case (with a hole drilled in the side wall) and an anvil, that held it in place.

When the cartridge was fired in the test barrel, the copper cylinder was squashed by the pressure. The shortened cylinder was measured and compared to a chart called a tarage table. That was the test results of that particular production lot of cylinders and told you how much pressure it had been subjected to. This was listed as PSI-CUP. Or just CUP. Pounds per square inch, copper units of pressure.

A lot of people think that if you go over pressure, you break an AR-15 like this. Not really. This is from a steady diet of over pressure, but manageable (barely), ammo. No, if you go past the AR strength, you bust upper receivers.

When a new lot of cylinders, crushers, came in, you filed the old tarage table and used the one that came with the new lot. Yes, the "squishiness" of the little cylinders varied from lot to lot. That was life in the "good old days."

The limit of the copper crushed (shotguns, generating less pressure, used lead cylinders, and they were recorded as LUP) was that it produced one data point. It only told you the maximum pressure the cartridge had produced. It did not tell you how quickly that pressure had been produced, and it also had another problem: inertia. It takes time to squish a copper cylinder.

If the pressure mounted too quickly, it could spike past the allowed ceiling, and yet happen so quickly that the cylinder did not have time to react.

The response rate of a piezoelectric transducer is almost unlimited. You can measure the pressure every thousandth of a second if you wish. The limits are basically how quickly you can generate a clean, precise electric charge in the crystal, and how much of the resulting data your computer can gobble up. In today's systems, the data flow that can be generated is hundreds to thousands of times greater than we need.

This, however, caused problems.

The first problem was that each cartridge had to have its loading data regenerated and retested all over again. The "fit" of the pressure data generated electronically, compared to what had been generated in the old CUP method, wasn't exact. So, ballisticians had to retest all the old standard loads in order to get a rough approximation of what pressures to expect.

The second problem arose from the first, in that there was no "universal translator." It wasn't possible to apply a "multiply the old by XYZ to get the new" pressure conversion chart. Not only did each load have to be tested, but each cartridge had to have all of its data regenerated.

The third problem was the precision of the data. All of a sudden, ballisticians could see spikes, jagged lines and pressure excursions in the data. They had been there all along, but now that they could be seen, some loads had to be deleted from suggested loading manuals.

The copper crusher inertia also caused problems. Loads that had seemed (or even been) well-behaved under the old CUP method, now showed pressures, electronically measured, past allowable limits.

Oh, the screaming. The change caused a lot of complaining that old standards were being "watered down" and loads that had worked for decades were being changed.

What were they supposed to do? The old loads, measured with the new, more-precise methods, showed that they were over the pressure specifications laid down by SAAMI, and for the cartridge. Were they supposed to just ignore the data they had, because "It always worked in the old days"? Nope.

DESIGN

OK, you have a case, and you want to make a wildcat. Decide how long it needs to be, how large a bullet, re-form it to the shape you need, and have chamber reamers made. Ream a barrel, install it in your receiver and develop load data for it.

So far, relatively easy. (Well, easy for the mechanically inclined; for many it is arcana of the highest order.)

Since you are making your ammunition, and have designed it, you can use it relatively safely, since you know what is what. Just don't loan it to someone else.

SAAMI doesn't have that assurance. So, when a new cartridge is designed, based on an existing cartridge, it has to look into a few things.

Consider taking a .30-06 and necking it down to, say, something like a .277-inch bullet. Let's be traditional and call it the .270 Winchester. By making it out of a .30-06 case, we have an easy solution to brass production. Interestingly, when we squeeze the neck of the .30-06 case down from the diameter to hold a .308 bullet, to one that will hold a .277 bullet, the brass can get longer. The solution is to define the .270 as having a longer case. Otherwise, those who are being cheap, and necking brass down, would find the now-longer case bumping into the end of the neck section of the chamber.

The neck walls will also get thicker, but that is a reaming operation, and not something the factory can handle. Were they to make the chamber neck diameter large enough to handle a necked-down .30-06, the extra space would hinder accuracy of proper .270 brass. (Always a problem for wildcatters, that one.)

So, easy. But, what others? Let's do something wild. Let's take the .30-06, shorten it, and use a denser powder to gain the same performance. And we'll call it the .308 Winchester. How do we keep the .308 from chambering in a .30-06 rifle? We give it less taper.

Taper?

Yes, the diameter of a case at the shoulder is going to be smaller than the diameter of the case at the rim, or base. This has to do with what's called "secondary extraction." When you fire a round, the case expands. Brass being brass, if you have not exceeded the elastic limits of the brass, the case will spring back toward its start dimensions, but not fully. (That's why you have to resize brass, to reload it.)

The movement of the bolt begins breaking the brass free of its frictional fit to the chamber walls. The bolt turning attempts (and often succeeds) in turning the brass slightly, and that breaks the grip on the walls.

Then, the tapered case does the rest. Basically, the tapered case is a funnel inside a funnel. Were the case a cylinder, with no taper, the front end of it would drag the full length of the chamber as it was extracted. By including taper, as soon as the case begins to move, it breaks fully free of the chamber walls. The extreme example of this is the AK round, the 7.62x39. The Soviets put that much taper into the case because they planned from the start to be loading ammunition using steel cases. Steel, in this use, is not so good for friction or extraction, but it had one attribute the Soviets dearly loved: It was cheap.

So, cartridge designers are expected to pay attention to the possible unsafe combinations of their new cartridge, and existing ones. As a result, while a new cartridge might come from a parent case, the

There was an immense pile of rifles on that range, in a host of calibers, and keeping it all straight wasn't easy. Someone got a .308 round into a .30-06 rifle and managed to wrestle the bolt closed. The firing result wasn't as dramatic as some other combinations can be. The bolt was locked tight. It fell to me, the resident gunsmith, to pound the bolt handle open with a piece of lumber. (Situations like that are why most gunsmiths work in the back room, out of sight of their customers. I was using a piece of lumber on a multi-thousand-dollar rifle, because we needed it. And there was no back room to go to.)

shoulder might be moved, or the taper changed, so that the unsafe combinations will be unlike enough that you can't get the wrong one to chamber, and close the bolt.

The designers of the .308 (meant to be the U.S. military replacement of the .30-06, with its performance, but in a shorter package) went with a less-tapered case to increase capacity. That decreased taper keeps a rifle chambered in .30-06 from accepting a cartridge of .308 Winchester. Well, mostly.

I was at an industry function a few years ago when someone had that happen. OK, we were all experienced gun writers. (And no, I didn't do it.) There was an immense pile of rifles on that range, in a host of calibers, and keeping it all straight wasn't easy. Someone got a .308 round into a .30-06 rifle and managed to wrestle the bolt closed. The firing result wasn't as dramatic as some other combinations can be. The bolt was locked tight. It fell to me, the resident gunsmith, to pound the bolt handle open with a piece of lumber. (Situations like that are why most gunsmiths work in the back room, out of sight of their customers. I was using a piece of lumber on a multi-thousand-dollar rifle, because we needed it. And there was no back room to go to.)

The case was blown to an almost straight cylinder. The extractor had been blown out. Once open and with the empty extracted, (it took a cleaning rod, punched down the bore) the rifle functioned fine. Well, it functioned as well as you'd expect, lacking an extractor. We had to test-fire it and punch the empty out with a cleaning rod again.

And it is situations such as that, that compelled SAAMI to compile a list of unsafe cartridge combinations. These are combos where you must be on your highest guard, if you happen to have them at the range, or on a hunt, together.

One that wasn't so fraught came into the shop when I was gunsmithing. The owner had a lever-action rifle, a Marlin 336, that wouldn't shoot straight. I wrote it up, and in due time took it apart, scrubbed it clean, and took it to the range. It plunked three shots into a cloverleaf at 50 yards. Happy, I wrote up the bill and racked it. The owner picked it up the next Saturday morning, and that afternoon he was back. "This rifle doesn't shoot straight," was his declaration. Curious, I started asking the questions I perhaps should have asked when he first came in. Where did he get it? At a gun show. Was the ammo factory? Yes. Did he get it with the rifle? No, he bought it a couple of aisles later. Did he have the ammo?

He produced an elderly box of .30-30 soft points.

Mystery solved. The rifle was chambered in .35 Remington. He had had no idea that lever action rifles came chambered in anything but .30-30, so as a result that was the ammo he bought after buying his rifle. I gave him a box of the same .35 Remington I had used, and he was happy. He came back just after hunting season to show the photos of the whitetail he'd shot.

The .30-30 and .35 Remington cartridges are close enough in length that the rifle would feed them from the tube. The rim of the .30-30 was close enough to that of the .35 Remington that the extractor would hold it. In loading the magazine tube, and working the action, you might not notice that there was anything wrong. But the bullet was not close enough to the bore to let the rifling have any effect. The bullet, at .308-inch diameter, was basically ricocheting down a tube of .350-inch diameter, and then flying like a knuckleball after that.

The bullet had no contact with the bore, so the pressure was a fraction of the designed pressure.

Not all combinations are so lucky.

The exemplar here, for our purposes, is the .223/5.56 and the .300 Blackout.

The .300 Blackout, and its predecessor, clone and not-a-copy, the .300 Whisper, are type-accepted (Blackout by SAAMI, Whisper by CIP) cartridges that started life as .223/5.56 brass. The idea was simple: provide the largest, heaviest bullet that could be fit into whatever was left of a .223 case, in order to provide a subsonic thumper. This maxed out at .30 caliber, although you could (as later happened) fit a 9mm/.357 bullet in such a case.

The first one, the .300 Whisper, came to us from the fertile mind of J.D. Jones. He took .223 cases, lopped them off, necked them down, reamed the case mouths and loaded them. The idea was to make a handy, convenient, subsonic cartridge. Well, reality got in the way, as it often does. You see, that far down in the case, the case wall thickness is not rigidly defined. Brass makers were free to use whatever thickness they wished, provided their brass worked.

J.D. described to me the arduous process of working up a chart to determine what brands, markings and even production lots of .223/5.56 brass would work, and how much effort each would take. He finally gave up on trying to make .300 Whisper brass inexpensively, and just placed an order with a brass maker for brass to his specs.

The .300 Whisper had to fit into regular AR magazines, or else there would have been no point to the conversion. In order hold the bullets, the case had to be shortened so the neck would be clenching the body of the bullet. The body is that full-diameter portion between the base, or boat-tail, and the beginning of the curve of the bullet nose, known as the ogive.

The only way to keep the .300 Whisper, and the later .300 Blackout, from being chambered in a .223/5.56 rifle, is to have the nose of the bullet as far forward as possible, and to ensure that the ogive of the bullet would impact against the shoulder of the chamber of the .223/5.56 rifle.

This works. But it is not an absolute. In reloaded ammunition, if the neck tension is not great enough, feeding impact can allow the .300 bullet to set back in the case on chambering. Even if the neck tension is sufficient, if the reloader uses an incorrect bullet, one with too much taper in the ogive, there could be clearance.

This situation is known enough that you can hardly go to a gun club and fail to find someone "who was there" or "knows a guy" who had it happen. The reality is that it is a rare occurrence, but one that can easily happen if you are not careful.

But the .300 Blackout/.300 Whisper evolution points out one of the important aspects of cartridges for the AR-15: They have to fit the magazine. They have to feed from the magazine. They have to fit a bolt that fits the receiver. If a new cartridge that you are dreaming of doesn't do all of those, then you will find a small audience, or customer base, for your rifles. And they won't be AR-15 or AR-10.

4
FIRE

RIMFIRES

The rimfire method of cartridge priming was the first. Invented by Louis-Nicolas Flobert in 1845, the process is simple: The case holds the priming compound in the rim, and when the rim is crushed, the priming compound ignites, setting off the cartridge. And Flobert's cartridges didn't even have gunpowder in them. The priming charge was all that was needed to hurl the bullet. This, of course, meant it was a low-powered round, essentially the progenitor to the CB cap, but that was enough. You could practice your marksmanship in your parlor, if you wished. No kidding, people did that. It was even part of the origin stories of Sherlock Holmes, where he would plink a large "VR" on the wall of his room. (Victoria Regina, Latin for Queen Victoria.) I think Holmes did it with a larger cartridge, not a Flobert. It was viewed as eccentric, but not monstrously unsafe, anti-social and cause to call out the local SWAT team. Oh, and in case you were worried about the lead exposure, and the powder byproducts, the wallpaper of a Victorian-era home out-gassed enough arsenic, formaldehyde, and other vile byproducts that a little lead was almost healthy by comparison. And lath-and-plaster walls are almost like concrete, not the spongy wallboard we use today.

the common cartridge of today. So common that the last time I checked, the various ammunition companies were making 30 million rounds of it a day. A day.

If we simply go with a five-day workweek, and 48 weeks a year, that's 7.2 billion rounds of .22 LR a year, and it does not pile up on the shelves, even now that ammo prices are normal again.

If you go out and spend a day practicing with .22 LR, you can quite easily burn up 500 rounds. Do that once a month, and you have fired 6,000 rounds for the year, a not-bad practice rate. If 1.2 million of us do that, there goes all the .22 LR ammo made each year. Hey, I'm doing my part. Who among you is the slacker?

The priming compound on a rimfire is in the rim, no great surprise. But the firing pin has to crush the rim with enough force to set off the priming compound, and that means the rimfire case can't be as strong as a centerfire case.

The power limitation with a rimfire cartridge is the rim. You can't make the rim strong enough to withstand much pressure or make it too big. If you make the rim stout enough to be a powerful cartridge, the firing pin can't crush the rim and set off the priming compound.

The Henry Rimfire and the Remington Derringer both used rimfire cartridges (the Henry in .44, the Remington in .41), but still they were both low-powered. The listed spec for the Henry Rimfire is a 200-grain bullet at an optimistic 1,125 fps. As if, even out of a rifle. The .41 Remington? A 130-grain bullet at 425 fps, if you really need to know. In the days before antibiotics, no one wanted to get shot. But even then, the .41 Short (as it was also called) was a pipsqueak. It didn't take long for the rimfire process to be limited to the original, the .22. The big seller originally was the Smith & Wesson No. 1, a revolver chambered in .22 Short. Then, before the end of the 19th century, we got the .22 Long Rifle, which is

As an aside, there was a run on .22 LR ammo a few years ago. It got to the point that you simply couldn't find ammo anywhere. The Interweb was all aflutter with various conspiracy theories, how the government was restricting sales, the companies were ripping us off, and if they just made more, we'd have enough.

No, the math above makes it clear. When a store got a shipment of .22 LR, it wasn't uncommon for buyers to descend, and buy it all, 5,000 round cartons for each one in line. That's right, guys who hadn't shot more than 200 rounds a year for any of the years or decades before, were buying 5,000 round cartons of .22 LR, and stacking them in their basements or garages. That was why you couldn't find any. Once the panic subsided, and the makers had a chance to catch up, prices drifted down. Then President Trump got elected, and all thoughts of "the gun-grabbers are after us" faded, and prices sagged even more. (Until it begins again, as it has so many times in the past.)

As I type this, the current price for .22 LR ammo is sitting at $180 to $195 for 5,000 rounds. That's two-and-a-half cents per shot, not a bad price, and well in line with my growing-up experience of finding ammo at a penny a shot.

Once it was passed over in favor of centerfire cartridges, the .22 Long Rifle became a great little training cartridge, target cartridge and small-game cartridge. It was so well thought of as a training cartridge that military organizations around the world used to build special .22 Long Rifle rifles that duplicated their service rifles. Or even made conversion kits that would fit into a standard rifle. They are now mostly collectors' items, but the idea was sound. There is even a company offering a .22 LR conversion for AK-47s, as if 7.62x39 ammo wasn't cheap-enough practice.

For less money spent on ammo, (the training rifles cost money) and without needing a full-sized range, the troops could practice their marksmanship with rifles that handled just like the service weapons they'd use in combat. Alas, in most Armies, the choice was even clearer; they could save even more money if they just didn't practice. Ammunition costs money, and there will always be plenty of time just before the next war to let the troops actually get in some trigger-pulling time.

But that doesn't work for us. We like to shoot. Right?

Some of the rimfires you can wrestle into an AR platform. Left to right, .22 LR, .22 HMR, .17 WMR, .17 Winchester Super Magnum

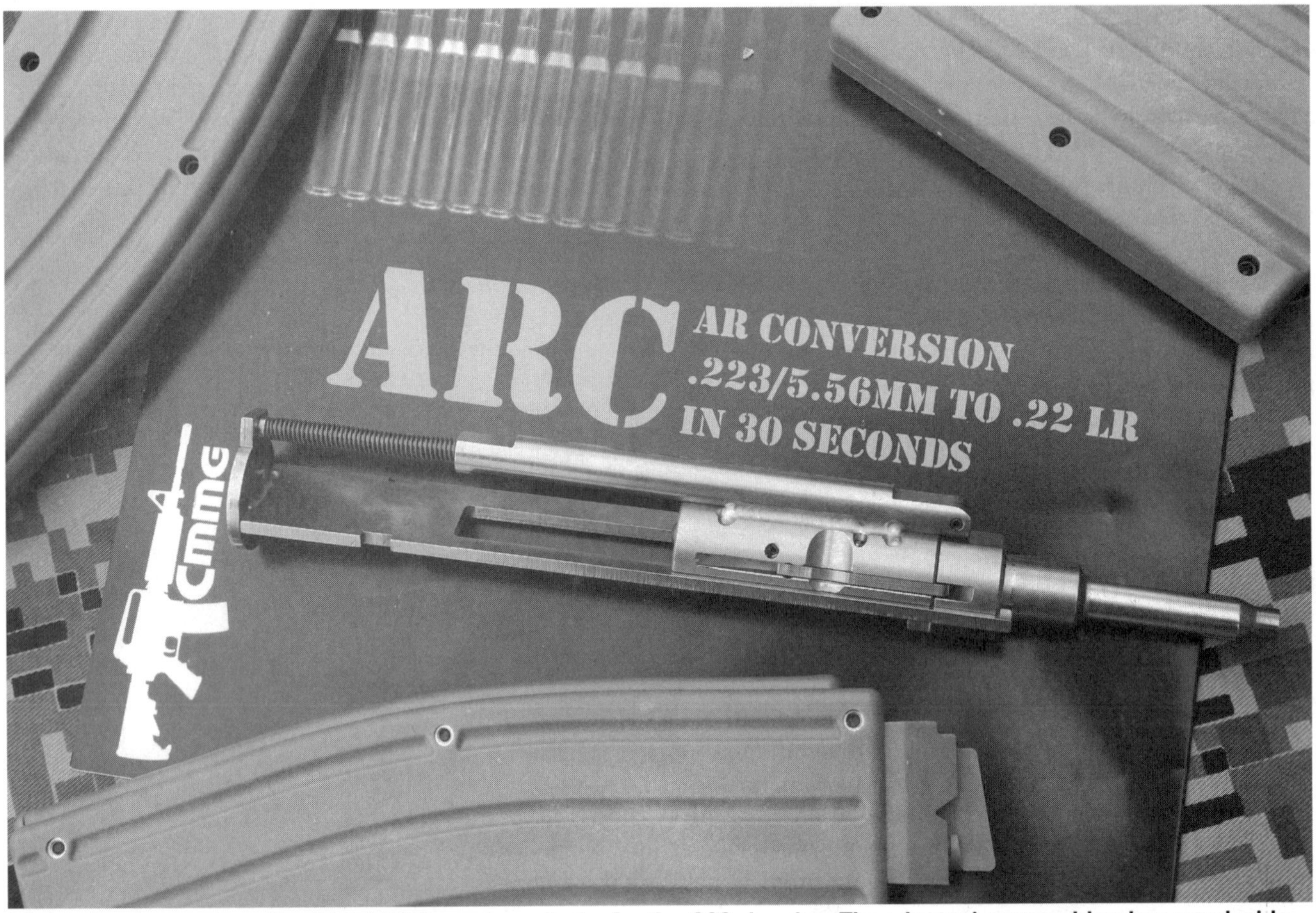

ARC
AR CONVERSION
.223/5.56MM TO .22 LR
IN 30 SECONDS
CMMG

The earliest conversion, like this CMMG, used an adapter for the .223 chamber. The adapter is removable when you decide to go to a dedicated .22 LR barrel.

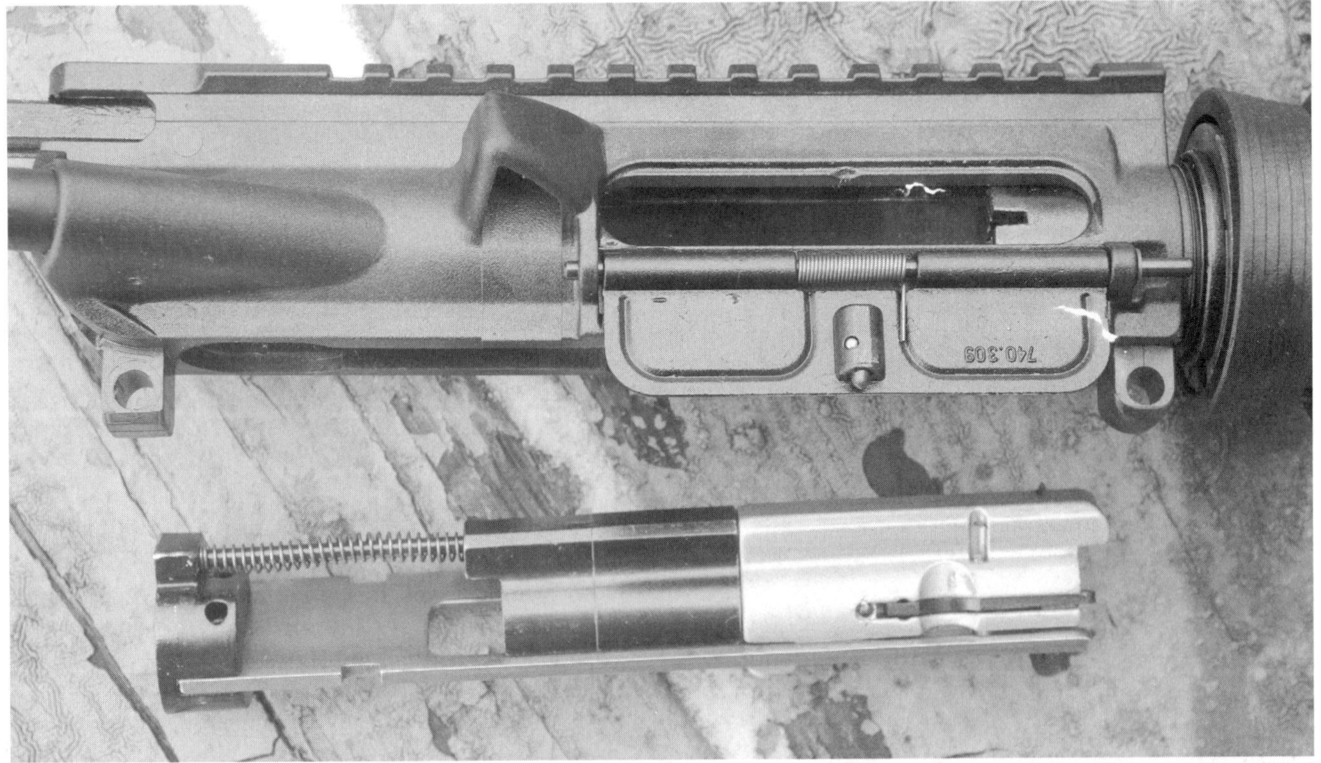

Here is a .22 LR bolt, with the adapter removed, showing the lack of need for a buffer spring and weight. Yes, a .22 LR can use a folding stock, and still function reliably.

When it comes to rimfires, we have three basic rim/cartridge sizes to deal with. There is the .22 Long Rifle, the .22 Magnum, and the .17 Winchester. That is, the Winchester Super Magnum, just in case you weren't impressed by a 20-grain bullet at 3,000 fps.

Let's start with the oldest first, since it is the easiest and the most common, and then check the others once we have the basics.

The .22 LR is a short rimfire case, with a 40-grain bullet as standard. The bullet is lead, usually with a wax lubricant coating, and sometimes with a "wash" of copper on it. The bullet is a nominal .221 of an inch in diameter, but since the bullet is soft lead, and often has a hollow base, even a bit smaller is no big deal to a .22 LR barrel.

The rim is .287 in diameter, and the loaded cartridge is only one inch long. The operating pressure is around 21,000 PSI. The bullet is the diameter of the case, and the case mouth is crimped into what is called a "heel" on the bullet. This is a reduced-diameter section of the bullet, extending below the crimp and inside of the case. It both provides a location for the crimp to grab and adds a bit of weight and length to the bullet.

Since the bullet is not inside the case, .22 LR ammunition has a lubricant applied to the bullet. This can be a waxy coating, or a copper wash, or both. It is there to reduce leading. It also collects all sorts of dust, lint, grit and smut. Do not let your ammo get dirty, because that dirt will be scraped down the bore at 1,000 fps or faster when you shoot it.

The earliest .22 LR AR-type rifles weren't. They were replacement bolts for the AR-15/M16, bolts that had a bolt face to handle the .22 LR rim, and a false cartridge extension on the assembly, to fill the chamber of the .223/5.56. The chamber adapter was not rifled. So, you had a soft bullet, first skidding down a smooth tube, before it jumped through the leade of the .223/5.56, and then into the rifling. There, it met with a bore using a nominal .224-inch groove depth, and a .220 land height. If you think this is a strong candidate for leading, you would be right. Especially if the .223/5.56 bore was already a bit rough from having seen a bunch of centerfire ammo. Oh, and to make matters worse, the original rifling twist of one turn in 12 inches in the AR-15, was faster than a .22 LR needed, which is 1/16. The later A2 and M4, with a twist of 1/7 just aggravated an already marginal situation.

The early conversions, often known as the "Air Force" conversions, or the Army M261, or the Atcheson conversions, were what we had back then. These all used the rimfire bolt with guide rails, internal springs (the .22 LR has no hope of cycling the buffer and spring of the AR on its own) and the false chamber. They differed mainly in the style of magazine used, with some being sheet metal .22 LR magazine tack-welded to an AR-magazine sized sheet metal shell. Or a plastic shell (called the "Teflon" even though it had none) magazine, which used .22 LR spring and follower inside the larger shell. The Air Force version even used a .22 LR magazine assembly that was stuffed into the regular shell of an M16, after you took out the M16 magazine guts.

Later came the Ceiner conversions, which used the skinny .22 LR magazine welded to the conversion shell, exclusively.

The expense of centerfire ammo has made for some changes in the marketplace. Also, the leading headaches, and the desire for improved accuracy, have brought about changes in design. First, the magazines.

The big change here was Black Dog Machine LLC magazines. The idea was simple. Take the follower and spring that will properly feed 25 rounds of .22 LR ammo and design a shell that is the same size as a regular 30-round AR magazine. Now, make the .22 LR magazine as a shell with two halves, and bolt them together, holding the spring and follower in place. You now have a large (the same size as the "real" AR mag) durable magazine that reliably feeds .22 LR ammo. There is plenty of room in the outline of the AR mag to provide the built-in curve you need for the stack of .22 LR ammo, from 10 up to 30 rounds.

The last step was to sonically weld the two halves together, making the setup even more durable. You can even get designs where the cartridge stack is exposed, or with "smoke" clear plastic as the shell, so you can see at a glance just how many rounds are left.

After Black Dog proved the concept, lots of other people started making them that way. That design is now the new standard, and if someone makes a .22 LR conversion bolt, they make it to use that magazine design. There's just no point in designing and making your own, proprietary, magazines, when you can depend on the BDM magazines or their clones.

On the bolts, the makers went a different way.

The big headache for users was the chamber conversion adapter. When people were only ever shooting already-built ARs, then that was what you did. But when people started building their own ARs, another avenue became possible: a dedicated .22 LR barrel. Instead of a .220- to .224-inch centerfire bore, and a smoothbore chamber adapter, they could make a proper .22 LR chamber, and a .218 (land height),

Black Dog now makes AR rimfire magazines for the .22 WMR, so you can feed your rimfire magnum.

.222 (groove) bore, with the correct twist for a rimfire cartridge.

The adapter makers simply changed the rimfire bolt design so the chamber adapter was removable (which most were, anyway, for cleaning) and the barrel makers just had to make the new rimfire barrel stick back into the receiver a bit more, so it would properly mate up with the .22 LR bolt.

This is now the standard combination, as it provides accuracy with reliability, and it fits in the AR platform.

This is not, however, the only .22 LR AR-15 to be had. Companies such as S&W make .22 LR rifles that look like an AR, but are not interchangeable with them. The M&P 15-22 is a close copy of an AR-15, but none of its parts will interchange with the converted AR-15. Why? Ease of manufacture. The S&W M&P 15-22 lists for $450, which until recently was half the cost of a regular AR-15. A regular AR-15 in .223/5.56 would differ in cost from the rimfire variant only due to the cost of the barrel, a .22 LR in place of a .223/5.56. So, you can (or could) get an S&W M&P rimfire for a lot less than a purpose-built rimfire AR.

The price fluctuations in ARs, however, can at times bring the cost of a real-deal AR, in rimfire, close to the M&P.

A case in point is the HK 416 rimfire, made by Umarex. (Licensed, inspected and approved by HK, in case you had any doubts. I didn't.) The list price is $499, which to those accustomed to buying HK products, is dirt-cheap.

I built my .22 LR AR-15 using a CMMG conversion kit and has run flawlessly since I wrenched it together.

The beauty of the dedicated rimfire AR is that you can have identical uppers. You can build a low-ammo-cost training upper that has the same handguard, sights and accessories as your centerfire one. You can shoot the rimfire indoors in the wintertime, and not be subjected to the muzzle blast of a .223. Well, at least not your own, who knows who else is on the range.

COST

OK, just out of curiosity I spec'd out an AR upper in .22 LR. That is: receiver, barrel, conversion. The optics and handguard I leave up to you. You can duplicate your centerfire upper exactly, in which case the extra cost is your problem. The bare-bones upper in rimfire would simply have regular handguards and a cheap Chinese knock-off red-dot scope. The upper runs $62. The barrel and conversion bolt run

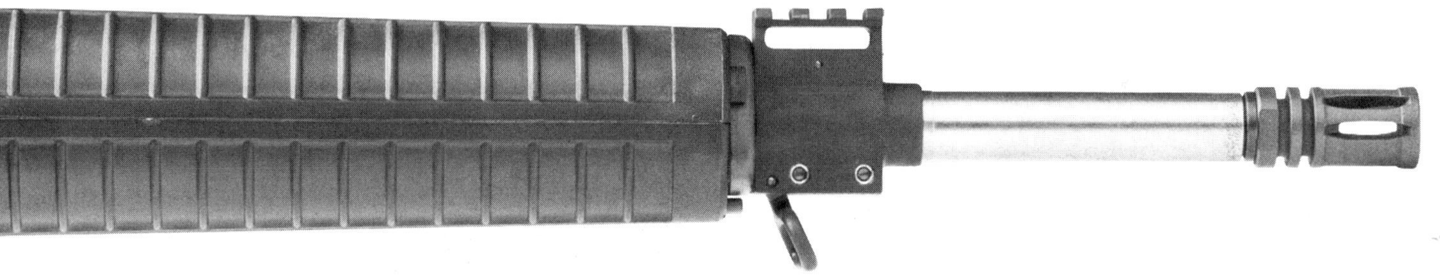

The standard .22 LR AR-15 no longer depends on the adapted chamber gizmo. It comes with a dedicated .22 LR barrel, and the conversion bolt closes up to the breech of that barrel. This is a Rock River .22 LR, and if you were to close the ejection port cover, you might be hard-pressed to tell it from a .223/5.56 carbine.

$330. Handguards and the hardware will run you an additional $50 or so. The red-dot scope can be had for less than the handguard and parts. So, for something like $500, you have a ready-to-go .22 LR upper.

That might seem like a lot, but compare ammo costs: .223 is currently $185/1,000 and.22 LR is $38/1,000. So, every thousand rounds of .22 LR you shoot saves you $147. You have recouped your investment well before you finish that 5,000-round carton of .22 LR you bought, the carton that cost you the same as 1,000 rounds of .223.

AMMO COMPATIBILITY

OK, while some firearms can be picky about the ammo they like, .22 LR firearms can be almost psychotic. It is essentially useless telling you which ammo is best/most accurate/most reliable, because your rifle will be the final arbiter of what is good or not. You must, and I mean you MUST, try various types of ammo in your rifle, to determine what is reliable, and what is accurate, before you plunk down a big wad of money for a truckload of ammo.

Buying something because it is on sale or recommended by the club's best shot is a good way to have a pile of ammo that your rifle doesn't like.

STANDARD

This can also be called hi-velocity. You get a 40-grain bullet that is going (you hope) some 1,200 fps out of a rifle-length barrel. There will be a sharp crack to the report, and that is fine. This ammo is made by the truckload, and ammo companies find they cannot make enough of it. And, they can't make a profit on it. We all shop price, even when we're searching for what our rifle likes, and won't spend a nickel more than we have to.

This is, or should be, your regular, go-to practice, plinking and having fun ammo.

TARGET

Here, the 40-grain bullet is not allowed to exceed the speed of sound. This can also be the "subsonic" load that some companies make. Why? Simple, a bullet that starts at 1,200 fps will slow down, and as it passes down through and below the speed of sound (called the trans-sonic region) its accuracy might be diminished. Target shooters want all the accuracy they can get, and they don't need to worry about power. So, they want slower ammo. Since they are paying more for performance, they expect it, and are charged for it. You can easily pay twice as much for target ammo as standard. The primo target ammo can cost as much as centerfire. ELEY test-fires each production lot of its ammo, and you can go online and see what your particular lot did in testing. No kidding. The company provides the printouts of groups for your review, online.

HYPER, STINGER, SUPER

Here the bullet weight drops to 32 grains, more or less, mostly less. The case is lengthened a smidge, and the velocity is upped. However, the delicate balance that is the .22 LR is not readily changed. You might find that the super-speed ammo is unreliable in your rifle. Or inaccurate. Relatively speaking, of course. How much you give up, for what you get, is a decision you have to make for yourself.

SUPPRESSORS

A .22 LR suppressor is a compact thing. At the smallest, they can be a one-inch diameter tube that is maybe four inches long. With standard or subsonic ammunition, it is so quiet that the bolt clattering back and forth might be noisier than the sound of the shot. And the clang of the bullet on steel is definitely louder than either.

There's a reason suppressor makers report lopsided production numbers, rimfire suppressors compared to centerfire. Rimfire is giggle-worthy fun.

Here you see the diminutive .17 Hornet, next to a .223. The .223 is considered small, so the Hornet is tiny. Compact. Elegant. But not as handy as a rimfire. And difficult to fit into an AR-15.

THE .17s

The idea with the various .17-caliber rimfires is to produce the performance, ideally, of the .17 Hornet. Originating from the .22 Hornet, the Hornet was the first varmint cartridge. It allowed for low-noise and low-recoil pest control, and is an elegant little cartridge. The .17 variant of it reduces recoil, extends range, but calls for very fussy reloading. By going with a rimfire .17, shooters can have some or much of the .17 Hornet performance, without the reloading needed.

And, fitting the Hornet, either .22 or .17, into an AR-15 would be a gunsmithing task of the first order.

.17 MACH 2

The Mach 2 is essentially the .22 Stinger case, necked down to accept .177-caliber bullets, and loaded for speed. Unlike the heel-type bullet of the lead .22 LR, the .17 bullet is jacketed, and crimped in the case mouth like a centerfire cartridge. We're looking at a 17-grain bullet at 2,100 fps (hence the Mach 2 name).

This came about in 2004, when Hornady brought it to market, following the .17 HMR, of which we will cover more in a bit. Bullet weights vary from 15.5 grains to 17 grains. Not a huge spread, but enough.

The .22 WMR is a robust little rimfire, and it hurls a bullet heavy enough for varmint dispatching. It is not a long-range cartridge, so if you need to go past 100 yards, or so, you'd best find something else.

.22 WMR

This is a Winchester cartridge (obviously) and came about in 1960. It uses a longer and larger-diameter case than that of the .22 LR, and a larger-diameter rim, so it can't be forced into a .22 LR firearm. The idea was to provide an inexpensive step up in performance from the .22 LR. So, the 40-grain bullet was supposed to be hot on the heels of 2,000 fps. It has settled down to a bit less than that, and can be had in weights from 30 to 50 grains.

The bullet, unlike the heel-type of the .22 LR, is a plated or jacketed bullet, with neck tension holding it in place like a centerfire cartridge.

.17 HMR

The .17 HMR is another Hornady development, and takes the .22 WMR case. Hornady necked it down to .17, and produced a zippy rimfire cartridge. The .17 HMR uses bullets from 17 grains to 30 grains, and the lightweights can be going over 2,600 fps.

.17 WINCHESTER SUPER MAGNUM

Unlike the other rimfires, which evolved from an earlier, or the earliest, rimfire, the .17 WSM came to the shooting sports from a nail gun, of all things. Nail guns use rimfire blanks to drive a nail without having

The .17s, either HMR or Mach 2, are necked down .22 WMR and .22 LR (in order). They generate more velocity, which is why they come with jacketed bullets, not lubricated lead ones.

The .17 HMR, with a pair of fired cases, to show the firing pin impact.

to swing a hammer. Carpenters, after decades of swinging a hammer, can end up with all sorts of joint problems, and using a nail gun not only speeds the construction process, but saves their elbo ws and shoulders.

Winchester took the .27-caliber nail-gun blank (which it makes for the construction industry), necked it down to .17 and made it work as a cartridge. The .27 nail-gun blank was for driving nails into concrete, something no carpenter could do with a hammer.

A brief aside: Nail guns are dangerous. Originally, they used compressed air, but now there are "powder-actuated" ones that have been around for some time. Despite the fact that they are construction tools, they should be treated as if they are firearms. Which they are, to a certain degree. Thousands of people end up in hospital ERs with nail-gun injuries each year. Safety message off.

The result of using this larger case, at a higher pressure, is to drive a .17-caliber bullet of 20 grains to 3,000 fps. This came out in 2013, and most of the firearms that use it are bolt-action rifles. However, in 2015 Franklin Armory unveiled an AR chambered in .17 WSM that is gas operated, not blowback.

The two hot .17 rimfires, the HMR and the WSM.

RIMFIRE DIMENSIONS

CARTRIDGE	BULLET DIAMETER	CASE LENGTH	RIM	OPERATING PRESSURE
22 LR	.223″	.613″	.278″	24,000 MAP
17 M2	.177″	.714″	.278″	24,000 MAP
22 WMR	.224″	1.055″	.294″	24,000 MAP
17 HMR	.177″	1.058″	.286″	26,000 MAP
17 WSM	.177″	1.200″	.333″	33,000 MAP

BUYING

You can buy a complete and AR-15-correct .22 LR easily. One was recently announced from Rock River, a complete rimfire AR-15. You can get it in three different versions: a tactical model, looking like the latest in cool AR carbine with a free-float handguard; the M4 model, with regular handguard and front sight; or the National Match A4 CMP Trainer, which is a rimfire rifle that fits the rules for National Match competition. If you really wanted to make a mark in next year's competitions, get this rifle and find what ammo it likes. Then spend the whole winter practicing with it. When the snow melts and you are ready to start with the centerfire, you will be tuned up on holding and squeezing.

CMMG also offers a raft of rimfire ARs, from pistols and SBRs to carbines, in its Banshee and Resolute lines, but not the Endeavor full-sized rifles. And across the series; 100, 200 and 300. It does not offer them in any rimfire caliber but .22 LR.

BUILDING OR CONVERTING

OK, the process of building a dedicated .22 LR upper is pretty easy. If you have any knowledge or experience of assembling ARs, then the process goes like this: Take the .22 LR barrel and slide it into the upper receiver. Tighten the barrel nut. Install whatever handguards or forearm you desire. Slide the .22

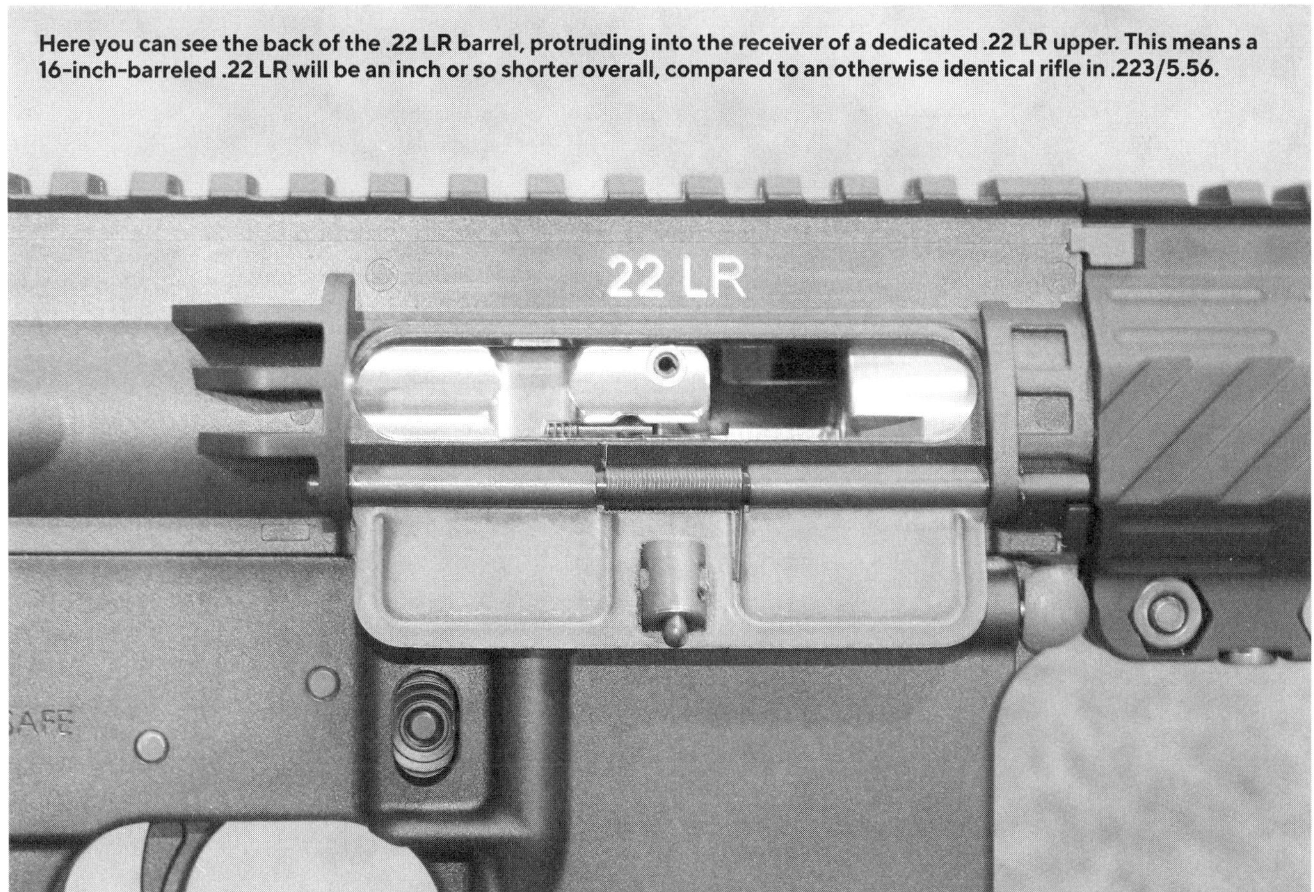

Here you can see the back of the .22 LR barrel, protruding into the receiver of a dedicated .22 LR upper. This means a 16-inch-barreled .22 LR will be an inch or so shorter overall, compared to an otherwise identical rifle in .223/5.56.

LR bolt assembly (minus the chamber adapter, if you have an integral .22 LR barrel). Check to make sure the .22 bolt extractor does not impact or bind on the slot in the barrel for it.

Close the receiver, load magazines and shoot. Really, that easy.

Now, if you are using the chamber adapter to use the .22 LR conversion on an upper with a .223/5.56 barrel on it, then you simply remove the old bolt and carrier, leave the charging handle in, install the new .22 LR conversion (with chamber adapter) and close and shoot. Remember to thoroughly scrub your bore clean afterward, however.

Now, if you want to shoot some other rimfire caliber, things can get a bit more complicated.

The easy one here is the .17 HMR. You just have to

order an upper from Alexander Arms, and its lower conversion parts. The AA .17 HMR upper comes with the bolt, barrel, receiver, handguard, everything on top you need. The system does not use magazines anything like the AR mags, however. The magazines are .17 HMR (and one supposes .22 WMR as well) specific. They are made of a very hard, and slick polymer. The magazines need the slickness due to the increased bolt speed of the .17 HMR. Alexander Arms can also provide you with a complete rifle. And a point to be aware of: Unlike the .22 LR systems, with a self-contained bolt and recoil springs, the Alexander Arms .17 HMR uses the rifle or carbine buffer tube. It has its own spring and buffer weight, not the little springs a .22 LR has, in order to control the high bolt speed the .17 HMR generates.

The Alexander Arms .17 HMR, with a few groups.

A rifle in .17 Mach 2 might be more difficult. Finding a barrel is the hard part. As far as I know, there are no AR-specific .17 Mach 2 barrels to be had. However, a good gunsmith with a lathe could adapt a Ruger 10/17 barrel to the AR, by fashioning a proper barrel extension for the new barrel. The .17 Mach 2, since it is the same length as a .22 LR, could use the same magazines. There is, however, the matter of bolt thrust and velocity.

Blowback systems operate by balancing the power of the cartridge with the mass and spring rate of the bolt and its cycling spring. Chamber pressure is the key here, but bullet mass also enters into the problem. With a .22 LR, we have a Maximum Average Pressure of 24,000 PI. The .17 Mach 2 has a MAP (Maximum Average Pressure) of the same. So, the pressure component of bolt thrust is the same. However, the lighter bullet of the .17 Mach 2 might cause the bolt of a converted rifle to cycle with insufficient force, and not eject, or feed, properly. This will call for experimentation.

For the .22 WMR and .17 HMR, the problem is different, and more of a puzzle. Comparing just the .22 LR and .22 WMR, we find a higher MAP with the HMR, and the same on the WMR, compared to the .22 LR. However, those pressures are leveraged through a larger-diameter case head. The rim of the WMR/HMR is 12 percent larger in area than that of the .22 LR. This might matter. Whether it matters a little or a lot, only experimenting can determine. The .17 HMR, with essentially the same rim diameter (the dimensions are the max allowed, they can all be smaller by a few thousandths), is coupled with an increase of pressure of more than 8 percent.

The problem with the .22 WMR and .17 HMR is not the mechanics. Again, a good gunsmith could fit a proper barrel to a receiver. He (or she) if good with a lathe, could even open up the bolt face to accept the new rim diameter. The question is: Where are you going to find magazines?

The problem was one faced by Bill Alexander, when he was developing the .17 HMR AA carbine. He ended up making his own magazines, to deal with the cycling speeds and feed problems that the bolt and spring could not handle on their own.

And then there is the .17 WSM. Add in an even

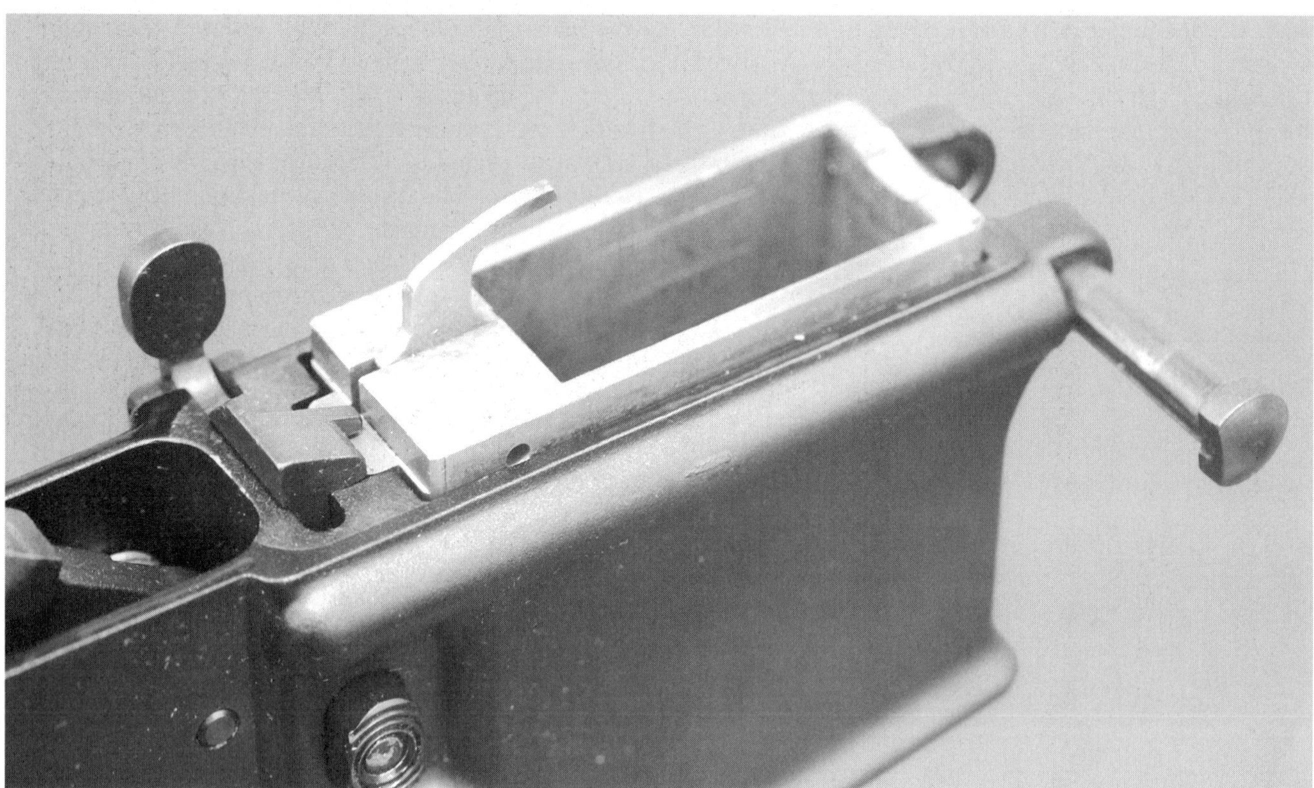

Here you see the magazine adapter in the Alexander Arms .17 HMR, so it can use the proprietary magazines for reliable .17 HMR feeding.

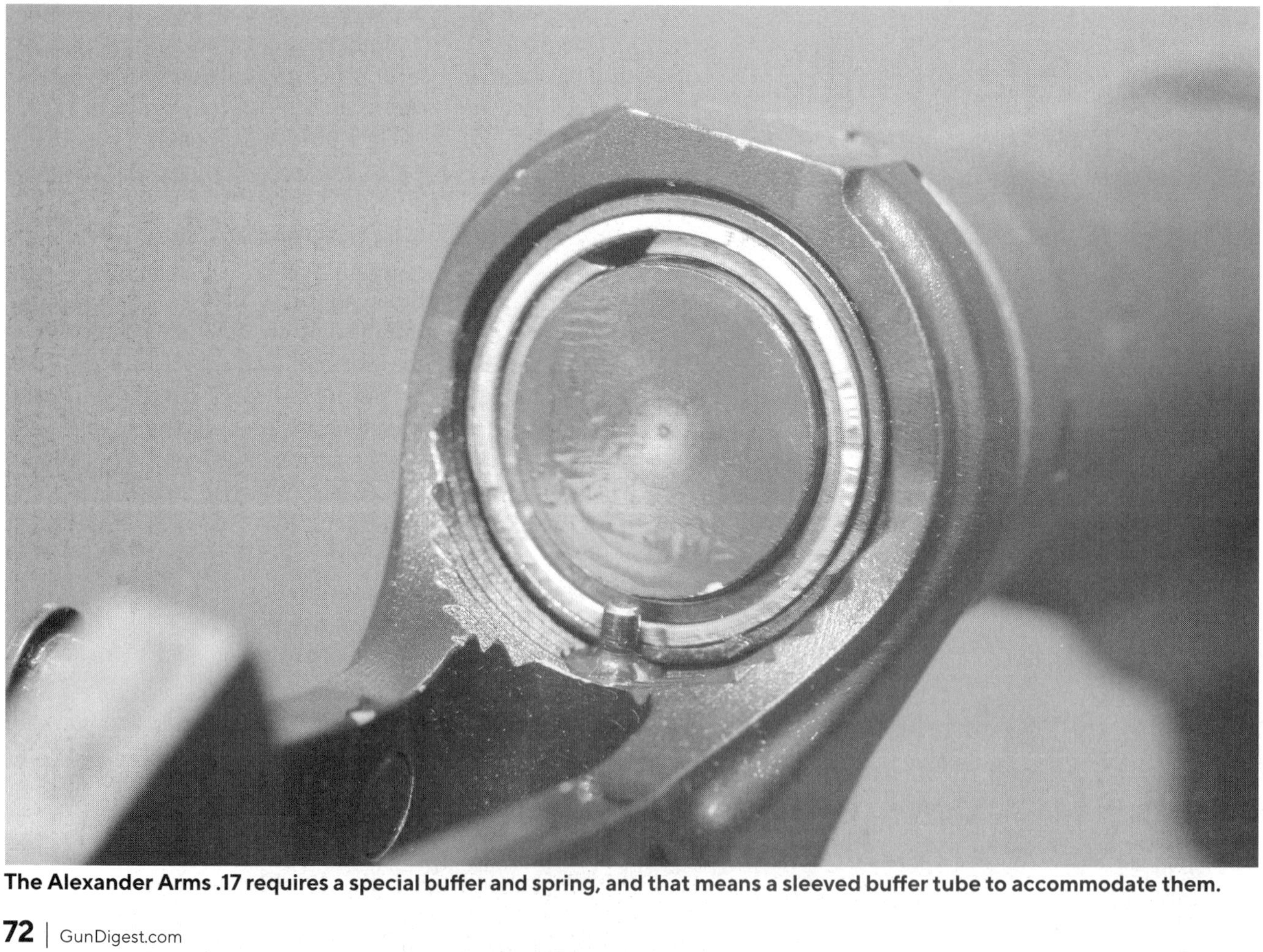

The Alexander Arms .17 requires a special buffer and spring, and that means a sleeved buffer tube to accommodate them.

larger rim diameter, and a big jump up in operating pressure, and you have a cartridge that can't be handled with just a blowback system. You probably need a gas system, a piston system even. And then how do you shepherd a relatively stubby rimfire round (the .17 WSM is 1.440 inches, overall length, a quarter-inch short of the empty case length of a .223) past the locking lugs of the barrel extension?

(above) The Alexander Arms .17 HMR is clearly marked on the bolt. So, you have no excuse if you get to the range and find you only packed .22 LR.

(below) The Alexander Arms .17 rimfire requires a heavier bolt than that of the .22 LR. Which explains why it also requires a buffer and spring in the stock, plus the extra cyclic travel.

GARROW FIREARMS DEVELOPMENT

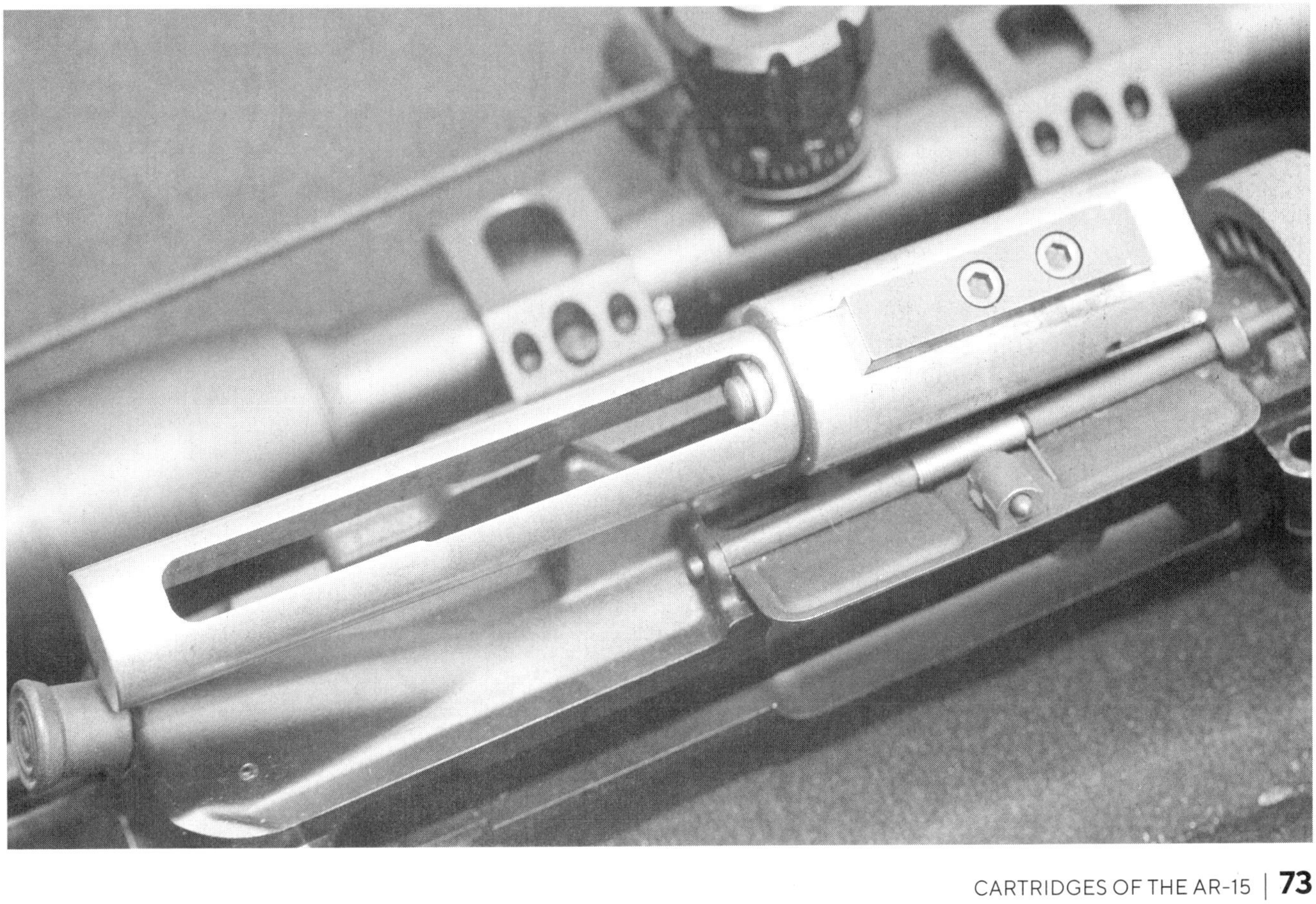

Garrow found an absolutely clever way to make a gas-operated, blowback rimfire that handles the .17 HMR. The process is rather involved, mechanically, but works just fine. It is a variation of the roller-lock system used by the West German G3. The spring-loaded carrier has a pair of ball bearings in it, that are pressed outward by the carrier key as the carrier (which is the bolt) closes. Those ball bearings ride in holes drilled through the receiver. In firing, the cartridge case thrust on the bolt cannot overcome the ball bearings. The lever arm is far too short of that to happen. However, the gas tube delivers a jolt of gas back to the carrier key, and movement of the carrier key allows the ball bearings to now roll back into the bolt/carrier. This begins the carrier movement. Then blowback takes care of the rest.

To call this clever is to discount clever people. This is great.

A RIMFIRE ADVANTAGE

In addition to the low cost, negligible recoil, and easily managed muzzle blast, a rimfire AR has another advantage: There is no need for a buffer system. The bolt/conversion system has its own spring system (usually a pair of springs, on guide rods) and they do not extend back into the buffer tube.

So, you could make an AR-15 clone, in .22 LR, with a folding stock, and it would function with the stock folded. The actual added usefulness of this is up for debate, but it certainly is cool.

The Garrow Firearms Development conversion for .22 magnum is a complete upper, magazines, and a recoil spring and buffer replacement.

The Garrow conversion uses a pair of ball bearings that act not unlike the roller bearings on an HK G3.

(below) The gas key slides, forced by the gas coming back from the gas tube, and that movement allows the ball bearings to come out of lock. After that, it is simply a blowback system.

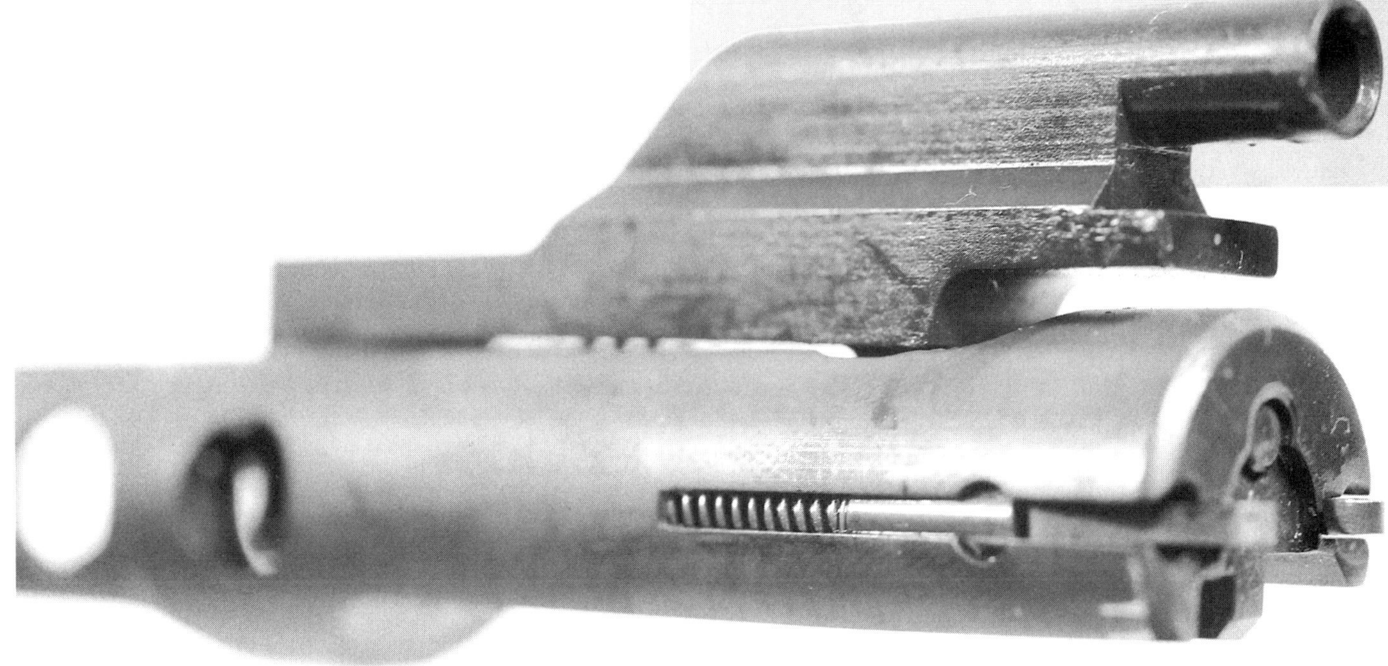

5.7x28

The 5.7x28 cartridge came about because of a NATO requirement. That requirement was part and parcel of the NATO hand-wringing and near pants-wetting over the prospect of Soviet troopers wearing body armor. The thought of armor-clad troopers bailing out of BMPs, and then assaulting the objectives, impervious to the lowly 9mm Parabellum, was enough to cause the creation of a new idea: the Personal Defense Weapon (PDW).

We will overlook the penetrating abilities of the rifle rounds then in use: you know, the "inadequate" 5.56, and the "obsolete" 7.62 NATO. This was a couple decades before ceramic plates, so anyone who wanted to "armor up" with something that would stop rifle rounds would look like the Michelin Man.

Left to right: .45 ACP, .40 S&W, 9x19 and four loads of the 5.7x28.

The armor they were going to test against was called CRISAT armor, named after the "Collaborative Research Into Small Arms Technology" program. The test panel was a 1.6mm plate of titanium, backed by 20 layers of Kevlar cloth. There was even a NATO standard for this, STANAG 4512.

Honestly, they expected Soviet troopers to be clad in this armor, probably back-and-breast plates of it, and they needed something that would get through it. Really? The Soviets couldn't afford to upgrade the AK-47, and settled for the AK-74, a slightly improved rifle in a new caliber, and they were going to equip all their troops in titanium and Kevlar?

Oh, and good old steel core 7.62 NATO, and any kind of a similar 5.56 round, would have sliced through such a setup like nobody's business back then.

And how was the standard selected? My suspicion is that this combination was just enough to stop standard 9mm ball ammo. I can easily see a test crew phoning back from the test range: "The hottest stuff in the warehouse goes through 16 layers of Kevlar, we'd better make the standard more than that."

Of course, if you simply loaded 9mm ammo with a thicker gilding jacket, and a steel core, you could almost certainly poke it through a CRISAT panel, but

The P90 when equipped with a suppressor, can be very quiet indeed. Of course, it is quiet while still being a minuscule cartridge, so keep that in mind.

that wasn't the plan. I want to point out at this time that an improved .30-carbine loading, a 100-grain bullet, also with a steel core, would have probably made Swiss cheese of a CRISAT panel, but that was even further from the plan. Would have been fun, though.

The end result was a PDW unveiled in 1990 by FN: the P90 and its ammo.

The original loading, the SS90, was a 23-grain bullet, which featured a plastic core in a gilding metal jacket. It achieved 2,800 fps out of the P90 PDW. The terminal ballistic plan was for the bullet to penetrate, and then "J-hook" causing a more severe wound than simply a 5.7mm hole through the unfortunate Warsaw Pact trooper. A J-hook is when the bullet yaws, or tumbles after impact, and the wound track deviates from a straight line, into a curve. A J-hook.

This lasted a few years, and was replaced by the SS190, a 31-grain bullet at 2,130 fps. The SS190 could be used in the Five-seveN pistol, while the SS90 could not.

The testing and production continued. I visited the FN plant in Liege, Belgium, in 2000, and had a chance to shoot the P90, the Five-seveN, and even assemble one of each, there in the assembly area. (I'm sure they took them back apart when I left, so don't worry you got "the one Sweeney made.")

Interest in the PDW concept continued, and HK got into the act, with its 4.6x30 cartridge, and the MP7 pistol/PDW/SMG, and a pistol for the same cartridge. In the testing, the testing board determined that the 5.7 was the superior cartridge. The Germans disagreed, and since the board had to agree, and the Germans had to adopt whatever was agreed to, the whole matter was tabled. Where it remains today. As an aside, I've since fired both cartridges. I visited Blackwater (back when it was so-named) and had a chance to shoot the MP7. Interesting.

The MP7, as a pistol-sized hole-punching firearm, is cool to shoot. Would I be enthusiastic about shooting various terrorists, enemy combatants and orc-like bad guys, with a cartridge that really is a mildly loaded .22 Hornet? No, not really. If it were the only option I had, I'd be a lot more enthusiastic about it than, say, a baseball bat. If I had to be packing a firearm, as a backup to a radio, laptop computer with satellite linkup, or other modern bad-guy-whacking tool, I think I'd rather have a 1911 (hey, I'm an old guy, with settled preferences) or a really, really compact AR-15.

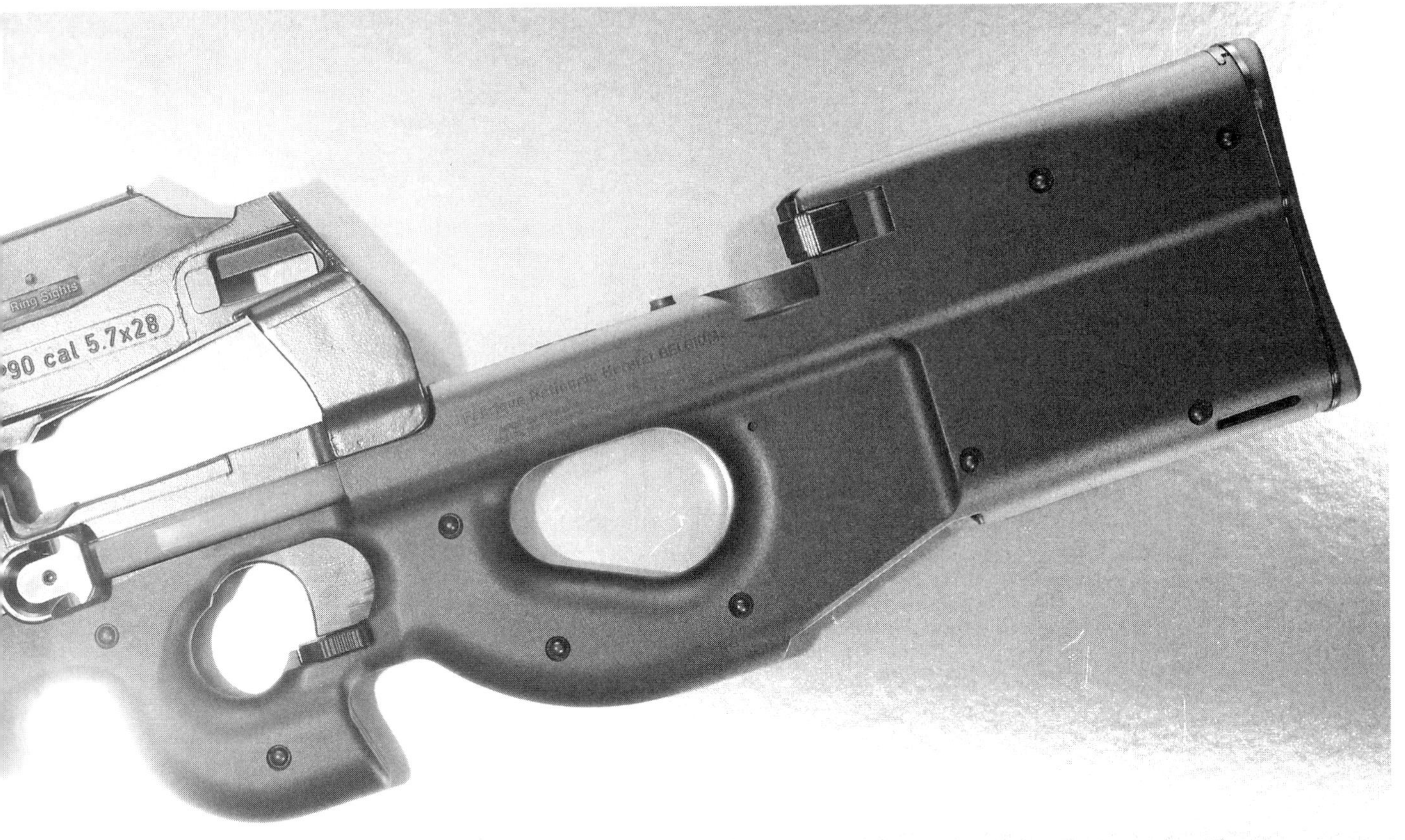

The MP7 is not a lot bigger or heavier than a government 1911, but somehow, I'd gravitate toward the latter.

The MP7 can also be suppressed, and the Germans make a goodly selection of ammo for it.

The MP7 does have one option the 1911 doesn't: It is select-fire. If that matters to you.

Snark aside, the 5.7 can also be thought of as a rimless .22 Hornet, or a really hot .22 WMR. It isn't actually either, being made on a new case dimension, and not converted from something else. It also is somewhat restricted in availability. The really hot, mil-spec ammo is not generally found "loose on the street" as it were. That is, you cannot walk into a big-box sporting goods store and find or order a carton of SS190. That's because it is the stuff that will go through body armor, and since there is a handgun made to chamber the 5.7, AP is off the table for the rest of us.

The P90, and the semi-auto version of it, the PS90, use a different magazine and operating system than we are accustomed to.

The question is: How to get this to work in an AR-15? There are two ways.

AR57

The AR57 is a simple setup, really. It consists of a modified upper receiver, with a barrel chambered in 5.7x28. There's a bolt, a heavy blowback bolt (the P90 and PS90 are also delayed blowbacks) and all of this rides on top of a regular AR-15 lower assembly. Then it gets odd. The magazine is not an AR-15 magazine, nor a modified one. It is the same magazine used in the P90/PS90. How does it fit in the magazine well, you ask? It doesn't. It rides on top of the barrel, with the cartridges feeding down, just like the P90. The feeding part of the magazine points back toward the shooter, just as it does on the P90 and PS90. The difference is the magazine on the AR57 is much farther forward. That particular geometry is dictated by the location of the chamber. On the PS90, the chamber is to the rear, since the firearm is a bullpup. On an AR-15, the chamber is forward of the PS90 location, so the magazine has to be designed to ride more forward to meet up with the AR57 bolt and feed properly.

The empties, when they have been produced, simply fall down through the open magazine well, to the ground.

The result is interesting, if odd. The AR57 assembly is as large as, and heavy as, an AR-15 in .223/5.56, yet it fires a cartridge that is a decided step back in power. However, were you to bob the barrel to a length no longer than needed to keep the magazine in place, and put it on a pistol lower, it would be a very compact firearm.

Conversion is simple: an AR57 upper. Can you make one? No, not really. There are no sources for 5.7x28 barrels for the AR-15 that I know of. And you'd have to make your own bolt from scratch. So, a conversion upper it is.

You acquire an AR57 conversion upper from, no great surprise here, AR57. At this writing, the company seemed not to be making uppers, but you can find them from various wholesalers and firearms shops. Magazines are easy, you simply lay hands on FN P90/PS90 magazines of various capacities.

As a less-expensive firearm than the FN PS90, the AR57 upper assembly can be had for $500 or greater, less than a PS90 costs. That's a lot of 5.7x28 ammo.

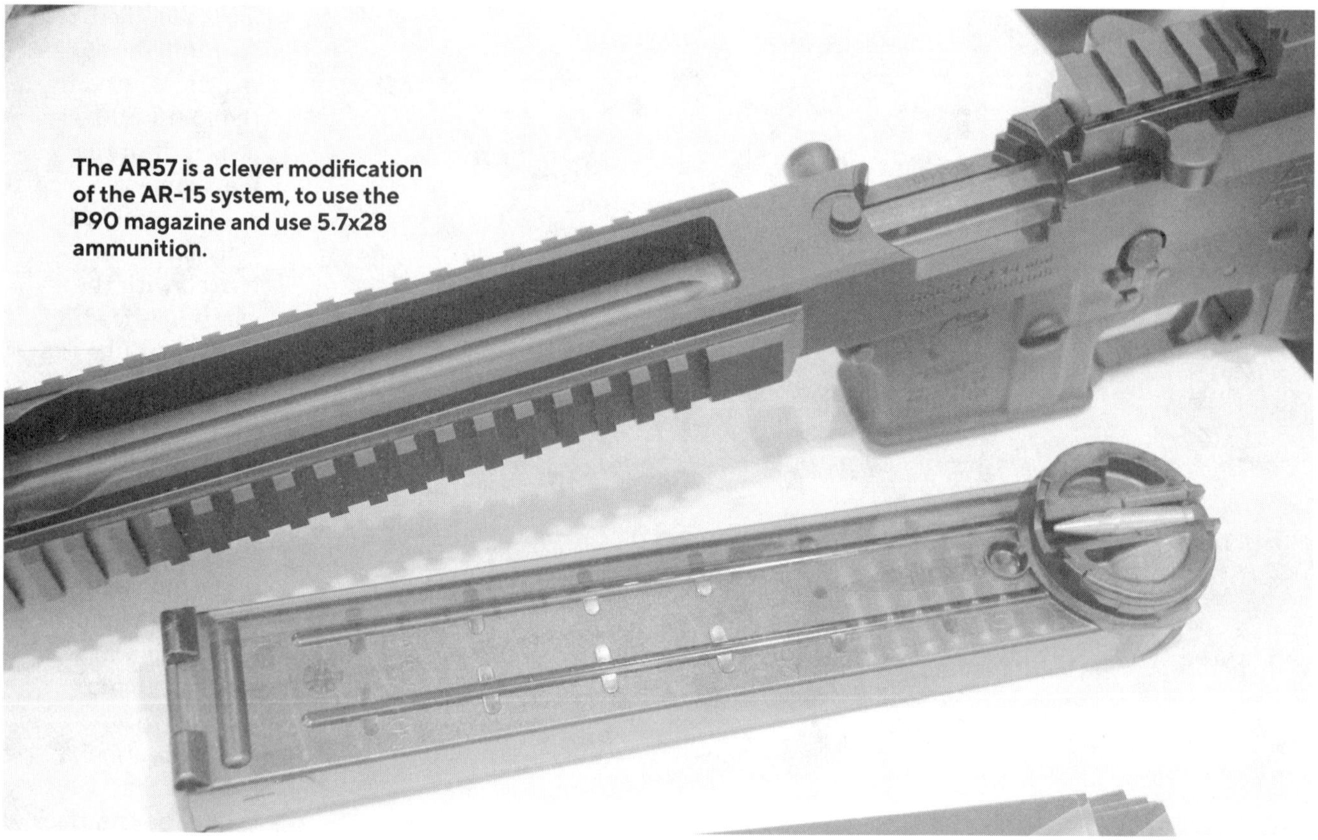

The AR57 is a clever modification of the AR-15 system, to use the P90 magazine and use 5.7x28 ammunition.

The AR57 is accurate and delivers everything the little 5.7 can generate.

CMMG offers the Banshee, an AR pistol or SBR (or carbine, if you prefer a longer barrel) chambered in 5.7x28. The first detail to know is the magazine: not the P90 2x4 magazine, but the Five-seveN magazine, made for the pistol.

CMMG

CMMG offers the Banshee, an AR pistol or SBR (or carbine, if you prefer a longer barrel) chambered in 5.7x28. The first detail to know is the magazine: not the P90 2x4 magazine, but the Five-seveN magazine, made for the pistol. CMMG broaches a lower that accepts this magazine without any adapters, and even manages to build in a magazine release and last-shot hold-open.

The other change is the bolt design. The FN P90 is a delayed blowback system, where the barrel slides to the rear for a short distance, along with the bolt, before the barrel stops and the bolt continues onward.

CMMG uses its Radial Delayed Blowback system. The angled rear faces of the bolt lugs create poor leverage for the cartridge to simply blow the bolt open. That disadvantage allows the bolt to open later, slowly and under control, and this gives two advantages. One, the bolt-carrier-buffer weight combo doesn't have to be as heavy as on a blowback system. The 9mm, for example, uses a buffer that is as heavy as that of the full-sized rifle. So, recoil is reduced, recoil from the mass of a blowback system bottoming out in the rear of the buffer tube.

Second, the bolt hold-open lasts longer. One weakness of the 9mm systems is the mass of the bolt-carrier-buffer crashing into the bolt hold-open when the 9mm is empty. That can end up breaking the hold-open lever, which is a different part than the .223/5.56 one is.

The end result is a pistol or SBR that has a barrel no longer than that of the select-fire P90. And the Banshee is nearly as compact as the P90, without the somewhat awkward ergonomics of the FN PDW. And if you do not want an AR pistol, or SBR, then the carbines have full-length barrels, complete with free-float handguards, so everything is just like a regular AR-15.

You want a small, light, compact package? The CMMG Banshee in 5.7 delivers that and won't abuse your shoulder or ears.

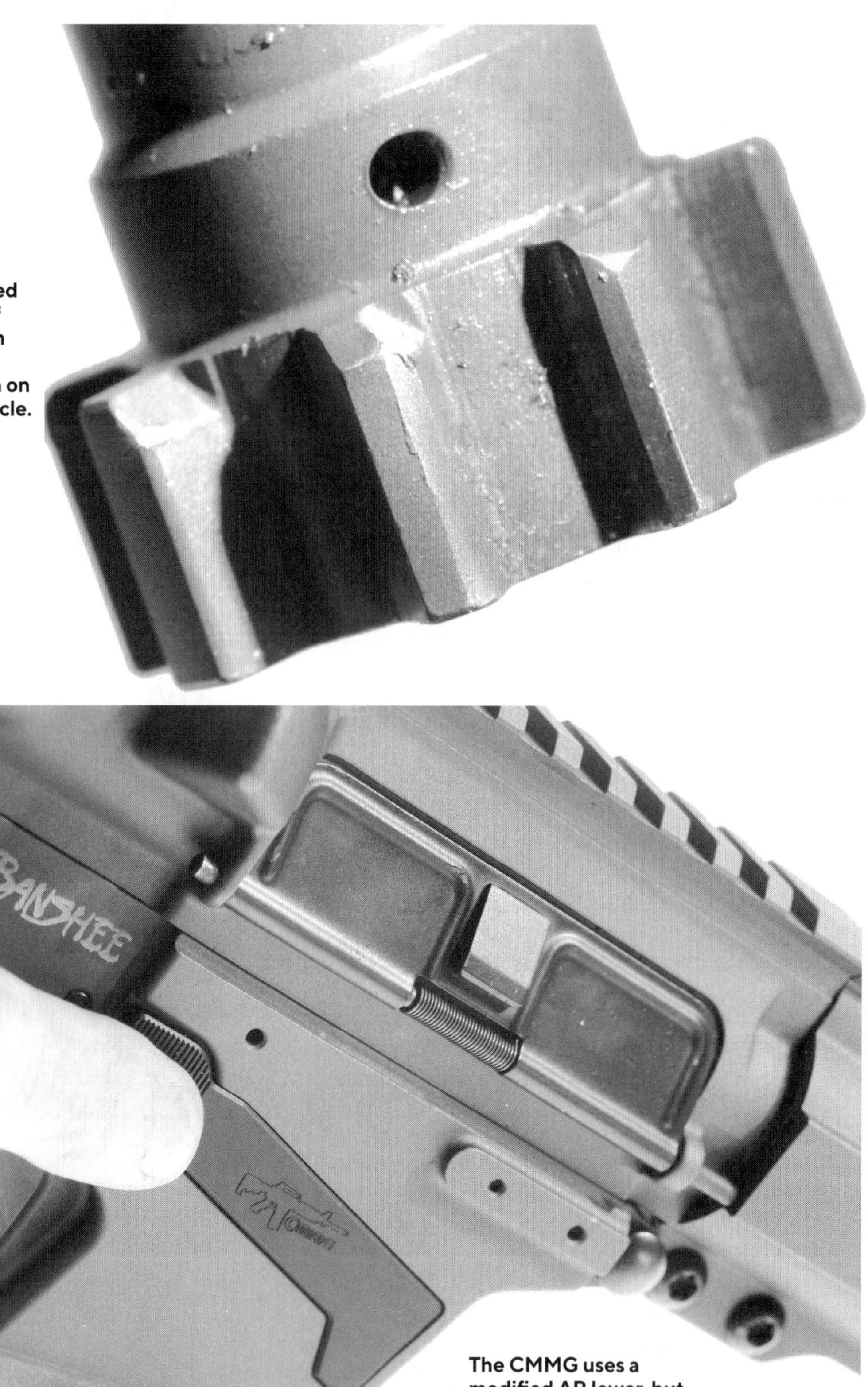

The CMMG radial delayed bolt has the rear faces of the locking lugs cut at an angle, and the cartridge has to cam the bolt open on those lugs, in order to cycle. Which it does.

The CMMG uses a modified AR lower, but the magazine button is still in more or less the same place.

The CMMG Banshee uses FN Five-seveN magazines, not P90 magazines.

The CMMG Banshee, with the Five-seveN magazine, feeds like any other AR-15.

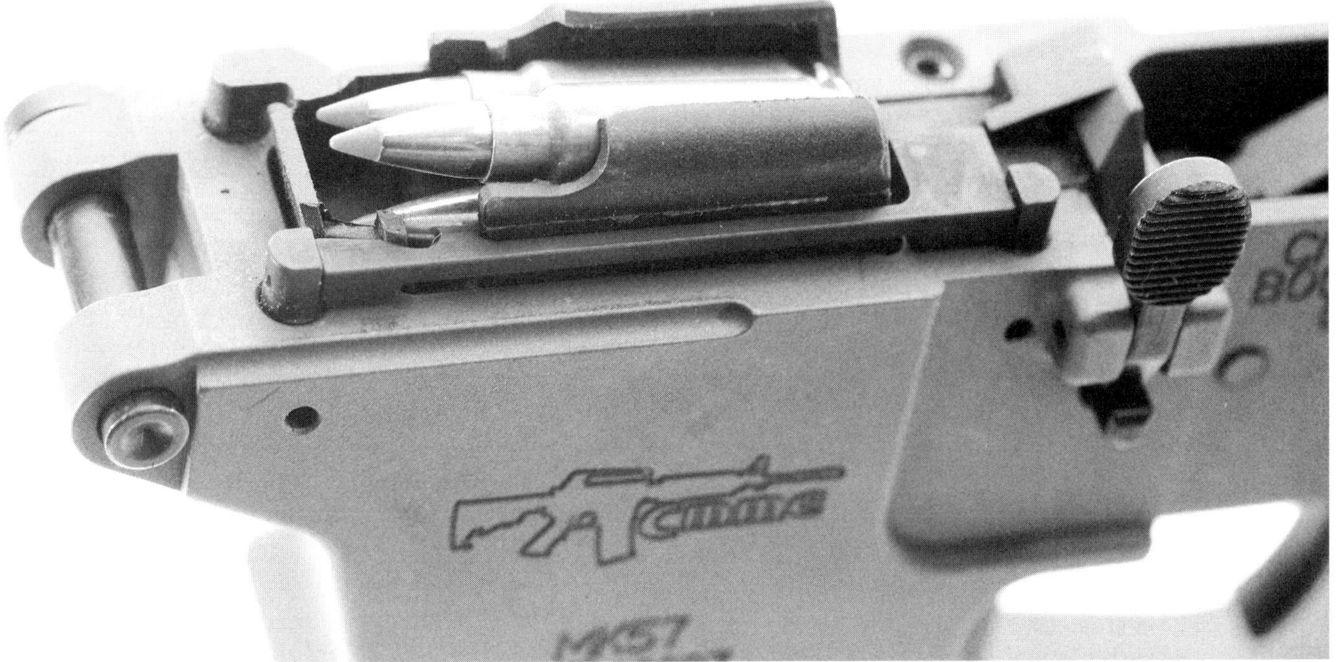

The magazines are more expensive than .223 magazines are, but that is more a matter of economies of scale than anything else. Anything that has been made in the bazillions is going to be as cheap as dirt. You can buy three or four 20- or 30-round AR magazines for 5.56, to the cost of one Five-seveN magazine of the same capacity. But that is not as big a deal as you might think. You are not, after all, equipping a police force, or an infantry company. You are buying magazines for yourself. How many do you need? As long as you don't abuse them, they will last a good, long time.

But the rest of the firearm is so AR-standard that you could treat it as just another AR-15.

5.7x28

The cartridge itself, intended for a delayed blowback design, is not all that easy to reload. In fact, it is very difficult, and probably not a good idea. The delayed blowback aspect of the FN firearms means that the shoulder of the 5.7 blows forward. The amount is small, but then it is a small cartridge, so as a percentage of the overall length, it blows forward a lot.

When you resize a case, you have to set the shoulder back so the new round will chamber properly. The stretching of the case does not happen as a simple balloon-like expansion at the shoulder. No, the case is bound near the front, so the case expansion comes at the expense of the case wall near the base. Fire and reload a case enough times, and it will break at the expansion point. This is a well-known phenomenon in other cartridges. The exemplar here is the .303 British.

So, theoretically yes, the case can be reloaded. But the miniscule size, the pinch of powder charge, the case being worked so hard, all make it a dicey proposition. I reload a lot of cartridges. I do not reload 5.7x28.

Not a problem, as it is commonly loaded. Federal and FN both offer loads for the 5.7, and they do not limit the choices to a single bullet design.

(below) The 5.7 in a compact AR pistol is a real handy tool. It can be a bit flashy in low light, but a good flash hider or a suppressor easily takes care of that.

Either bare or suppressed, the CMMG Banshee is as short as the originator, the FN P90. Granted, the CMMG only holds 30 rounds to the P90 holding 50, but unless you are dealing with waves of zombies, that should not be a problem.

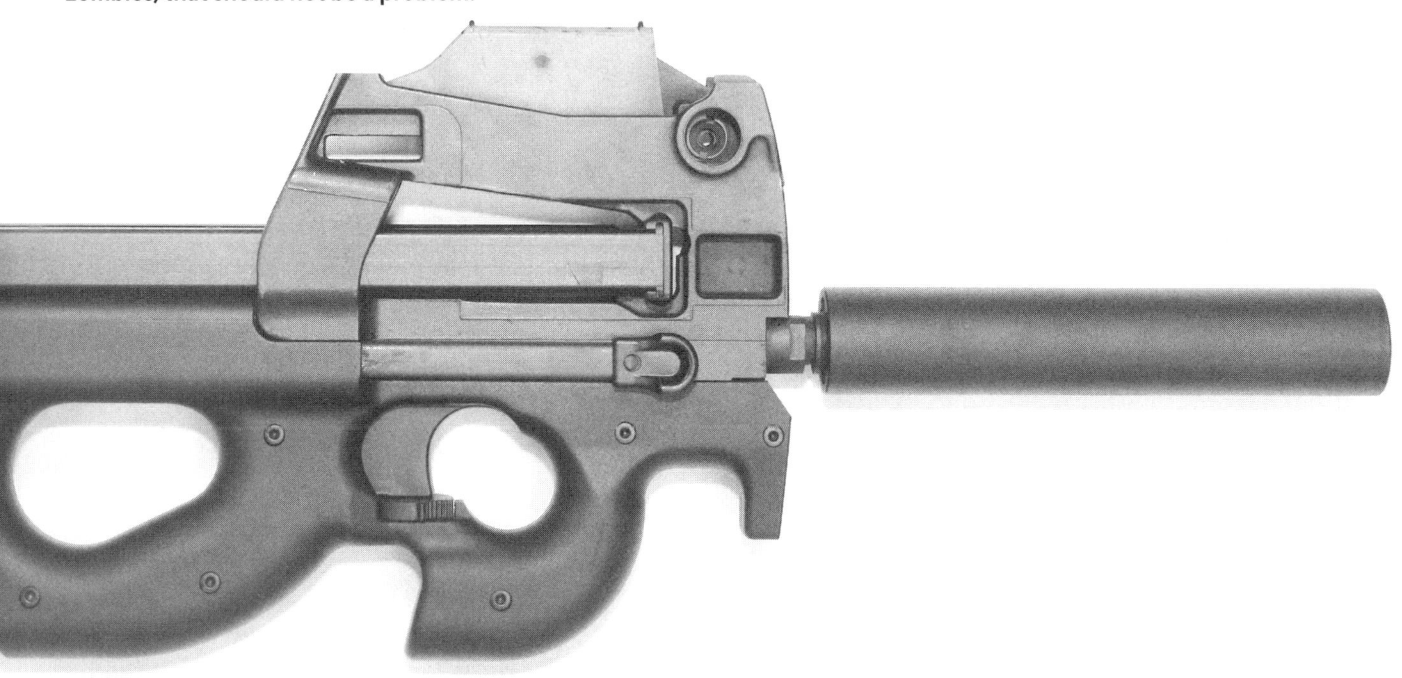

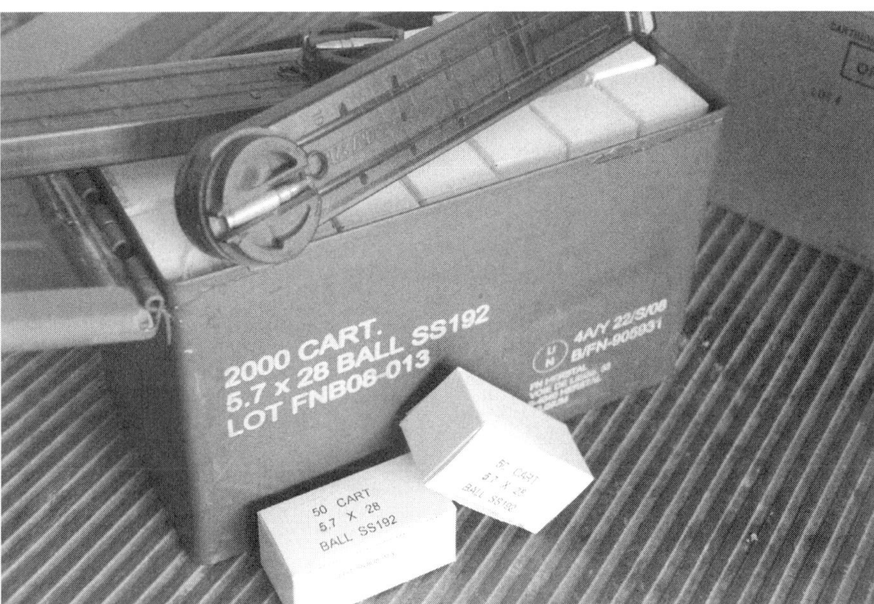

Reloading the 5.7 empties is a task in frustration. So just look for deals, buy in bulk, and have fun. Oh, and pick up your empties anyway. No one likes a messy range.

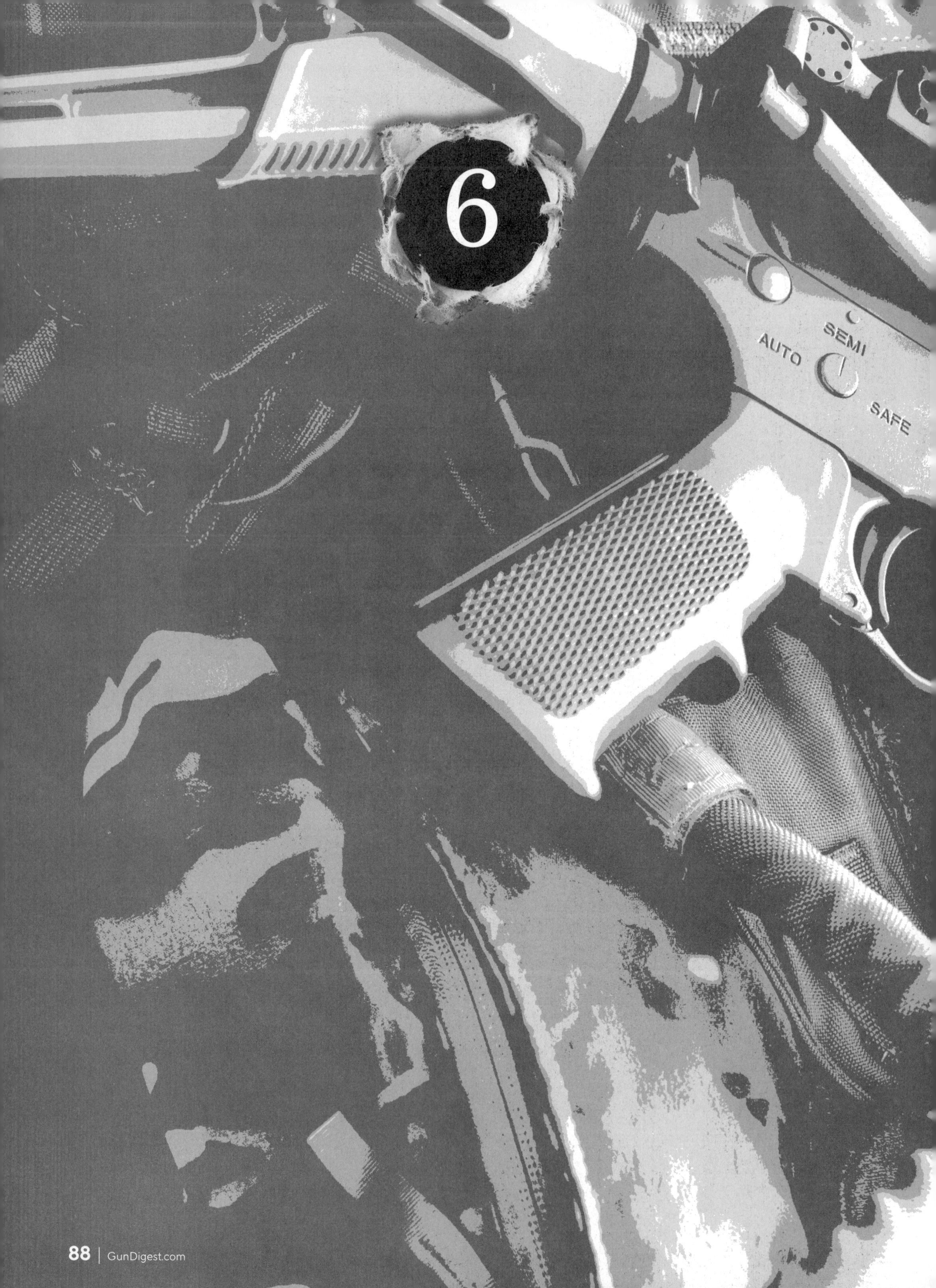
6
SEMI
AUTO
SAFE

5.45x39 THE LITTLE COMMIE

This was going to be the future. Well, it was going to be the future for the Soviets at least, and it was going to be the future for AR owners 30 years later.

The 7.62x39 was a great idea for the war the Soviets had fought and won, World War II. But 30 years on, it was getting a bit long in the tooth. Also, the experience of the Americans in Southeast Asia had shown that the small-diameter, high-velocity bullet idea had legs.

The Soviets were all full of enthusiasm and excitement. They were going to leap ahead. They were going to adopt a new cartridge that out-did the American one, and they were going to put it into a rifle that did everything better than the decadent capitalist rifle did.

As usual, reality sneaked up behind them and pummeled them pretty seriously. Basically, the Soviet economy could not deliver a new service rifle with all those advances, and a new cartridge, and new planes, tanks, missiles, while at the same time also producing cars, houses, clothes and food. They had to settle for what they could do, which was basically make the AK-47 accept the new cartridge.

The AK-47 was supposed to be a great leap forward. Instead, it was as much as the Soviet Union could do, with the money it had. They might have been communists, but they still were bound by the laws of economics.

That's how they ended up with the 5.45x39, a cartridge that's pretty much the same length as the 7.62x39. If they changed the cartridge length, they would have had to change all the stamping dies, trunnion specs, magazine dimensions and all the rest. The new cartridge also had to work with a steel case, and with steel-jacketed bullets, because steel was one of the two materials you could build things out of in the Soviet Union. The other was cement.

Also, the cartridge case could not have the same base/rim diameter as that of the 7.62x39. Doing so would cause a severely tapered case, and the magazines would be awkward. So, the 7.62x39 has a base and rim diameter of a nominal .447 of an inch, while the 5.45x39 has one of .394.

Thus, the AK-74, with its muzzle brake and visibly different magazines, operates the same way as the AK-47, so training is training.

Fast forward a couple of decades, and the Soviet Union has fallen apart. Oligarchs are stealing everything in sight, factories built to provide 100-percent employment now find themselves on the Procrustean bed of efficiency and cost containment, and yet have nothing to make that anyone wants to buy. Firearms, however, as durable goods, are always something you can sell. Those crazy American collectors would love to buy AK-47s and 74s, but the fact that they are select-fire is a problem. There's also the pesky problem of import laws.

Now, the Chinese had figured a way around that many years before. There was a time when you could buy Chinese AKs, pistols and ammunition pretty much by weight. No, really. I remember a time (now I sound like I'm old) when you could go to a gun show, and buy an SKS for $79, and a case of Chinese ammo for it for $79. A case would be somewhere from 1,200 to 1,600 rounds of ammo. So, the Chinese could get cash, American dollars, by selling ammo and guns.

Basically, it was because of the old Vulcan maxim: Only Nixon can go to China. The Chinese got favored-nation status, and were allowed to begin trade with America. At that time, the only thing they made that we wanted were AKs. So that's what they sold.

The Russians couldn't do that, because by the time the Soviet Union fell, and the survivors were looking to sell, import restrictions had been slapped on firearms. But they could sell de-milled parts kits. So, take a warehouse full of AK-47s. Get the accepted instructions from the ATF and State Department for what cutting had to be done where, disassemble, chop, sweep everything back into a greasy box, and ship to America for money. American collectors would do the rest: buy, clean, replace and assemble.

The ammo was even easier, as it just had to be loaded into Conex containers.

To get an idea of the volume involved, consider this: A motorized rifle division in the Red Army, had about 13,000 men in it. The Soviets had 150 such divisions in the Red Army. Each man needed an AK. Then there were the armored divisions, military police, training units, in all, the estimates of active strength of the Soviet Union during the Cold War was between 2.8 and 5.2 million men. (You can see the problem with replacing all the AK-47s with a new, expensive, updated rifle.) Then you need as many rifles in storage as you think you'll need for the reserves, when you call them up in case of war.

Rifles get used and worn out or lost in training and action, so you have to make more. Oh, wait, there are also the armies of the Warsaw Pact. East Germany, Poland, Hungary, Romania, the Czechs and the Slovaks, they all have men under arms as well.

There were tens of millions of men, and they need-

The external impression of the 5.45 in an AR is pretty darned good, especially if it is an LWRC. (Excellent rifles, always.) While ammo was cheap and plentiful, things were good.

ed many more rifles than that. The Soviets needed warehouses full of ammunition. Last, there were the various overseas support efforts of the "people's struggle for liberation" which meant shiploads of arms and ammo heading out.

Once things got up to full steam, it was clear there was going to be a tsunami of arms and ammo into the U.S.

The 7.62x39 is an awkward, ugly, fit in the AR-15. We'll get into that later. But the 5.45x39 was a much better fit. The bore was almost the same, as it needed a groove diameter of .221 of an inch compared to the .223 which uses a groove diameter of .224. The rim diameter of the .223 Remington is a nominal .378, so a bolt opened up to accept a 5.45x39 rim has had a minimal amount of steel removed. You could even use the same magazines, although it was always a roll of the dice. If you built an AR in 5.45, you tested magazines, and once you found ones that worked in that rifle, you kept them with it.

There was only one problem: the gas system of the AR. It blows gas back into the receiver. The 5.45x39 ammo loaded by the Soviets was corrosive. Oh, you will have people say it isn't, or wasn't, and today that might be true. But the original stuff, the military-production ammo, the ammo that was going to be so cheap, was as corrosive as the promises of sirens.

The short-term solution was simply to clean your rifle after shooting. Having built up an AR in 5.45x39, a shooting session involved hot water, ammonia, brushes, lots of scrubbing, a heat gun to dry things, and lots of oil.

The best of the 5.45 ARs came from Bill Alexander, of Alexander Arms. But Bill, an engineer of exemplary skill and knowledge, despaired of making a rifle that could handle the wildly variable quality of the Soviet-production ammunition. He compared the Soviet selection of powder to "bridge sweepings" and "whatever came from the powder mills." The gas system of the AK, either 7.62 or 5.45, is a lot more

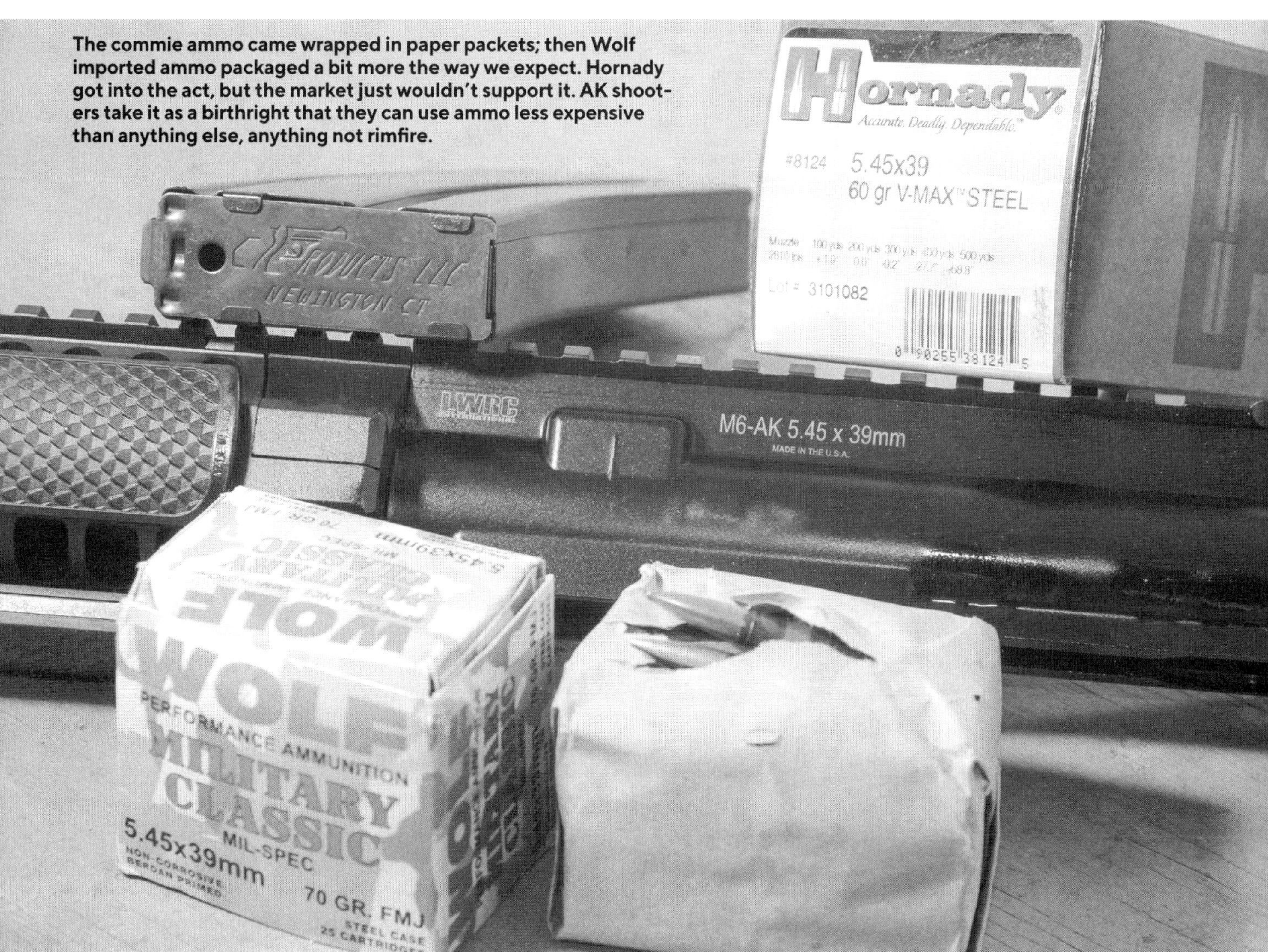

The commie ammo came wrapped in paper packets; then Wolf imported ammo packaged a bit more the way we expect. Hornady got into the act, but the market just wouldn't support it. AK shooters take it as a birthright that they can use ammo less expensive than anything else, anything not rimfire.

The recoil was the same as .223/5.56. The accuracy wasn't as good, but when ammo was cheap, who cared?

accommodating of variant powder burning rates. The system is designed to be over-gassed, and almost as soon as the piston begins moving, it vents to the atmosphere. So, as long as the powder worked the action, who cared about powder burn rates, right comrade?

The best AR-15 solution to this was the LWRC one, a piston gun. That kept the corrosive gas products (the primer was the culprit, as it always is) out in the gas system, and made things easier to clean.

Accuracy was good enough, depending on which particular production lot, and from what arsenal, your ammo was.

However, it was not to be. The problem was three-fold: desire, cleaning and cost.

The serious AK collector had to have one of each, and ammo to feed them. But the vast majority of shooters who wanted to be shooting, and using an AK, wanted it to be chambered in 7.62x39. The 5.45 was only a curiosity to them. I suspect that the ease and volume of manufacture of 7.62x39 ammunition also played a role. After all, they had been making it by then for over half a century. There was probably so much on hand that everyone in the former communist countries who wanted to pocket some cash could sell an aisle's worth of it, and no-one would notice. If they had to make more, it was cheap. For the 5.45, however, there was less of it, and in order to be accurate enough, it took a bit more work and skill to make.

And the AK is notorious for being unconcerned with a little bit of corrosion. ARs, on the other hand, don't like it very much.

There was another hitch in the AK as AR-beating rifle, the ban on imported 7N6 ammunition. This is the infamous "poison bullet" for the AK-74, that allegedly had much greater terminal ballistics. Not really, but that was enough to get it banned for import. So, all that wartime stock, in warehouses, was no longer importable to the U.S. Suppliers had to provide newly made ammo, and not using the 7N6 bullet.

When the prices for ammo inched up, manufacturers stepped in to provide newly made 7.62, but the 5.45 wasn't. There were some attempts to provide newly made ammo in 5.45, but the variables were all against it as a marketable product, and it just faded away. Hornady has announced it will be offering 5.45 brass, Berdan-primed, for reloaders, but that's a pretty niche market. The number of AR and AK owners who want to load up their own 5.45 ammo is going to be small.

As an example, a search for current ammo turns up 5.45x39, newly made, at a price of $260 per 1,000 rounds. I suspect you would be hard-pressed to find any of the old "spam tins" of Soviet ammo for sale, anywhere. For 7.63x39, however, newly made, can be had for $190 per 1,000. So, $70 per 1,000 rounds might not seem like much of a difference, but there is one aspect of the AK set that had endured: They are cheap. They are being worn down by the reality of newly manufactured rifles, and it is hard to find one still who will grumble about "when parts kits were under $100," but they still want AKs for less than what ARs cost.

The conversion of an AR-15 to 5.45x39 involved a bolt and barrel. Once you found reliable magazines for that arrangement, you were set. Since the build was specialized, I suspect that there are no more sources for bolts. If you have an AR in 5.45, you might still be able to find "new-old" stock of replacement barrels. But they won't last, and as the demand dwindles, the barrel makers who can make them will do fewer and fewer special runs.

The good news is that an AR in 5.45 can be rebuilt back to another caliber, since the only changes were the bolt and barrel.

It was nice while it lasted, and the promise was alluring, but it turned out to be a dead end.

The good news is, when the supply of cheap ammo is gone, or the barrel is worn out, you can rebuild your 5.45 AR into some other caliber. Which is what this book is all about.

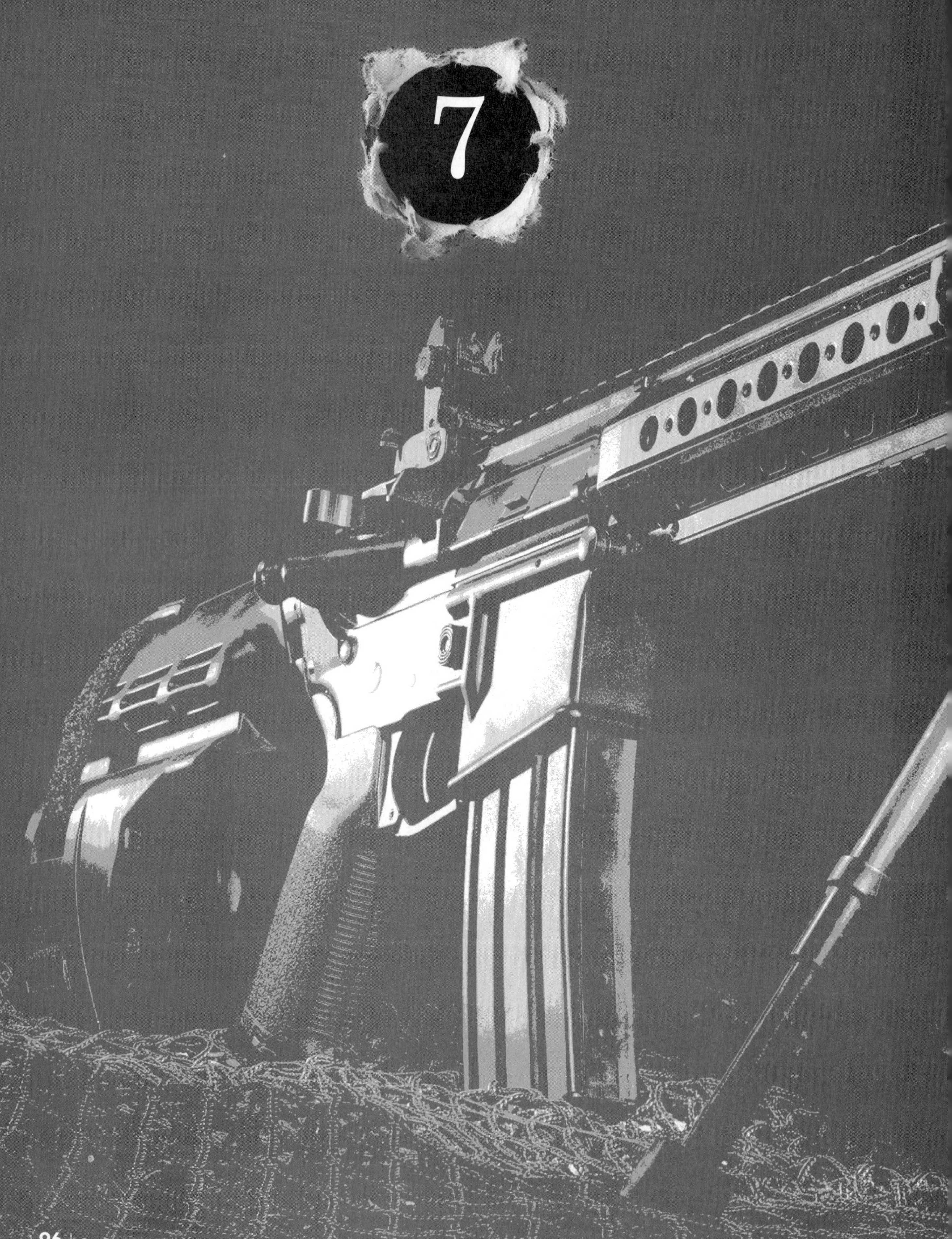
7

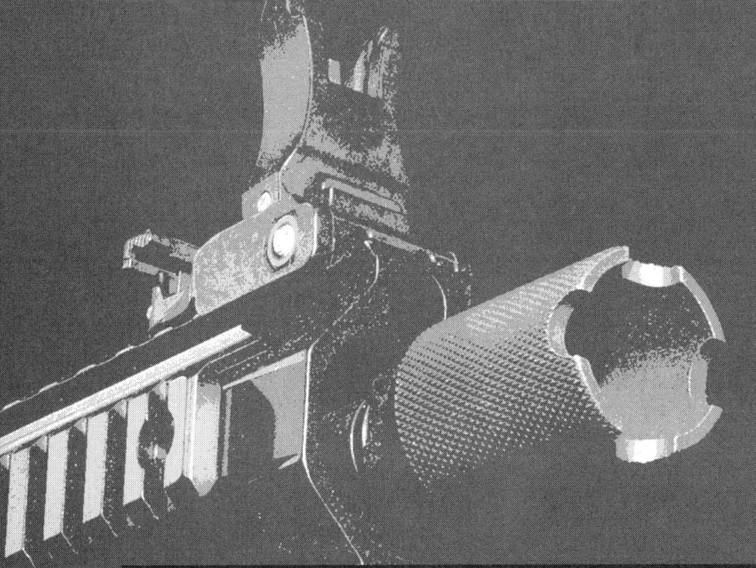

.223 BIGGER AND SMALLER

OK, let's dive right into the easiest conversion: one that simply uses a cartridge that is the base cartridge, the .223, necked up or down. All you really need here is a new barrel, because the bolt is the same and you can even use the same magazines.

I first ran into this back at Northwest Gun shop, when we had a customer come in with a "malfunctioning" Colt HBar in the late 1980s. He had bought it at a gun show and bought a bunch of ammo (reloads) to go with it. None of them worked. The bolt wouldn't even close. I wrote it up and stuffed it in the rack, with the full expectation that I would find the ammo the culprit. The first thing I did, after I brought my Wilson case gauge from home, was to gauge the ammo. Surprisingly, it was fully within spec. Go figure, gun-show reloads that actually fit. I then popped headspace gauges into the Colt, and sure enough, they would not close. Well, what have we here? The barrel is Colt, and marked, what? Wait. What does that say?

What was on the bench was a Colt AR-15 chambered in .222 Remington. Well, ah do declare.

OK, a bit of background. Some countries are very picky about what their citizens can own. Not just semi-auto rifles, and that sort of thing, but even calibers. Italy comes to mind, where you simply cannot own a firearm chambered in a military caliber. This was such a Colt, made, I later found out, for a contract to a French importer. Colt had an order for "X" number of rifles, so it made X plus some more rifles. Once the shipment was made, and accepted, they sold the extras to a wholesaler, who shoved them off on gun shops, and this one ended up in the hands of our customer.

I laid it all out for our customer. "I can make this one work with your ammo. I'll have to pull the barrel

and replace it with another. I can't just ream the chamber, because it is chrome-lined (true, it was) and that just won't work. I can simply trade you another Colt for this one, and your ammo will work." He was fine with that. He simply wanted an AR-15 and didn't care about "collectors' status" iron.

After he left, we called a couple collectors, who practically got into a fistfight over it, and ended up selling the rifle for more than twice what the Colt we'd traded was worth. Everyone was happy.

Changing the .223 AR to something else that uses the .223 case as the starting point is easy. Well, easy once you know your way around receiver clamps, barrel wrench, and so on.

The hard part has been done for you. The replacement barrel will have been chambered by the barrel maker so it will use a vanilla-plain mil-spec bolt. No rocket science here. Also, the gas port will have been drilled the correct diameter for the cartridge, at least in factory (if there is factory ammo for it) spec. So, let's get started listing them.

Stick around AR shooters long enough, and you will see pretty much everything. As calibers go, the 6x45 is not at all an unusual one, as it is such an easy conversion.

.17 REMINGTON

Talk about a laser. The .17 Remington is simply a .223 necked down to accept a bullet of .177-inch diameter. Well, not simply. The designers also shoved the shoulder back a bit on the .17 case. Why? So, it would be absolutely impossible to close the bolt on a .223 cartridge, in a .17 chamber. That would be bad. So, by setting the shoulder back just a bit, they made it impossible for even your iron-pumping shooting buddy to close the bolt.

This happened in 1971, and the idea was to make a bolt-action varmint rifle that has a laser-beam trajectory. Which it does, until the tiny little bullet starts to lose steam, and then it almost falls to the ground harmlessly. OK, slight exaggeration.

The specs on the .17 are pretty impressive. It will boost a 20-grain bullet to over 4,400 fps. That's half the felt recoil of a .223, which can get a 55-grain bullet to 3,200 fps.

Why do this? Varmints. A 20-grain bullet, with low recoil, will vaporize prairie dogs out to whatever distance you can hit them. For most shooters, 300 yards is full distance, and the .17 is still red-hot that far out.

The drawback is heat. It takes a lot of powder to drive even that light bullet that quickly. So, barrels will heat up quickly. But, the enthusiastic varmint shooter will have a pair (or even three) rifles to rotate through. Or some sort of powered barrel-cooling system, like compressed air or a fan. Hey, you're 300 yards from the varmints, they aren't going to notice a fan pushing air down the bore of your rifle, cooling it.

There's also a .17 Remington Fireball, which is the .22 Fireball necked down in a similar fashion. But since the Fireball is a much shorter case, there's no point in putting it into an AR-15. Even if you were to solve the feeding issues, you gain nothing, not velocity, case life or barrel life. Well, perhaps a marginal decrease in the powder used. But when we're talking 4,000 fps, who cares?

.204 RUGER

Unlike the .17, the .204 is not based on the .223 case. Instead, it is based on the .222 Magnum case. The difference? Nothing, really. Oh, when stuffed with .224 bullets, the .223 and .222 have different shoulder locations. (The .222 is farther forward.) But when you neck it down to hold a 20-caliber bullet, the .204 Ruger fitting into an AR-15 magazine doesn't care whether you made it from .222 or .223 brass. Actually, the best way to get brass is to buy ammo and shoot it, or new brass from Starline.

The performance is stellar. A 32-grain bullet was pushed at 4,225 fps, in the Hornady factory load. This was with a powder not available to reloaders. Reloaders had to "settle" for only 4,100 fps with their 32-grain bullets.

The weight range for bullets runs from 32 to 45 grains.

The .204 is another varmint cartridge (big surprise there) and as a result, a good rifle is a definite sub-MOA performer. That means ground squirrels are fair targets to 300 yards and beyond, assuming you can call the wind well. Tiny bullets are not good wind-bucking projectiles.

.222 REMINGTON

As I've mentioned before, Colt made a short run of AR-15s chambered in .22 Remington, for overseas sales. I've come across them in a couple of European firearms museums, and each time they have been something of a surprise.

6x45

When we move past the .223, the next step up in bullet diameter is 6mm, or .243. This is the bullet diameter of the well-known deer-hunting cartridge, the .243 Winchester. The 6x45 is not, however, the equal of the .243 Winchester. That latter cartridge commonly pushes a 105-grain bullet close to or past 3,000 fps. The 6x45 is the .223 Remington necked p to accept a .243 bullet. As such, it has a much more limited case capacity. It is also limited in overall length, the magazine. So, the 6x45 is stuck at or under 2.260 inches of overall length, while the Winchester (a necked-down .308 case) can be as much as 2.71 inches long. (The .243, however, is a fine candidate for the AR-10.)

The 6x45, or cartridges like it, have been proposed as replacement military cartridges in the past. The U.S. Army even experimented with a 6mm Saw

(above) The 6x45 conversion is simple, you swap barrels. As for the brass, you can make it from .223 if you're cheap, but it is easy enough to find 6x45 marked brass and ammo.

(left) This rifle was supposed to be chambered in .223, but in order to sell it overseas, Colt had to chamber it in .222 Remington. Was it stamped "222" by Colt, or by the importer, or by the European Proof House? Nobody I asked knew.

(Squad Automatic Weapon) with performance not unlike the 6x45. Th heaviest bullet it can use is 100 grains, and that has a not-blistering velocity of only 2,400 fps. You can gain more speed with lighter bullets, but they will have poor ballistic coefficients (BC), due to their short length. BC is a measure of the drag a bullet experiences as it travels through the air. The higher the BC, the less drag, and the less deceleration as it travels to the target.

However, the 6x45 does have attributes. Because of the small case and relatively large bore, it does not need a lot of powder to gain the velocities it generates. That means less heat, and longer barrel life.

The 6mm bullets are also known for accuracy, so you will have a very accurate, soft-recoiling rifle, should you build one in 6x45. The exemplar use here would be a lightweight hunting AR, for women or youngsters, where the chambering would satisfy the DNR (not a .22), be enough for deer, and not be so noisy or hard-kicking that it discouraged hunting and shooting.

It is always prudent to mark a non-standard caliber receiver with the correct caliber. No, firing .223 in a 6x45 is not going to break anything, but it can mean a wasted range day.

SHARPS .25-45

The next step up from 6mm is .25 caliber, and the Sharps company has an AR-15 for that. Another necked-up .223 case, the Sharps gets an 87-grain bullet to about 2,800 fps. Which makes it a very fine deer hunting cartridge for wooded areas. The short .257 bullet is not going to have an exemplary BC, but for most hunters, who will be whacking their deer inside 200 yards, high BCs are just advertising points.

Making brass is as simple as running .223 brass into a .25-45 sizing die.

.277 WOLVERINE

OK, now we're just getting to the point of doing things because we can. The .277 Wolverine uses (you guessed it) bullets of .277 diameter. However, because we are using the .223 parent case, and we are limited to the magazine overall length, the result is a cartridge with really stubby bullets. Yes, they are 85 to 110 grains, but they are really short for their weights.

It might be tempting to consider the .277 Wolverine a 6.8 SPC competitor, without the larger case

Necking cases up or down to create new cartridges is as old as the cartridge case itself.

and the need for a different bolt. But if you simply consider the case capacity, the smaller .223 case can't hold as much powder as that of the larger 6.8 SPC.

For me, the .277 crosses over the line of a bigger bullet gaining advantages, and it starts to step backward.

.30

Here we have a slew of bullets and cartridges, and they will be covered in their own chapters. While the 6mm, .243, .25 and .277 are wildcats or proprietary cartridges, the .30 ones we will be discussing are either proprietary and supported by established firms, or they are fully SAAMI-approved cartridges.

So, we jump right past the .30s, and go to:

.350 LEGEND

With the .350 Legend, we've reached the end of the line with the .223 case.

The Legend is a new cartridge designed for a very special application. It is, essentially, a .223 case without a neck, using a bullet that is the full diameter of the case mouth. The details are a bit more involved than that, but if you think of it that way, you will be starting from the right point.

Back when I began shooting, the idea of handgun hunting was still pretty much considered a stunt by old-time hunters. This would have been the early 1970s, and "old-time" hunters at that point in time grew up in the Depression. To their minds, one hunted then for food, or a trophy rack. And since trophy racks were rare, you hunted for food.

Deer were considered scarce, (and indeed, they were) and you didn't risk wounding one by shooting it with something so puny as a handgun. How scarce? At the time of the discovery of the Americas by Europeans, the estimated deer population in the U.S. was something like 44 million. Poor land management, over-hunting and habitat destruction brought the deer population of the U.S. down to near-extinction levels. As in, one million for the entire country. Maybe a million. By the time the veterans came back from overseas, there might have been 10 million deer. Their fathers essentially knew no deer. The vets saw them rarely.

By the 1970s, the whitetail population was back up to around 30 million, there were plenty of deer, and the .44 Magnum was known, and immensely popular due to a certain actor and movie. It had plenty of power for the task. After all, it was more powerful than the .44-40, and in some circles the .44-40 was still considered an entirely suitable woods cartridge for hunting. So, handgun hunting gained acceptance.

As handgun hunting moved from stunt to curiosity, to new adventure, to common exercise, the various state DNRs had to adapt. They did so by adding handgun-only areas or adding handguns to the shotgun-only areas. The question that consumed a lot of time and hot air was one you'd think was easy to answer. What was a handgun? At first glance, not a difficult question. But look a little deeper, and you can see how hard it might have been for them. Sure, a .44 Magnum revolver with a six-inch barrel is a handgun, and entirely suitable for hunting. But, a single-shot pistol, like the Thompson-Center Contender, chambered in .30-30, equipped with a scope on top is a handgun also. It is, however, also not very much less effective than a lever-action rifle in .30-30. If the idea of handgun hunting is to be more difficult, then the single-shot isn't. If the idea is that a handgun round is

The new .350 Legend is meant to be a hunting cartridge for the AR, in areas where you have to use a straight-walled case.

like a shotgun slug, and won't travel three counties over, then the T/C in .30-30 isn't a handgun.

The real problem most DNRs had with the .30-30 (and I'm using ".30-30" just as a place-holder for all the other rifle-common calibers in use or available) was range. A .44-Magnum bullet, while it will travel farther than a 12-gauge slug, it isn't as powerful and ranging as the centerfire rifle cartridges. So, the almost universal rule for handguns for hunting was that they had to be a straight-walled cartridge case.

There were also other, common but not universal restrictions as well. Some added a requirement that the handgun be a repeater, leaving out the single-shots. Some added a caliber limit, usually one of .357-bullet diameter. And some required a factory load that delivered more than a certain number of foot-pounds of energy. The idea was to require sufficient power.

The eventual result will be that DNRs will adopt all of them, if they haven't already. I mean, if you insist on a diameter of at least 9mm, and a straight-wall case, and a repeating action, then a Walther PPK in .380 meets the requirements. There has to be a power threshold, to get the hunters up to at least the .357 Magnum.

While it looks like it is just a straight-wall .223 case, there are differences in dimension that make it not so. You can't make .350 brass from .223, nor vice-versa.

When ARs became popular, they of course were adopted for hunting. The Mauser 98 and Springfield '03 of earlier generations had done the same thing. Most DNRs prohibited hunting deer with .22 rifles (an attempt to forestall poaching) and as a result that left the .223 out of the caliber options. But it was entirely possible to use an AR-15 in 6.5, 6.8, 7.62x39, and anything else that wasn't a ".22" bullet.

When the .450 Bushmaster came out, it opened the floodgates. You see, along with the adoption of handgun hunting, a lot of states opened their shotgun-only areas to straight-walled rifle calibers. The intention was to let owners of lever-action rifles in .45-70, and the like, hunt as well. What happened was they hunted, but so did a lot of other shooters.

All of a sudden, with AR pistols available, and hunting allowed in shotgun areas using rifles with straight-walled cartridges, that the AR-15 chambered in .450 Bushmaster became a hot property. But this is about the .350 Legend, so why does it exist?

Simple. The .450 Bushmaster might be a straight-walled case, it might fit the bill for handgun hunting, but one thing you can't say about it: It is a pussycat to shoot. It isn't.

If you want to introduce a new shooter to hunting, you do not hand him or her a firearm chambered in .450 Bushmaster if the goal is to gain a new shooter and new hunting partner from the experience. The .450 Bushmaster, in a normal factory load, drives a 250-grain bullet at 2,200 fps or a bit more, depending

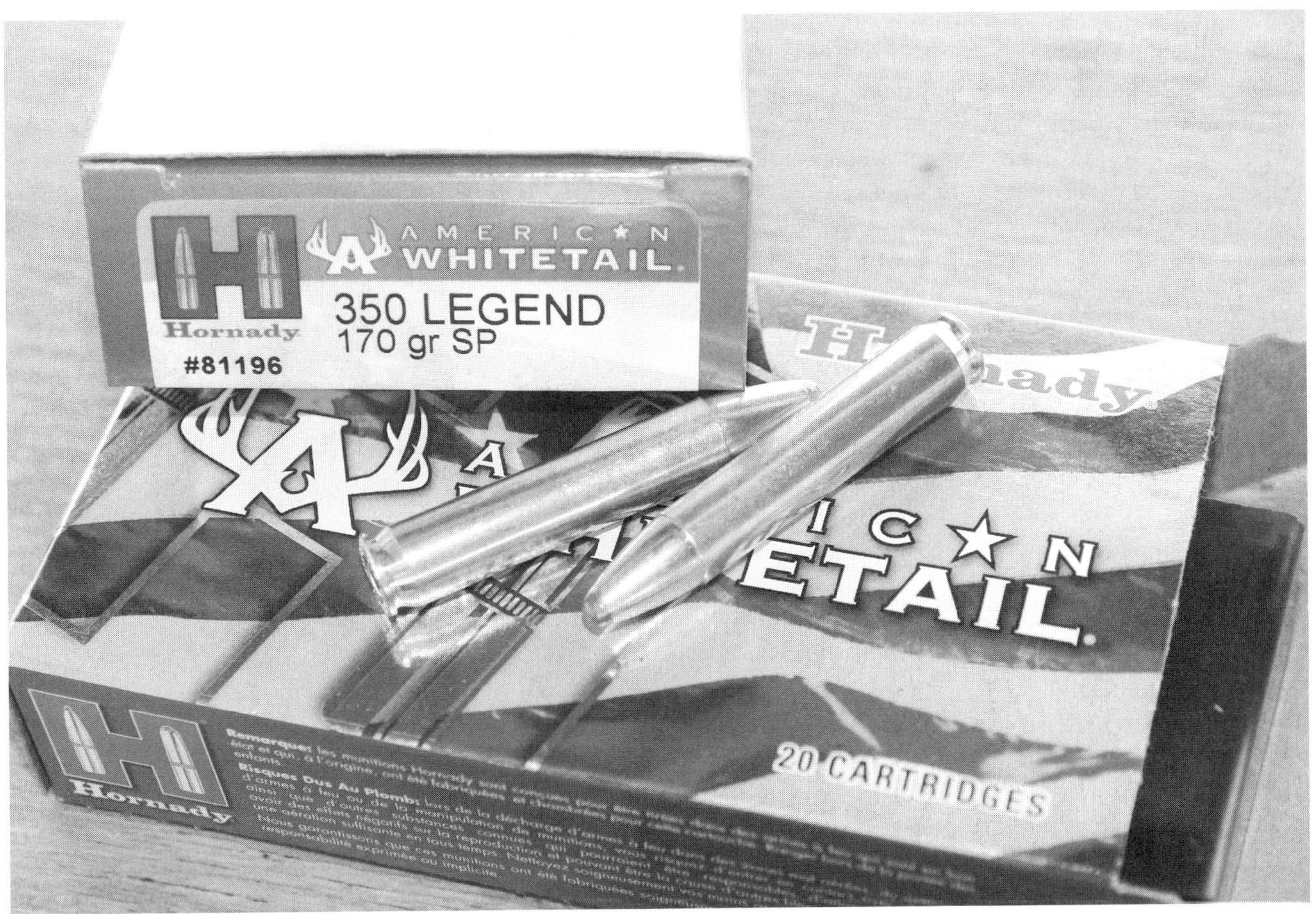

The .350 Legend is new, but it is being pushed hard because it is so useful. And if it catches on, then there will be an established base of users for a couple of generations.

on barrel length. That's a Power Factor of 550. Ouch.

So, the .350 Legend, with a smaller and lighter bullet, offers more than sufficient deer-slaying power, without the recoil. A .350 legend factory load suitable for deer will push a 180-grain bullet at 2,100 fps. That's a 378 PF, and one that is a lot more manageable.

The .350 Legend case looks like an un-necked .223 case, but it isn't. The rim and extractor groove are the same, but the base diameters differ. The SAAMI specs for the .223 Remington base are .379, while the .350 Legend base is .390.

The .350 Legend headspaces on the case mouth, and the mouth diameter is .378. As a result, you can see that the case has a small but measurable taper to it. It is not absolutely straight-walled, but it is not a necked case. Some might quibble about it not being straight (and I'd bet there were some in DNR officers who did), but a close look at the chamber drawings of the .45-70, approved by SAAMI, shows that cartridge having more taper than the .350 Legend does. If a state DNR were to disallow the .350 Legend because of insufficient straightness, then the .45-70 would have to go as well, and that just isn't going to happen.

The .350 Legend is rated for 55,000 PSI max pressure, which puts it right in the same ballpark as the .223 Remington. Which makes sense, as the case rim is the same diameter, and that means the .350 Legend, despite firing a heavier bullet, will not generate more bolt thrust than the .223.

The slight taper to the case means extraction will be easier, as the first movement of the case means the case breaks free of the chamber walls right at the start. Were the case actually absolutely cylindrical, the case mouth would be dragging along the chamber walls for the entire length of the case on extraction. The wider base of the case also makes it clear that the .350 Legend is not going to chamber in a .223 rifle, not in the slightest. However, without having tried it (there are some things I just don't feel the need to test) I suspect the .357 bullet is going to wedge in the .223 chamber neck, long before the case base has anything to say about it.

For deer hunting, the trajectory of the .350 Legend is entirely adequate. No, it isn't a 300-, 400-, or 500-yard cartridge. But, for the deer hunter, having to use the aforementioned 180-grain bullet at 2,100 fps and a sight-in distance of 100 yards, that 180-grain bullet will be about 10 inches low at 200 yards. With laser rangefinders now being common, and software to calculate drop within a fraction of an inch, it is not very difficult at all for hunters to calculate and write range cards for their hunting blind, and be spot-on for distance.

Reloading promises to be pretty straightforward. The SAAMI specs call for a bore groove diameter of .355, which means a 9mm bullet. Wait, what? Yes, a 9mm bullet, to accommodate the case taper. But why not a .357 groove diameter, which would allow the use of .357 bullets? Or even .358, to take advantage of all those .35-caliber rifle bullets out there?

Because the .350 Legend requires new bullets, regardless of the diameter chosen. Those who want to use .357-diameter bullets, keep in mind the velocities we are generating. Let's take a 158-grain .357 bullet designed to expand at 1,350 fps out of a handgun, and fire it from a cartridge that generates 2,200 fps at that weight bullet. That is just asking for trouble. OK, then, let's bump it up to .358 diameter, and use one of the 200-grain bullets available. Hmmm. The .350 Legend, with a 200-grain bullet, is going to be hard-pressed to get velocities up to 1,800 fps. More likely will be the low 1,700s. So, we're going to use a 200-grain bullet from the .35 Remington, are we? Those are designed to expand at 2,100 fps, so shooting a deer with them with a muzzle velocity of 1,700, or even 1,750 fps, means they will act like solids. No expansion.

Every other .358 bullet meant for rifle use is going to be worse.

No, the Legend isn't going to be able to use any existing bullets for either 9mm or .38/.357, due to the velocity differences between what the existing bullets were designed for, and the velocities the Legend will be launching them at. Now, I can see some bolt-action shooters who reload using heavy 9mm bullets as practice and plinking, lower-velocity loads. But those probably likely won't cycle an AR-15.

Will the .350 Legend catch on? The tacti-cool folks can hardly contain their disdain. It doesn't have range, it doesn't have low recoil, it doesn't offer them anything the .223/5.56 doesn't already offer. However, for the hunter, the .350 Legend offers a lot. I suspect that what it will do is not sell trainloads of ammunition for the ammo makers. Hunters are notoriously sparse in ammunition consumption. Some I knew back in my gunsmithing days were even proud of making a box of 20 rounds last a decade of hunting.

I suspect that what it will do is sell a lot more AR-15s. Or AR-15 uppers. An enterprising tacti-cool AR owner who wants to hunt, will find it easier to buy a new upper, and a five-round magazine, than buying a new bolt-action rifle, to go hunting. The bolt-action rifle makers will be offering rifles in .350 Legend (I've already seen a bunch of them) so the bolt-action hunters will have that choice for areas where it is

allowed, as well.

If you are planning to build one, the conversion is easy and straight-forward. The .350 Legend uses the same bolt as the .223/5.56. The magazines for .223 will feed the .350 Legend. All you'll need is a barrel chambered in .350 Legend. And a magazine that passes muster with your local DNR.

If you aren't looking to build, there are plenty of AR makers who will gladly assemble an AR-15 of any size, chambered in .350 Legend, for you. A five-round magazine, and the OK from your DNR, and you're ready to hunt.

8

6.8 REMINGTON SPC

OK, as I've said before, the U.S. Army has been trying to replace the M16, and the 5.56 cartridge it is chambered in, since before it was forced to adopt it.

The terminal ballistics, and performance, of the 5.56 will be argued endlessly, but in a lot of situations, for a lot of uses, it serves just fine. It took getting involved in a grinding CQB war, namely, Iraq and Afghanistan, for some end-users to become dissatisfied with the 5.56. Now, to be clear, we're talking about the performance of the M855, or "green tip" loading. Time for a short history and ballistics section, on the 5.56, a chambering I promised this book would not cover, much.

The 6.8 Rem SPC (Special Purpose Cartridge) can be very accurate. Accuracy depends more on barrel and bullet quality than the cartridge, but the 6.8 is plenty accurate. Does it deliver what the advocates wanted? Perhaps, but the Army has moved on to something else. We'll see what.

The M855 is the loading adopted in the 1980s for the M16A2. It uses a 62-grain bullet, with a two-section core. The front tip is a steel penetrator, and the rear is lead. The steel tip is a small cone of 10 whole grains in weight. The extra length added by the lower-density steel makes the M855 unsuited for use in old barrels with a 1/12 twist. Well, worse than unsuited, it is hopelessly inaccurate.

The problem is twofold: The twist adopted with

the M855 is one turn in seven inches, which over-stabilizes the bullet. Second, the bullet is stoutly constructed, and even were it to overturn in time (it can penetrate and exit a human torso before it begins to yaw) it is not likely to break apart like the M193 or XM193.

In talking with veterans from the dusty places, the M855 performance is wildly variable. Sometimes it would perforate, create a narrow wound, and pass through, to little or no effect. And sometimes it would be like a boulder fell from the sky. There was no way to know which result you would get, from shot to shot, and bad guy to bad guy. You got what you got, and you had to deal with it.

The load was developed in the early 1980s, as a response to an expected threat. That threat being the impending Soviet invasion westward, across Europe. The Soviets had large amounts of titanium ore, and the new soft body armor cloth, Kevlar, could be used with titanium to create effective body armor. So, NATO developed an expected body armor, and the standard, referred to as CRISAT (Collaborative Research Into Small Arms Technology), was the one new-rifle ammo was tested against. It was found that the M855 would defeat this prospective armor, and that was what we adopted.

The mid-bore lineup. Left is the 6.5 Grendel, center the 5.56 and right the 6.8 Remington SPC.

The idea was that when the Soviet mechanized infantry units dismounted from their armored personnel carriers, we'd be able to reach through the body armor they would be wearing.

Well, it turned out the Soviets not only didn't have enough of an economy to equip all their troops with body armor, they didn't have enough of an economy to have an economy. But we were stuck with the M855.

The battle of Mogadishu, Somalia, in 1993, had the participants reporting on the ineffectiveness of the M855, but as that was just a two-day fight, and we weren't going to be in a war ever again, its lack of performance was shrugged off. The sweep into Iraq was so overwhelming the effectiveness, or ineffectiveness, of rifle ammunition wasn't a concern. It wasn't until we were there for years, in daily (and nightly) slugfests, that the up-and-down nature of the M855 became a problem.

There are several ways you can increase the effectiveness of a rifle cartridge. You can increase velocity. You can increase bullet weight. You can increase bullet instability, leading to yaw and fragmentation. You can increase bullet diameter, that is, caliber.

The 5.56 is already at the limit of velocity. You can't get more without increasing chamber pressure. (Which the Army, in a misguided effort to increase M855 effectiveness, has done with the M855A1 loading.) You can't do much to increase bullet weight, due to magazine size and case-length limits. There is also the matter of barrel twist. Make a bullet too long, and the twist rate of the barrel will not stabilize it. Changing twist means changing barrels.

Instability is part of that, but it means either a new barrel, or a much longer bullet.

That leaves bullet diameter, or caliber. The problem here is case capacity. You need enough room for the powder you need to push a bullet fast enough to work. Simply plugging a larger bullet into the case can often lead to a bigger, heavier, but slower bullet, ending up with the same terminal effectiveness. We covered

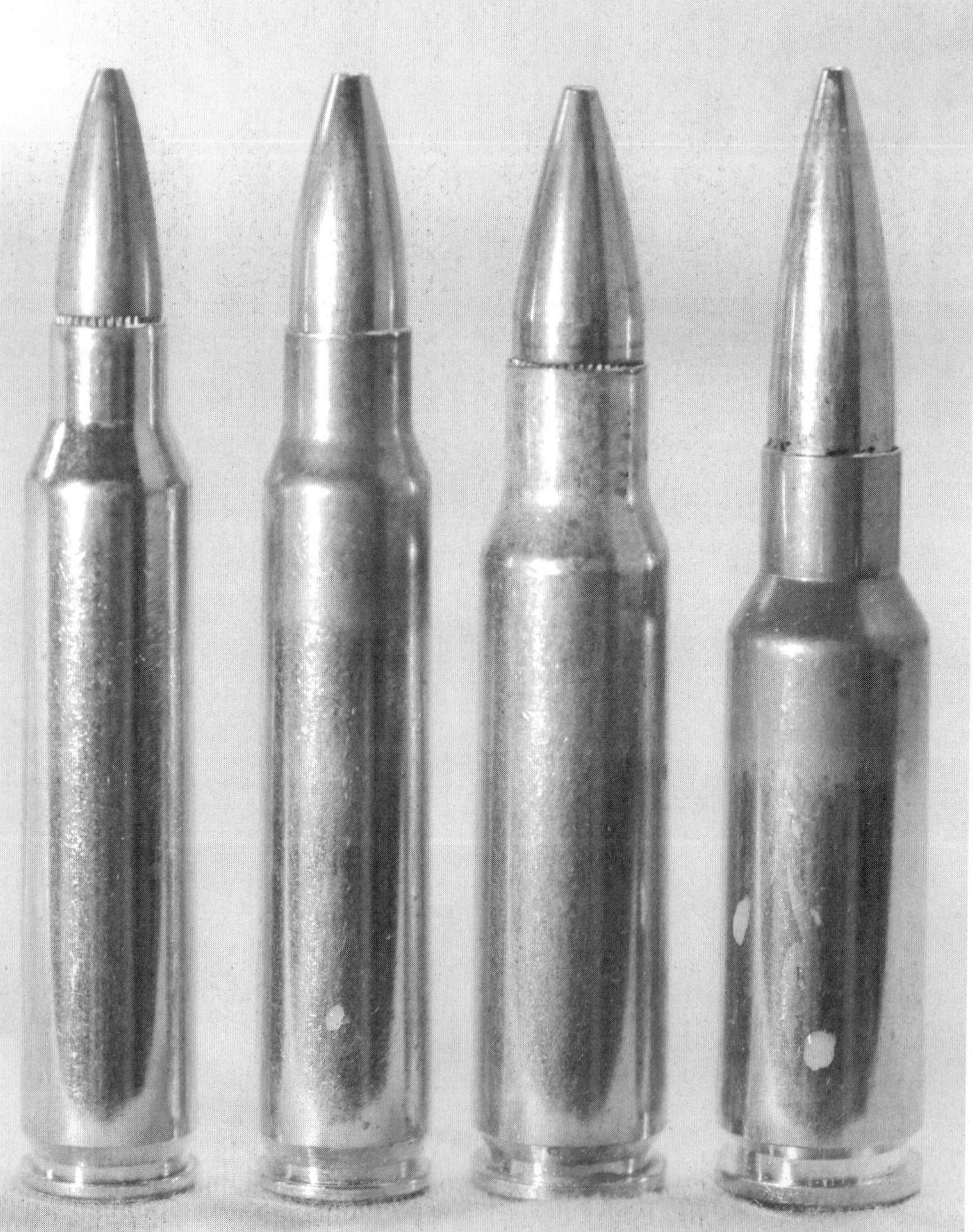

To increase the performance of the 5.56 (left) you can increase bullet diameter, as with a 6x45 (second from left). Or, you can use a bigger case and a larger bullet, like the 6.8 SPC (second from right). Eventually you end up with a bigger bullet, a bigger case, and a sleeker bullet, like the 6.5 Grendel (right).

that in an earlier chapter, where we increased the bullet diameter in the .223 case, step by step.

So, the U.S. Army Marksmanship Unit, working with Special Forces members, came up with a solution: a bigger case. The parent case they settled on was an oldie, the .30 Remington. The 5.56 case head has a diameter of .378 of an inch. The .30 Remington has a case head diameter of .422. Those with a good memory will note that the rim diameter of the .30 Remington is the same as that of the .40 S&W. Yes, because the .40 also came from the .30 Remington.

The origins of the .40 date to the early 1970s, when Whit Collins and others, at the urging of Jeff Cooper, worked up a .40 pistol cartridge, using the .30 Remington case as the starting point.

So, we come full circle. The rim and case body diameter of the .30 Remington allows for a usefully larger case capacity, without over-stressing the AR-15 bolt. Were you to go much larger than that (and the 7.62x39/6.5 Grendel is about it at .440) the bolt can't stand up to the pressures the AR-15 needs to generate the velocity you want.

So, a larger case, now what about bullets? The experimenters settled on .277 bullets, which easily gets you bullets of 110 to 125 grains in weight. The pressures of the case permit velocities of 2,550 fps with 110-grain bullets, and 2,450 fps with 120 to 125 grains.

The velocities are high enough to be useful, and the lowest weight is twice that of the basic 5.56 load, at 55 grains for the smaller one.

The plan was to require only a barrel change to gain the improved performance. As with so many situations, it was found that while most 5.56 magazines would work, for best results it would be a good idea to use 6.8-specific magazines.

The problem with the plan was exactly that. You see, if you were to start changing calibers, and use the 6.8, how would you keep things straight? With all magazines able to use both, and all rifles and carbines able to use all magazines, how would you keep ammo supplies straight? Mixing ammo means ineffective rifles, because there is no inter-operability.

The Japanese had this problem in WWII, with two different rifle cartridges, and four or five light machine gun cartridges to keep track of.

The Remington SPC, since it is based on the .30 Remington case, has to have a larger bolt face. This leaves little room for an enclosing rim, but there's enough.

The SPC got named because Remington designers developed it. They brought it to SAAMI, so they got to name it. The 115-grain OTM (open-tip match) is a common weight for this, and a good bullet design.

Then, we have two cartridges, the SPC and the SPC II.

When Remington developed the SPC, not only did it use the .30 Remington as the parent case, with its large-rifle primer, it used the .223 Remington leade design as a template. (The suggestion is also mentioned that there was some error in the drawing submitted to the reamer maker, errors that were not noticed or were overlooked in subsequent testing and development. I'm not sure which way it happened is a "better" mistake

Next, the name. The 6.8 Remington SPC, or Special Purpose Cartridge. The .277 is pretty much a 6.8 caliber, in metric terms. Remington designed it, with input from the Special Forces community. And it was not meant to be a general hunting cartridge, hence the "SPC" addition.

Then, we get further confusion, in ammunition and rifles. First, the ammunition. Remington, as the originator of the load, and the parent brass, uses large-rifle primers, because that's what the case it used to develop it had. The .30 Remington uses large-rifle primers, so the 6.8 was going to use large-rifle primers. However, other ammo makers, such as Hornady, use small-rifle primers, for the simple reason the case doesn't need the oomph of a large-rifle primer. So, if you plan to reload, you'll have to sort your brass, or simply stick with one brass brand or the other. And no, SAAMI does not specify primer size.

I find I have a pile of each, and have to sort, and be careful.

The loading data doesn't care about which primer size you use, so it is simply a matter of what primer-feed system you have in your press, and the cases being used.

The SPC II is a longer-leade version of the basic SPC, sometimes with a change in barrel twist (to a slower twist) to ease pressure.

The twist rate on a 6.8 barrel will/should be marked, because it matters. This DPMS has a 1/11 twist, good for the 6.8.

This Noveske barrel has a slower twist, a 1/12, and it will have greater terminal ballistics due to a faster onset of yaw.

The 6.8 Remington SPC magazines differ from 5.56, and you cannot interchange them. At least not and expect reliable function.

The LWRCI Six8. A handy carbine (this happens to be a pistol) it delivers a big punch for a small package.

than the other. They are both serious oversights.) The relatively short leade was seen by some as a handicap, so designers used the 5.56 leade as a template, and the SPC II was born. In an exact pattern with the .223 and 5.56, so we have the SPC and SPC II.

In delving deep into the history of this cartridge, and the specs of the cases and chambers, I found, to my horror, that there are not just two, but actually as many as six or seven chambers, all differing in the leade. The original has a freebore of 0.050 of an inch in length. The SPC II has a freebore of 0.100 length. Other variants have freebores from 0.080 to 0.115, and small variations in the freebore diameter and neck diameter.

Basically, if you have the original, you have a chamber that is limited in bullets and pressure, in exactly the same way a .223 leade is, compared to a 5.56 leade. All the others are fine with higher-pressure 6.8 ammunition.

When you load, you have to know which leade you have, and that means checking the length forward from the case mouth. There are several ways to do this, from a chamber gauge, to simply sacrificing a bullet and case, using the rifling starting edge to press a bullet back into a case as you chamber the primer-less and powderless case.

Building a 6.8 is as simple as replacing a worn 5.56 barrel with a 6.8, and using a new bolt in your carrier. Magazines will work reasonably well, but if you want complete reliability you can source 6.8-specific magazines. The magazines do not care about SPC or SPC II, that's an ammo in the chamber situation. The 6.8-specific magazines cost a few dollars more than 5.56 magazines do, and they look very similar, so you'll want to clearly identify your magazines to avoid mixing them up.

After all this work, the promise of the 6.8 SPC faded, and it is a niche cartridge. Part of the fade was the lack of interest in the military. Yes, the 6.8 SPC (almost no one uses the whole name, it is just called the "six-eight SPC") does offer more than the 5.56 does. But, and this is important to remember in a service-wide military adoption context, it doesn't offer enough more to warrant the cost. Yes, it is "just a barrel and magazines," but that's not enough.

The 6.8 also has most of its advantage at closer distances. The case length and case capacity (even with the larger case) mean bullets are not as streamlined. While a 6.8 is a real hammer inside 100 yards, by the

The need for caliber-specific magazines led one firearms manufacturer to look at the cartridge with a task in mind: Make a rifle that fits the cartridge. That would be LWRCI, and the rifle is the Six8. The company re-dimensioned the magazine to correctly hold the 6.8 round, and to have the correct curvature for the case taper and stacking dynamics.

time you get to 300 and farther, the better 5.56 loads, like the Mk 262, have closed the gap to just about nothing.

The cost also entails testing, detailing the specifications, and then producing new ammunition. That means, ball, AP, tracer, dummy, proof and any other special loadings. New targets, new training manuals and materials. Also, the new round would have to be tested to determine maximum range. Why? If the new round has a maximum range that exceeds the safety fan (the space behind and to the sides of the targets on a range) of a given range, then that range has to either be closed, or expanded.

Then, what to do with all the receivers marked M16A1, M16A2, M4, etc.? They are all marked as being 5.56. Do you call the new rifles M16, or something else? How do you change the markings, for the model and caliber, in warehouses with millions of M16s?

And you have to be thorough, so you don't mix the two.

The 6.8 SPC is an exemplary hunting cartridge, and it would serve well in a defensive role.

LWRCI designers changed the receiver dimensions to better fit a 6.8 cartridge, and while they were at it, they made it ambidextrous.

LWRCI

The need for caliber-specific magazines led one firearms manufacturer to look at the cartridge with a task in mind: Make a rifle that fits the cartridge. That would be LWRCI, and the rifle is the Six8. The company re-dimensioned the magazine to correctly hold the 6.8 round, and to have the correct curvature for the case taper and stacking dynamics.

Then LWRCI re-dimensioned the lower to hold this proper magazine, and adjusted the upper to work with the new lower. The end result is a rifle that is a bit larger, but only in the areas that matter, than a standard AR-15. The company uses its most-excellent AR parts in the build, and an SPC II chamber. The end result is what the services probably should have done: adopt a piston-driven AR in 6.8, with all the advances in materials, heat-treatment, coatings and design advances we've learned in the half-century since the M16/AR-15 was first formalized.

The LWCRI Six8 uses proprietary magazines, made by Magpul. Be sure and mark your 6.8 mags, because if you just toss the 6.8 into a bin full of 5.56 mags, you'll be all afternoon finding it again. (You know how I know this, right?)

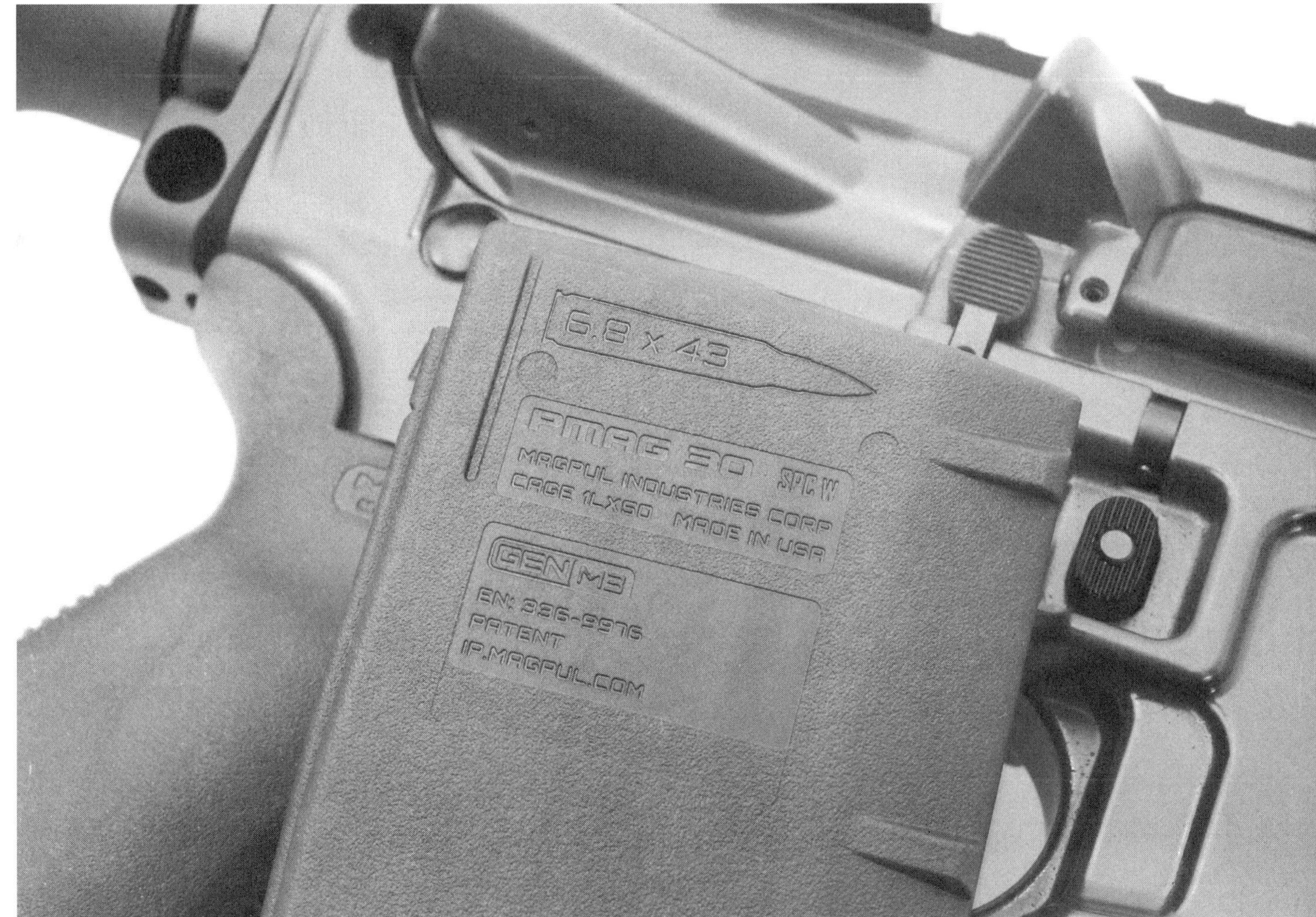

9

BATTLE OF THE HOT .224s

Back when I was into street racing, we all knew the rule: The only reply to how fast do you want to go was: "How much fast can you afford?"

How fast you want to go with rifles is pretty much the same proposition.

.22 NOSLER

OK, Nosler was for a long time a maker of bullets. Just bullets. It made its reputation on the Nosler Partition, a hunting bullet offering both expansion and

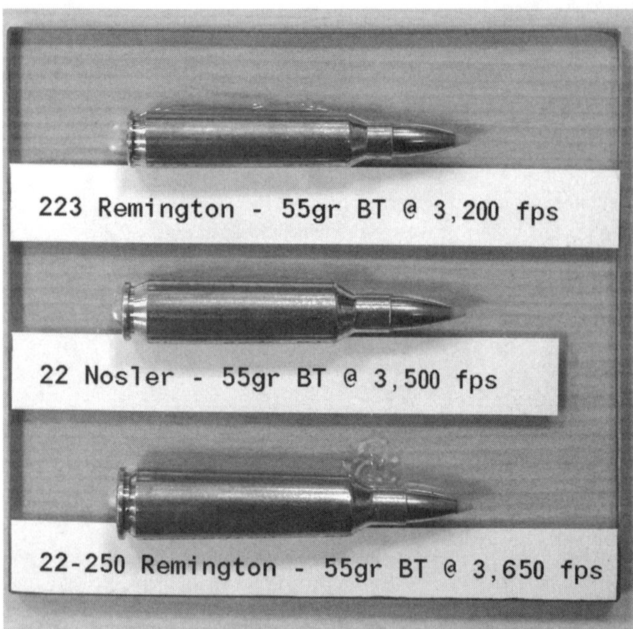

The lineup of the usual and the Nosler. The Nosler comes close to the old standard, the .22-250. The label for the top round indicates a .223. It is not a common .223 that pushes a 55-grain bullet to 3,200 fps. Usually you have to have a 5.56 load to get that figure.

penetration. Then Nosler started to make rifles, and ammo, and now it is designing cartridges. The first ones the company designed used the case dimensions of a cartridge that most shooters haven't heard of, and almost none of them had seen: the .404 Jeffery. The .404 was designed at the beginning of the 20th century by W.J. Jeffrey & Co, to duplicate the performance of the .450/400 Nitro Express 3-inch, but in bolt-action rifles. The loaded cartridge is about the same length as a .30-06, but the case has a rim of .543 of an inch and a case base to match. The bullet is .422 in diameter, and common loadings run from 400 to 450 grains.

The result, in 1905, was that .422 diameter bullet of 400 grains, going 2,325 fps, or a 450-grain bullet going 2,150 fps. Ouch.

There is no belt on the .404 case, unlike the .375 H&H, a contemporary cartridge. The big advantage of the .404 Jeffery was that it could fit into a standard-length bolt-action receiver (with the bolt face opened up to accommodate the .543 rim) and deliver a crushing blow without resorting to high pressures. High pressures were bad if you were hunting in the tropics. So, standard, not magnum-length action, plenty of power, no worries about over-pressure loads wedging a fired case in the chamber, and everyone was happy. Except for the big game being hunted.

So, Nosler took that case, with its huge capacity, and necked it down to accept .338, .308, .284 and .264 bullets. The velocities of such cartridges are greater than the previous big cartridges using the same bullet diameters.

However, such cartridges clearly are not something you can put into an AR-15, or even an AR-10, since the Noslers are all 3.340 inches long.

So, for the AR-15, Nosler designers went and did something few others have done: They came up with an entirely new case diameter. The case body maxes

You have to be careful with the AR-15. This CMMG can be chambered in a multitude of cartridges. If it happens to be chambered in .22 Nosler, you'll want to have that ammo with you when you go to the range.

Sometimes the caliber is marked on the barrel, instead of the receiver. So, make sure you know where yours are marked, to keep them straight.

out at .420 of an inch just above the extractor groove. However, to make conversions to the AR-15 easier, and to make sure bolt life was not decreased, they rebated the case rim, and the rim is the standard AR-15 .378 in diameter, just like an AR-15 in .223. The overall length is the same as well, at 2.260 inches. As a result, to convert an AR to .22 Nosler, you just need a barrel.

The results are impressive. You can gain as much as 400 fps advantage over the .223, using a .22 Nosler.

The .22 Nosler has a sharper shoulder angle than that of the .223, 30 degrees compared to 23 degrees. This wrings a bit more case capacity out of it. The shoulder of the Nosler sits at 1.389 inches forward of the base, compared to the .223 at 1.438 inches. What this means is you cannot get a .223 to chamber in a .22 Nosler rifle. Were it possible, the smaller-diameter .223 case would split on firing, and that would be bad. Hot, expanding, uncontained gases can wreak havoc on an action. Conversely, the wider .22 Nosler case has no hope of fitting into a .223 chamber.

The .22 Nosler, despite not being derived from the 6.8 SPC case, needs to use magazines for the 6.8 to function. The fatter cases won't work properly in a .223 magazine.

As Nosler is an ammunition factory, the .22 Nosler is SAAMI approved, and the operating pressure is listed as 55,000 PSI, same as the .223. That makes sense, with the rim and bolt face being the same for the two.

TWO NEW NOLSERS

OK, just when it seemed like the world was going to get back to normal, Nosler has to go and upend things. It used the basic .22 Nosler to produce two new cartridges: the .24 Nosler and the .20 Nosler. The .22 Nosler pushes a 55-grain, .224 bullet at 3,500 fps. The .24 Nosler pushes a .243 bullet of 55 grains at just over 3,400 fps. The .20 Nosler uses a .204 diameter bullet, and a 32-grain bullet leaves the muzzle at over 4,200 fps.

The cases both use the same parent as the .22 Nosler, but the shoulders of each are adjusted for proper neck length and to make mixing them up and getting the bolt closed not a safety issue. Clearly the .20 is meant to be the ultimate laser-beam varmint cartridge. Let's take the most-excellent Hornady V-Max 40-grain varmint bullet leaving your immediate vicinity at 4,250 fps is still going 2,046 fps at 600 yards, and has dropped seven inches. Seriously: 600 yards, with seven inches of hold-over, and it is still arriving with almost as much steam as a .22 Hornet at the muzzle?

Varmints beware. Had the .20 Hornet any more speed, you'd need a forward observer to deal with varmints at its max range. And the recoil is going to be nothing.

.224 VALKYRIE

Federal designers decided that since the AR-15, the Modern Sporting Rifle, was getting a lot of new calibers, that they'd jump in, and boy, did they. The basic case of the .224 Valkyrie (Valkyries are the maidens who decide amongst the fallen, who goes to Valhalla, and who goes with Freya to Folkvangr) is the 6.8 Remington SPC.

And basic is the catchword here. In order to wring the utmost out of long-range performance from the .224 Valkyrie, Federal decided to go with the heaviest of .224 bullets. As a result, the low end of bullet weights for the .224 are the 75- and 77-grain match bullets. Oh, you can find, or load, lighter bullets for the .224, but when you are pushing a 60- to 65-grain

LWRCI makes it abundantly clear what a rifle is chambered in. Not only is the upper marked, but the lower has the "V" for Valkyrie logo LWRCI puts on its rifles.

bullet at 3,400-plus fps, it had better be stoutly constructed, or it will spin itself apart before it gets to the target.

The normal bullet weights for the .224 Valkyrie are in the 85- to 90-grain range.

It is possible to push those bullets to over 2,600 fps, something utterly impossible to do with the .223/5.56, unless you are willing to risk case breakage, and rifle breakage.

In order to do this, Federal had to really massage the 6.8 case. The shoulder is shoved back, the neck is long enough to hold a long, heavy bullet, but the end result is a case that is shorter overall than the parent case, the 6.8. The case also is given less taper, and the shoulder angle is sharper. It approaches the dimensions of the old "improved" case design, popularized by P. O. Ackley three-quarters of a century earlier.

Obviously, the .224 Valkyrie cannot use a standard AR-15 bolt, it must use one with the breechface opened to the rim diameter of the 6.8. Ditto magazines. You will have to hunt down 6.8-specific

Since the .224 Valkyrie uses the .30 Remington (actually, the 6.8 Rem SPC) case as the starting point, you have to be using magazines meant for that case. Standard 5.56 magazines will not be a lot of fun.

magazines for your AR-15, and fight for them with the guys shooting 6.8 SPC rifles and carbines. That's life.

The barrel twist is one turn in seven inches, but you will find custom-barrel makers who will make one in 1/6.5 twist for you, as that is more likely to fully stabilize the 90-grain bullets. And 90-grain bullets and 1/7 twist barrels are right on the edge of stability. If you want to go heavier (and yes, Virginia, there are those who do make heavier than 90-grain, .224 bullets) you absolutely must go to a 1/6.5 twist.

To give you an example of the performance that can be had, there is a new (as of this writing) bullet from Hornady, an 88-grain version of its ELD Match. As in Extremely Low Drag. The BC of this bullet is .545. Where your normal 75-grain, .224 bullet would have a G1 drag of .395, the ELD version of a 75-grain bullet has a G1 of .467.

So, let's start the 88-grain ELD-Match bullet at a brisk but doable 2,650 fps. That bullet stays supersonic out to 1,400 yards, depending on atmospheric conditions. The 75-grain ELD drops subsonic at 1,200 yards, even with a 100 fps faster muzzle velocity. And the 75-grain BTHP, the old standard? That one goes subsonic at a smidge over 1,000 yards. If long range is your game, the .224 Valkyrie is the answer.

Now, an interesting comparison comes to mind: the .224 Valkyrie vs. the 6.5 Grendel. Since the bullets for each are high-BC, and start at similar velocities, then the results, trajectory-wise are much the same. Drop, for example, out at 1,000 yards has the two (a 90-grain Valkyrie load and a 123-grain A-Max out of the Grendel) within two percent of each other. Not even a click of adjustment difference between them. That small margin goes to the Valkyrie. However, the A-Max is better at wind drift than the 90-grain Valkyrie bullet, 10 inches less drift at 1,000 yards (full-value wind), but the 10 inches comes out of over 100. So, the Grendel is 10-percent better at wind drift than the Valkyrie.

Of course, the Grendel is doing this with a 123-grain bullet, versus the 90 grains of the Valkyrie, so you are delivering more horsepower. But to do that, you have to deal with more recoil.

Now, there's a great rule that the science-fiction author Robert Heinlein came up with, and created the acronym for: TANSTAAFL. "There ain't no such thing as a free lunch." The .224 is going to extract a price for that extra yardage. To start, the powder charge that gets you the 2,650 fps out of the 88-grain bullet is 27 to 28 grains in weight. You can get 2,750 fps out of a .223 with 23 to 24 grains of powder. So, you get 43 fewer rounds out of a pound of powder, with the .224 Valkyrie, compared to the .223.

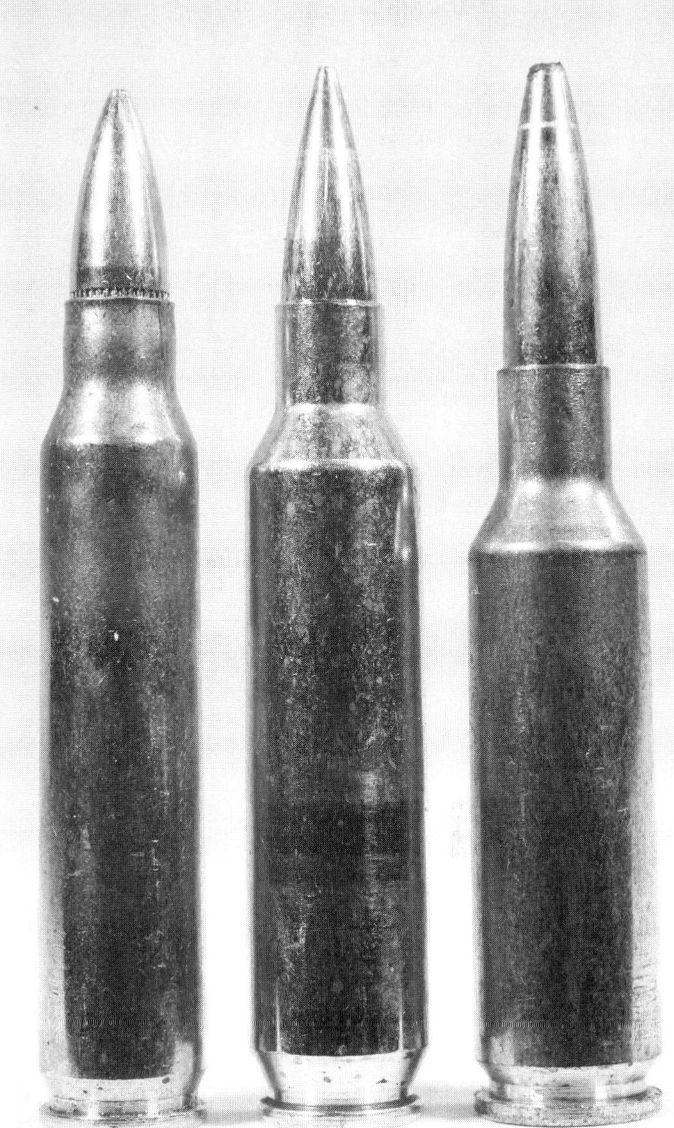

Left to right, we have the .223, the .22 Nosler and the .224 Valkyrie. How much speed do you want?

All that powder going down the bore is going to create heat and friction. Barrel life with the .224 is going to be shorter, with identical shooting schedules, than with the .223.

But, like sports cars, if you want the performance, you have to be willing to pay the price.

Who wins?

It depends on what you want to do. If you are looking for the best long-range performance, and "long range" is as far as you can reach, then the Valkyrie. If you want a varmint round, the Nosler can be had with factory ammo using bullets as light as 55 grains.

Neither is going to have a long barrel life. Depending on how OCD you are about cleaning and avoiding over-heating, you might get 3,000 to 4,000 rounds out of a barrel.

You want speed? You have to pay the price.

10
FIRE
SAFE

.300 WHISPER AND .300 BLACKOUT

The beginning of the subsonic revolution in ARs came to us from J.D. Jones. To call him a prolific inventor is to use "prolific" lightly. He has always endeavored to expand the borders of firearms performance, from the smallest to the largest. The .300 Whisper was his AR-15 cartridge for quiet shooting. The idea was simple: take a .223 case, expand the neck to hold a .30-caliber bullet, shorten it so the neck would hold the bullet at the proper place, and fit it all into an AR-15 magazine. A shortcut would be to take the .221 Fireball case, and neck it out to .30. The Fireball itself was essentially just a shortened .223, meant for use in single-shot bolt-action pistols, primarily the Remington XP100. It was the varminting answer to "How do I use a handgun to shoot varmints?"

J.D. was aided in this work by the continuing efforts of rifle target shooters. When I began shooting in the early 1970s, the bullets available for .30 rifles for target shooting were not many. You could find a 168-grain match boat tail. You could, if you were lucky and persistent, score a supply of 175-grain FMJ-BT bullets, which were used for decades before by the military.

Heavier than that, there were only hunting bullets. There were 180-grain soft points, and 220 FMJ or soft-point bullets, but they were round-nosed, and meant for use on large game. You'd have the 220s loaded in your .30-06 or .300 H&H, for use on bear, moose or elk on a hunt in Alaska or Canada.

But long-range target shooters wanted more. For long-distance shooting, the competitor has two problems: distance and wind. Distance is easy, as the targets are a known distance away, and that distance does not change. Wind, however, does.

If we assume a bullet design has the same ogive, and boat tail, then the only way to change weight is to make it longer. This is good, because a longer and heavier bullet will have a larger ballistic coefficient, or BC. BC is a measure of a bullet's drag, compared to a theoretical object that is a standard. The higher the BC, the more efficiently a bullet passes through the air.

We're getting a bit involved here, so stick with me. For any given cartridge, operating at a certain pressure, adding weight to a bullet means you have less velocity. You simply cannot push a (to use as an example) 168-grain .30 bullet and a 240-grain .30 bullet at the same speed. The 240, in any given cartridge, has to be going slower, simply because the pressure limit of the cartridge determines the maximum amount of energy you can use to push the bullet.

Target shooters don't care. A bullet with a higher BC loses less velocity as it goes downrange, so the net is not to lose as much when it reaches to the target. The real boon for target shooters is that a higher-BC bullet is less affected by wind.

A high-BC bullet is said to have less wind drift. So even with a lower starting velocity, the 240-grain .30 bullet will drift less than a 168-grain bullet in the same wind. In target shooting, riflemen must estimate the effect of wind drift in real time and adjust for it. The smaller the amount they have to adjust, the less effect an error, or change in wind, will have on their scores. They don't care about trajectory differences, because the targets are always the same distances. Well, they were for NRA High Power. All that changed with the development of the Precision

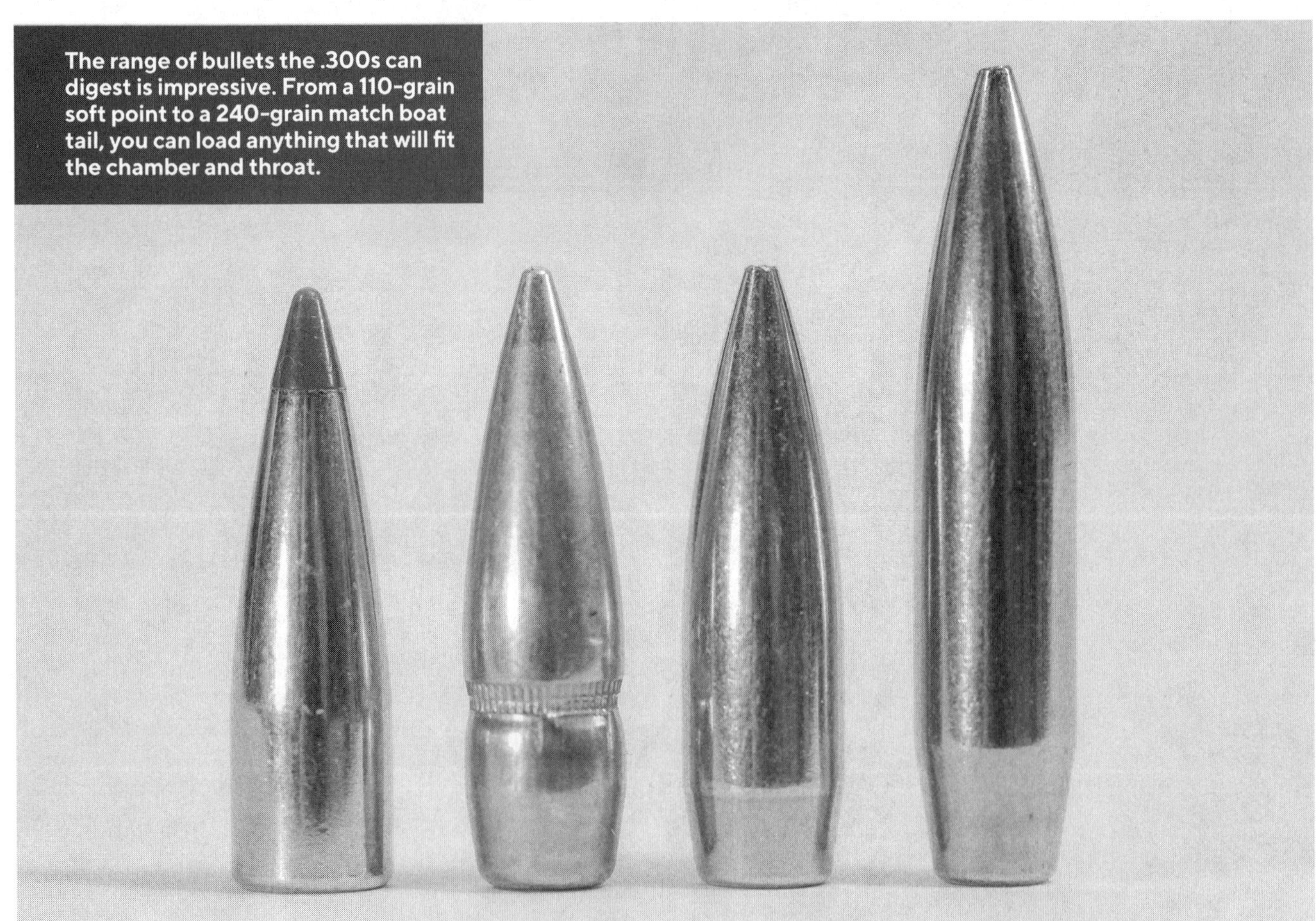

The range of bullets the .300s can digest is impressive. From a 110-grain soft point to a 240-grain match boat tail, you can load anything that will fit the chamber and throat.

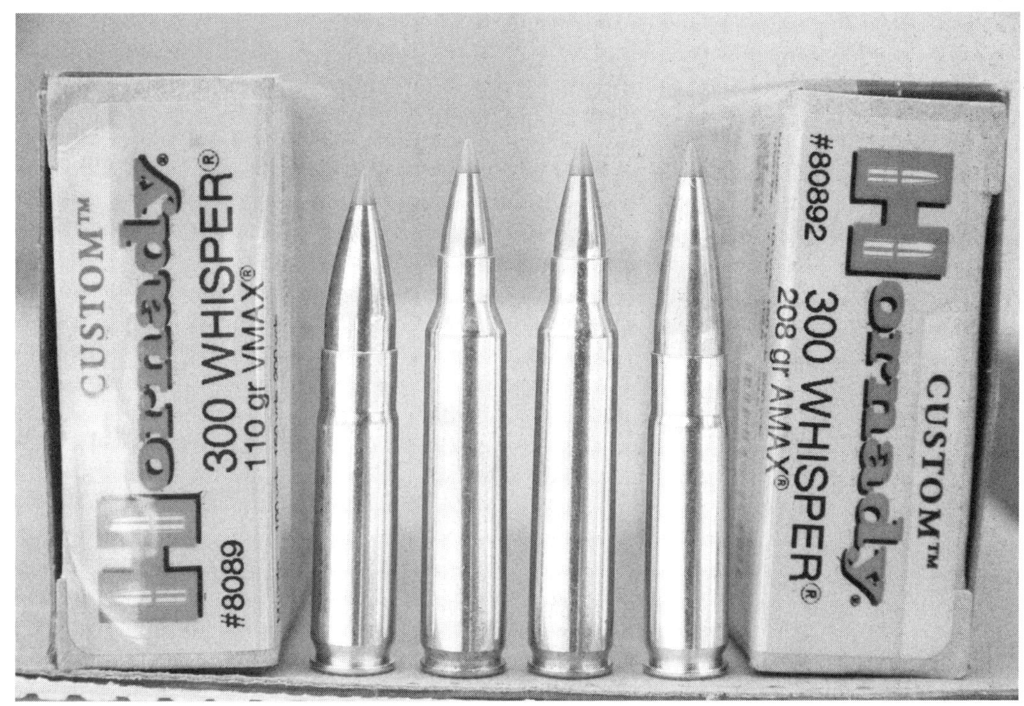

J.D. Jones was first, and he got his invention type-certified by CIP.

Rifle Series, where targets are at odd and differing distances. But we risk wandering, so back to it.

OK, so from the early 1970s, to the late 1980s, the heaviest .30 bullets that could be had went from 168 grains to 220 grains. And those were pointed, match bullets.

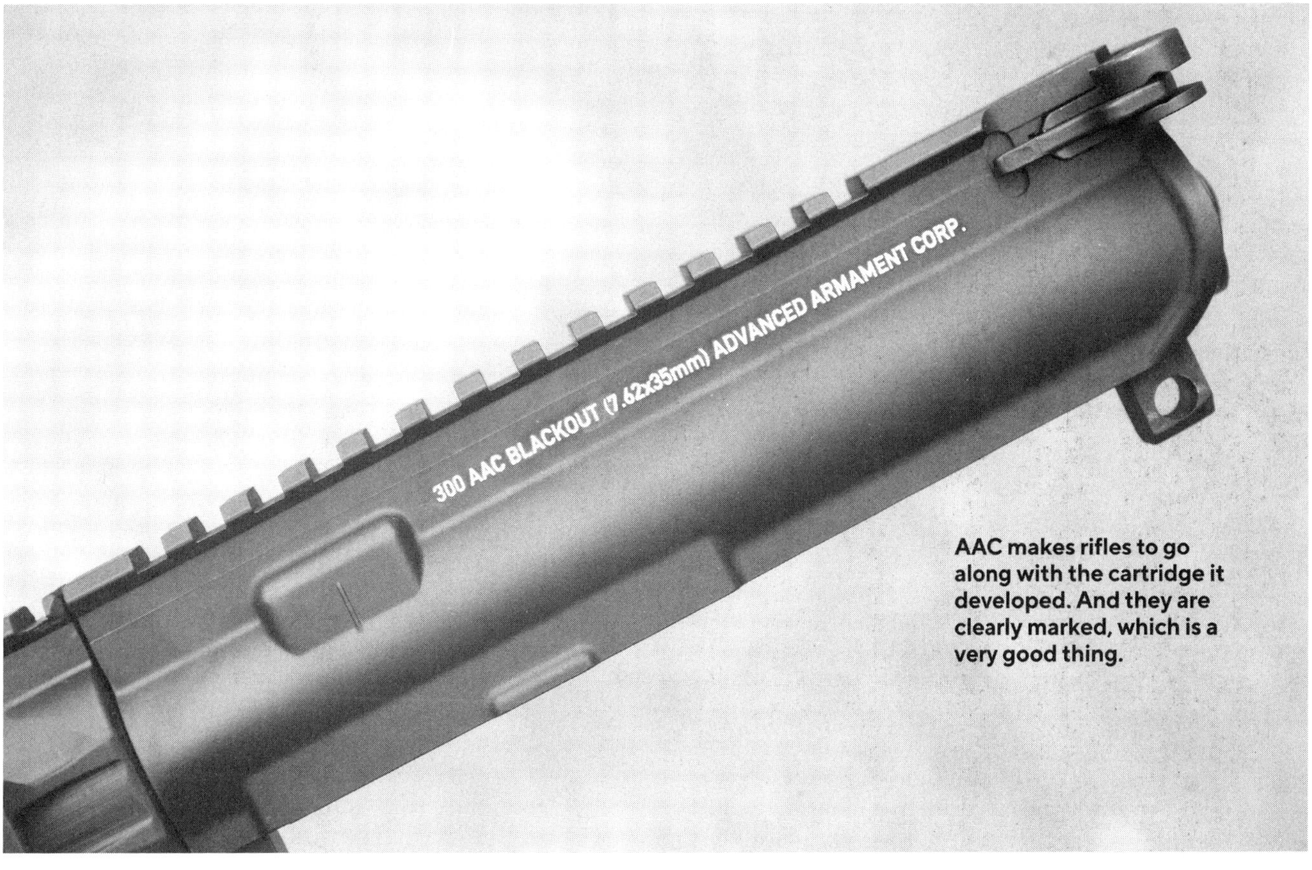

So, J.D. designed the cartridge, modified brass, trademarked it as the .300 Whisper, and began offering rifles and ammo. His work on modifying brass was a continual headache. The internal thickness of .223 and 5.56 brass is not a rigid specification once you get down past the case neck. So, he found that he had to ream some lots and brands of brass more than others. The reaming was required because the new neck was formed in the middle of the body of the original case. Differing wall thicknesses meant some rounds would not chamber unless the formed case was reamed.

When the volume of ammunition produced re-

AAC makes rifles to go along with the cartridge it developed. And they are clearly marked, which is a very good thing.

quired by customer orders got to be great enough, he simply went to an ammo maker, had the company get his ammunition type-certified by CIP, and then could have brass made.

The ammo maker was Hornady, and I had the opportunity to be one of the first testers of factory ammo in a J.D. Jones-built upper for the AR-15. This was in 2011, and life was good.

Then, controversy erupted. A new ammo maker burst onto the scene, in the form of the .300 Blackout. Developed by Advanced Armament Company, or AAC, the Blackout was brought into being because of AAC's military customers. Those customers (or a certain subgroup of them) wanted a subsonic, heavy bullet, autoloading cartridge that would work with in their platform. That platform was the M4, so the new cartridge had to fit into AR-15 magazines, and work with AR-15 bolts.

Remember earlier, when we discussed pressure testing, and certification agencies? AAC could not use CIP loading and certification, because the parent company of AAC, Remington, is a SAAMI member. So, the engineers at AAC had to start essentially from scratch, to design, refine, test and offer for certification, a new .30 cartridge to fit the bill.

The end result was that the .300 Blackout and the .300 Whisper, for almost all concerned, were interchangeable.

The .300 Blackout was type-certified by SAAMI, and Remington and everyone else began making ammo. The controversy?

The .300s can be loaded with many different bullets, but you have to be careful with overall length. They have to fit the magazine, regardless of bullet weight.

Some people think the design team at AAC just made a few minor changes in the dimensions to the .300 Whisper, and then handed it off to the acceptance committee. Well, they didn't. I've talked to people involved, and they did their due diligence, and worked it up properly.

The problem is, the design specifications are so narrowly defined, it is hard to be different. As an exercise in cartridge design, I dare you to design a cartridge that does what the Whisper and Blackout do, and doesn't come so close to either that it would seem to be a duplication.

Or, assuming you could find someone who didn't already know about either, and who knew enough about cartridges, pose them this problem: a .30 bullet, as heavy as possible, in a parent .223 or .221 Fireball case, that has to fit an AR magazine, feed reliably and use an unmodified bolt. They will, just as you had, come up with a clone of the Whisper and Blackout.

The positives of the .300 (I'm not going to type "Whisper and Blackout" dozens of more times) are obvious:

You can shoot subsonic ammo, and that makes the rifle or pistol very quiet. A subsonic 240-grain bullet is going to be going, at most, at 1,050 fps. That puts it squarely in the realm of a .45 ACP+P load. However, it does it with a carbine or pistol that holds 30-round magazines, and can be teamed with a red-dot or magnifying optic. There are even .300 loads that offer expanding bullets. If you do not have one of the expanding bullets in your .300, do not fear. I tested the Hornady subsonic .300 Whisper load when this was all new. They use a 208-grain A-Max bullet for that load. It clocks in from just under supersonic out of a carbine-length barrel, to just over 1,000 fps from a stubby eight-inch pistol or SBR tube.

Testing in ballistic gelatin uncovered some very interesting results. Each shot

There are now expanding bullets for the .300s, but for many applications a non-expanding one works just fine.

would travel about 10 inches into a gel block, and then the yawing bullet would veer to the top, bottom or sides of the block, and exit. In order to recover bullets, I had to wrap the block on all sides with Kevlar vests. You might not like that, and want deeper penetration, but I have to think that a 208-grain, .308 bullet, going sideways, is going to get a lot of the job done, if not all of it.

All the heavyweights, fired at subsonic velocities, will do much the same. I'm not sure you can make a barrel with a twist rate fast enough to keep them point-on in ballistic gel. Or living targets.When fed subsonic ammo, the .300s can use a compact and lightweight suppressor, to make them even quieter. Jumping up to supersonic loads is too much stress for the lighter, more-compact suppressors, so do be careful.

If you want a different performance envelope, you can switch to .300 loads using 110- to 125-grain bullets, which will be delivered as much as 2,300 fps out of a 16-inch barrel. For deer hunters, this is perfect. A modern, expanding, .30 bullet of 110 to 125 grains, out of one of the .300s is soft in recoil, not overly noisy, and more than enough to bring down a whitetail. If your DNR permits deer hunting with suppressors, then you have your answer: A lightweight AR, in .300, with a suppressor is just the ticket for getting new shooters introduced to hunting.

It won't hurt their shoulders, it won't hurt their ears, and it will certainly bring down a whitetail.

In either loading, the .300s do not use much powder per shot, so if you reload, powder costs are about as small as they get. This is offset by the greater cost of the bullets, as a 240-grain .308 jacketed bullet is going to cost you more than a 230-grain lead bullet for a .45 ACP. (The ballistic performance similarity.)

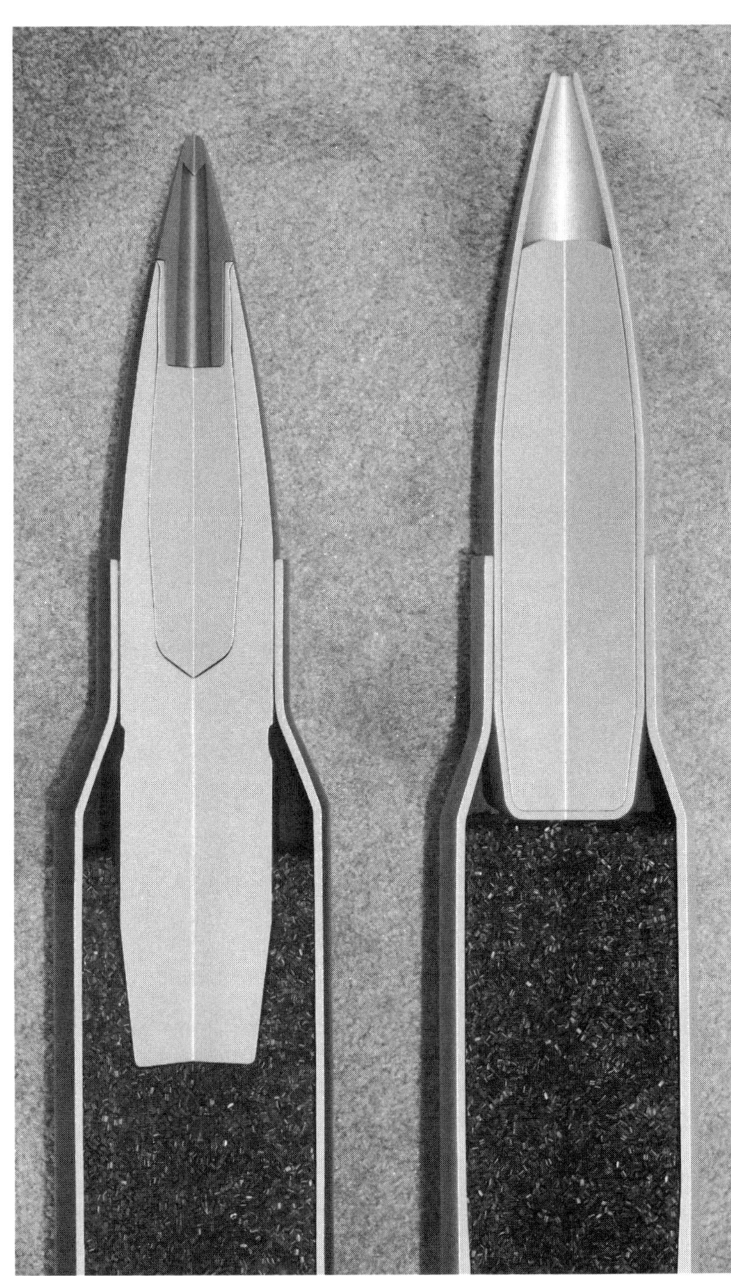

Here you can see the difference bullet weight makes. These two dummy cartridges show the distance a heavy bullet protrudes back into the case. This takes up case capacity, but since we are looking for subsonic performance with heavyweight bullets, reduced case capacity is a good thing.

THE DOWNSIDES:

As rifle brass, reloading the .300s is more involved than reloading pistol ammo. For a .45 ACP, for example, you simply have to clean the brass, then run it through your reloading press.

If your brass was relatively clean, having fallen on the floor of an indoor range, or on the sand or grass of a dry-enough outdoor range, cleaning is simply running it through the vibratory tumbler for two hours. Then feed it into your carbide or T/C sizing die, and ammo falls out the other side of your progressive press.

The .300s have to be cleaned more aggressively, since they run at higher pressures and will have the carbon-firing on the outside that rifles get. Also, you will have to attend to brass trimming details. Trimming .45 ACP is a waste of time, as it is all too short to start with. But .300 brass isn't, and you have to have a relatively exact case length, or else you can run into real pressure problems.

Finally, necked rifle brass does not usually have carbide sizing dies available. So, you'll have to lube and size the cleaned brass, then clean the brass again and trim it, before loading. Yes, you size, then trim. Resizing can change brass length, so you trim after.

The other downside is the risk of getting a .300 into the chamber of a .223 (or .17, .20, .25, etc.) AR-15. This is disastrous to the rifle, and can be hazardous to the shooter. While the photos are spectacular, I have not heard of any severe or permanent injury to shooters who have experienced such a mix-up.

CONVERSION

The conversion of an AR-15 to .300 is easy. You need a barrel. It would be prudent to consider some sort of marking, or specialty setup, to minimize the chances of a mix-up. This would be particularly important if you are going to the range with friends, and some have .223s, and some have .300s.

WHEN THINGS GO WRONG

It is not difficult to find the "Ooops" of someone firing a .300 Whisper/Blackout cartridge in a .223/5.56 rifle, and the end results are not good.

How does this happen? What happens? Is anyone hurt? How can this be avoided?

How is easy: the two are similar in size and use the same magazines. You'd think, looking at them "there's no way someone would mix them up" and yet, rifles get busted across America now and then. It is pretty simple to pick up a magazine loaded with .300 and try to make it work in a rifle chambered in .223/5.56. I haven't tried the opposite, but the results there have to be pretty unspectacular, if it works.

The question arises: If the bullet it too far forward to allow the bolt to close, then how does the bolt get closed enough to lock up and fire? I can see a number of possibilities. One, the bullet was not sufficiently given neck tension or crimp. The momentum of the bolt closing just seats the bullet deeper into the case, making the coming detonation even worse.

The other is the bullet is not long enough to start with. A short-loaded heavy, or a short medium-weight .308 bullet, that doesn't protrude far enough forward to prevent bolt closure, could be the problem.

A bolt not fully closing, but coming very, very close to locking up, and someone hammering on the forward assist might make the difference. This gets back to one of the AR basics: Don't Use The Forward Assist. Ever.

Here is the bolt of a rifle that had a .300 fired in a .223/5.56 chamber. The bent extractor was the least of the damage.

Finally, there is the "bubba load." This is when someone, with the bolt locked open, drops a single loaded round into the chamber, and then lets the bolt fly forward. This might not close the bolt on a regular round, but it will certainly close the bolt on one with weak neck tension or crimp.

If the bolt is not fully closed, and the bolt and carrier are held back far enough, the hammer can't reach the firing pin, and there is a click instead of a bang. Whew. You escaped that disaster. This is a good place and time to have had an M16 carrier (yes, it is legal) in your AR-15. The lower lip of the carrier shields the firing pin from the hammer until the bolt is fully closed. The AR-15, semi-auto carrier, not so much. There is a certain distance where the hammer can reach the un-closed bolt firing pin, which makes the coming loud noise even worse.

What happens when the .300, is in the .223/5.56 chamber, and with the bolt fully closed, and you pull the trigger? The fired cartridge pushes the bullet out. Well, it tries. The bullet has to be ballistically swaged down from .308 to .224, and this just isn't going to happen without strenuous objections to, and comment by, the AR.

In the 1960s, the NRA publication, *The American Rifleman*, had a tech column entry on a returned Japanese rifle that had been "sporterized" for its owner. The owner found that Japanese ammo was hard to find (no kidding) so he had the gunsmith re-chamber it to .30-06. Generally, this is no problem as the Japanese 7.7 round used a .311-inch bullet and had a shorter case than that of the .30-06. Such "conversions" (translation: butchery) were common back then.

The owner was reasonably satisfied, and bagged his fair share of deer, but complained about the recoil.

As it turned out, the rifle had not been chambered for 7.7 Japanese (7.7x58 Arisaka), but 6.5 Japanese (6.5x50 SR Arisaka). The gunsmith, when tracked down, recalled the work, because he had had to grind down the reamer pilot to make it fit the bore. Clue, clue!

NRA shooters test-fired it (they found the headspace, despite the reaming and shooting, to still be within specs) and the firing produced an elongated bullet. No kidding. A 150- to 180-grain .308 bullet, being rudely shoved down a .264 bore, is going to be elongated.

The heavy .308 bullet, shown the distance down the bore it traveled before the rifle came apart. Next to its halves is an unfired .224 55-grain FMJ.

Well, that's what happens with the .300 in a .223. Except, the AR, not being as strong as the Arisaka, breaks apart before the bullet has traveled more than a few inches down the bore.

A friend of mine, Ned Christiansen, laid hands on a blown-apart AR, and used a wire EDM setup to split the barrel down its length.

Having read of a bunch of these incidents, the amazing thing is that no one was seriously hurt. Yes, some scrapes, sore hands, but the force of the breaking case is directed at the mechanism itself. The extractor is bent and often blown out of the bolt. The bolt seems OK, but without a manufacturer's setup to measure dimensions, and conduct magnetic particle inspection, there's no way of knowing if the bolt can be used again. I wouldn't. I would simply make a display case or stand for the bolt and keep it handy every time I was going to be loading .300 ammo.

The carrier has the bottom rail, the pickup rail, broken loose and bent downward. It sometimes breaks off. The upper receiver is split and bent. Depending on how the break happens, the barrel nut can be broken, and if it is, the handguards end up trashed as well.

The force of the explosion is directed down into the magazine well, and the magazine is usually bulged, disassembled and the parts (follower, baseplate) often broken. The spring is twisted.

The lower receiver might survive in a reusable condition, but the force of the explosion often bulges the magazine well. In short, the only parts that can be salvaged are usually the trigger mechanism and the stock assembly. Optics on top might be OK, but since the usual reaction to such a mix-up is for the shooter to drop the rifle/carbine, the optics might be busted just from falling out of his hands.

With one trigger pull, a $1,000 or $2,000 rifle can be reduced to less than $100 of spare parts.

How can this be avoided?

You start by making sure your .300 ammo is too long to fully chamber in a .223/5.56 chamber. So, you do not load (if you reload) bullets so short they will fail to keep the bolt open in the event of such a mix-up. You make sure you have the tightest possible neck tension with standard loading dies, and a generous crimp. These steps help avoid bullet set-back.

Then, you color-code or otherwise mark your magazines. Mark your rifles as to caliber.

And finally, if you do take new shooters to the range, you take one or the other. You do not take

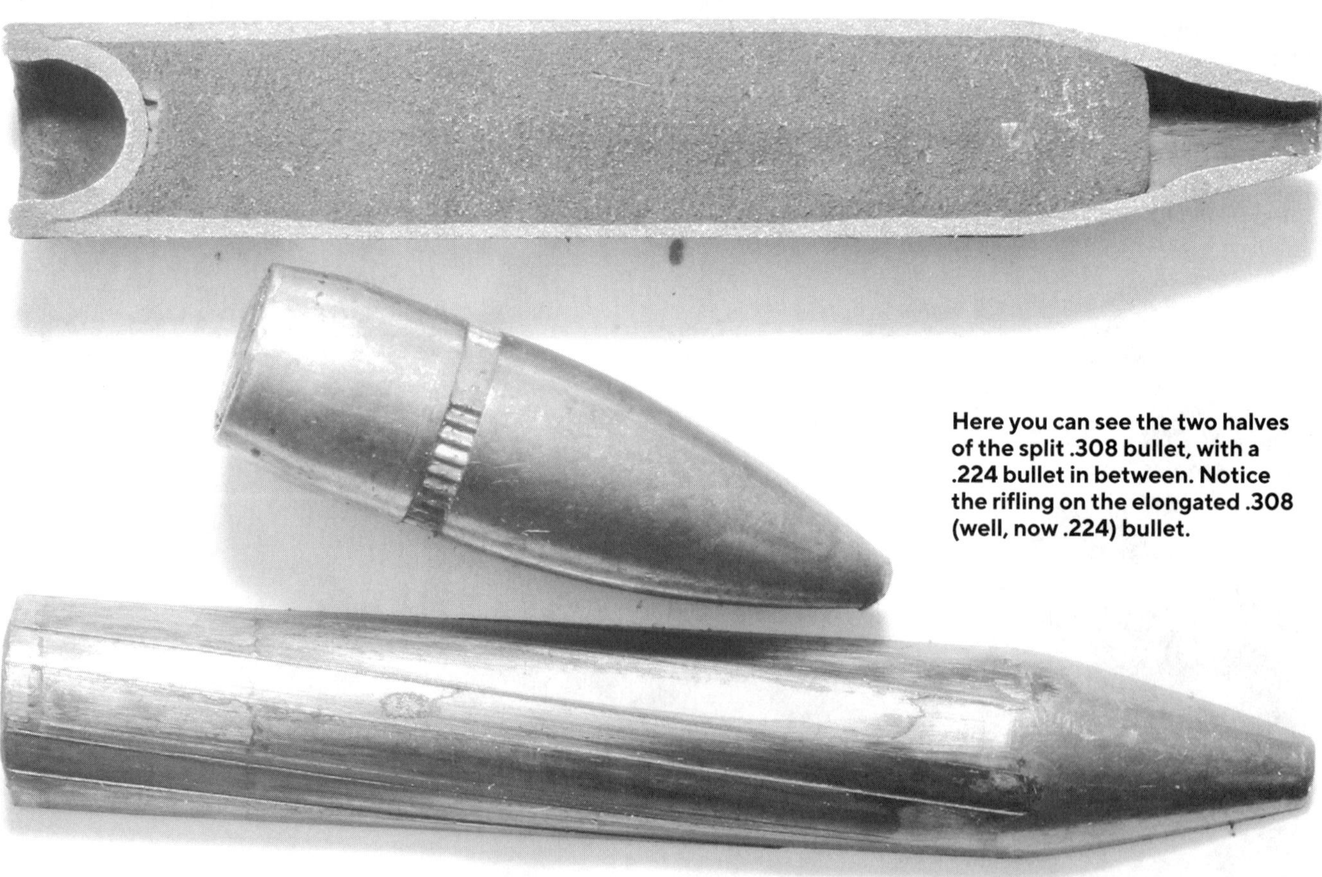

Here you can see the two halves of the split .308 bullet, with a .224 bullet in between. Notice the rifling on the elongated .308 (well, now .224) bullet.

both .223 and .300 rifles to the range. If you must, separate them by type. Shoot one, then pack away everything for the first ammo/rifle used, then break out the next one. When you take out the next, make sure all the magazines you bring out are empty. Explain to your new shooter what you are doing, and why.

The two cartridges are not going away. The .223/5.56 is too deeply embedded in the user base and has too much usefulness. To give you an example of usefulness inertia, the .30-06 cartridge was invented in 1906. It ceased to be the official U.S. military cartridge in 1956. It had a 50-year run and has been off the military scene in any large way for 64 years. If the 5.56 were officially replaced today (after a 50-year run) it would be the year 2084 before it was in the same situation as the .30-06 is today. No, it's not going anywhere.

The .300 Whisper/Blackout is far too useful to be replaced anytime soon. In fact, it serves a niche that is surprisingly large, and as long as people have ARs and suppressors, there will be a solid base of users who will want to be putting a silencer on their .300.

So, be careful out there.

GAS SYSTEMS

There are two gas systems for the .300s, compared to three for the carbines and rifles. (Some AR pistols use a fourth gas system, but they are not common.)

The two are a carbine-length gas tube, and a pistol-length gas tube. The carbine is just that, a regular carbine-length gas tube. This is just fine with a supersonic load for the .300s. It permits reliable function and reasonable recoil. It, however, does not cycle with subsonic loads. The miniscule powder charge does not generate enough pressure at the gas port to pressurize the system and cycle the carbine.

The pistol-length gas tube and system works just fine with subsonic loads. It, however, works the system much harder with supersonic loads. The pressure at the gas port, in a pistol system, is much higher when you use a supersonic load.

So, you have a choice to make: which length system, and what is the price you pay for it. If you are primarily going to be using your .300 with subsonic loads, and supersonics will be rarities, then go pistol. If you will be using it as a hunting rifle/carbine,

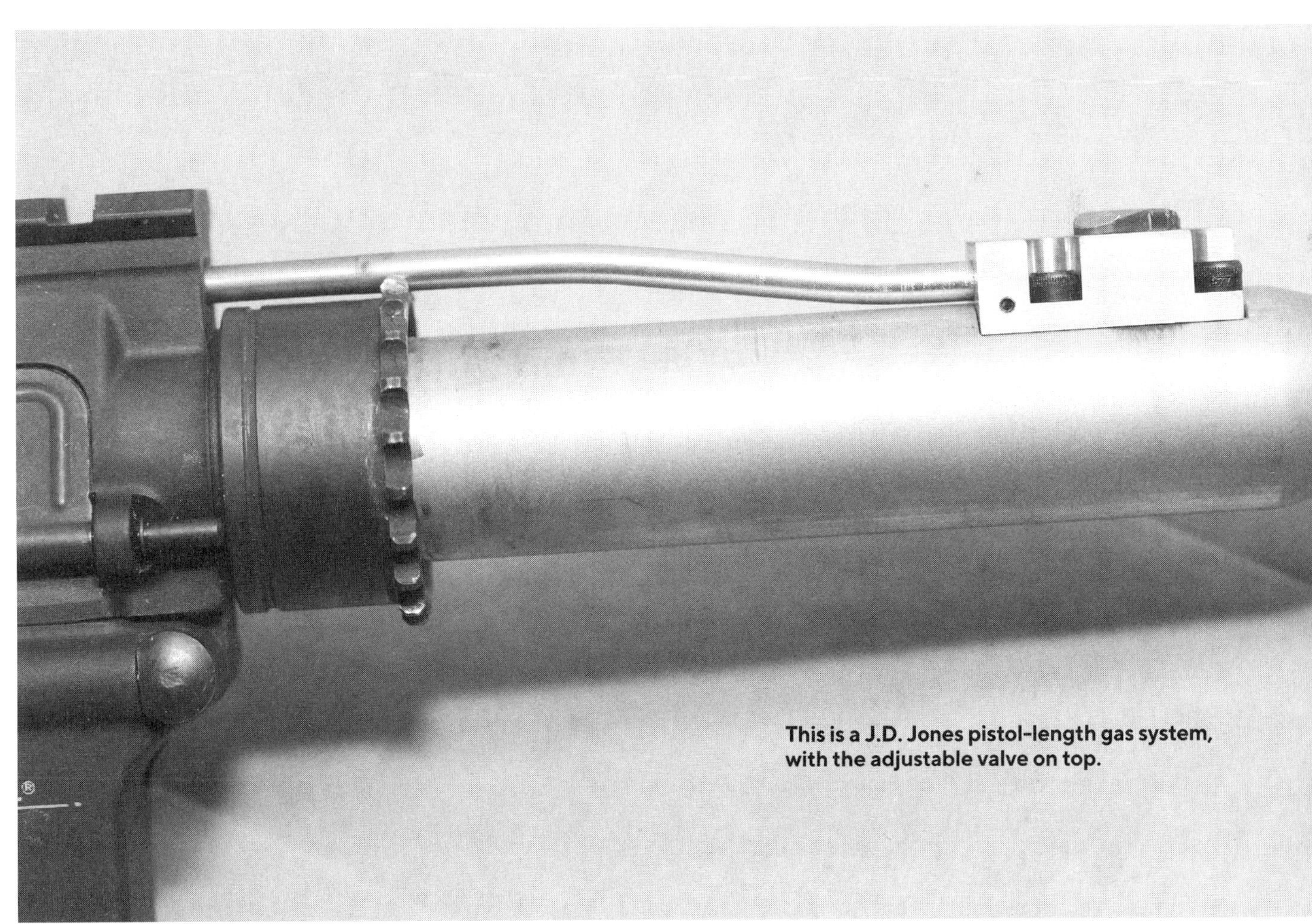

This is a J.D. Jones pistol-length gas system, with the adjustable valve on top.

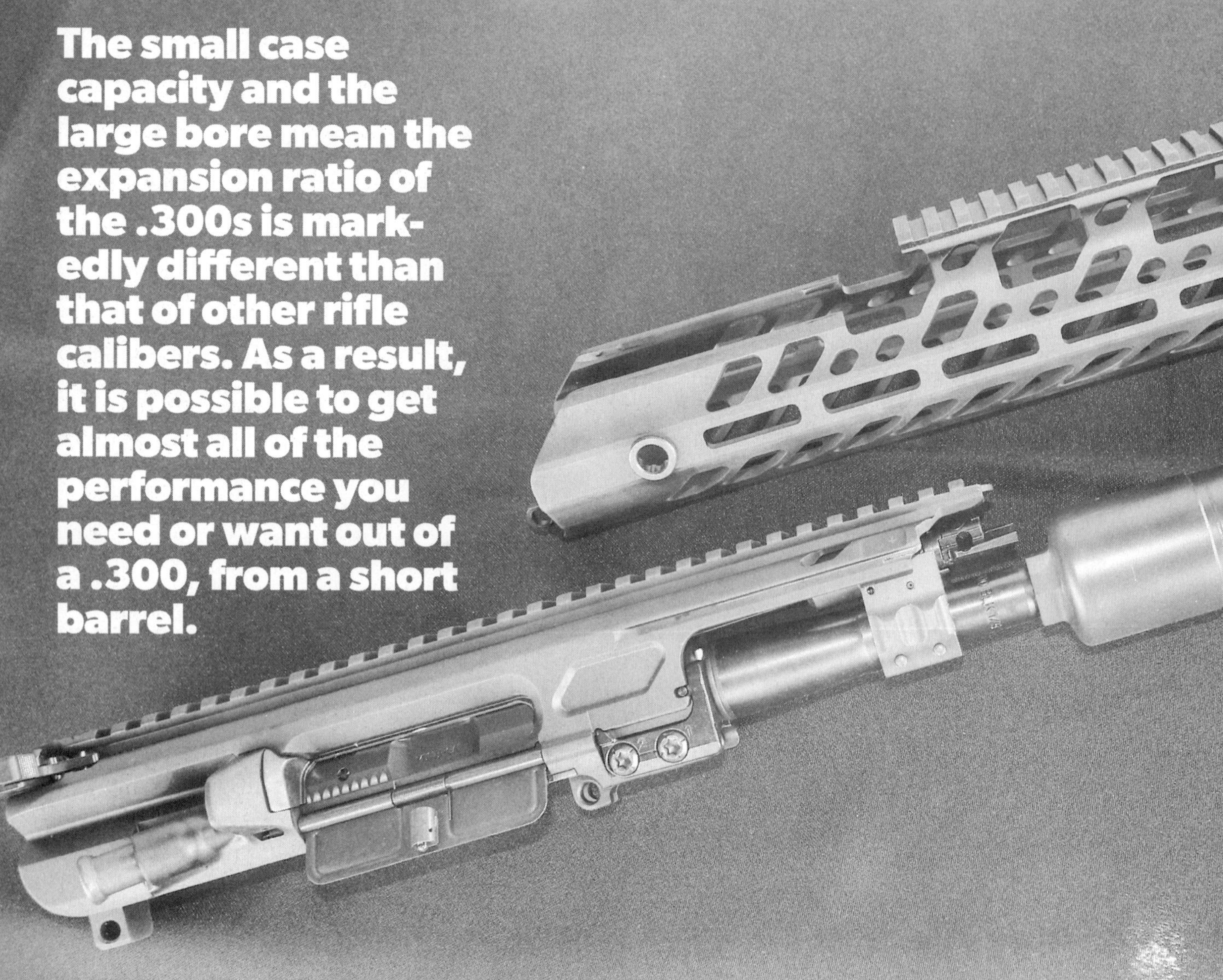

The small case capacity and the large bore mean the expansion ratio of the .300s is markedly different than that of other rifle calibers. As a result, it is possible to get almost all of the performance you need or want out of a .300, from a short barrel.

and will primarily feed it supersonic ammo, then go carbine.

You can, however, have both. J.D. Jones makes barrels and uppers with switch-valve pistol systems. The gas tube is a pistol-length one, but on the top, there is an adjustment knob you can turn, and throttle back the gas flow for use with supersonics.

You just have to keep track of which setting is for which load. But, the first shot will tell you if you have it right.

.300 PISTOLS

It is not uncommon for .300 barrels to be offered in eight-inch lengths.

A .300 with an eight-inch barrel is a very handy tool. And it lends itself to an AR-15 pistol. If you have an eight-inch barrel, and you put an arm brace on the back end, you have a very compact package that delivers much of the performance of a much larger carbine.

And if you want to do double-duty, then you simply get something like the Sig integrally suppressed upper and put that on a pistol lower. Sig is not alone in making such a beast, and since you are building a pistol you don't have to paper the firearm as an SBR. That means, however you do it, it is one transfer tax stamp.

The compact size, soft-ish recoil and excellent accuracy have led a number of shooters to build such pistols for use as truck guns, or just fun range guns.

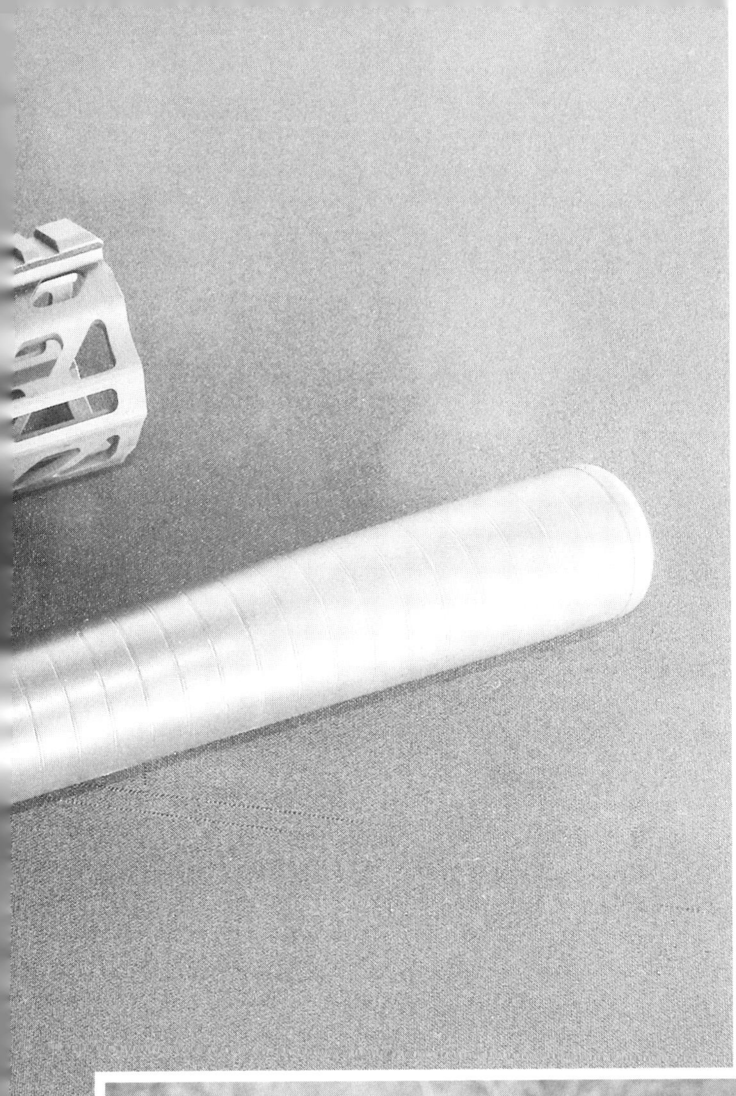

(left) The Sig integrally suppressed upper, in .300 Blackout. This is way cool, very handy and just one tax stamp if you put it on a pistol lower.

(below) An AR-15 pistol, chambered in one of the .300s, equipped with a suppressor, is fun to shoot. And quiet.

11

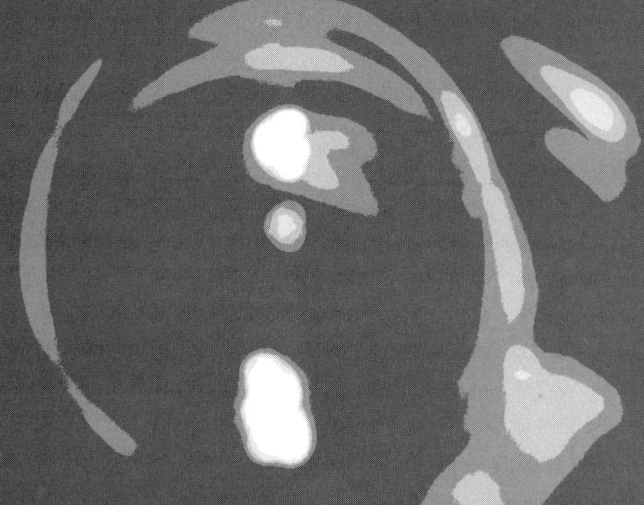

7.62x40 WILSON AND .300 HAM'R

The two Wilson Combat cartridges are the other end of the quest for a .30-caliber bullet in a .223 case cartridge. The whole idea, and the sole intent of the .300 Whisper was to hurl the heaviest .308 bullet at subsonic velocities. The fact that it can also be loaded to get special 115-grain bullets to supersonic velocities is a bonus. A bonus some take advantage of and others view as a distraction.

The 7.62x40 Wilson Tactical was just the opposite. It was designed to get as much velocity out of a .308 bullet of hunting weight, while still perhaps having some subsonic utility. The result was very pleasing for hunters who wanted to use the AR-15 in areas where deer hunting with a ".22" was prohibited.

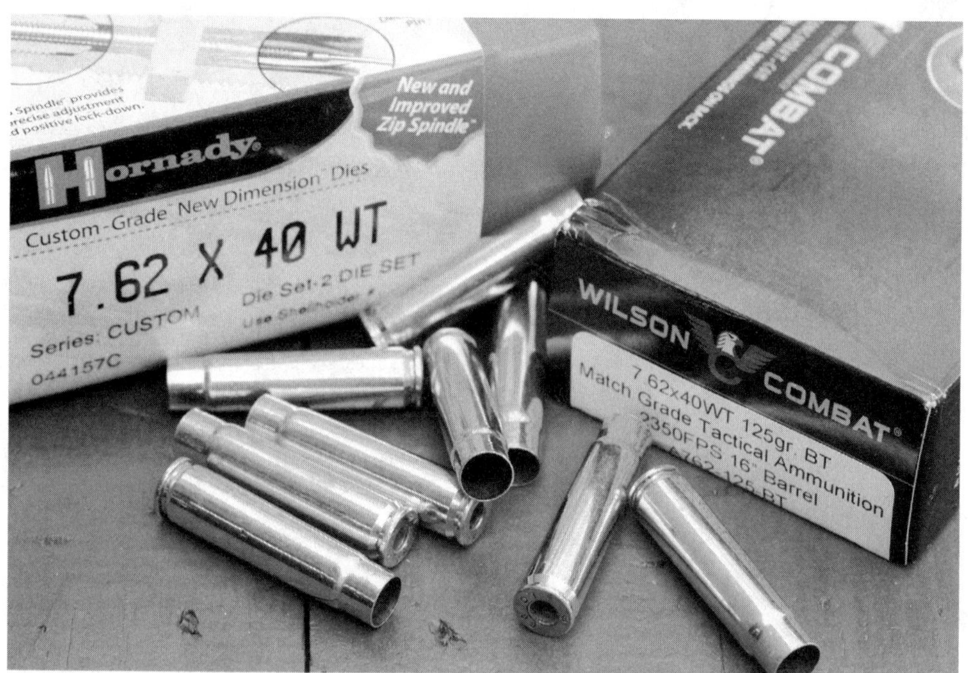

You can make 7.62x40WT brass from .223 or 5.56, but why would you? You can get ready-to-go brass and ammo from Wilson Combat.

Introduced in 2011, Bill Wilson wanted a hunting cartridge that could readily take down a deer or hog, and not require a lot of special products. So, it used relatively normal 110- to 125-grain .308-caliber hunting bullets, and pushed them to 2,600 fps (110-grain bullet) to 2,350 fps (125 grains) out of a carbine-length barrel.

As far as deer-level performance is concerned, this is not out of line with what a .30-30 can produce, and no one questions its utility in whitetail bagging. A .30-30 with a 150-grain bullet might be able to generate 2,300 fps. Oh, the book specs might list a higher velocity, but when I was sighting-in customers' deer rifles, I'd occasionally chronograph them just for fun. I never had a 150-grain load that produced an honest 2,300 fps from a carbine-length barrel.

Brass for the 7.62x40WT could be made from .223 with only a little effort. And bullets of the correct weight and construction were already in the bullet-makers' catalogs. So, it only requires a barrel change to create a 7.62x40 hunting rifle. The brass required neck-expanding, and had to be trimmed to length (a bit shorter than what an expanded .223/5.56 would end up as), but the trimming also ensured the case mouth was concentric. Expanding a case from .224 to .308 could lead to the mouth being a bit titled, shorter on one side than another. Trimming evens that out.

Or, just buy ammo from Wilson Combat. The company make lots of it.

There was one small problem, in that the loaded cartridge was wider at the neck than a .223/5.56 would be. The internal ribs on magazines that are there to control movement of the smaller cartridges

The original Wilson .30 AR cartridge works reasonably well in standard AR magazines, but for the best feeding, use 7.62x40WT-specific magazines.

caused the front end of the cartridge stack of 7.62s to be crowded together. This could sometimes cause feeding problems and could decrease the capacity of a magazine. Bill Wilson worked with Lancer to create a 7.62-specific magazine, with the ribs adjusted for the new cartridge, to ensure absolute reliability.

Now, the performance of a deer-hunting cartridge is a big deal. As with so many things, there is an accepted, and usually older-than-dirt, standard, and for deer hunting it is, as mentioned, the .30-30. With that cartridge, bullets tend to be heavier than the 7.62x40. A customary .30-30 factory offering would be 150 or 170 grains. The velocities would be 2,100 fps for the 170, and 2,290 for the 150-grain bullet. The 7.62x40 Wilson, with a 125 at 2,350 fps, is clearly a step behind that, but only a small step. And to a hunter who does not have a long history with a .30-30, a family tradition, the difference is not enough to be worrisome. Also, the 7.62 is going to be in an AR-15, and the .30-30 in a lever-action. Yes, I'll grant you that 150 grains weigh more than 125 grains, but a 125 just under 2,400 fps, versus a 150 just over 2,200 fps? No deer will know the difference.

The Wilson cartridge (left) has the neck and shoulder forward of where the Whisper/Blackout has them. This provides a bit more case capacity. The idea is not subsonic, but the best supersonic hunting energy that can be generated.

Building a complete upper, set up for deer hunting, an upper that can be swapped out for the 5.56 upper for competition, training or defense, allows a shooter to hunt with the same trigger and stock, the same feel, as the rifle he/she competes and trains with. That is a big, and good, thing.

Reloading the brass is normal, and if you need more you can make more from once-fired or new .223, or just get more ready-made 7.62x40 brass.

.300 HAM'R

If the 7.62x40 was so good, why did Bill decide to up his game? Simple: No one wanted, or needed, a subsonic 7.62x40 load, or wanted to reload for it. Everyone who wanted a subsonic load was already using the .300 Whisper or Blackout, and for good reason. The 7.62x40, in subsonic mode, was limited in bullet weight. Once the bullet ogive became long enough that you could not fit it into the Wilson case, in a magazine, and keep all the ogive outside of the case, you could not load it.

Basically, the curve of the heavier bullets would extend down into the case mouth, and the game was over.

If you wanted a bullet heavier than 150 grains, the limit you could fit into a 7.62x40WT case, for subsonic shooting, the 7.62x40 was not an option. With subsonic loadings now commonly 200 grains or more, and going up to 240 grains, the Whisper/Blackout was the winner here.

Bill had tested the .300 Whisper on game. His ranch in Texas has plenty of hogs, so he uses them as his test subjects. It isn't so much hunting as pest control. With the .300 Whisper tapped out (this was before the .300 Blackout, but the results would have been identical there) he shifted to the 6.8 SPC. But it didn't deliver the performance he wanted.

The light bulb moment was when he saw the .30 Remington AR. At last, the kind of performance he wanted. Too bad it was with a proprietary upper receiver, bolt and magazine, plus the fact that Remington dropped it soon after introducing it.

So, Bill looked over the bullets that were suitable for hunting, in .308 diameter, on the lighter end, and

The beauty of the Wilson conversion is that it can be done with just a barrel. Or you can have a complete upper that parks right on top of your AR-15 lower. Your choice.

redesigned the 7.62x40WT case to move the shoulder forward. He also lengthened the throat, the leade, so bullets could be loaded to the full magazine length, and with a blunter ogive, in effect pulling the bullet base forward. This way he could gain a bit more case capacity, and get more velocity out of his loadings. The result is the .300 HAM'R, and it can push a bullet of 125 grains to 2,540 fps. With this kind of performance available in a carbine that weighs less than seven pounds, we all of a sudden have a new .30-30. A 21st century .30-30. If you have a new shooter who is recoil sensitive, then a compact muzzle brake on a .300 HAM'R will offer a soft shooting experience and yet more than sufficient deer-hunting power.

The .300 HAM'R is an auto-loading equal to the .30-30. It is not a step behind, even though the bullets are lighter. I got the lowdown on this during a visit with Bill at his ranch, when the various HAM'R calibers were being introduced.

If you need to tame the noise, then a .30 suppressor (and a lot of states now permit hunting with suppressors) will knock back the noise and take some of the recoil out as well.

The .300 HAM'R, like the 7.62x40, uses the .223/5.56 case as the parent case. However, the shoulder is forward of where it is on the 7.62, so the .300 won't chamber in a 7.62. I suspect that a good gunsmith could ream the 7.62 chamber to .300 HAM'R specs, but why do that? If you already have a 7.62x40WT, then load it, shoot it and be happy with it. Wilson Combat still lists 7.62x40WT ammunition on its web page, and you could go your whole life and not wear out the barrel that is there. You could even bring home a deer each year for as long as you can get yourself out to the hunting blind, and even practice, and still not wear out the barrel. No, really. Let's say a barrel lasts only 5,000 rounds. (A pretty shabby barrel, if it is only that good.) That's 20 years of hunting and practice at 250 rounds per year. The average hunter might shoot 100 rounds a year if they are really keen on practice, and that's a 50-year barrel.

Up the service life to 10,000 rounds, and that rifle will last two to three generations of hunters. Not that I'm trying to interfere with Bill's plan to sell lots of rifles, but that barrel is going to last a long time.

If you want to start now, then the .300 HAM'R is

Left to right we have the 5.56, 7.62x40WT, .300 HAM'R and 7.62x39. Note the shoulder location of the .300 HAM'R. Just enough to keep it from chambering in a 7.62x40WT.

the way to go, as you can load it right up to full specs, or even load it down a bit, to 7.62x40WT performance, and save a bit on powder costs and recoil. In full .300 HAM'R trim, you are going to get more than 100 fps over the 7.62x40WT, and almost 300 fps over a .300 Whisper or Blackout, with the same 115-grain bullet weight.

While visiting Bill at his ranch when the .300 HAM'R and other HAM'Rs were being unveiled, we went out in search of hogs. At the feeding station we set up on, a pair came out in the dimming evening light. One shot each put them on the ground right where they stood, and a second shot each stopped their movement. A second shot was probably not needed, but I was back on the first one, after having shot the second, right away, and I'm not the type to let a game animal spend any more time at the end than I can manage.

The .300 HAM'R has the same sometimes-problem that the 7.62x40 has, with magazines. That is, if the magazine in question, in the rifle being used, has a problem, then it has a problem. If it doesn't, then it doesn't. If it does, then the Wilson 7.62-specific magazine will solve that problem. And if you are using your 7.62/.300 for hunting, then you'll need a five-shot magazine anyway. Get a Wilson.

HISTORICAL ASIDE

When the AR-15 was new, and for a long time after, the idea of a ".30 AR-15" was a non-starter. The only "acceptable" .30 cartridge back then was the .308/7.62 NATO, and that could only be had in an AR-10. Since no one was making an AR-10, then there wasn't any point to it. The idea of an AR-15 in a chambering other than .223/5.56 was still in the future. Really, if, back in 1989 you had suggested expanding a 5.56 case to .30, and load bullets for deer hunting, the laughter would have ranged from polite to derisive. And oddball bullet diameters, like 6.5mm, .270 or others would have been just as bad. "Hunt with an AR?" The sneering would have been epic.

The German idea of a suitable rifle on the Eastern Front is the Stg44, the bottom firearm in this photo. Firing the 7.92 Kurz, it was powerful enough, held plenty of ammo, penetrated better than 9mm, and was select-fire.

Not because, like modern anti-gun legislators claim, the AR is "unsuited for hunting," but instead because the cartridge was not traditional.

But with modern powders and modern bullets, the performance on deer-sized game is more than good enough for modern hunters, deer and DNR authorities. And modern hunters are not all that concerned about traditional cartridges, unless they are. And then they go right back to the 19th century for inspiration.

Once the floodgates were opened in the 21st century, every usable bullet diameter came under scrutiny, and I suspect that no diameter has gone uninvestigated.

I have a Wilson-barrel 7.62x40WT upper in the rack, and while I think the .300 HAM'R is better for hunting, I don't see any point in changing this upper, or selling this for a .300. (I have a slew of those as well.) As I mentioned before, if you have a 7.62x40WT, then there's not much need to move up. (Sorry, Bill, I have to call them as I see them.) But if you are looking to get a lightweight, compact, .30-caliber hunting rifle on the AR system, then the .300 HAM'R is the cartridge for you.

7.62x39

But there was one .30 cartridge that was actually a contender. Well, kinda-sorta a contender. That was the commie one, the AK cartridge, the 7.62x39.

The '39 came about because the Bolsheviks were willing to lose soldiers. They could send soldiers to the front, and at the Germans, faster than the Germans could shoot them, and at times even faster than the Germans could resupply ammo. That changed when the Germans fielded the Mkb 42(H), a "machine carbine."

The idea the Germans had was simple, and one they also had to hide from Hitler. If a bolt action was too slow, then use an autoloading rifle. If it didn't hold enough ammo, use a box magazine that holds more. If the 7.92x57 rifle cartridge was more powerful than you needed, then use one with less, but enough, power. In short order, they had a 10-pound carbine with a 30-round magazine that fired the 7.92x33 round. The 125-grain bullet was going 2,250 fps, compared to the 7.92x57, with its 195 at 2,600 fps.

The Haenel Mbk 42(H) had all kinds of problems, but working them out and competing with other manufactures for the contracts caused the creation of the MP43, MP44 and Stg44/Stg45. Oh, and they were all select-fire.

With captured samples, the Soviets didn't take long to figure things out, and adopted the M43, the now-famous 7.62x39 cartridge.

The '39 differs from a lot of other cartridges, then and now. The '39, like the German '33, has a severe taper to the case. This is for two reasons: feeding and extracting. Feeding a cone into a tapered hole is easy and slick. Once fired, the tapered case, as soon as it has moved just a bit, breaks completely free of the chamber walls, and is easily extracted and ejected.

On the left we have the 7.92 Kurz, or 7.92x33. That's the one the Germans were shooting at the Russians. On the right is the Russian response, the M43, or 7.62x39. And some people have the nerve to suggest the Soviets came up with the 7.62 all on their own. Really?

The idea was also popular with the Soviets because they were going to be making the casings out of steel. Compared to copper, steel is cheap and readily available. I've joked that the only reason the Soviets made AKs, and ammo for them, out of steel, was that they couldn't make the concrete R&D samples work well enough. The only thing cheaper than, and which the Soviets had more of, than steel, was concrete. So, steel it was.

In the earliest days of the socialist era, when the future was so bright good commies had to wear shades, each of the newly socialist countries actually thought that that was the way things were going to be. The Czechs, in particular, in Czechoslovakia (now two countries) developed a line of small arms. They made a rifle and light machine gun, chambered in what they thought was a suitable cartridge: the 7.62x45. This was obviously a bit longer than the 7.62x39, and the ballistics were pretty good.

The various vZ 52 firearms (rifle, carbine and LMG) fired a 130-grain bullet at just over 2,400 fps. This was less than the previous rifles had fired (the .30-06, 8mm Mauser, .303 British and 7.7 Jap were all pretty much identical) but more than what the AK round did.

Well, the Russians weren't having any of it. If the Czechs were going to be suitable second-line Warsaw Pact troopers, and battle replacements, they were darn well going to be using 7.62x39 ammo.

So, the carbines and rifles were changed to 7.62x39, the LMGs were mothballed, and the carbines already made in 7.62x45 were also mothballed.

Some decades later, I noticed a news item of the Warsaw Pact supplying some group in Central or South America with carbines. Dog-gone if they weren't vZ 52 carbines, and the magazine shape clearly indicated they were of the 7.62x45 variety. Thanks for the "Help," comrade, since there was no ammo available. But, back to the AK round.

The design of the 7.62x39 case poses particular problems for the AR-15.

The tapered case makes magazines a real problem. The taper of the case causes the stack to tilt on the follower after more than just a few rounds. The AK,

The advantage of the CMMG approach with the Mutant is that you get a really hefty bolt, on the right, instead of the smaller AR bolt, left, that has to be opened up even more.

with its continuous-curve magazine, shows you just how much the rounds want to angle as they stack. The AR has a straight magazine well. The magazine has to be straight until it has left the well. The common 20-round AR mags are straight, but the angled bottom shows you how much the .223 round wants to angle as it stacks, and it is much straighter than the AK round.

As a result, magazines for the 7.62x39, for the AR, have an almost ludicrous curve once they have left the magazine well. It is necessary, in order to keep the tapered cases under control.

The second problem is the rim diameter. The rim of the AK round, at .447 of an inch, is much larger than the .223, at .378. The bolt face of the AR has to be opened up to accommodate the AK rim. This does not leave a lot of steel around the perimeter of the bolt face. However, using good steel, and proper heat-treatment, bolt makers can manage that. It also helps that the 7.62x39 operates at a lower chamber pressure than that of the 5.56.

The steel case of the AK round was for a long time thought to be problematic in the AR, but extensive use in 7.62x39 and .223/5.56 has shown that steel causing problems with extraction are not the case.

The bigger problem is the Soviets were not all that interested in ammunition uniformity. That is, any powder, it seems, that delivers the expected velocity, or near-enough to it, was used. The AK gas system is biased to over-gassing. Severely over-gassing. The AK gas system vents almost immediately upon piston movement, unlike the AR, which drives the system until the gas key uncovers the end of the gas tube. The pressurized system dwell time for the AK is minimal, for the AR it is much greater. The AR is much more sensitive to gas-port variations, and those are caused by powder burn rates. The variability of AK ammo loading can cause some ARs to be reliable with one batch of ammo, and not with another.

This was more of a problem back when what we were getting was real-deal, surplus Soviet ammo, made over the course of decades by various arsenals in the Warsaw Pact. Now that most of that has been shot up, we've got new-production ammo that is more closely controlled.

Another problem with the older ammo was that it was corrosive. Oh, we were assured that it wasn't, but you trusted their assurances at your peril. Or rather, the peril of your rifle's bore.

The last problem is bullet diameter. The Soviets settled on .311 of an inch, more or less, but American .30 rifles use .308-caliber bullets. Add to that the Soviet willingness to accept variances, and you might see an AK bore with grooves from .310 up to .314. American makers are more likely to consider a variance from .3075 to .3085 as the maximum spread in grooves. Bullets? Even tighter specs. So, accuracy can be variable, depending on the bore diameter of your rifle, and the bullet diameter.

To make an AR-15 in 7.62x39, you need barrel, bolt and magazines. To make an AR in 7.62x39 is a bit of a kludge, as it really wasn't intended to use that round. Why did it get done, then? To gain the alleged "better stopping power" of the 7.62x39, with the obviously better ergonomics of the AR-15. While the ergonomics of the AR are obviously superior, opinions vary on the stopping power of the AK. When I was early in my gun shop working career, I met more than one vet who could show you the scars from where he had been shot with an AK. "And killed the bastard who did it, too!" was the usual result, and gleeful memory. Now, that is a small, and obviously self-selected sample, but it does indicate that the 7.62x39, in Soviet trim, is not the hammer of Thor.

One approach taken by CMMG is to rebuild the AR to the round. Called the MK47, or Mutant, it

Left is the Czech 7.62x45, next the 7.62x39, the 5.56 and the 6.8 Rem SPC.

The CMMG Mutant has not much in common with a vanilla-plain AR-15. The stock assemblies and the trigger parts, that's about it. That's part of the cost of going all-in on an AK cartridge.

has a larger-diameter bolt, to accommodate the AK rim. It has a reshaped lower receiver, to accept AK magazines. It keeps the AR ergonomics, solves the mechanical problems and gives you 7.62x39 performance.

One can argue as to whether it is an AR-15 or not, but there's a lot of AR DNA in there, and it does work the way they say it will. If you want an AR-15 in 7.62x39, and you have a stash of AK mags (and who doesn't?) then the Mutant is an obvious choice.

THE AK AR TO BEAT THEM ALL

CMMG makes an AR it calls the Mutant. The idea was simple: take an AR-15, make the bolt big enough to actually handle the AK cartridge, and modify the lower to accept AK magazines. So, the ergonomics of the AR, with the performance of the AK, but more accurate.

If what you want is the 7.62x39, then this is the approach you take.

The bolt of the CMMG is more the size of an AR-10 than the AR-15, and this provides plenty of safety margin. Not that there has been a run of broken bolts on ARs chambered in 7.62x39, but more is more, right?

AND, FINALLY...

There's a subsonic cartridge out there called the .338 Spectre, designed by Marty ter Weeme of Teppo Jutsu. It is a magazine-length .338 bullet cartridge, based on the 10mm magnum case. I didn't know where else to place it, and since it has pretty much the same case capacity as these .30 cartridges, but with a .338-caliber bullet, I figured why not here?

As cartridges go, it is interesting, but what it does is done by a host of other cartridges. On the subsonic side, you can do almost as well with the .300 Blackout or Whisper. If you want heavy and subsonic, the .458 SOCOM (also designed by Marty) has weight all over the Spectre.

As a high-velocity hunting round, the .300 HAM'R is much better. And for hunting in places where you need a straight-walled cartridge, well, it isn't.

But Marty is beyond clever, the cartridge has a following, and I figured you'd want to know about it.

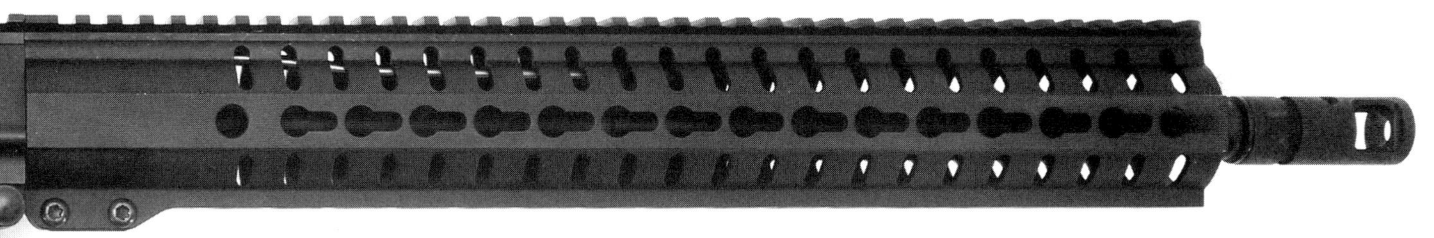

The CMMG Mutant is an AR that uses AK magazines and fires the 7.62x39. The ergonomics of one, and the performance of the other.

12

6.5 GRENDEL AND .264 LBC

There are, or were, back when such things were being argued over, people who pitted the 6.5 Grendel against the 6.8 Remington SPC. This despite the fact that the two cartridges came about for different reasons, with different purposes in mind.

The 6.8 was intended to be a military cartridge, to replace the 5.56 in the same package, offer more oomph, and not require much more to rebuild than a few components. The intent was a new barrel, a new bolt, and maybe new magazines, and the military could get more performance out of the rifles and carbines they were already using. And, we covered it back in Chapter 8.

BC, the less drag, and the less deceleration as it travels to the target. As an example, and this is a cartridge we'll be discussing in another caliber chapter, but if you take a 147-grain, 6.5mm bullet, with a high BC, such as one by Hornady, it just doesn't seem to slow down. The example I worked up when testing barrel length was that if you started this bullet at just over 2,000 fps (a relatively low muzzle velocity for a rifle bullet) it will remain supersonic past 1,000 yards.

The 6.5 Grendel can use bullets up to 130 grains, and they are all high-BC bullets. So, they don't have to start with as much velocity, to retain velocity downrange.

(above) The 6.5 Grendel has more recoil than a .223/5.56 simply because it delivers more. In a compact package, it can be a really useful tool in an emergency.

(below) The Alexander Arms 6.5 Grendel uses bullets with high ballistic coefficients (BC).

The starting point is the AK-47 case, in a kinda-sorta way. The 7.62x39 case has a larger taper to it, and is usually loaded in steel cases. However, back when the Olympics still had an event called Running Boar, the Russians used the AK cartridge as a start-

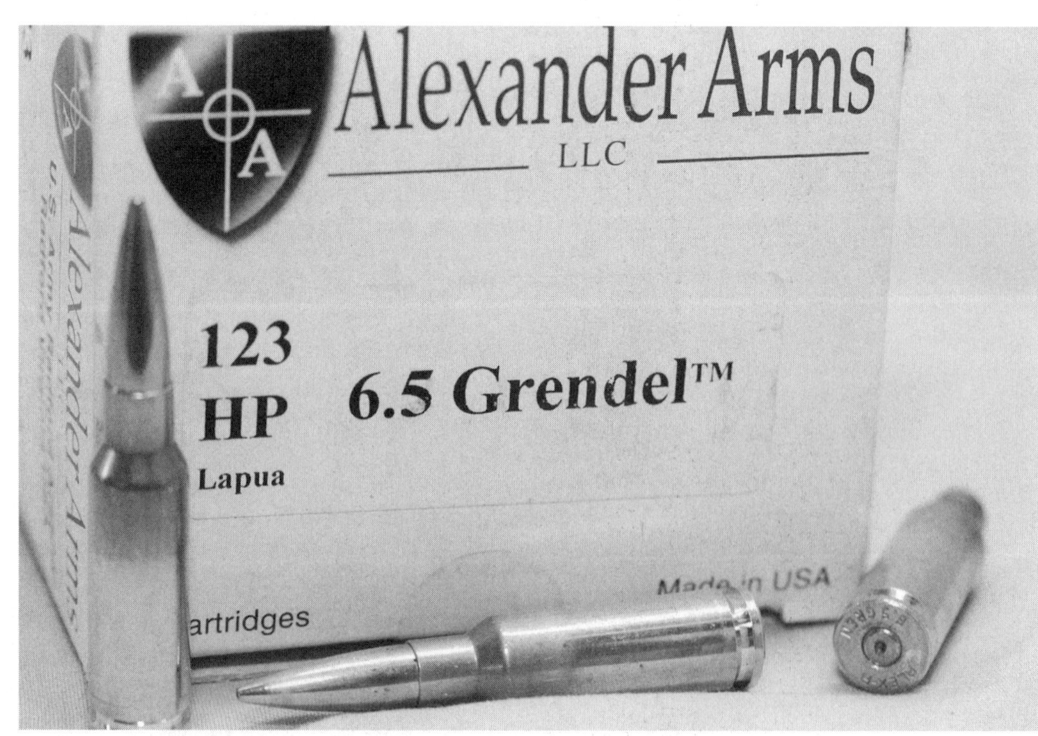

The 6.5 Grendel was designed by Bill Alexander as a hunting cartridge for the AR-15. Instead of a relatively stubby .277-inch-diameter bullet, Bill went with the 6.5mm, a .264 bullet, to gain the high-BC performance of the 6.5mm.

BC? Ballistic Coefficient. It is a measure of the drag a bullet experiences as it travels through the air. The higher the

You can clearly see the origins of the 6.5 Grendel, from the 7.62x39. Necked down, blown out, and using bullets with impressively high BCs, it has it all over pretty much anything else for its size. To do more you have to move up to an AR-10-sized rifle.

ing point. They took the case, changed the primer to a small rifle from large rifle, and necked it down to their .22 rifle bullet. Called the .220 Russian, it was an accurate, low-recoil cartridge for the sport.

As a short, wide cartridge case, it offered promise in other areas. The sport of benchrest shooting thought it was useful, so brass cases made in Finland (getting ammunition from the Soviet Union back in the 1970s would have been a job for the CIA) of .220 Russian were imported for use in benchrest competition, and called the .22 PPC. (After the two originators: Louis Palmisano and Ferris Pindel, benchrest competitors in the 1970s.) Those two also changed the shape of the cases (ordered that way, not modified here state-side) by giving the case body less taper, and making the shoulder a sharper angle than the Soviet angle. In due time, it was also necked up to 6mm, called the 6mm PPC.

To make the case work in the AR-15, Bill Alexander teamed up in R&D with Arne Brenna and Jahnne Pohjoispää to adjust case length, neck length,

A lineup of 6.5 Grendel loads, including a steel-case Wolf load, for less-expensive practice.

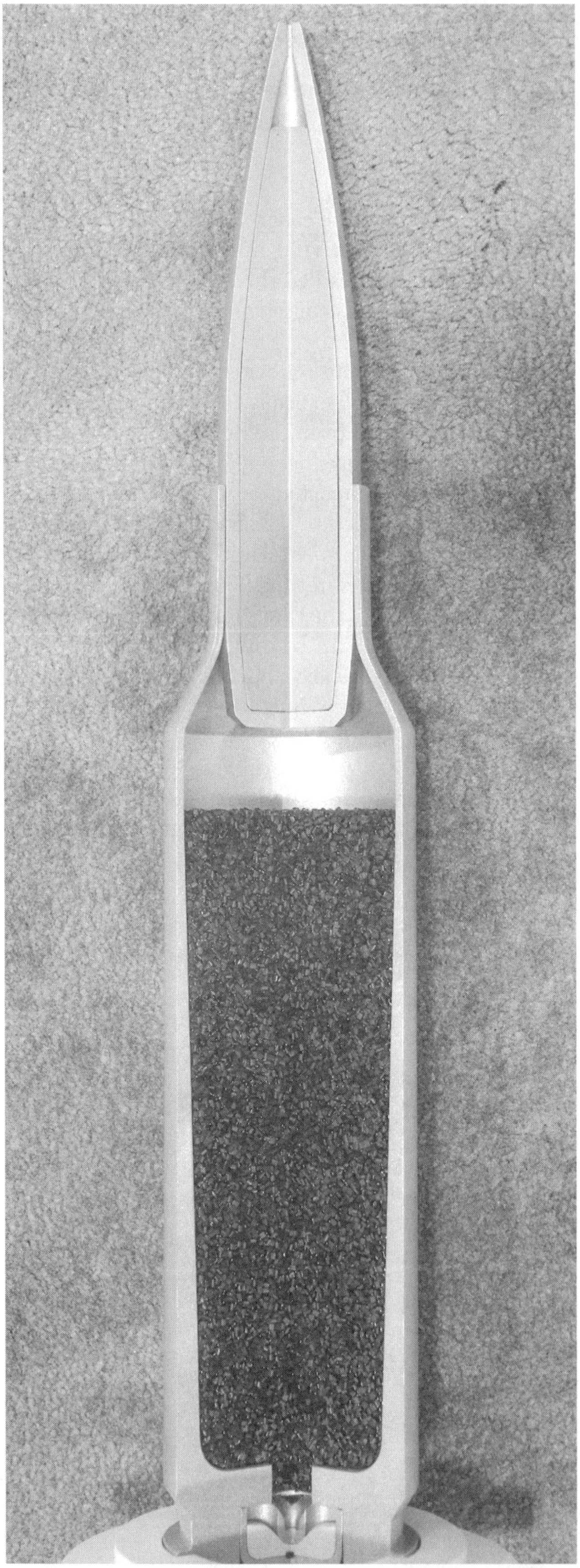

Here you see what a case with high loading density looks like. The closer the powder charge is to the base of the bullet, the better.

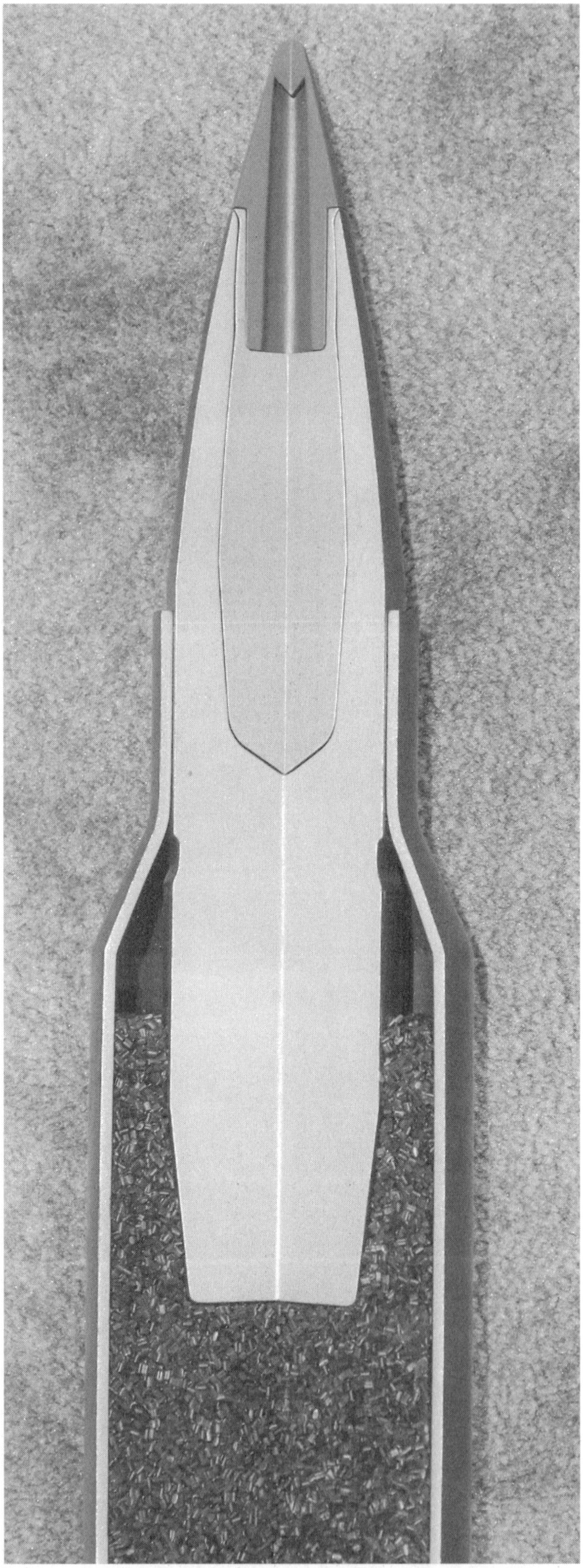

The drawback to a short case is when you load heavy bullets they can protrude back into the powder charge. This isn't bad, but it does limit the amount of powder you can use.

shoulder location and angle, and an important detail for Bill, the length and shape of the leade.

The result is a great-performing cartridge.

The high BC means bullets do not lose velocity like others do. One example specific to the 6.5 Grendel is the .123-grain Lapua Scenar bullet out of a rifle. With a starting velocity of 2,600 fps, it remains supersonic out to 1,200 yards, and shoots sub-MOA that far.

The relatively short, fat case means that you can get more powder behind the bullet, but also that the powder will fill that case and there is less air gap behind the bullet. This is called "loading density" and the closer it is to 100 percent the more consistent the ammunition can be.

I had an opportunity to shoot an Alexander Arms rifle in a competition with gun writers. The target was a half-scale silhouette at 640 yards. We had a rifle and a pile of ammo. So, what could we do for a contest? How many hits out of five shots? We'd all get five hits, so no contest there. Time? We could shoot fast, but how? We decided that the contest would be five shots, winner with the most hits, but any shot past 10 seconds wouldn't count. We could use anything on the range to build a shooting position. I finally found a shooting position that let me see my hits and misses, and correct for wind, etc. I got five hits in just over seven seconds.

Accurate, low-recoiling, low-drag bullets, and built like a tank, that's an Alexander Arms AR-15.

Now, the 6.5 Grendel requires a new barrel, bolt and magazines. The rounds will not work properly in a standard 5.56 magazine. So, you have to have 6.5-specific magazines. The bolt is the same one that you'd use for a 7.62x39 conversion, at least dimensionally. The 6.5 Grendel benefits from a better-built bolt, and Alexander Arms makes better bolts.

The end result is that for any given situation, the 6.5 ends up having as much energy or velocity on target, as the next-sized AR in 6.8. That is, if you have a full-sized rifle in 6.8, it delivers a bullet at 200 yards with the same power as a 6.5 carbine does.

No, really. Let's take a 6.8 120-grain bullet with a BC of .400. Leaving the muzzle at 2,460 fps from a rifle, that bullet arrives at 200 yards with 2,050 fps, and at 300 yards with 1,859 fps.

The 6.5 Grendel, launching a 123-grain bullet with a BC of .510, only needs a muzzle velocity of 2,325 fps to match the 6.8 at 200 yards (with 2,010 fps) and beat it at 300 (with 1,861 fps). Past that, it is all 6.5 Grendel. And a carbine is going to give you more than just 2,325 fps, it will be closer to the 6.8 rifle velocity. More to the point, the 123-grain bullet is the 6.5 bullet with the most drag that isn't a varmint

An AR pistol in 6.5 Grendel can deliver the performance of a 6.8 carbine, but in a more compact package.

bullet. The heavier 6.5 bullets (weights the 6.8 cannot use) have BCs that go up to .578. That's getting almost to the point where a bullet gains velocity as it travels onward. OK, mild exaggeration.

Similarly, if you use a 6.8 SPC carbine as your baseline, then an AR pistol chambered in 6.5 Grendel performs the same high-BC magic. Hard off the muzzle, the 6.8 has a small edge, but the 6.5 catches up so quickly that at any distance much past the length of a Buick, the Grendel is in the lead.

The much-less-tapered 6.5 case means that the rounds will still stack properly in a regular AR magazine tube, and the changes that are needed for 6.5-specific magazines are in the feed lip dimensions and follower shape. Also, being a larger cartridge, with rims of .440-inch diameter, compared to the 5.56 at .378, you can't fit as many in a regular-length magazine. So, you end up with a full-sized magazine holding 25 or 26 rounds, compared to 30 for the 5.56.

The bolt on the 6.5 Grendel has the bolt face opened to accommodate the rim, and this has lead Alexander Arms (and others) to improve the AR bolt: improved steel alloys, better heat-treatments, lug shapes that better handle the stress, and extractors that have a "lobster tail" end, with two extractor springs to drive it.

The improvements on the 6.5 bolt are examples of what could have been done to the AR-15 bolt for .223/5.56 firearms, if the Ordnance department was actually improving the M16/M4. Instead, they are looking to churn program after program to replace it, and not bringing the half-century of improvements that have been developed to the existing platform.

Wolf makes 6.5 Grendel, and it is good ammo.

Les Baer wasn't interested in complex leade shapes, and simply wanted what would deliver tack-driving accuracy with hunting-weight bullets. Ammo is interchangeable, and both AA and LBC loads are superbly accurate.

The main reason for that is simple: Anything new to replace the M16 has to have a marked improvement over the old. If they kept improving the old, they would just be lifting the bar higher and higher.

OK, soapbox mode off.

You can buy complete rifles, uppers, or just barrels and bolts, should you want to build your own 6.5 Grendel. You will have to have 6.5-specific magazines. There is no way to make a .223/5.56 magazine work with 6.5 Grendel ammunition.

Reloading ammo is no more difficult than any other cartridge, and there is plenty of loading data to be had. Even a cursory search turned up two dozen loads in a variety of bullet weights.

The 6.5 Grendel was a trademarked cartridge, and there is one detail about SAAMI, and that is, it won't spec a cartridge that is trademarked. So, Alexander Arms released the trademark, and in 2011 it became a SAAMI-recognized cartridge.

If you find that AA ammunition, loaded with Lapua bullets, is too rich for your wallet, then you can use Hornady ammo. Or Wolf ammo, as well as Barnaul.

.264 LBC

Les Baer took a look at the 6.5, and took a slightly different approach. The leade details that Bill Alexander worked on used the Scandinavian experience with 6.5 rifles, and his desire to make the Grendel accurate with any and all bullets to be had in 6.5mm. So, the 6.5 Grendel leade shape will work with both 130-grain match bullets and 90-grain varmint bullets.

Les figured varmint shooters would be using the less-expensive .223/5.56 rather than the 6.5, so he uses a leade shape that is intended to be used with heavy match and hunting bullets. The chamber shape and dimensions are the same, and the performance is as exemplary.

Les builds superbly accurate rifles (as well as brilliant 1911s) so you can count on tack-driving accuracy.

The Les Baer hunting rifle chambered in .264 LBC, which is 6.5 Grendel.

13

.30 REMINGTON AR

Say what? Sometimes the people who are in charge just don't seem to grasp what the buyers want. The .30 Remington AR is a case in point. The idea was simple: create a hunting cartridge for the AR-15, a cartridge that fulfills the requirements for DNR agencies, and fits with the idea a lot of hunters have regarding using a "proper" deer-hunting cartridge in an AR-15 if one is using .30-caliber bullets.

Now, the idea of firing a .308-caliber bullet from an AR-15 was not new when Remington came out with the .30 Remington AR (and I have to find a contraction for that, it is just so clumsy) in 2008.

The idea was to make the .30 Remington AR (center) nearly the equal of the .308 (left) while fitting it into a rifle that was as handy as those chambered in .223 (right).

Oh, and let's get right to the historical point, that every gun writer mentioned at the unveiling: .30 Remington. The .30 Remington is/was a cartridge designed to be an exact competitor to the .30-30. Since Winchester had developed the .30-30, and it was inexorably linked to the Winchester 1894 lever-action rifle, Remington had to be different. So, when it developed the .30 Remington, it was for the Remington Model 8, an autoloading rifle designed by Browning. (Yes, Browning designed both the 1894, and the competitor's Model 8. He was a genius, and a savvy marketer.)

Since it was made for an autoloading rifle, and later a pump-action rifle, the .30 Remington is rimless. And it is the parent case for the 6.8 Remington SPC, as well as the case head and rim diameter of the 10mm-pistol cartridge. It would seem that no matter where you go, you cannot escape the John Moses Browning legacy.

For those who have let the numbers slide, the ballistics of the .30-30 and the .30 Remington are simple: a 150-grain bullet at 2,200 fps, or a 170-grain bullet at 2,000 fps. Newer loads in the .30-30 exceed those by a small margin, but not much. If you can find .30 Remington ammo, it will work hard to match or exceed those figures.

Anyway, the .30 Remington was a historical cartridge, and one that a lot of older deer hunters (and the inheritors of their rifles) would be familiar with. Naming a new cartridge almost the same would be confusing. The last thing a new cartridge needs is confusion with an existing, even near-obsolete, one.

The starting point for the .30 Remington AR (and let's call it the .30 RAR, just to shorten things) was the .450 Bushmaster, the case for which was itself a development from the .284 Winchester case. By 2008, Remington had conglomerated a number of companies together including DPMS and Bushmaster, both AR makers. The .450 is a large-diameter case, but to make it fit into the AR, Remington had to make the rim a bit smaller than the case diameter. So, the case for the Remington has a rim of .492 of an inch, but the body has a diameter of .500. The .450 Bushmaster case is too long, so they had to shorten it, but that's easy when you are making brass.

The case also has to be quite short, so you can fit the bullet into the case, inside the magazine and have a suitable bullet positioned in the case. But that's part of the reason the .30 RAR is so wide, to maintain case capacity.

This means the magazines can only fit a single stack of cartridges, not the double-stack of the

The short, fat .30 RAR meant magazines were not going to hold a lot of ammo.

original 5.56. Since Remington saw the .30 RAR as a hunting cartridge, and hunting requires a five-round-magazine limit, that wasn't a problem.

The problem was designers overestimated the velocity needed, and the recoil tolerance of their prospective buyers. The factory specs called for a 125-grain bullet at 2,800 fps. Now that might not seem like much. After all, were you going from a .30 Rem to a .30 RAR, you are trading 150s at 2,200 fps (a 330 Power Factor) for 125s at 2,800 (a 350 PF), which isn't much on paper. But, the higher velocity will mean a sharper recoil, and the higher pressure will mean greater muzzle blast. Both of those are off-putting to new shooters.

If you are going to offer a low-recoiling .30-caliber hunting cartridge, you only need a 125-grain bullet at something more like 2,400 fps for effective whitetail performance. That puts your prospective cartridge at the upper end of 7.62x39 performance, and represents a 300 PF. That, as a slightly smaller-diameter case, would have been a wicked-performing hunting rifle, especially if you could make it as light and handy as a Winchester '94, or a Model 8.

If you are trying to lure hunters used to the .30-30, then you might need to be using heavier bullets. A .30 RAR with a bullet of the same weight, and same velocity as the .30-30 would have been an even easier sale. "Like the .30-30, but now with autoloading."

So, an oddball bullet weight for the traditional deer hunter, at a velocity that did not offer less recoil

The .30 RAR rifle we tested at the unveiling was little more than an anvil. No wonder the assorted gun writers were cool on it, at best.

The Remington R-15 rifle for the .30 RAR is a combination of a .223 lower, with a .308 bolt up top.

than traditional hunting rifles. Combine that with a non-traditional appearance, less handiness, and a bit more weight, and it is no wonder that it was unveiled to a resounding yawn.

I was at the Remington PR event where they first showed it to gun writers. The collective shrug of the shoulders we gave it was not expected. The AR-centric shooters looked at the cartridge and thought "Why?" The traditional-cartridge and rifle writers looked at it and asked "What for?" And we all thought "The brass doesn't come from anything we can make, so who wants to load it?"

The rifle they had us testing wasn't a strong point, either. With a mixture of .308- and 5.56-rifle features (the magazine is an AR-15 tube, but the upper receiver is made to fit a .308-sized bolt, to handle the pressure and case rim) the rifle was not exactly handy. With a fixed stock, a stout barrel, and a cylindrical aluminum handguard, it was more of a barge than a speedboat. As the gun writers picked it up, you could see them assessing the handling and balance, and perhaps even comparing it to the last time they handled a handy hunting lever gun or carbine.

All of which explains why it is no longer a Remington rifle, and ammo is not being loaded. If you have one of these rifles, you had best stock up on brass for reloading, because you will have to do that for your shooting and hunting in the future. You cannot make a rifle in .30 Remington AR, because no one besides Remington made bolts for it. You can, however, replace the .30 upper with one chambered in any other AR cartridge, and with the appropriate magazines, use it like any other AR-15.

If you have one, it will work just fine. But there's no future for it.

I did a quick check for ammunition availability. Remington still lists it on its web page. And miracle of miracles, it shows a 150-grain load as well as the initial 125-grain load. This is the Core-Lokt bullet, which is a traditional cup-and-core construction. Nothing wrong with that, it has served perfectly well for a century on deer-sized game. It also shows the .30 RAR in its premier-bullet lines, but with a single load each.

The .30 RAR is not going to wear out barrels anything like a training 5.56 would. With a modest supply of cases, and reloading tools, you can keep a Remington R-15 in .30 RAR running for the rest of the century. Even if Remington stops making ammo for it tomorrow.

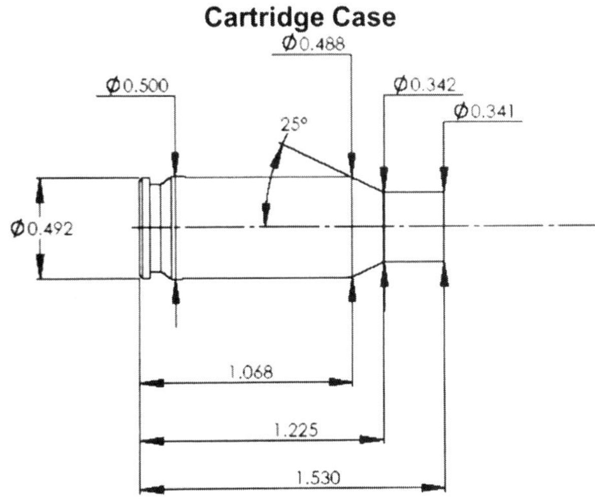

Reloading the .30 RAR is not a big deal, it presents no problem. It is just another bottlenecked rifle cartridge, and reloading will be easy.

Finding ammo is not so easy. A search turned up this outlet with one load, and another outlet with a different load, a third outlet with one of the previous loads, etc. On the good side, the .30 RAR is not the rifle and cartridge you are going to be shooting five-gallon buckets of ammo through, practicing for a match or defense. It is a hunting cartridge. So, if you have 100 or 200 cases (loaded, or fired and ready to load) and the reloading equipment needed, you have a lifetime hunting supply.

Even at a brisk 100 rounds a year of practice and hunting, and even if you only count on five firings per case, you have 10 years of practice and hunting, with 200 cases. If you are considerate of your brass, and get 10 loadings out of each (an easy task) you now have 20 years of hunting with what's on hand. And the barrel will have seen 2,000 rounds, which is essentially nothing. A good barrel, at 100 rounds per year, is going to still be minute-of-whitetail when the 22nd century rolls around.

By then we may well have phased-plasma rifles in the 40-watt range, and might have other problems to deal with than "Is my .30 RAR still suited for hunting?"

14

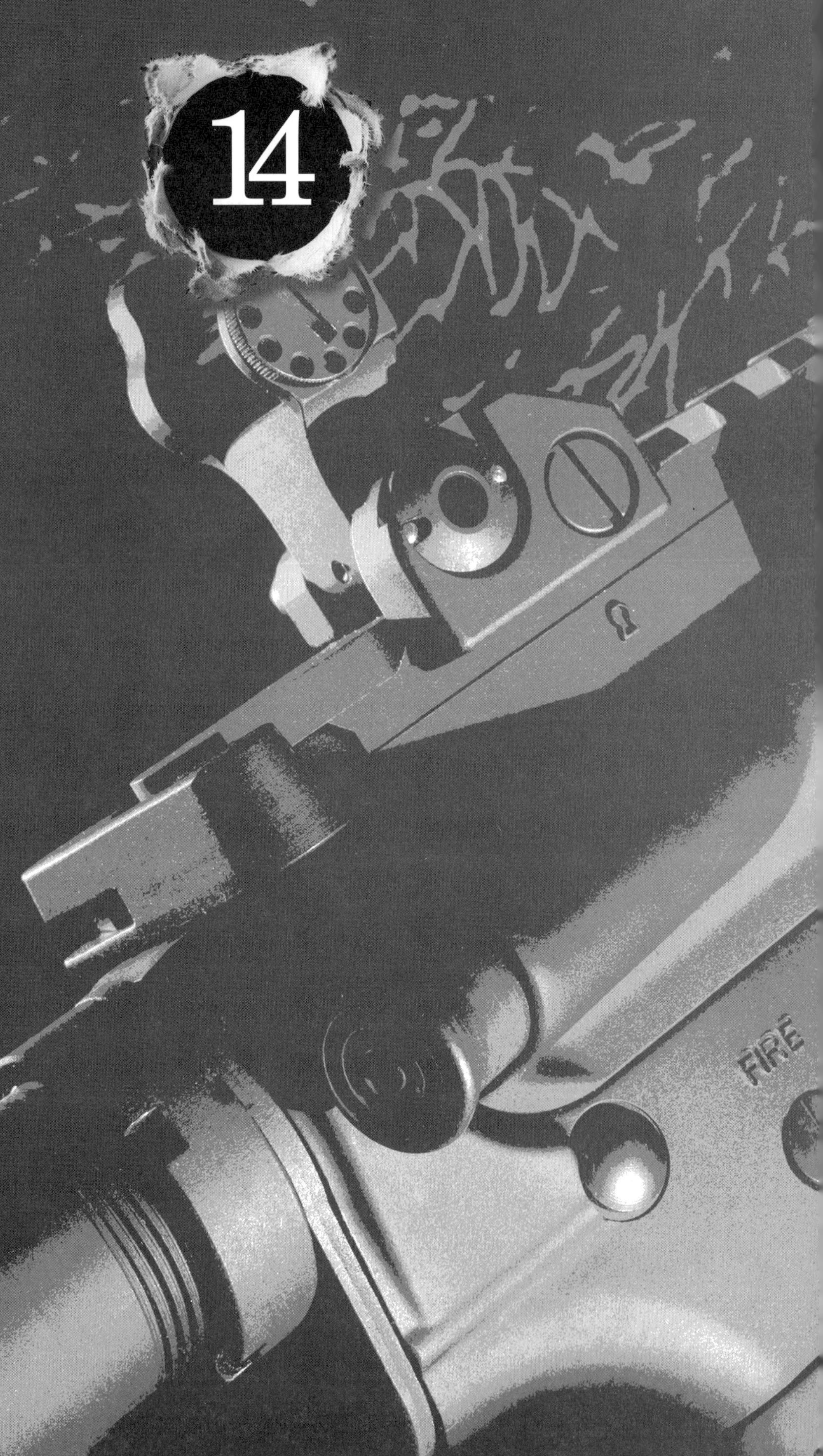

.308 THE REAL DEAL

The AR in .308 is actually the original, and not the AR-15. The origins come from the very early 1950s, when the U.S. Army was looking for a replacement for the M1 Garand. While the Garand had served well (and was much-loved, then and for a long time after) it had its faults. The eight-round en-bloc clip was an all or nothing proposition. You either loaded up with eight, or you didn't. If you were partway down in ammo, you had to jettison the rounds you had, to replace them with another eight-round clip.

Also, the long, unsupported operating rod was prone to bending if you used ammunition with the wrong powder. For the military this wasn't a big problem, but it did mean there were limited (or no) options as far as improving the ammunition was concerned.

We went from the .30-06 (left) in the Garand, to the .308 (center) in the M14, to the 5.56 in the M16 (right) in less than a decade.

So, Ordnance Department officials set about finding a new rifle. One thing they didn't want to change was the terminal performance. Regardless of whatever else they did, they were going to retain the 150-grain, .308 bullet, at something around 2,700 fps. Yes, they were sticking with a powerful, long-range round.

This, despite the experiences of the war that had just happened, when both the Germans and the Soviets had found that what a lot of troopers needed was more ammo, less recoil and 300 yards was the maximum distance desired.

So, despite the Germans having adopted the 7.92x33, and the Soviets adopting the 7.62x39, we stuck with a full-power .30.

What ended up happening was the new rifle was basically an improved Garand, with a 20-round box magazine, a new gas system that was a bit more forgiving of powder selection, (a bit, but not a lot) and a shorter .30-caliber round. While shorter, the new round, the 7.62x51, was not that much less than the .30-06. And it was shorter due to improved powder chemistry and formulation. The new ball powders, with a denser formulation, meant the same weight powder took less volume, and thus a shorter cartridge could deliver as much velocity.

And having adopted it, we were going to force it upon our allies.

Our allies, in the midst of developing their own rifles, rifles with moderate power, lessened recoil and smaller-diameter bullets, were livid. But, since the USA was the big dog of NATO, they had to adopt it. The Germans adopted the G3, pretty much everyone else adopted the FAL. The Germans would have adopted the FAL, but the Belgians were not going to license its manufacture, the Germans had to buy them from FN if they wanted FALs. The Germans weren't going to be treated that way, and went with the roller-lock design, and the G3.

I find it amusing that the Germans were not willing to purchase rifles from their next-door-neighbor, and fellow NATO member, but rather than simply make a knock-off of the FAL, they went with something else entirely.

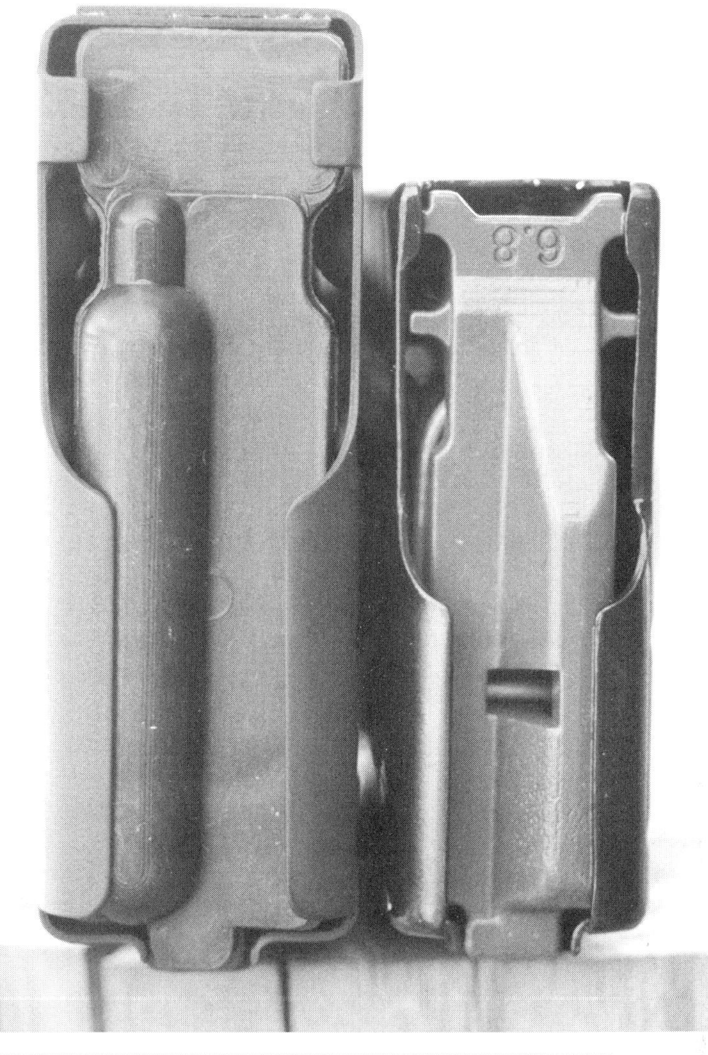

(right) You can see how much bigger the magazine has to be to hold a .308, on the left. The M16 magazine on the right is what everyone is used to now.

(below) Despite the lessons learned in WWII, we stuck with a full-powered cartridge. We just shortened the .30-06 and gave it a new name.

The AR-10 was in development during this fracas, but came along at the end of the adoption of the M14 (the U.S. rifle) and had it been out a few years earlier, it might have had a chance. On second thought, nope. Ordnance Department officials wanted what they wanted, and they were going to get it; and they even went so far as to rig the Arctic tests in order to disqualify the FAL entrants in the testing.

The AR-10 was radically different from all the others, but since it is the origin of the AR-15, you know that. It was adopted in a small way, and a few thousand were made. They ended up being a cult subject all through the 1970s and 1980s, when we were working the bugs out of the AR-15. After all, if you wanted a .308 rifle, but not an M14/M1A, then your choices were really limited: FAL, G3 (in the form of the HK 91and not much else) and the good old Garand. One of those choices was an AR-10 parts kit, built on a new semi-auto AR-10 lower. Not easy back then, when AR-10 lowers were one-at-a-time custom machining operations.

As the problems and details of the AR-15 got

One of the original AR-10s made in the Netherlands. The parts kits from these were what we were building on in the 1980s.

worked out, the desire of the shooting public as a whole over a "must have" .308 rifle faded a bit. And with it crept in the ongoing problem of the AR-10: lack of standardization.

OK, if you want to build an AR-15 in your basement, you can buy all the parts you need, and assemble it yourself. Why? Because everyone who makes parts has to hew to the mil-spec dimensions as best they can. Some of them have the actual blueprints and dimensions, called the Technical Data Package, or TDP. A manufacturer who has the TDP (and this is something you can get only on government contracts, and only if you are making things for the government) tells all. And it is closely held. Even those who hold a TDP and a contract can't just make extras on a government run, and sell them as "mil-spec." I am not privy to the exact details, but there has to be some separation between military work and non-military work.

The number of manufacturers who have actual, real, copies of the TDP (and being found having one, and not having a government contract, is a sure way never to get a contract) can be counted as very few.

Others simply measure 10, 20, 50 parts bought from one of those gold-standard makers, figure out their own drawings and dimensional variances, and then make parts. But the desire is always to fit every and all proper, mil-spec receivers.

That is why in the AR-15 world, "parts is parts." Quality varies, but the dimensions are held closely enough that they all work.

Not so with the AR-10. There never was a TDP for the AR-10. The Dutch-made guns are not of help, because there were so few made, and when they got rebuilt decades ago, there's no telling what was "adjusted" where to make each one work. Four sample rifles made 60 years ago, and used who-knows-how-much, are not a statistically valid sample to build a blueprint from.

When it came time for each AR-15 manufacturer to build and offer for sale a .308 version, they had to pretty much do it all themselves. Now, makers such as Knight's could pull an original AR-10 off the wall, copy it, test and improve it, and then offer it for sale to the government. Hence the M110 sniper rifle you can find photos of.

But, having done that, Knight's isn't going to let just anyone else see the blueprints or working drawings. Not just because they see no point in giving away all that work and knowledge, but also because it is a product purchased by the government. They can't give the info away; the contract forbids it.

The details matter. For instance, unless you have a drawer full of like-new magazines, how would you know what dimensions the magazines require? Designing magazines from scratch is hard work. Having a magazine manufacturer make them is expensive, especially if you are still in the R&D stage and aren't exactly sure what the magazine needs to be. And again, 60-plus-year-old samples aren't of much use.

As a result, when you, the end-user, the shooter, decide to go to a .308 rifle, an AR-10, you are locking yourself into a given ecological niche. Like buying lenses for your camera, once you're in one system, it

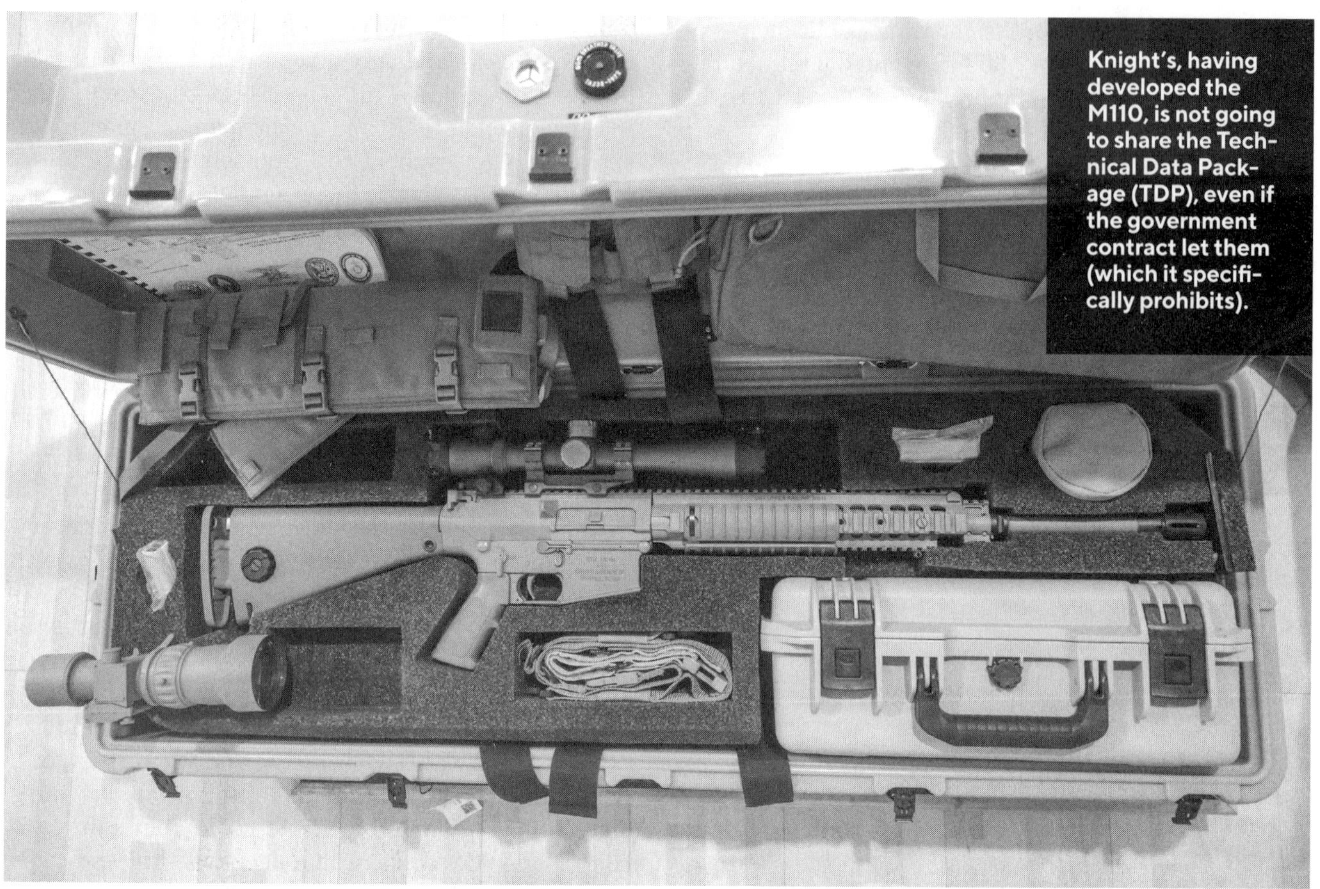

Knight's, having developed the M110, is not going to share the Technical Data Package (TDP), even if the government contract let them (which it specifically prohibits).

isn't easy to use equipment, parts or all accessories from another. Need a replacement .308 barrel? You have to buy one from the rifle maker of your rifle.

Magazines? Oh my. The originals were copied by Knight's for the M110. Then, they were copied again by DPMS, and you can find magazines that are "DPMS pattern." When Armalite (the modern company, not the original, 1950s maker) decided to make an AR-10, it took a different path. Armalite modified M14 magazines to work in an AR-10 lower, called the AR-10B. At the time, this was a clever approach. M14 magazines were common and inexpensive.

To give you an idea, when I was still in my own .308 phase, I had a match-conditioned M1A I was shooting in matches. I got a flier for a magazine sale for M14 magazines. New, in the wrapper, $4.99 each. New, unwrapped, $3.99 each. Used, serviceable magazines, $2.99 each. Even just a short time after, I wished I had bought a whole lot more of them.

So, Armalite could buy literal truckloads of M14 magazines for not much, alter them, re-Parkerize them, and offer them with its AR-10B rifle.

Rock River Arms took a different tack. For a similar while, a decade after my M14 magazine episode, FAL magazines were dirt-cheap. Even less expensive than the M14 magazines I had bought. Rock River thus designed and built an AR-10 rifle that used FAL magazines. I did not have an FAL at the time, or I would have filled the trunk of my car with surplus FAL mags.

A new magazine company showed up, called Magpul. At first, it offered only AR-15 magazines, then AK-47 magazines, but once it had the details worked out, and it had customers asking, Magpul began making AR-10 magazines that fit the DPMS/M110 pattern. The magazines follow the original AR-10/DPMS dimensions well enough that they will work in those, but what Magpul ended up doing was establishing the new standard for AR-10 magazines, and to a small extent the rifles for them.

If you have a modern-built AR-10, odds are it will work just fine with a Magpul or a Lancer (another new magazine maker) magazine. Older rifles, there's no telling until you try. Still, with the AR-10, you test, and you keep the magazines with the rifles they like to work with, and do not swap them around.

On the rest of the rifle, there are a few other areas of commonality. Almost all will work with regular AR-15 stocks. On the outside, not the inside, more on that. Most will work with regular AR-15 trigger parts or packet triggers, the drop-in kind. The top rail is mil-spec Picatinny rail dimension, simply because no one is stupid enough to make something proprietary, and lock their customers out of the wide-open optics market.

But handguards? That depends on the barrel nut and the barrel, and those are proprietary. Bolts and bolt carriers? Ditto. Thank goodness muzzle threads are common, but that is more because the suppressor makers would revolt if someone used something different.

So, in summary, when you decide to go Ten, as in AR-10, you are going to be in a particular .308 or .308-based rifle environment, and you won't be able to swap willy-nilly when it comes to upper, lower and parts.

Yes, that's the last bit of relatively unpleasant news: Unlike the AR-15, where you can swap uppers and lowers between brands, you can't do that with .308s. Now, it might be possible, but it would be a case-by-case basis, and there would be no guarantees. If Brand X .308 upper and Brand Y lower happened to fit, and even work, there's no guarantee the next X and Y pair you try will fit. And AR-10 maker Z? Cross your fingers and try the fit before you buy.

Nope, you buy an AR-10, you are working on that one, and that one only, for the future.

However, let's look at a few, and the options.

THE RECEIVER LINEUP, THEN AND NOW

Back in the beginning, or the 'aughts as some call them (the 2000 to 2009 period) we had three types of receiver setups. We had the Armalite (and they split with the change from M14 mags) the DPMS LR-308 and the Rock River LAR-308. Now, who can keep track?

Most are more-or-less DPMS-compatible, but you have to be careful. Some will have the top rail of the receiver higher than the DPMS receivers, while being compatible in things like barrel shank size and pins locations.

Later ones, like the Mega Arms were as compatible as manufacturing tolerances permitted. (Some hand-fitting might be called for.)

ARMALITE, OLD SCHOOL

The Armalite AR-10 of the 21st century first used modified M14 magazines. Since then, with the universal adoption of the Magpul magazines, Armalite

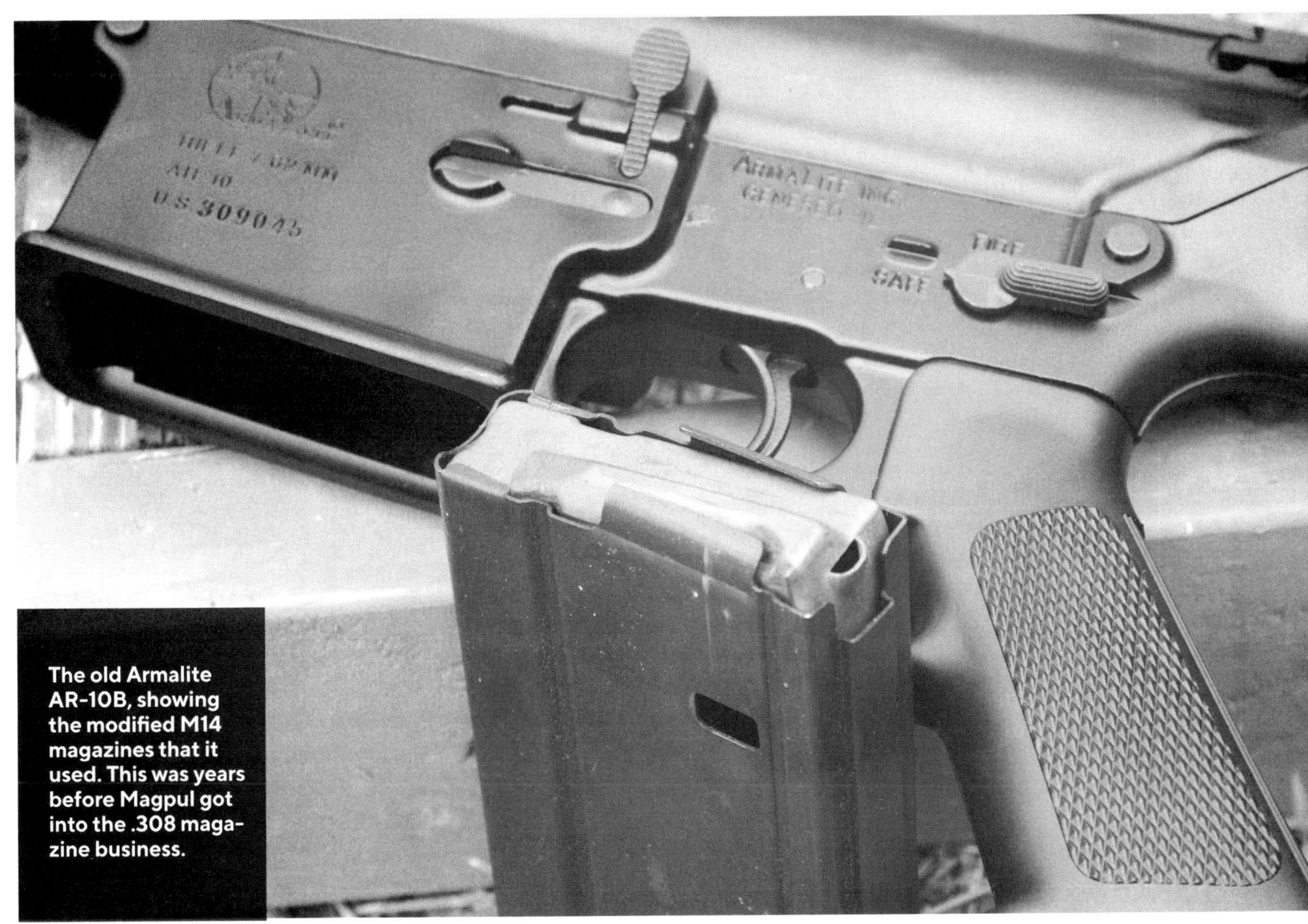

The old Armalite AR-10B, showing the modified M14 magazines that it used. This was years before Magpul got into the .308 magazine business.

has changed its rifle to work with Magpuls. But the old rifles still work, even though they can only work with modified magazines. The handguard and delta ring assembly use a proprietary thread pitch, so you'll have to specify that to whomever you get updated handguards from.

And, just to make things more difficult, the height of the handguard varies from Armalites to others.

S&W, NEW SCHOOL

The S&W M&P 10, an AR-10 descendant, is pretty universal. It uses Magpul magazines, but it does have a proprietary buffer. Buffers are not such a big deal on the AR-10, because there just aren't as many options to building. For example, not many people want to build themselves a 10-inch AR-10 pistol.

When ordering parts, just make sure you use the pull-down menu, or tell the order-taker "I have an M&P AR-10" and they will make sure you get the correct parts.

Not only is the M&P 10 clearly marked as such, you'll notice it has ambidextrous controls. That's part of the many improvements that have come about in the last half century in the AR world.

An S&W M&P-10, being wrung out on a damp and brisk November morning.

ROCK RIVER, COOL SCHOOL

Rock River has made AR-10 rifles using the FAL magazine, proprietary RRA magazines and now Magpuls. Getting accessories isn't a problem because Rock River makes all of them for its own rifles. You can hardly come up with a configuration you'd want, that RRA doesn't list as its own. Which is good, because most aftermarket makers have focused on other brands.

A Rock River back when the company was building on the FAL magazines. If you have one, keep using it, because it runs like a champ.

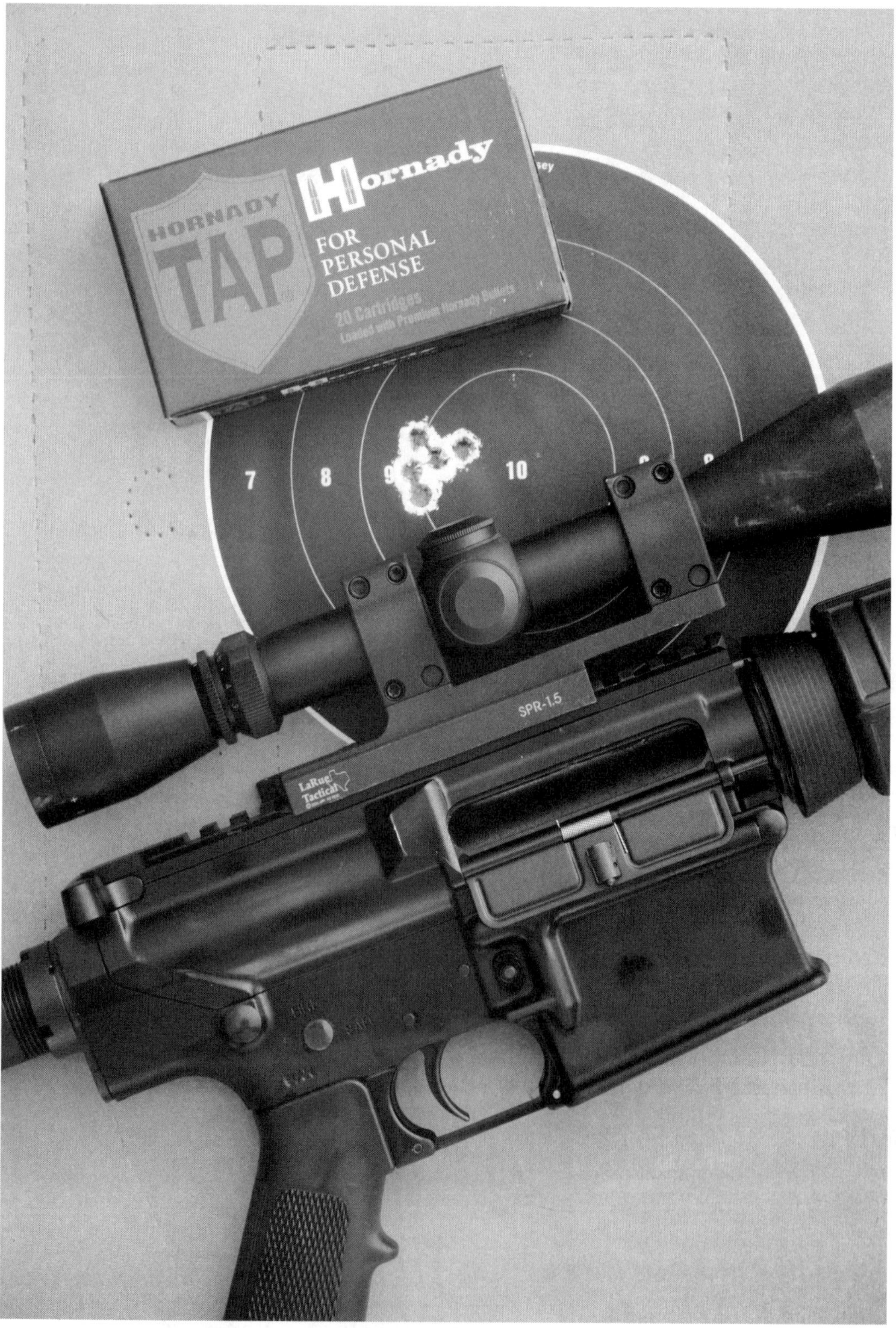

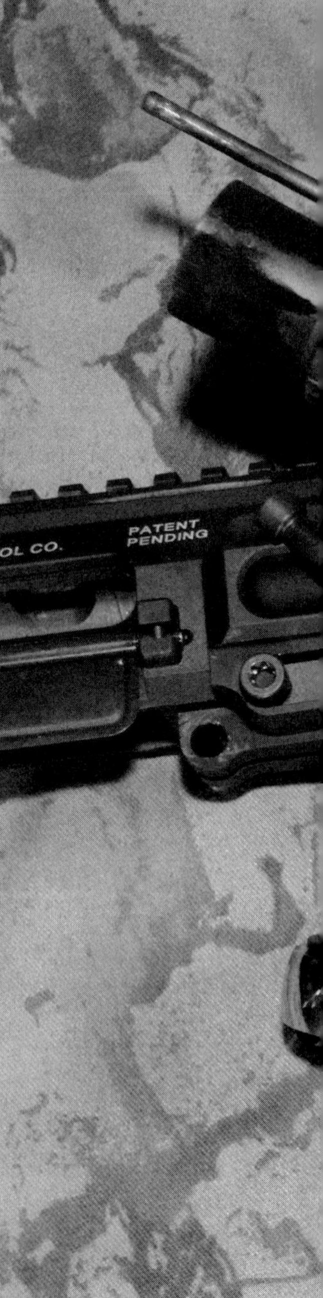

LMT, TACTI-SCHOOL

LMT has a leg up on the others in that it has actually sold .308 rifles to military organizations for use. LMT rifles are engineered like bridges, and some might say about as heavy. Two details LMT has in spades over the other designs are: a one-piece upper receiver, and easy-swap barrels.

LMT pioneered, and patented, the upper receiver that was also a handguard. One piece of aluminum. The barrel swap is accomplished by using two larger bolts crossways through the integral upper, passing through notches in the barrel. Loosen and remove the bolts, then pull out the barrel. Stuff in a new one, install and tighten the bolts, and you're good to go.

Now, the overly tacti-cool set views this as a way to carry a sniper-length barrel on the way to an objective, then change to a CQB-length barrel on arrival. Morons. The real advantage is that worn barrels don't require the whole rifle be sent back to depot-level workplaces, to be re-barreled. The unit can simply have new barrels sent along with the water, food and ammo coming on the next chopper or truck. And they can swap it themselves.

The rest of us can easily change an LMT chambered in .308 to one chambered in 6.5 Creedmoor. Or back the other way.

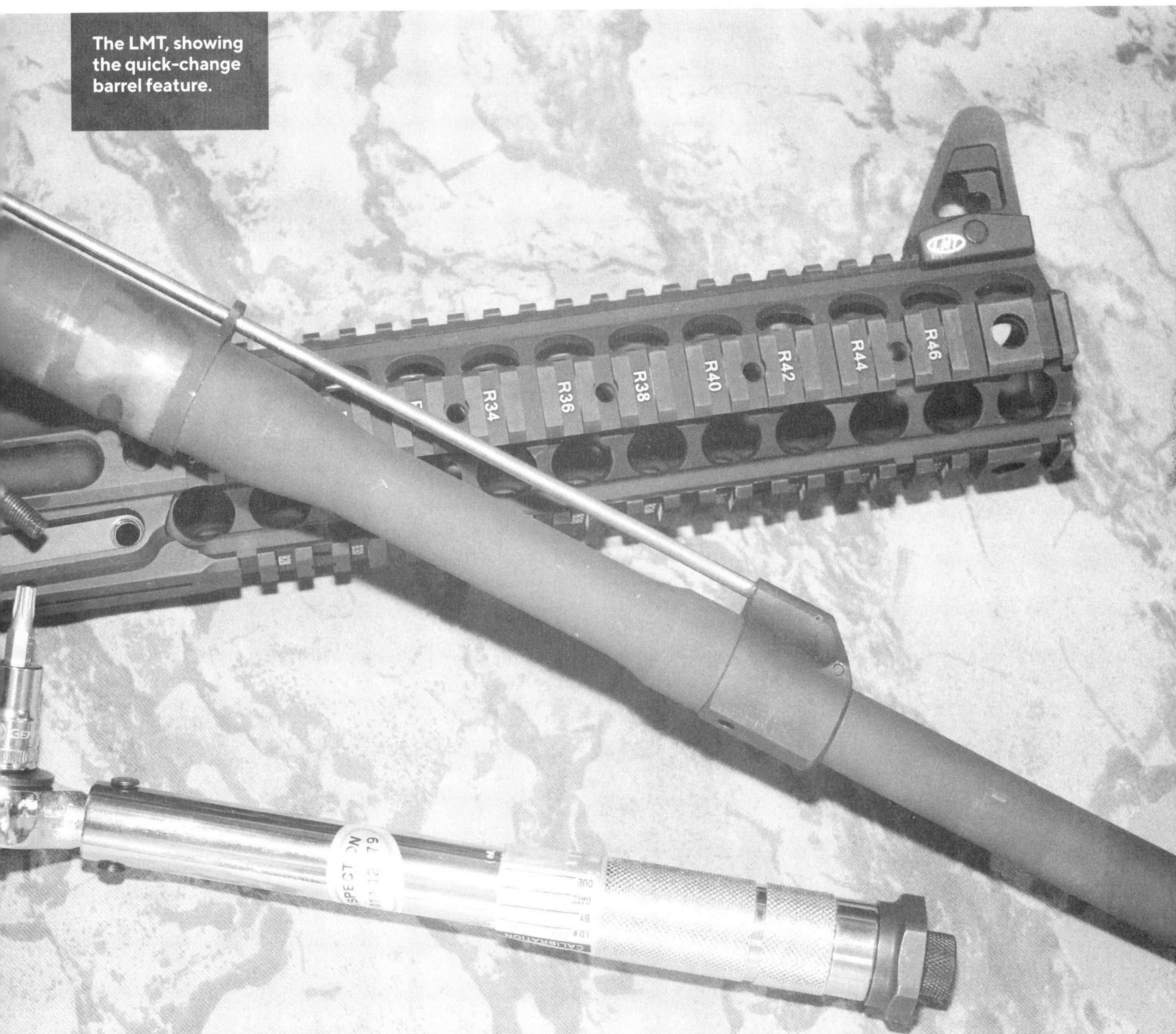

The LMT, showing the quick-change barrel feature.

Bill Wilson went all-in on an AR-10, and since he makes all the major parts himself, he makes them the way he wants them to be made. As in, excellently.

WILSON COMBAT

Bill Wilson went all-in on an AR-10, and since he makes all the major parts himself, he makes them the way he wants them to be made. As in, excellently. No forgings for him, his are made from pre-hardened billets of aluminum, and since he's doing that, he can sculpt them any way he wants.

Plus, you have your choice of .308, 6.5 Creedmoor, 6mm Creedmoor and who knows what else.

The Wilson Combat AR-10, this one in .308.

COLT

Yes, Colt made/makes/who knows an AR chambered in 7.62x51. It offered it as a modified AR-10, with several interesting features, such as the .308/7.62 had a sleeved/changeable lower, so you could use the same lower with an AR-15 upper in 5.56 or .300. Colt calls it the Modular Carbine, and the original 7.62 chambering is not listed, instead it is now shown as a 6.5 Creedmoor firearm.

Colt being Colt, there's no telling if it is actually in production, or in inventory, if you want one. But if you do, and one is available, the price is attractive enough that you probably should just jump on it.

(right) You can tell the Colt .308 by the funky lower receiver magazine well shape.

(below) The Ruger SR762 bolt and carrier, showing the piston shoulder.

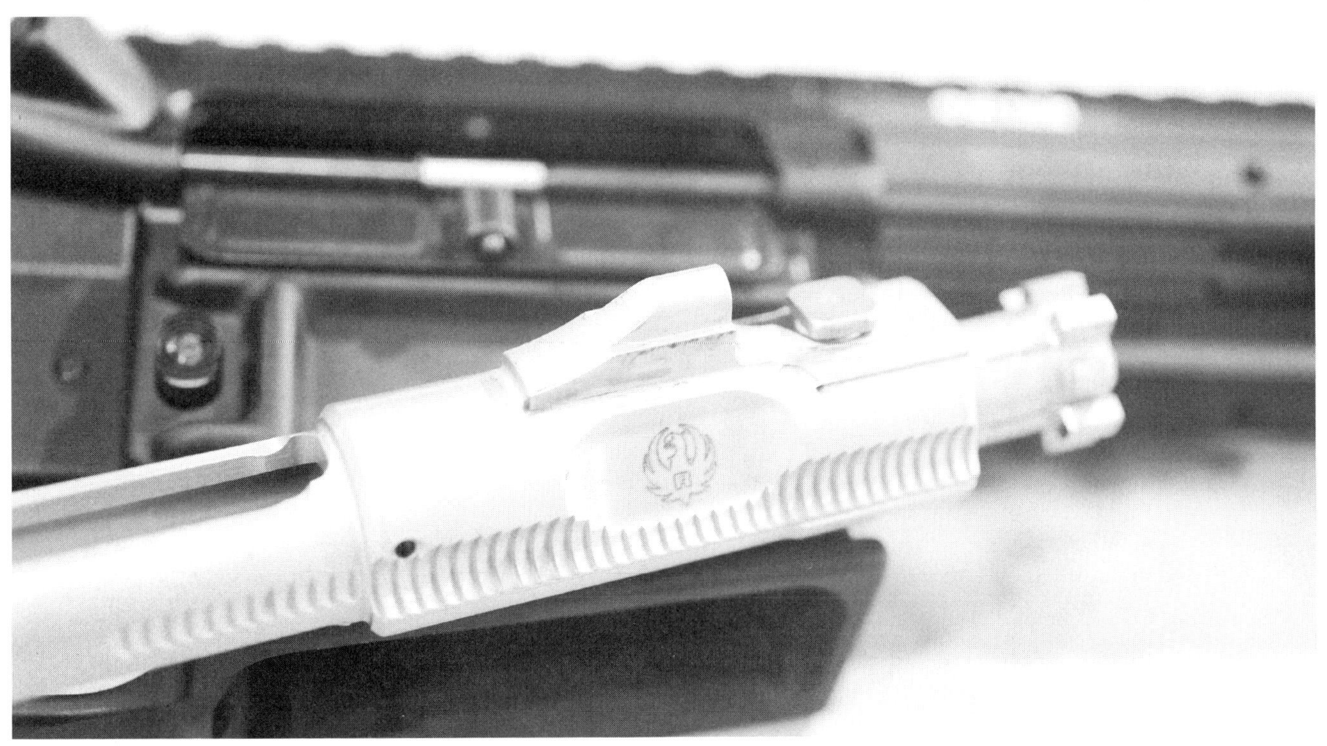

RUGER

Yes, Ruger. If you had said, when I was learning the gunsmithing trade, that one day Ruger would be making not just hi-cap 9mm pistols, but also ARs and suppressors, I would have snorted coffee out of my nose. And laughed myself silly as well.

But no, the Ruger SR762 is a ready-to-go .30 AR rifle, and you can have it once you find one. Ruger discontinued it as of the writing of this book, but there are plenty out there. It is a piston gun, unlike a lot of the others which are DI, or gas guns. As a bonus, the gas system is adjustable, one thing piston guns can offer that DI guns cannot.

The Ruger SR762 and its adjustable gas system.

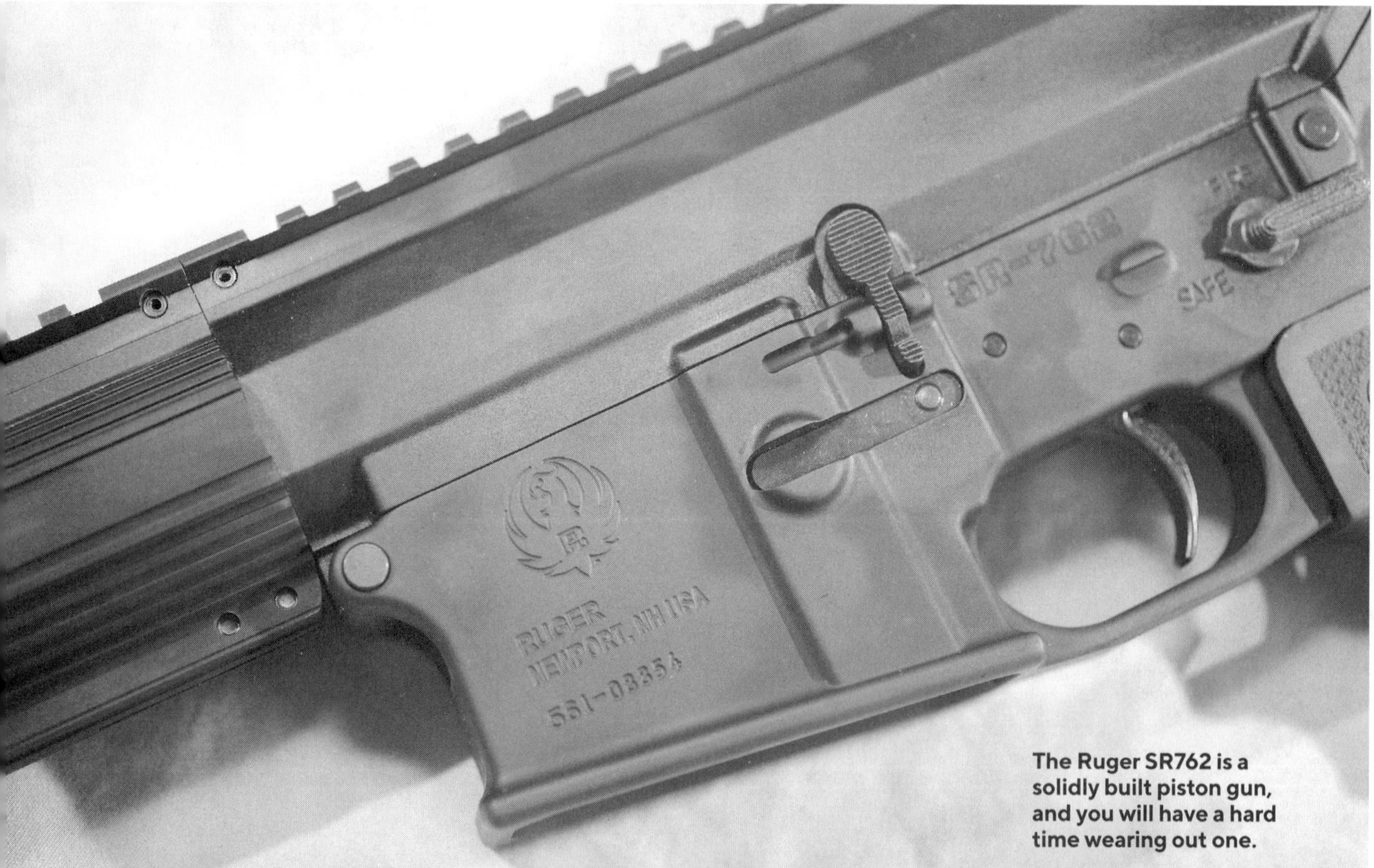

The Ruger SR762 is a solidly built piston gun, and you will have a hard time wearing out one.

LARUE

The LaRue OBR is a fully featured, DI rifle that you can have in .308, 6.5 Creedmoor or .260 Remington. Yes, LaRue, the maker of scope mounts, also offers complete uppers as well as complete rifles. Mark LaRue, being Mark LaRue, will not make anything that isn't the best that can be made, so if you fancy yourself a good shot, then you need to try a LaRue.

PATRIOT ORDNANCE FACTORY

Frank DeSomma, at Patriot Ordnance Factory (POF), makes excellent rifles; and he is more than willing to push the boundaries of engineering and design. One such detail is the bolt cam on his rifles. He designed and uses a roller-bearing system, to reduce friction. That's the sort of incremental improvement the DoD would have been doing for the last half-century, if the people in charge actually knew anything about small arms. I'd be happy to list Frank's rifles, but he improves them at such a fast clip that the list would be out of date before this book got to print. Just know that he makes really good rifles, and you can't go wrong with a POF choice.

BOLTS AND CARRIERS

Fuggedaboudit. If you have a given receiver set, and a barrel that works with them, then you stick with the bolt and carrier of that receiver set. That is, S&W with S&W, RRA with RRA, you get the idea. There is no guarantee of interoperability whatsoever here. None.

(above) Here's a POF .308, with all of the improvements Frank DeSomma had to offer when it was made. Since then there have been more.

(left) A POF bolt carrier. You'll notice this is for a piston gun. Also notice the roller bearing on the cam pin head.

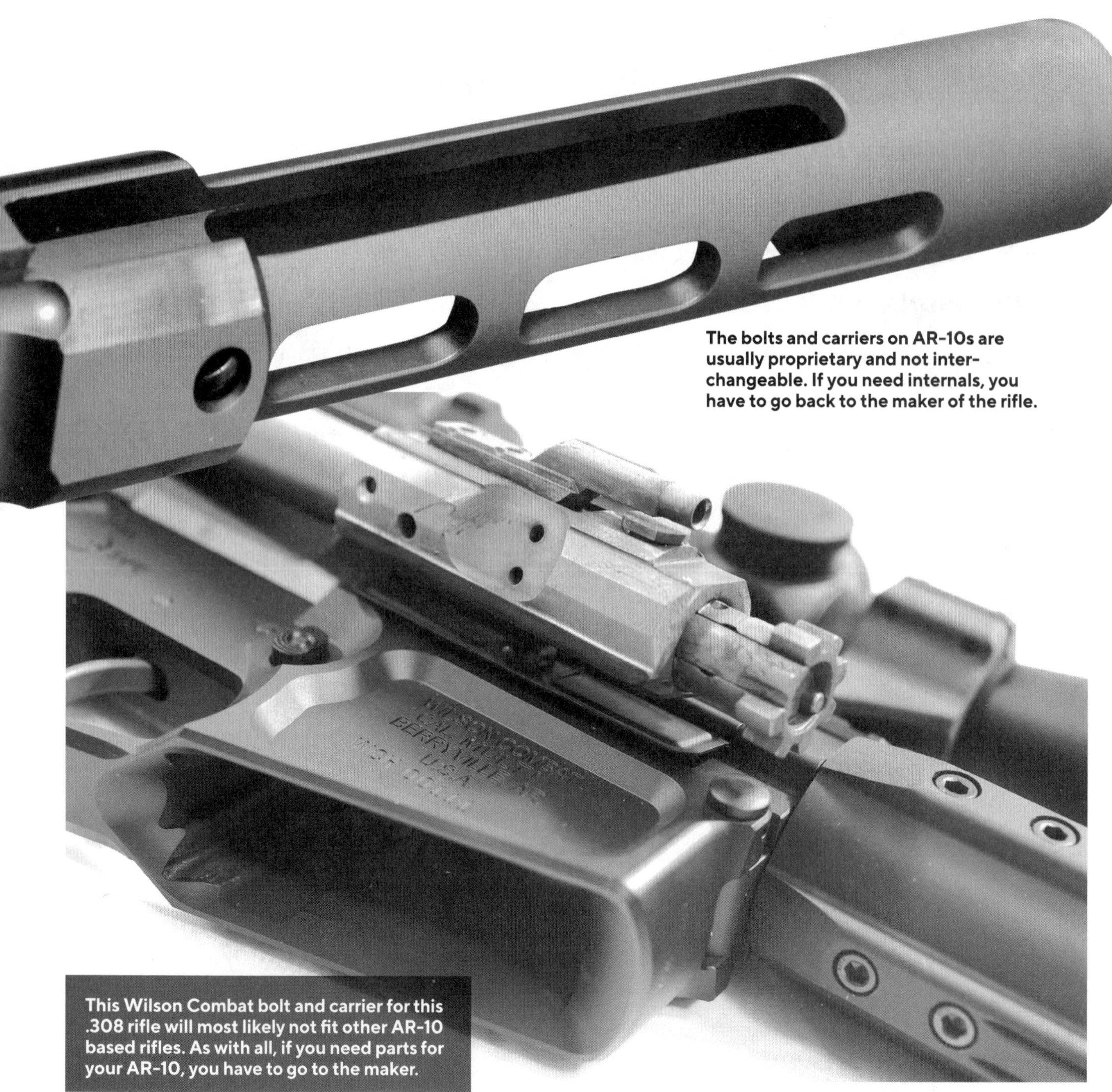

The bolts and carriers on AR-10s are usually proprietary and not interchangeable. If you need internals, you have to go back to the maker of the rifle.

This Wilson Combat bolt and carrier for this .308 rifle will most likely not fit other AR-10 based rifles. As with all, if you need parts for your AR-10, you have to go to the maker.

BARRELLS AND BARREL NUTS

Mostly we have the DPMS shank, but even there small manufacturing differences can matter. If a company makes a "DPMS compatible" barrel, but it makes the diameter half a thousandth or a thousandth larger than your receiver, you are out of luck.

As with other parts, you get the barrel the receiver-set maker offers, or you have a custom barrel maker fit the new one. Unless you are lucky, and the new one is indeed a drop-in replacement for the old.

The barrel has to be locked in with the barrel nut. Here we have a divergence of opinion. Armalite went with an 18-tpi nut, and DPMS went with a 16-tpi nut. (Grrr.) And these are just the threads on the receiver. The length of the nut, its fit to the receiver and handguard, these are all subject to manufacturers differences of opinion and design. If the setup is supposed to work, but doesn't, it might not be anyone's fault. Such is life.

Just when you thought it was safe, the issue of gas tubes comes up. The Armalite system uses a gas tube that is almost three-eighths of an inch longer than the rest of the AR-verse, so if you go Armalite you

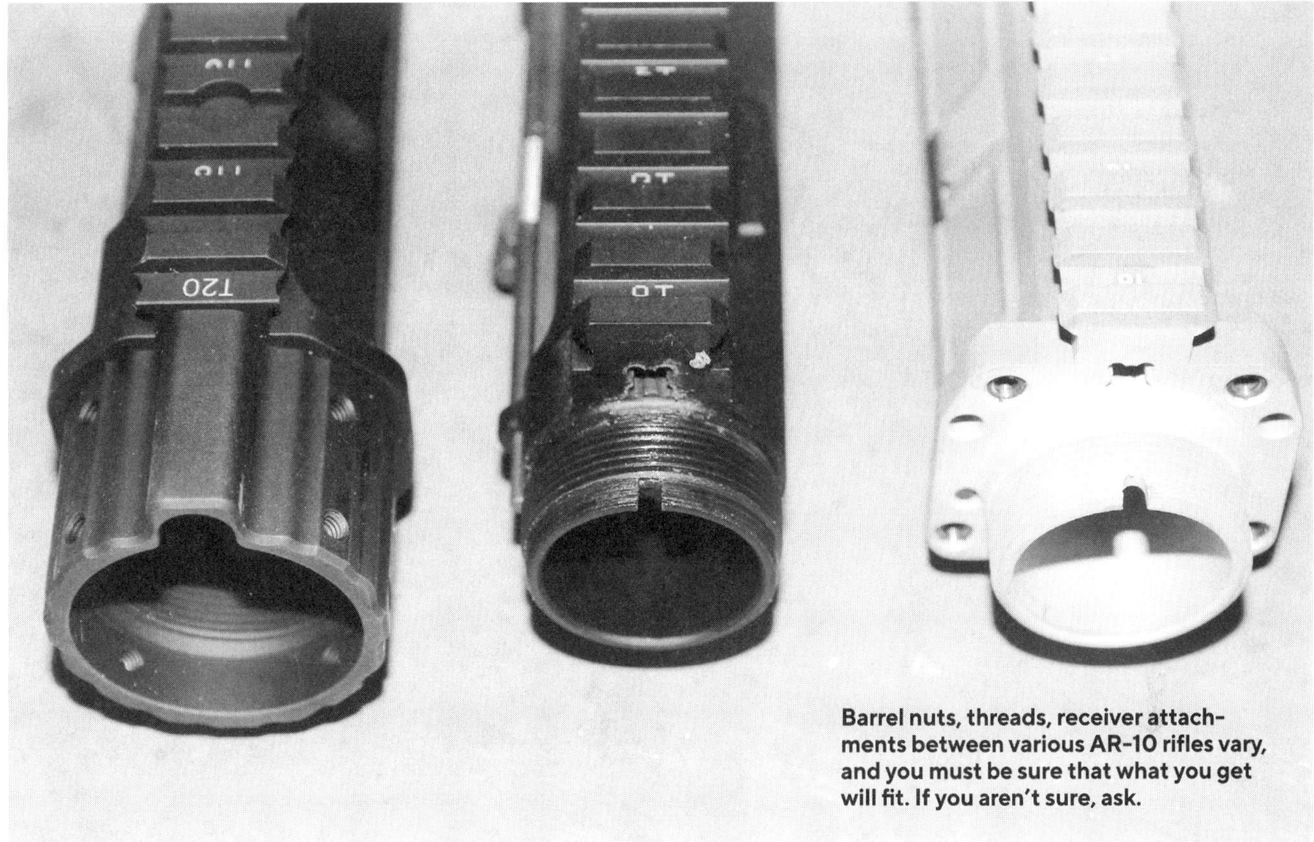

Barrel nuts, threads, receiver attachments between various AR-10 rifles vary, and you must be sure that what you get will fit. If you aren't sure, ask.

must use Armalite tubes. The rest are a pretty much everything fits setup, but you can't be entirely sure until you try.

BUFFERS, TUBE SPRINGS AND WEIGHTS

This is where things get even worse, if you can believe it. While a lot of AR-10 carbines use a buffer tube that is either the military dimension or the commercial, inside is a mess. The two diameters are 1.146 inches (more or less, it can easily vary .001) for the mil-spec and 1.168 inches for the commercial. This is important to know for reasons of fitting a new tele-stock slider on your carbine. If you want a Magpul, VLTOR or any other, you have to know if you have a mil-spec or commercial tube. Some of the commercial tubes have a slanted rear, but not all.

This is easy to measure, you just need a caliper, dial or digital.

Inside, every system has its own spring weight, number of coils, buffer weight and size, and you can't swap them without knowing in detail which one your AR needs.

And just to make things even more of a problem, the length a particular AR-10 system needs for its buffer tube might differ from the AR-15 as well. If a given carbine needs more length for the longer carrier to cycle, then installing a standard AR-15 buffer tube on it (assuming it fits the threads of the AR-10, will be setting yourself up for disappointment.

If you use a too-short buffer tube, because "they are all the same," then the carrier will bottom out inside the tube, banging the spring fully collapsed, slamming the weight of the carrier, buffer and spring onto the rear face of the tube interior. Something will break.

STEPPING BACK IN TIME

And if you just have to have a better-than-.308, but can't give up the .308, then Noreen Firearms can make you a long-action AR-10, chambered in .30-06, .270 or .25-06. I have to wonder just how far we can stretch the AR platform, and still call it an AR.

CALIBERS

OK, the first, original, and the one most desired for a long time: .308, aka 7.62x51, aka 7.62 NATO. The cartridge came about as the U.S. Army was updating its equipment, post-WWII. Type-named by Winchester, and approved by SAAMI in 1952, it was the cartridge that was adopted (forced by us) by NATO in 1954, as the 7.62x51mm T65.

The military still uses the M110 rifle, but it is being replaced as the originals wear out, and the military finally realizes there have been a veritable host of improvements since the M110 was bought. Photo by: Marine Corps Lance Cpl. Kyle Bunyi.

Split like the later .223/5.56, the .308/7.62 pairing is not like the smaller cartridge, in that they are each safe in the other, gas-port considerations aside. Some hunting loads, using slower-burning powders, might not be all that satisfactory in a gas-driven military rifle chambered for 7.62 NATO. The solution is simple: Find what works and stick with it. If something doesn't work, don't use it.

Yes, the old "Doctor, it hurts when I do this" joke applies here.

The standard military loading for the round is the M80, with a 147-grain FMJ-BT bullet at approximately 2,700 fps. More from longer barrels, but a lot of AR-10s are seen with 16-inch barrels, and that cuts down velocity. The real-deal military load uses what is called a "bi-metal" bullet. Basically, it is a steel-jacketed bullet with a gilding metal (copper and zinc, 95- to 5-percent, respectively) layer on top. This is so the bullet will still engage the rifling on belt-fed machine guns, when the barrel is so hot it is glowing. No, I kid you not. For the rest of us, it makes the real-deal M80 load one that can't be used on steel targets, as it is just too hard on the plates.

Match ammo, sniper-rifle ammo, is not like the vanilla-grade M80; it is precise, accurate and wonderful ammo.

There was also the problem NATO had with the loadings various arsenals used. OK, the M14 has a more-or-less self-regulating gas-piston system. On the M14/M1A, you leave it alone and you feed it what it likes. The FAL has a piston, but it is user-adjustable. You can dial the gas system to work with pretty much anything. The West German G3 used a delayed-blowback roller-locked system that didn't care one whit about gas ports, only the pressure curve and bolt thrust.

I have a stash of ammo from Radway Green. Marked RG 69, it was loaded by the British arsenal Radway Green, in obviously, 1969. I bought it long enough ago that surplus ammo was an actual, real thing. And this is surplus. It is also so lightly loaded that my M1A won't cycle with it. My FALs will, because I can dial their gas systems. My CETME will, because gas port pressure is nothing they care about. (The CETME is a Spanish-made G3, for all intents and purposes.)

The West German G3 and the Spanish CETME are pretty much the same, even though parts usually don't interchange. Using a roller-lock system, these rifles don't care one whit about port pressure, because there isn't any port.

The British didn't care, they could tune their FALs to cycle with whatever the arsenal produced. Just adjust the gas system. The Germans didn't care, because the G3 only cared about "area under the curve" the work the gas pressure curve produced. Of course, the cost for that was obnoxious recoil and brass often flung into the next zip code.

Even when the .308/7.62 NATO was king of the hill, the NATO armies had problems keeping the rifles all working with whatever arsenals produced. Don't expect your AR-10 to be any easier.

The recoil is marked on the 7.62 NATO. A 147-grain bullet at 2,700 fps produces a Power Factor of 397, where a 5.56 out of a carbine, with a 55-grain bullet at 2,900 fps is a 159 PF. The 62-grain M855, aka "green tip," has the same felt recoil as the 55-grain bullet.

That recoil was a big part of why the other militaries of the world left their similar to the .30-06 ballistic, for something lighter. (The .30-06 and the .308 are so similar in felt recoil, there's really no difference.) One big advantage of the M16 (besides the lighter weight of the rifle itself) was the decreased recoil.

The .308/7.62 is still highly thought of, but it is losing ground to other cartridges. In historical order:

.243 WINCHESTER

Winchester necked down the .308 to the .243 bullet diameter only a few years after introducing the parent case. This was to produce a dual-use cartridge. With heavy bullets (for the bore diameter) it was a light-recoiling deer cartridge. It would replace the .250-3000 and a host of other medium-bore hunting cartridges.

With lighter bullets, it would be a long-range varmint cartridge.

I suppose there were those who shot varmints

No military organization I have heard of ever considered the 7-08 as a replacement cartridge for any use. But as a hunting cartridge, it works very well.

with a .243 instead of something even faster, like a .22-250, but where the .243 really caught on was for deer hunting As a "ladies rifle" for deer hunting, rifle makers made and sold tons of them. Many went into the fields not in the hands of ladies or kids, but manly men who didn't like being beaten-up with recoil when hunting.

Rock River Arms lists its LAR-8M as being chambered in .243, in case you want something not a 6.5 Creedmoor or .308 Winchester. It is shown with a 20-inch barrel. If I was going to build an AR for hunting, for use by someone who was a bit sensitive to recoil, I'd rather it was a 16-inch barrel, to make it handily shorter with the suppressor I'd put on it. But that's just me.

7-08

This is simply the .308 case necked to accommodate a 7mm bullet. The 7mm bullet, if it has the same weight as a .308 bullet, will have a higher BC, and thus better long-range retained velocity. If you instead decrease the 7mm bullet weight until it has the same BC as a .308 bullet, then you have decreased recoil.

No military organization I have heard of ever considered the 7-08 as a replacement cartridge for any use. But as a hunting cartridge, it works very well.

.260 REMINGTON

Brought forth by Remington in 1997, the .260 was simply the .308 necked down to accept 6.5mm bullets, aka .264. Why not the ".264 Remington"? No idea. This was to make a moderate-recoiling hunting cartridge that took advantage of the high BCs of 6.5mm bullets.

I first heard of this hunting and long-range-target cartridge being used in practical shooting competition to make Major in scoring. And, interestingly enough, it was used in FAL rifles for this, because that experimental era was early enough that reliable and available AR-10 rifles were still the rarity.

Since then, the calibers used in practical shooting has diverged. In the regular divisions of 3-gun and Multi-gun, the minimum cartridge allowed is 5.45x39. Which means, here in the USA, 5.56 is it. Unlike in handguns, where the scoring of Major is so advantaged over Minor that no one shoots Minor when there is a Major option, in rifles it is the opposite. You don't get enough of an advantage with Major rifle scoring to make it competitive to 5.56.

And in the divisions made for the big bore, Heavy Metal Scope and Heavy Metal Tactical, you have to use a .308.

6.5 CREEDMOOR

This is the big one. Unlike the .260 Remington, the 6.5 Creedmoor, when it was developed by Hornady, was brought about not as a simple necked-down .308 case. The dimensions of the Creedmoor were adjusted to take into account everything that was known about wringing accuracy from a cartridge. Also, to make it as reliably feeding in autoloading rifles as possible. And to position the case neck and shoulder in the exact place that allowed the use of high-BC 6.5mm bullets.

As a result, it is now the cartridge used in PRS, the Precision Rifle Series. This is long-range target shooting on unknown distances, in non-standardized steel plate arrays. The competitors have to hike to each firing position with all their gear, find, range and shoot the plates, then pack up and move on. It is all scored.

Faced with odd distances, you'd think the hottest, flattest-trajectory load would be best. And it would, except you have to haul that rifle, and put up with its recoil, for the match.

The 6.5 Creedmoor is soft-shooting, flat-shooting enough, and easy to pack.

As a bonus, U.S. Army officials are considering adopting a 6.5mm cartridge. They, of course, are doing it the stupid way, and insisting on something with the ballistic performance of a hot-loaded 6.5-284 Norma, or even a 6.5 WSSM, were there such a thing. They want a high-BC bullet at 3,000 fps.

(opposite) LMT has figured out how to make an accurate and durable .308 for military use. It should not be too much of a problem for LMT to adapt this to 6.5 Creedmoor, once the DoD gets back to making rational decisions.

SPR-1.5
PATENT
PENDING
LEWIS MACHINE & TOOL CO.
LMT
FRONT FOCAL ILLUMINATED

But shooting for speed against the pro shooters, I needed an advantage. I found that if I pulled the bullets from Winchester 150-grain hunting ammo, and loaded 125-grain spire points, the rifle cycled 100 percent. This process is called making "Mexican match" ammo. The recoil was markedly lighter, and I managed to place first as an amateur in the 5-Gun standings.

I suspect that once recoil, barrel life, muzzle blast and ammunition weights are taken into consideration, the Army decision-makers will be settling on a standard, the 6.5 Creedmoor. They will then declare that the "new" 6.5 doesn't offer enough of a performance increase over the 5.56 and will decline to spend the billion dollars it would take to switch rifles. They've only done the same thing 10 or 12 times since they adopted the M16 back in 1966.

AR-10 AND AMMO CHOICES

OK, the first thing you have to be aware of when you decide to start feeding your AR-10 is this: Ammo isn't all just ammo.

Things weren't too bad back in the early days. There weren't that many powders to choose from, and the gas system of the M14 (our military rifle of the time) was reasonably adaptable when it came to those powders. However, our allies were not so situated. The piston of the M14 (aka M1A) is a hollow rod, one end closed, with a slot down the side. The slot corresponds to the gas port of the barrel. Once

The HK G3 (these made in Turkey, for the Turkish army) has one strong point: It really doesn't care about port pressure or pressure curves. As long as the work done by the powder is within operating parameters, the G3 is going to cycle.

the gas flows, it moves the piston, and when the piston slot has moved far enough, the end of the slot closes off gas flow from the gas port.

So, within the burn rate spread of the midrange powders available in the 1950s, the M14 could adapt. Even in the early 1990s it could do all right. I shot the 1991 Steel Challenge 5-Gun World Championships with my Springfield Armory M1A. It was built entirely with mil-surplus parts except for the receiver. I accurized it according to the USAMTU guide, and it produced one-hole groups at 100 yards. But shooting for speed against the pro shooters, I needed an advantage. I found that if I pulled the bullets from Winchester 150-grain hunting ammo, and loaded 125-grain spire points, the rifle cycled 100 percent.

This process is called making "Mexican match" ammo. The recoil was markedly lighter, and I managed to place first as an amateur in the 5-Gun standings.

The AR-10 might have managed, and might not have. Generally, the DI gas system is much less likely to handle marked powder changes. And now, with a panoply of bore-fouling-reducing powders, and extremely progressive-burning powders, the gas port pressure on your AR-10 might be so off-spec with commercial ammo that the rifle might not work.

I had one experience where a particular load simply ripped the rims off of rounds I fired, and refused to work properly. This is not the fault of the ammo. The ammo makers are doing what they do to provide the best performance for the vast majority of their customers who use bolt-action rifles to hunt with.

So, we're back to the "Doctor, doctor" joke again. If your rifle does not like a particular load, don't use it. There are plenty of choices, and you can even load your own ammo and tailor it to be 100 percent reliable in your rifle.

Now, this is the case with .308, but not so much with 6.5 Creedmoor. The 6.5 was developed when the AR-10 was becoming a big part of the marketplace. The 6.5 is also meant to be a precision round, and, as such, the last absolute final foot-per-second isn't expected to be wrung out of it. It is entirely likely that we will not see 6.5 Creedmoor ammo produced that won't run reasonably well in many AR-10 rifles. That is, after all, a big part of the market these days, for that caliber.

But keep in mind that the AR-10 is not the AR-15. In the AR-15-verse, anything that is .223 or 5.56 is expected to run reliably in any and every AR-15 ever made, even the basement-build done by your cousin who can't be trusted with sharp sticks.

MOVIN' ON UP — .338 FEDERAL

OK, if you want a big thumper in an AR-10 package, then the .338 Federal is just the ticket. A joint effort by Federal and Sako, coming to market in 2006, it is a .308 necked up to take a, you guessed it, .338 bullet. But that's the next chapter.

FINAL WORD

There will be those who just have to have the big boy of ARs, the AR-10 or some version of it. Good for them. But, if you decide to go down that path, be aware that each branch is its own path. There is no cutting across the field. Unlike the AR-15, where you can have a box of parts, no two of which came from the same source or maker, and rightly make a rifle from it, the AR-10 denies you that option.

You start with one, you are wedded to that one for as long as you own it. You can own AR-10s from different makers, but except for the magazines underneath, and the optics on top, there is no guarantee of interchangeability.

.338 FEDERAL

The .308 is a suitable cartridge case for a lot of conversions. That many of the bullet-diameter options for making a new cartridge either didn't happen, or didn't become popular, is a mystery. Well, not really. For instance, necking the .308 Winchester down to 7mm is not much of a change, when you consider that the 7x57 Mauser had existed for well over half a century before the .308 ever saw the light of day. But, what the 7-08 did, that the 7x57 couldn't, was fit into standard-length-action bolt-action rifles. That wasn't enough, it isn't selling like hotcakes.

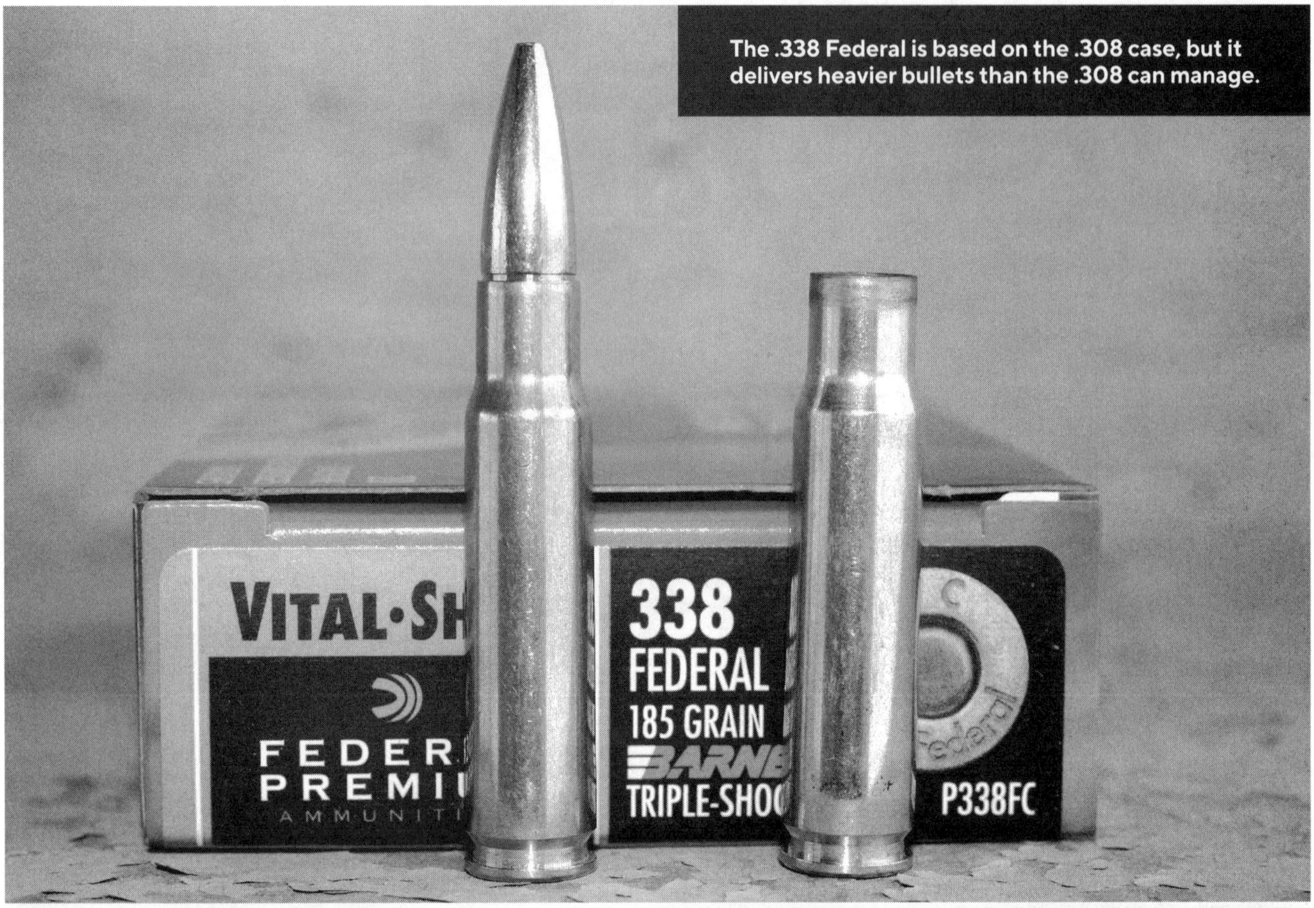

The .338 Federal is based on the .308 case, but it delivers heavier bullets than the .308 can manage.

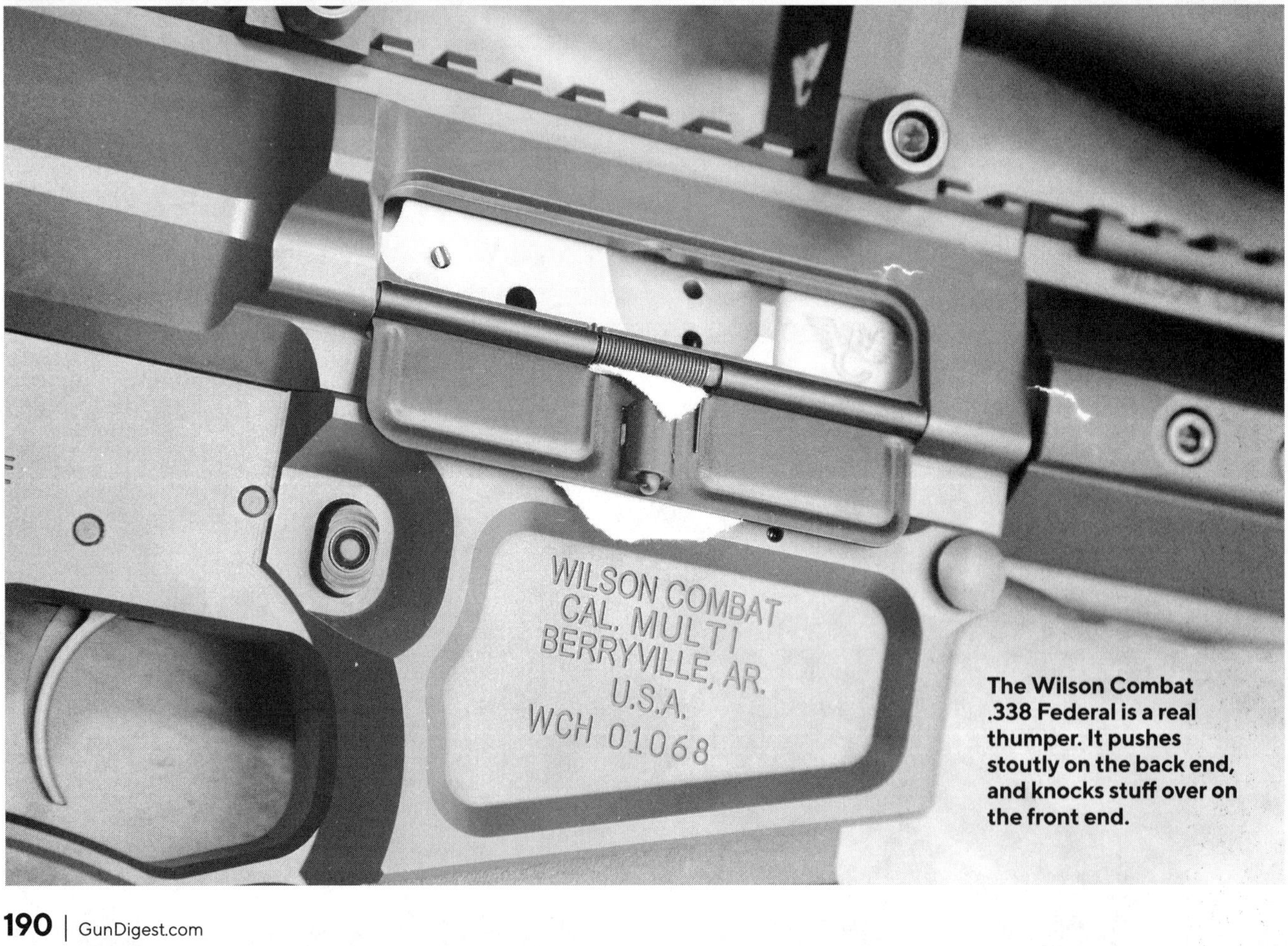

The Wilson Combat .338 Federal is a real thumper. It pushes stoutly on the back end, and knocks stuff over on the front end.

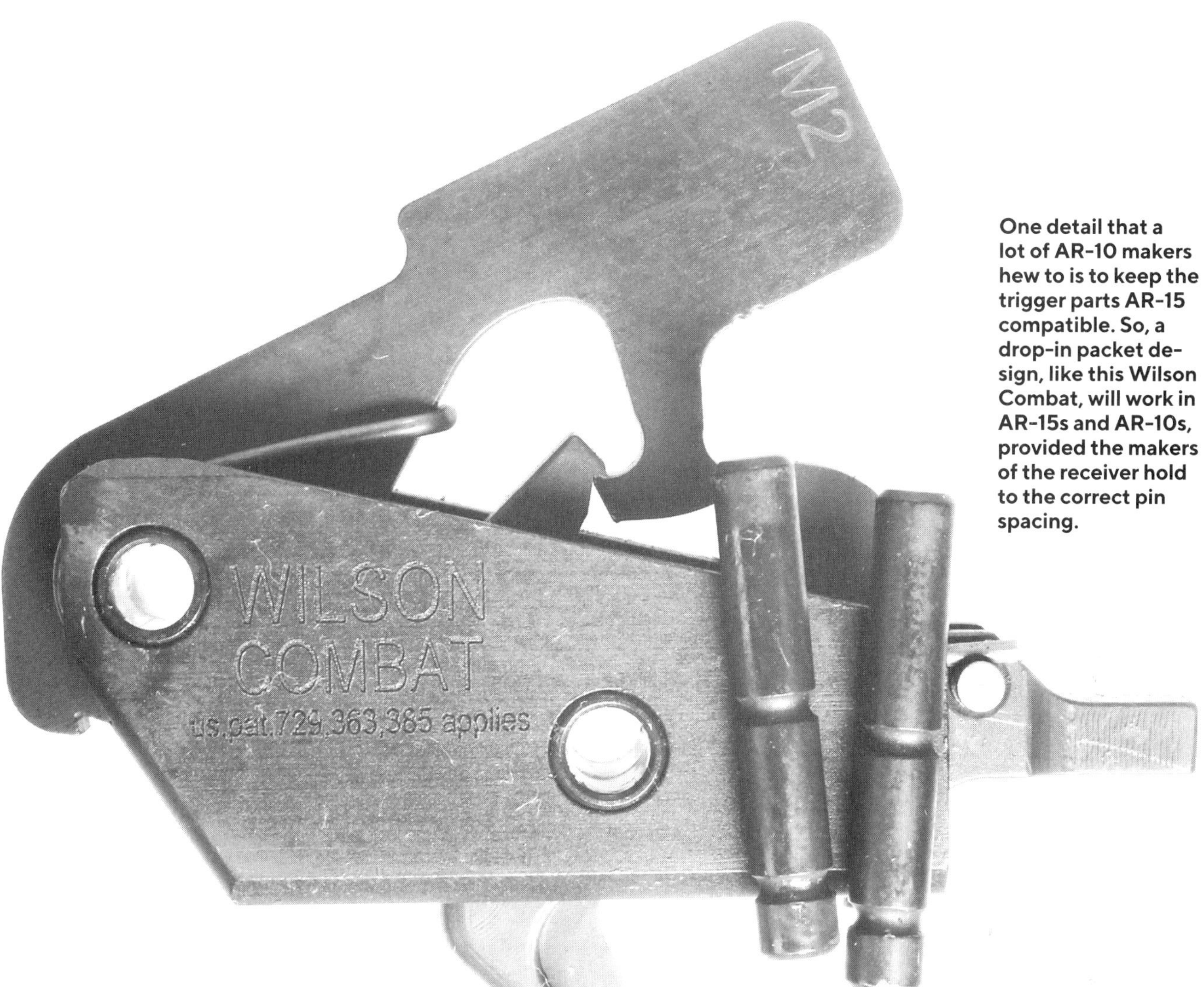

One detail that a lot of AR-10 makers hew to is to keep the trigger parts AR-15 compatible. So, a drop-in packet design, like this Wilson Combat, will work in AR-15s and AR-10s, provided the makers of the receiver hold to the correct pin spacing.

The .243, also a .308 case, had a good run, but it still struggled against competitive cartridges like the .250-3000 that had had a decades-long head start. The .243 established itself as a niche cartridge, the deer hunting cartridge that you let your wife use, or started your kids on. Or, you used when no-one was looking, because you didn't like recoil. Who does?

Remington designers found themselves even more in a pickle when they came out with the .244 Remington, aka, the 6mm Remington. They couldn't decide if it was a varmint cartridge, a deer cartridge or a multi-use cartridge. It didn't help that there wasn't a nickel's worth of difference between it and the .243. To steal a quote from Sean Connery in *The Untouchables*: It's as dead as Caesar now.

Winchester, along with necking down the .308, also necked it up. The .358 Winchester suffered mightily because it also didn't do anything that already existing cartridges didn't do. With a 180-grain bullet at 2,700 fps. It did exactly what a .308 or a .30-06 would do. Up the bullet weight to 250 grains, and the .358 suffers in comparison to the .35 Whelan, which is based on the .30-06 case. The .358 also suffers compared to the .35 Remington, a century-old deer cartridge invented by none other than Browning himself back in the first decade of the 20th century. The Remington tops out at a 200-grain bullet, but at the same velocity as the .358's 250-grain bullet, 2,200 fps.

No deer will ever notice the difference of 50 grains of bullet weight, between the two. And yet the hunter will, with the .35 Remington being softer on the shoulder than the Winchester.

.338 FEDERAL

The .338 Federal is simply the .308 case necked up to accept a .338-diameter bullet. How does it then differ from the other cartridges named?

For one, the .338 uses bullets with better ballistics than those in either the .358 or .35. The .358 has round-nosed bullets for the most part, due to overall length and weight. The .35 Remington has to use round-nosed bullets (and blunt ones at that) because it gets stuffed into lever-action rifles. Pointy bullets and tube magazines are not a good mix.

So, out of an AR, the .338 can have better ballistics, and a flatter trajectory than the .358 or .35.

Modern .338 bullets are designed for performance and work better at the velocities they are fired at. The .35 and the .358 generally use legacy bullets, often lacking the design advances of the newest designs.

Currently, the .338 Federal is chambered in a few bolt-action rifles, and three ARs; by LMT, DPMS and Wilson Combat.

The Wilson Combat .338 is not a big deal as far as recoil is concerned, as long as you know what you are getting into.

The WC uppers are clearly marked as to caliber, so there's no way to mix up this one with some other chambering.

I had a chance to thrash a Wilson Combat AR-10 in .338 Federal a short while back, and it really does the job. The .338 fires bullets from 180 grains to 210 grains, at hunting velocities. At the low end, the 180-grain bullet from the .338 is faster than a 180-grain bullet from a .308. Not by a lot, but enough to make a difference. If you wanted a heavy thumper for hunting, the .338 delivers. I'm not aware of a 210-grain bullet loaded for the .308, so if you want weight, and a autoloading rifle, then the .338 is your choice.

I was at an industry event where assembled gun writers first saw the .338 Federal cartridge and had a chance to shoot it. Things went pretty much as you'd expect. Those who wanted heavier bullets than they had previously been able to use, were pleased.

(right) One detail that Bill Wilson attended to was to put dual ejectors on the bolts of his AR-10 rifles. This ensures the empties will be tossed overboard. The brass is big, you don't want it loitering in the feedway.

And when you go big bore, with the .338 Federal, you can keep accuracy. Two loads, 100-yard groups, and everything is fine.

Everyone else saw it as not something they needed. I didn't view it as a failure, I mean, there's a reason we have paint in many colors. If you have ever even been in, let alone lived in, a suburban development where all of the house colors are carefully controlled, you know how boring that can get.

There's no need to be bored by our cartridges, too. So, .338 Federal, welcome.

.358 WINCHESTER

And speaking of the loneliest bore diameter in the American firmament, the .35,

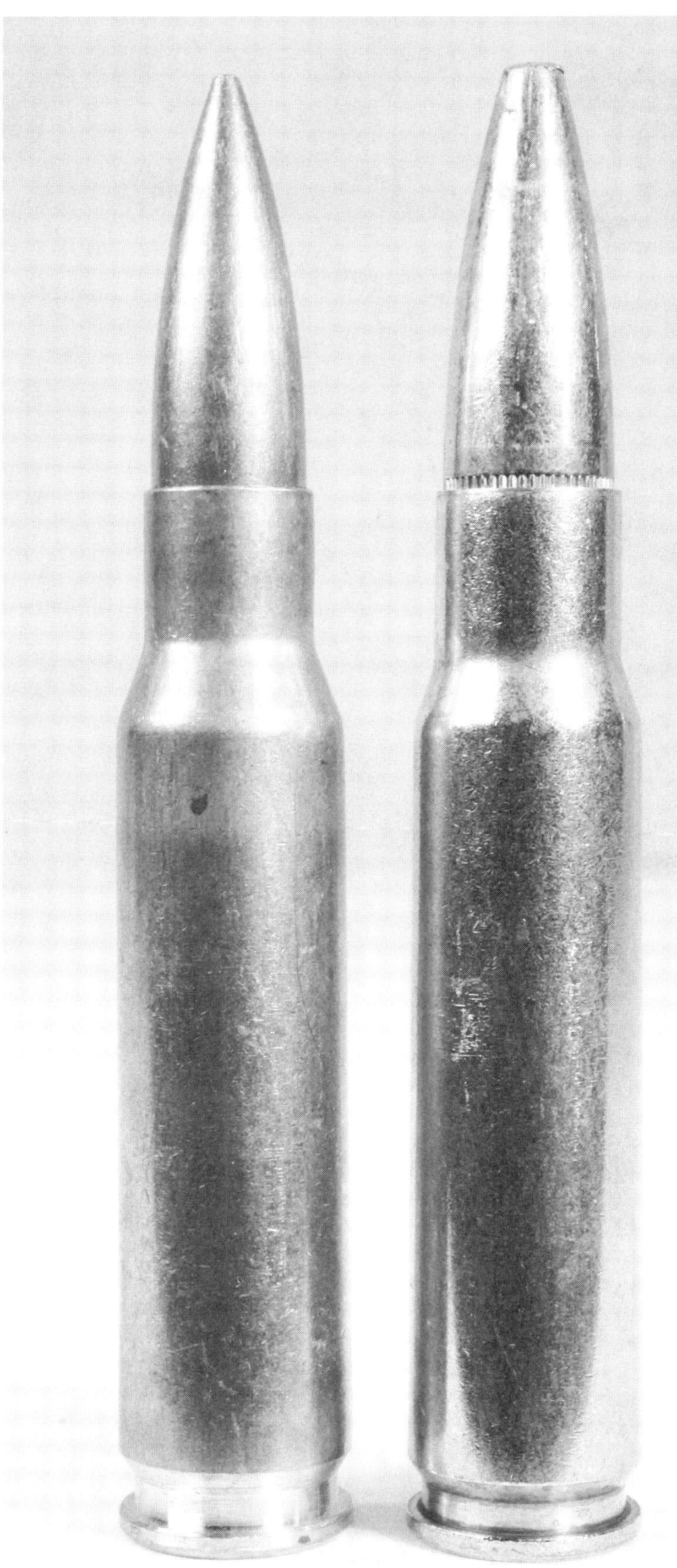

Bill Wilson also makes AR-10 uppers chambered in .358 Winchester. It can be counted on for a 200-grain bullet at 2,475 to 2,500 fps. This is not a long-range, flat-trajectory round. This is for delivering a heavy-for-caliber bullet at a useful velocity, to put a long winter's worth of venison or other game in the freezer.

And like all Wilson Combat rifles, it can be counted on to shoot better than most of those who own one.

Do you need one? Can you find a use for one? The answer to the former is simple: There you go again, confusing wants with needs. And secondly, there are a lot of hunters who prefer bullet weight over velocity, for delivering terminal effects on big game.

Now, if you have an AR-10 chambered in .308 (or other cartridge) and you want the other options, you can acquire another upper. As long as the new upper is compatible with the existing lower, life is good.

If the maker of your .308 doesn't offer the caliber you want, there is still an option. You see, the barrel on an AR-10 is threaded into a barrel extension just like the AR-15 barrel is. It isn't the same extension, but it works the same way.

If you can get the parts you need, an upper, bolt, carrier and barrel extension, you can have a gunsmith who is good with a lathe install a barrel for you. He/she simply has to thread the back of the barrel to fit the extension, chamber it, and torque it up to keep it tight. This is pretty standard gunsmithing work, even if it is beyond the home AR-15 gun-plumber.

The only real trick will be in drilling a gas port of the correct diameter. Start small and open it up if the original diameter doesn't produce enough gas.

If you have a basement full of .243 Winchester ammo, and you want an AR-10 chambered for it, this would be a way.

The .338 Federal, on the right, is noticeably different than the .308. But if you were in a hurry, or not paying as much attention as you should, you could get in trouble.

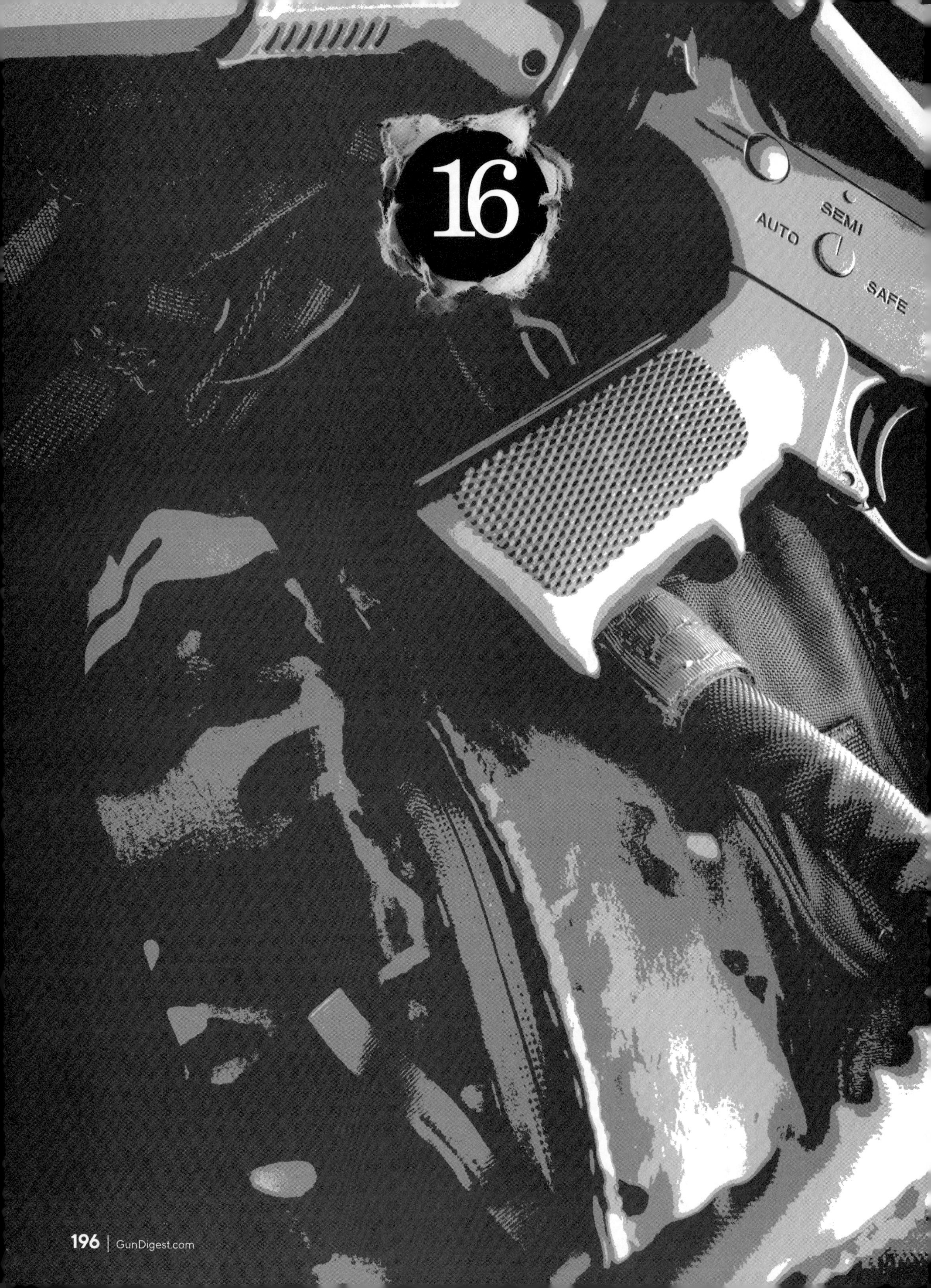

16

6mm AND 6.5 CREEDMOOR

The Creedmoors were not derived directly from the .308, like the .260 Remington, but you would be in good company thinking so. Yes, the case head and rim diameter are the same size, but that was intentional. The idea was not simply to neck down the .308 to those diameters. That had already been done. The .260 Remington, for example, was known for a long time as the 6.5-08, a conversion done by wildcatters who wanted a short-action cartridge that essentially duplicated the performance of the 6.5x55 Scandinavian cartridge.

There was a time when it looked like the .260 Remington was going to be the middleweight champ. It has been overtaken by the 6.5 Creedmoor, and the .260 will fade into history.

Remington necked it down and adopted it, and it was good. Not the best, but good. I had a rifle built for it a couple of decades ago.

The formation and growth of the Precision Rifle Series, a long-range marksmanship competition that was very demanding (both physically and accuracy-wise) called for better performance than what was available. And getting that performance without the usual costs would be a bonus. You see, in the PRS, shooters have to hike from one shooting position to another, with all their gear. Once they arrive at the shooting station, time starts and they have to then find all the targets, gauge distances, and hit them, under time pressure.

A really flat-shooting cartridge would be great, but not if it required a heavy rifle. Or pounded them with recoil in a light rifle.

There was a brief time when the .260 Remington was used in 3-gun competition. There, in the Heavy Metal Division, and as an alternative to the .308, some competitors used rifles chambered in .260 in some matches that allowed such.

In an interesting circle back to the past, some of them used FAL rifles chambered in .260. This was quite close in performance to the pre-war .276 Pedersen, and had the U.S. Army adopted the M1 Garand in .276, and then post-war adopted the FAL (both would have been clever decisions to have made at their times) we would have had the equivalent of an FAL in .260 Remington, but in the 1950s.

Instead, it took more than half a century more.

The 6.5 Creedmoor was developed by Dave Emary of Hornady, and Dennis DeMille, of Creedmoor

The 6.5 Creedmoor lineup is already impressive, and grows greater every week. This was a small part of what is available that I tested in a barrel-length review.

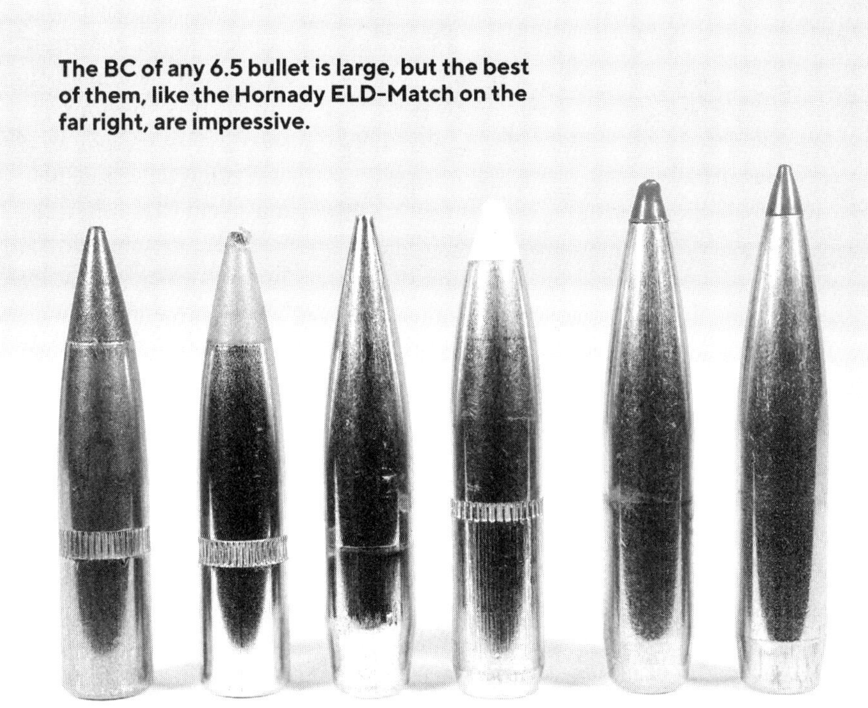
The BC of any 6.5 bullet is large, but the best of them, like the Hornady ELD-Match on the far right, are impressive.

Sports (hence the name). The idea was to start with the basic .308 case, but not to simply neck it down. They used every trick in accuracy development and case design that had been found out in the previous half-century, and made the resulting cartridge fit and feed reliably from .308 magazines.

Hornady also worked on bullet design and has since come out with some 6.5 bullets with eye-opening BCs. One example is the 147 ELD-match, with a BC of .697. Such a bullet, started at a miserly 2,000 fps, will remain supersonic to 1,000 yards. You did not read that wrong, and it is not a typo. A BC of .697. Compare that to the 7.62 NATO 147-grain FMJ-BT, which typically has a BC of .420. Were you to start the .308 147 at the same velocity as the 6.5 Hornady, 2,000 fps, at 1,000 yards, the velocity there will be 922 fps, and the .308 will have probably lost accuracy was well.

Lost accuracy? Yes, bullets that transition from supersonic to subsonic quite often demonstrate a loss of accuracy. The supersonic bullet is pushing the shock wave of the compressed air ahead of it. The subsonic bullet has the compressed wave behind it. As the bullet slows down, that shock wave has to traverse the length of the bullet, and also change in peak pressure.

Bullets with points have their center of gravity behind the center of pressure of the air pressing on the bullet as the bullet travels. As the pressure wave travels down the bullet, it changes the balance of the bullet, even with gyroscopic stability, and if the disturbance is great enough, the bullet stops being point-first balanced.

In the case of our .308 147-grain FMJ-BT, that transition happens just past 600 yards or so. For NRA High Power competition, this is not a problem, as the farthest target is 600 yards. But for matches past that, of which there have been many customary ones, the .308 with a 147-grain bullet is not an option.

In a recent test I performed, I chronographed 6.5 Creedmoor ammunition as I chopped the barrel down, inch by inch. Now, based on what I had seen

One thing I discovered about the 6.5 was its efficiency. Even trimming barrels down to absurd lengths, velocity held up.

Cut and test, cut and test. Sometimes the work of a gun writer can be downright boring.

The end result was to quickly sweep all other match cartridges off the board. It is so common to see 6.5 Creedmoor as the cartridge used in PRS matches, that other cartridges are notable when they appear. Except for the 6mm Creedmoor, which is the 6.5, but necked down.

I have a 6.5 Creedmoor AR, a LaRue OBR, and it is a tack-driver. I had a chance to test-drive a 6mm Creedmoor, a Wilson Combat Super Sniper. I first tested the 6mm at Bill Wilson's ranch. We soon found it was easy to get this on steel past the distance where we could hear the impact. We had to depend on closely watching the target for a new black spot, and a spray of dust at the bottom, in order to determine that we had a hit. And hit we did, with almost boring regularity, out to 1,200 yards. Past that, my wind-calling skills weren't up to it, but we could get hits past that.

with other calibers, I would have predicted that a carbine in 6.5, chopped down to SBR lengths, would be nothing but a flashy noise maker. I would have bet on velocities dipping below 2,000 fps soon after leaving the 16-inch barrel length. And that anything under 14 inches would be useless.

Well, what I found was that all the loads kept their bullets above 2,000 fps until I had the barrel down to 10 inches. And then, only the heaviest bullets dipped below 2,000 fps. So, a 6.5 Creedmoor SBR with a 12-inch barrel, keeps all of its loads supersonic out to, or past, 1,000 yards.

And the competition shooters are not using 12-inch barrels.

PRS matches routinely feature targets well past 600 yards.

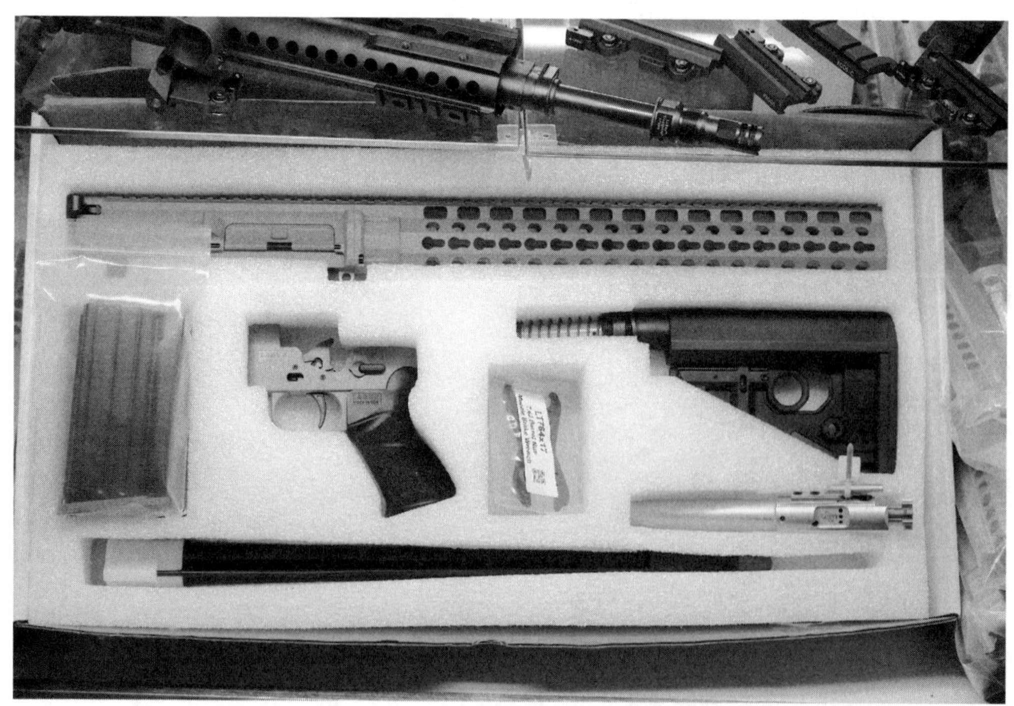

The LaRue lower completion kit, yours in 6.5, .308 or .260 Remington.

Getting an AR-10 in 6.5 or 6mm is easy: a new barrel. It uses the same bolt and magazines as the .308.

As mentioned in the previous chapter, if you wish to re-barrel an AR-10 from .308 to 6.5 or 6mm, you will have to make sure the barrel is compatible with the make and model of the AR-10 you have.

One option you might look into for ammunition is those self-same PRS matches. Ammo for the 6.5 Creedmoor is so common right now, and the factory ammo so accurate, that I have heard of competitors who do not reload their ammo. With the cost of components being a significant fraction of the coast of ammo (and the ammo prices not being so much elevated as in the past) that they will practice with factory ammo, sell the once-fired empties, and buy more ammo for matches.

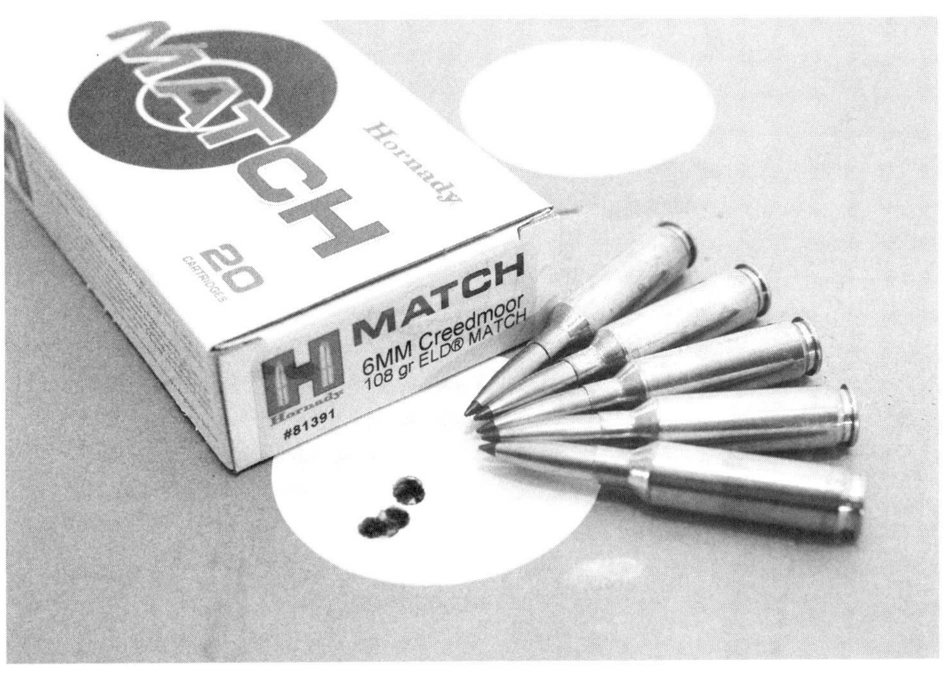

(above)The 6mm Creedmoor is brilliantly accurate.

(below) The Wilson Combat Super Sniper in 6mm Creedmoor, with which I found it absurdly easy to hit targets farther away than I could hear the hit on steel.

The AR-10 rifles have one point of mostly commonality: magazines. Lancer mags (shown here), Magpul mags and Brownells aluminum M110 magazines all will work. Still, test in your rifle before you go depending on any of them.

They also save the time of reloading, most of which is spent in brass prep.

Save yourself a great big headache, and time, and do not even consider "saving money" by re-forming 6.5 Creedmoor from .308 brass. Even if you could get buckets of brass for free from a range, there is the hassle of necking down the brass and establishing a new shoulder location. Then there is the question of neck thickness, and do you ream or outside turn?

No, save yourself the headache and potential heartache, and just buy new brass, or ammo, or once-fired brass.

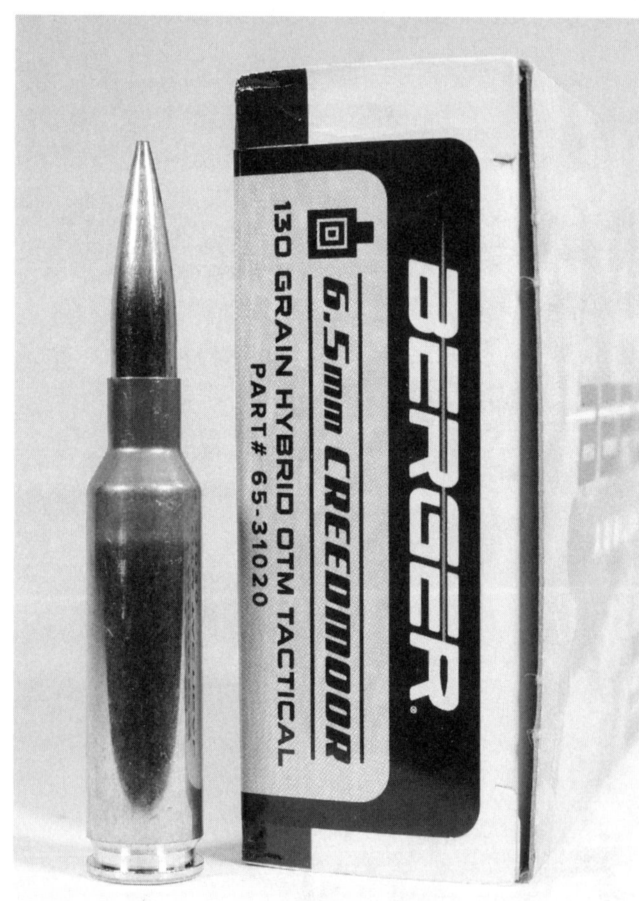

The 6.5 Creedmoor is so hot, and rifles can be particular, so you are not out of line trying everything, to see what your rifle likes best. This has been very good in several rifles already.

DIFFERENCES

The 6mm and the 6.5 differ in the bullet diameter, of course, but the shoulder has been changed between the two. The shoulder of the 6mm is a bit farther forward. This is in part because the smaller-diameter neck of the 6mm requires the shoulder be a bit more forward, so the neck ends up being the proper length. (Left where it is for the 6.5, the 6mm neck would be longer than needed or desired.) But, also for chambering.

The 6.5 clearly wouldn't chamber in a 6mm chamber, because the bullet and neck would be too large to even start past the shoulder.

But the 6mm, with its shoulder slightly forward, doesn't let the bolt close in a 6.5 chamber, so you don't have the embarrassment of "blooping" a 6-mm bullet down a 6.5mm bore.

However, you could probably make the 6mm "work" in a 6.5 rifle. You could probably, if the chamber is at the large end of dimensions, and cartridge at the small, and you were really heavy-handed and willing to pound on the bolt handle, get a bolt-action rifle closed. And all you'd manage to do is get miserable accuracy and lousy velocity out of a 6-mm bullet down a 6.5 barrel, and then not be able to get the bolt open. (The chamber pressure would likely wedge things tight.)

An AR-10 probably won't let you do that at all, as you have no exposed bolt handle to bang onto.

Still, keep sharp if you happen to end up owning a rifle in each cartridge.

Why 6mm?

Simple: recoil. Yes, the 6.5 recoils less than a .308, but that's like saying a middleweight hits softer than a light-heavyweight. The 6mm, pushing a 100-grain bullet at the same velocity a 6.5 would be pushing a 147-grain bullet, will have less recoil. If you are learning to shoot, shoot accurately and shoot at distance, then the less recoil makes the task easier.

You simply shoot your 6mm until you are better than the barrel (which will happen probably before you actually wear out the barrel) and then have the 6mm barrel replaced with a 6.5 barrel.

And then get on learning even more distance shooting.

FUTURE

The U.S. Army is talking about adopting a 6.5 cartridge for the future. This of course caused all sorts of glee on the part of the 6.8 SPC advocates, until they discovered the Army had no interest in going back over that again. And it also caused momentary glee on the part of 6.5 Creedmoor fans, who had thought it the obvious solution.

Alas, the Army is not so rational as that. As we've discussed, the attempt seems to be to adopt some sort of polymer-cased or dual-materials case cartridge, one that delivers the performance of a 6.5mm magnum of one sort or another.

I don't know if the people involved know so little about basic ballistics and physics that they really think they can get that performance (a 6.5 Remington magnum delivers a 120-grain bullet at 3,200 fps) at little or no cost, or they really think that silencers reduce recoil that much.

In any case, my bet (were there a line in Vegas for such things) is that they will find they can't get the performance the PowerPoint slides promised, and when they find the best they can do is a 6.5 Creedmoor, in a 10-pound rifle, with half as many rounds per combat load per soldier compared to the 5.56, they will decline the billion dollars such a changeover requires, and call the "study" done.

In the meantime, we'll keep shooting our 6.5 Creedmoor AR-10s, and the manufacturers will, we hope, begin to work toward parts compatibility.

The Army is talking 6.5, but it seems to want a 6.5 Super magnum. Once decision makers realize they can't have it, the Sig rifle is poised to jump right into contention. (This is one I'm testing on steel. The distance was 300 yards, the plate was small, hitting was easy.)

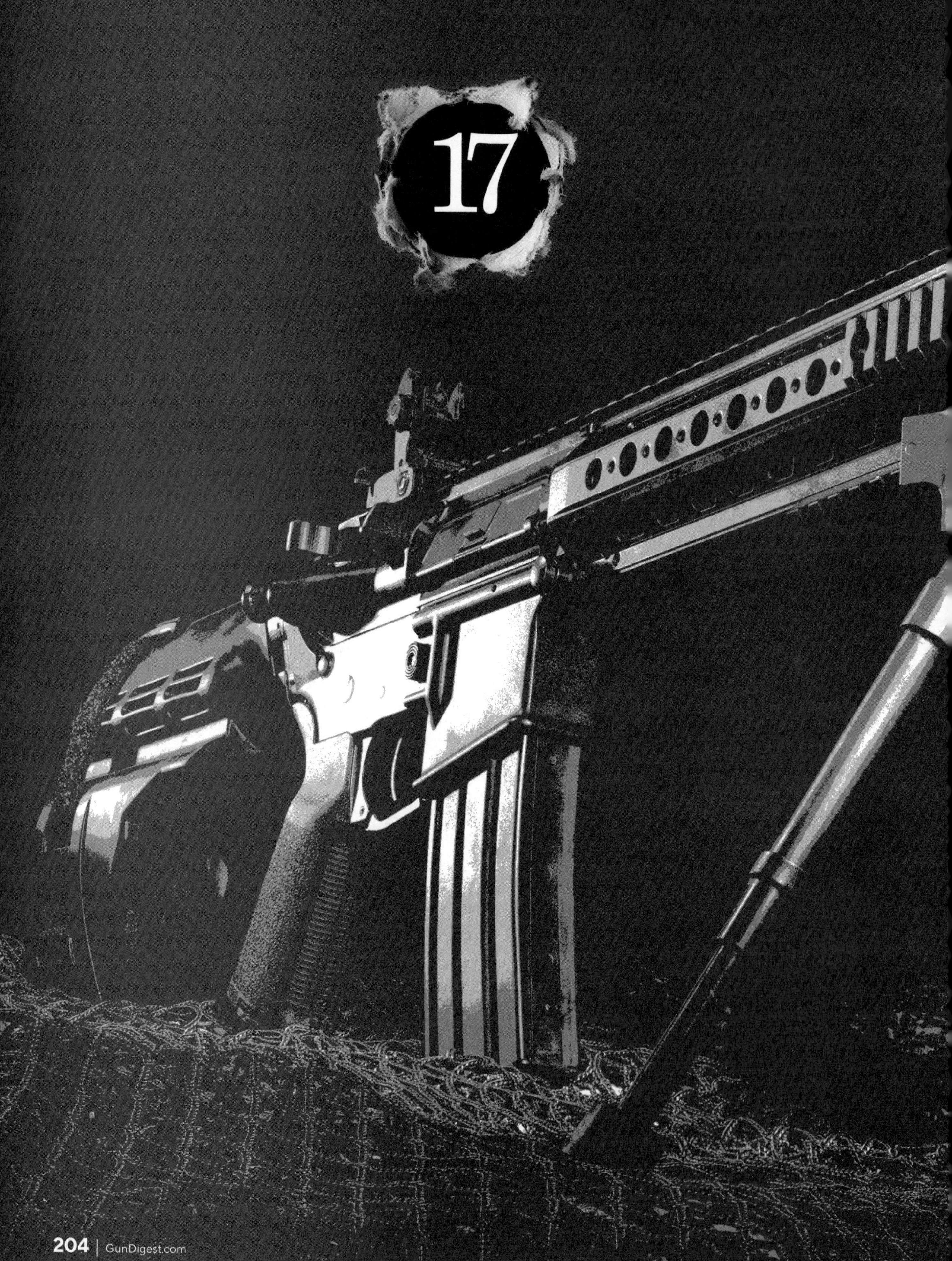
17

.450 BUSHMASTER

The big, big bore.

OK, you want to put the hurt to something, with a heavy bullet moving along at a pretty high velocity? The .450 Bushmaster to the rescue. When I first saw it, at the 2007 SHOT Show, the cartridge was so new the samples they had for us to shoot didn't even have a headstamp on them. The bases of the cartridges, where there would have otherwise been a headstamp, were blank, as if they had been made for some super-secret CIA plan in a foreign country.

The super-secret CIA assassination round? No, just ammo so new it is barely out of R&D, and not yet into production. The .450 Bushmaster, as we first saw it.

Nope, not the case. They just hadn't gotten around to making the brass with headstamps, that's how new it was. So new, we gun writers only got to fire a few rounds each, we couldn't snag loaded ammo for samples to write about, and each empty was tracked as it ejected and was picked up. Yep, that's how you can tell a cartridge is 15 minutes out of its R&D cycle.

In all fairness, the SHOT Show is when the SHOT Show is. They are not going to change anything about it, especially the dates, to accommodate a manufacturer, any manufacturer, no way. So, if your product is coming off the line just in time to pack it up and ship it to the show, that's what you do. Because if you don't, it is next year for your next opportunity to get your new product in front of a huge group of gun writers, the next SHOT Show.

The original cartridge was designed by Tim LeGendre of LeMag Firearms. The idea was simple: produce a hard-hitting cartridge in a compact form, one that was a real crusher at close range. The result, the .45 Professional. The impetus came from the late Jeff Cooper, who called such an approach the "thumper."

It was not new, in that there had already been lightweight carbines chambered in .44 Magnum, lever-actions and self-loaders, and there was even a short-lived run of M1 carbines rebuilt in .45 Winchester Magnum. I had an opportunity to shoot one of those particular specialties several decades ago. Once I had had a chance to inspect the sample carbine, and see how much steel had to be removed to fit the .45 case into the M1 receiver and barrel, I declined the invitation.

But by fitting that sort of a cartridge into an AR-15 receiver, the approach has a lot more strength.

The starting point for the .450 Bushmaster is the .284 Winchester case. A magnum in performance, the .284 does not have a belt, like so many of the belted magnums do. The lack of a belt, and the rebated rim, make it reasonably adaptable to standard-length bolt-action rifles, and those with standard (i.e. .473-inch diameter) bolt faces. The idea was to get .270 Winchester or .280 Remington out of a short-action rifle, instead of the standard-length actions those cartridges (based on the .30-06) required.

It might have worked, but Winchester intended it to be in, and introduced it in, the Model 100 and the Model 88. The 100 was a self-loading rifle, and the 88 was the lever-action version of the 100. Both duds, and both sought out by the few who wanted them, chambered in .308 or something with an even bigger bore.

Had Winchester introduced it in something

The .450 Bushmaster rifle they had us shooting at SHOT Show was equipped with a red-dot scope. That was all we needed to mangle targets at 100 yards.

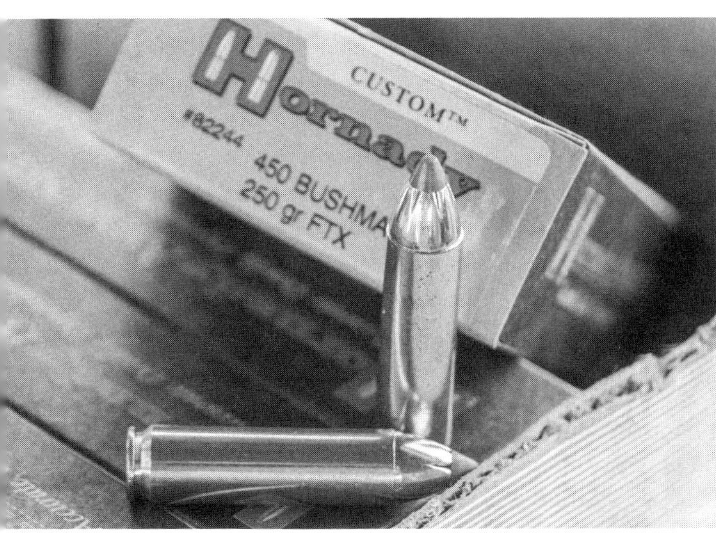

The .450, as designed, was intended from the start to have the Hornady FTX bullet as the projectile. And there is nothing at all wrong with that. This is a deer-hammering combination of bullet, cartridge and rifle.

like a lightweight Model 70 bolt-action, meant as a mountain rifle, it might have had a chance. But with two strikes against it, it faded away.

But as a parent cartridge for the big thumper, it was perfect. So, back to the .450 Bushmaster.

Initially loaded by Hornady, the company adjusted the case length to accommodate its new Flex-Tip bullet and AR-15 magazines. This bullet is one with a flexible polymer tip, not a hard one, as is used on other rifle bullets. The soft tip allows for the bullet to be used in lever-action rifles, where the bullet tip will rest against the primer of the cartridge ahead of it. Hornady had a great idea, and a great bullet, but it needed the case to be a specific length to fit and feed. No problem.

The bullet also, because of the polymer tip, can have a more-pointed profile. I wouldn't exactly call it a spire point, because you might have a mental image of a bullet much longer than the Flex-Tip is in this instance. However, the end result still improves downrange performance. The BC of the Flex-Tip used in the .450 Bushmaster is .175. Yes, it is miserable compared to the X-ELD Match 6.5, with a BC in the .600s. But you have to compare like to like. And the closest comparison to this would be a 250-grain flat-pointed .452-caliber bullet, and the nearest I can come up with as a comparison has a BC of .146. That's 20 percent better for the Flex-Tip.

The end result is a real thumper. In an earlier age, it would have been called an express cartridge. It is a .452 bullet of 250 grains, going just over 2,200 fps. A century and more ago, the British hunted all over the world with bolt action and double rifles, with the same ballistics. No Flex-Tip for them, however.

As a hunting cartridge in areas where a straight-walled cartridge is required, the .450 Bushmaster has been the choice. It does have recoil, however. The Power Factor, which is not a measure used by DNR for hunting purposes, but does correlate pretty closely to felt recoil, has the .450 Bushmaster at a 550PF. That's compared to a .44 Magnum, which can produce a PF between 280 and 330, and a 12-gauge slug, which can crank up a 700PF. I might be convinced to shoot a .44 magnum carbine that weighs a mere seven or eight pounds with ammo, sling and scope on board, but no way am I shooting a 12-gauge slug gun of similar weight. The .450 Bushmaster can recoil enough to create a flinch if you are not careful. The bright spot here is that it is easy to find a .450 Bushmaster that has a barrel threaded at the muzzle, and thus you can install a muzzle brake to dampen its enthusiasm.

The velocity is generated by a healthy chamber pressure, at 38,500 PSI max. The pressure limit is probably there as a result of the strength limit of the AR-15, but I have to think that even if the rifle could handle more pressure, more velocity would be too much of a good thing. I mean, an eight-pound AR recoils briskly enough with a 250-grain bullet at 2,200 fps. If you were to add another couple of hundred feet per second to that, who could stand to shoot it? Even with a muzzle brake, a 250 at 2,200 is sharp enough.

This is definitely an instance when you will want to swap out the mil-spec buttstock for something with a rubber pad on it. You won't find something with a Sorbothane pad, like the 12-gauge slug gun can come with, but you can find a non-slip buttstock. Even a small amount of rubber will make shooting the Bushmaster more fun than the hard plastic or aluminum of a mil-spec stock.

The .450 only fits into the AR magazine by slipping it under the feed lips.

You do not get the magazine capacity that a .223 will provide, but then you don't want that. The DNR will get very fussy if you have a magazine of more than five rounds, so leave the big mags home when you go hunting with a .450 Bushmaster.

The width of the case, at an even half-inch (.500 at the base, tapering down to .480 at the case mouth) means there is no chance whatsoever of it being a double-stack in an AR-15 magazine. No, magazines are single-stack only, which means you have a few choices. An otherwise 10-round magazine will hold four rounds of .450 Bushmaster. A Vietnam-era 20-round magazine will hold nine rounds, and a 30-round magazine will hold 12 or 13. You'd think it would be the same for all, but some I've tried will only hold 12. That's life.

The .450 Bushmaster, besides being a drop-on upper conversion, is an easy build. Use a .450 Bushmaster barrel and bolt, and build up one the way you want it to be.

This makes it simple for those who are planning on hunting with a .450 Bushmaster. You simply use any reliable 10-shot magazine, because it will only hold four rounds, and that is fine with DNR across the country. Well, except for those jurisdictions where four shots in a magazine are viewed with suspicion. OK, I'm being a bit alarmist, perhaps, but we can certainly understand that even if the magazines are OK, the AR-15 they would otherwise fit are not going to be allowed in some locales. Welcome to the 21st century.

Oh, and back a paragraph? Strictly speaking, if the case is .500 at the base, and .480 at the mouth, it isn't a straight-walled case. But it does not have a visible neck, unlike, say, the .458 SOCOM (more about that in a bit) and the DNR can just overlook the minor taper. Which they do.

The rim diameter is .473, the standard American rifle case rim, which started with the .30-06 (actually, the .30-03, but who ever heard of that one?) and selected so rifle makers who were making bolt-action rifles for the cartridge could use the standard bolt face dimensions they were using for other cartridges. That's one thing you have to consider if you are designing a new cartridge; what steps will the firearms makers have to undertake, to chamber their products in your new cartridge? Using a standard case rim diameter makes it easier for them, and more likely they will say "Yes" when customers ask.

CONVERSIONS

To make an AR-15 in .450 Bushmaster (besides the obvious, buy one) you need a .450 Bushmaster barrel, a bolt for same and magazines. Yes, the magazines should feed reliably, and if you have some, certainly try them. But if you are like any other .450 owner I have talked to, you will find some work and some don't, and you'll be sorting and marking your magazines.

Oh, and while the recoil is going to be tough on you, it is going to be just as, or even more, tough on scopes. So do not go cheap on mounts, and don't be surprised if your low-cost scope dies in a short while.

AVAILABLE AMMO

The standard bullet weight here is 250 grains, either the Hornady Flex-Tip, or a flat-nosed JHP or JSP. You can get 300-grain and even 350-grain ammo, the 300s from Federal, and the 350s from Buffalo Bore. The Buffalo Bore loads are listed as 350-grain bullets at 1,950 fps, and I'm more than willing to bet that out of a rifle they will do all of that. Out of a carbine, a bit less. But that's still a 680PF, and that is past my recoil limit in a lightweight carbine or rifle.

At 680PF, I'm not touching off a round out of anything that weighs less than 10 pounds, even if it has a muzzle brake on it.

For me, that is the very definition of "too much of a good thing" and I know my limits.

RELOADING

Reloading the empties is easy enough. Since the case is a straight-walled one (OK, again, it has taper, but really, not enough to be a problem with case stretching) you'd think you could reload without having to use case lubricant. Alas, such is not the case. You'll have to lube somehow; a good choice is to spray a tray of clean empties with Hornady One Shot before you proceed to the sizing step. Then clean off the lube before you go to loading.

Those of you who are usually loading your ammo on a progressive press might take the two-step approach. Use a single-stage press, a traditional old style, for sizing the lubed brass. Size and deprime lubed brass, then clean off the lube off ("Once more into the tumbler, dear friends" ... sorry) and feed the now-resized brass into your progressive press for loading. If you do this, have a sizing die in place at the first station, but don't screw it down all the way. Leave it high enough that it doesn't actually size the brass. However, make sure the decapping pin is long enough to poke through the primer hole.

That way, any tumbling media that might get wedged in the flash hole (and in hundreds of cases, there will be one or two; count on it) gets poked out by the decapping pin. You're welcome.

Crimping is taper crimp, of course, due to the case headspacing on the mouth.

The very good thing about reloading the .450 Bushmaster is that it allows you to dial back the recoil. If you take your 250-grain bullets and push them only 1,500 fps, you make the .450 a lot more fun to shoot. You might complain that that is a pretty expensive way to plink, considering the cost of jacketed bullets, but there is another solution: plated or coated. A plated bullet like the Berry's 250 LC 250 FP, a flat-pointed bullet meant for the .45 Long Colt, would make a very soft-shooting plinking load. You might find it too easy to exceed its velocity limit, in which case you simply switch to the Berry's 350-grain bullet meant for the .458 SOCOM.

Either, bought in bulk, would come at a markedly reduced price compared to premium jacketed bullets. And for practice and plinking who needs an expanding bullet anyway?

Acme Bullet Company, makers of coated bullets, has a polymer-coated 300-grain bullet meant for use in the .454 Casull or .460 S&W magnum. That one would stand up to use in the .450 Bushmaster for plinking and even getting up nearer the full factory recoil of regular ammo.

The trajectory of the .450 Bushmaster is flat enough for the hunting distances it is intended for. Once you get past 200 yards, the trajectory looks more rainbow-ish than flat. The recoil can be tamed by building your AR with recoil in mind. A muzzle brake on the front end will not make you any friends at the range, but will reduce the jackhammer effect on your shoulder and face. A stock with a rubber pad on it will also ease the impact, and if you keep an eye out for a design with a wider, larger surface area, that too will reduce recoil. Last, some have found hydraulic buffers to be of use in reducing the jolt. I haven't, but each of us has to find our own comfort in equipment.

From an oddball cartridge that the hard-core AR-15 shooters in 2007 looked at with some disdain, the .450 Bushmaster has gone on to become accepted as a hunting cartridge. Good going again, Hornady.

18

.458 SOCOM, .458 HAM'R, .50 BEOWULF

The even bigger big bores.

A lot of AR-15 development, and calibers, have come to see the light of day because of competition. But, some of the more interesting ones have come about because of bearded gents in dusty places. The .458 SOCOM is one of those.

Designed by Marty ter Weeme of Teppo Jutsu specifically for special operators, it had a big list of things it had to do.

For one, it had to fit into a standard AR-15/M16 magazine. That way, it would be a modified-upper only proposition. Hence the overall length of the .458 SOCOM cartridge is 2.260 inches, the same as the .223/5.56.

What bullet diameter? Back in 2000, when this was first being kicked around, the only jacketed bullets that were larger in diameter than .451 of an inch were designed for rifles. The pistol rounds were stubby; they were designed to expand at pistol velocities, and they just wouldn't do. The rifle bullets were .458 and they were designed to be hurled out of a .45-70 at the very least. That was a 1,500 to 1,800 fps proposition. The bigger and newer cartridges using .458 bullets were meant for big, dangerous game, and they started at 2,200 fps and went up from there.

Those .458 designs might expand at .45-70 velocities, and then again, they might be designed not to expand. Out of something you could fit into an AR, none would ever expand.

The idea is to make an AR that delivers the goods like the lever guns of old: the .45-70 and the .444 Marlin. We can do that.

So that was a small problem, but not an entirely deal-breaker one. After all, the guys who hunt at night with NVG don't need, nor mostly can't use, expanding bullets. And, if you are shooting people with a .458 bullet of 400 grains (as an example), how much expansion do you need?

A parent case of the .50 Action Express nestles nicely underneath the feed lips of an AR magazine, so that would work, provide case capacity, and even a shoulder to headspace on. Oh, wait a minute. The rim diameter of the 50 AE is .541? If you machine open the bolt face of an AR bolt to hold a .541 rim, there's no bolt left.

So, reduce the rim diameter. Called a rebated rim, this is an accepted practice in cartridge design when a problem like this comes up. The rim on the .458 SOCOM is .473. That should sound familiar, because it is the diameter of the .30-06, and every cartridge that has come to use since then, for what is called the standard (and not magnum) bolt face size.

The problems do not stop there. OK, you have a case, and bullets for it. What pressure can you run it at? The larger case means less steel around the chamber (you are stuck with the outer diameter of the AR barrel, regardless of what you want to do with it) and there's also the matter of bolt thrust. The thrust is calculated by chamber pressure times surface area of the case on the bolt face. (Case adhesion in the chamber alleviates that some, but they all do, and it is not a big variable in this equation.)

A lineup of .458 SOCOM loads. You can have everything from lightweight plinkers, to heavy solids for subsonic anvil-hammering impact.

The end result was a limit of 35,000 PSI, which is the same as that of the 9mm Parabellum.

Finally, what twist rate? Since the .458-diameter bullet selection includes heavyweights all the way up to 600 grains (and a thumper it is) you need a fast twist. Marty settled on 1/14.

If you have magazines that are caliber-specific, then mark them, and keep them separate from the rest.

The CMMG MkW-15, built to be a tank-like rifle, delivering a tank-like cartridge, the .458 SOCOM.

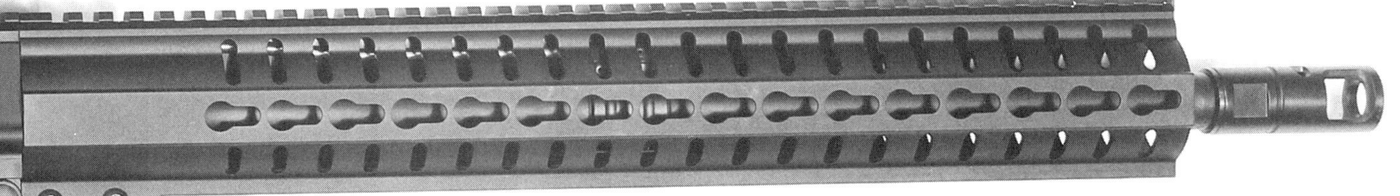

Oh, and one of the considerations was that it could be run suppressed. Yes, that explains a 600-grain bullet at 1,000 fps, or close to it. Basically, a suppressed 12-gauge slug, in weight and speed if not frontal diameter. And if the 600-grain bullet happens to be marginally stable from the twist rate of 1/14, well, is that a problem? A .458 bullet of 600 grains that yaws once it penetrates is going to leave a mark.

Now, if you are expecting to use .50 AE brass to make .458 SOCOM ammo, forget about it. (And it isn't like ranges are ankle-deep in empty .50 AE brass anyway.) Because the .50 isn't long enough. But brass is easy to come by, either as loaded ammo, or as new brass.

Loading is straightforward, there are no real quirks or potential stumbles in it. The long neck provides plenty of neck tension to hold the bullet. Bullets are common, albeit expensive. That's one thing you'll have to get used to, besides the recoil. Ammo is pricey, at $1,900 per 1,000 rounds. No, that isn't a typo. The ammo is almost $2 a shot, when bought in bulk. The brass is 65 cents per empty, direct from Starline, and bullets (I always go to Hornady first) run you between 40 cents each to $1.20 each, depending on weight and construction.

Using small rifle primers, and not a lot of powder, a typical load needs only 42 to 44 grains of powder, much the same as a garden-variety .30-06 load.

To build one, you need a .458 SOCOM barrel and bolt. The rest is all standard AR-15, of whatever variety you are in the habit of building.

The .458 SOCOM can actually prove to be too much of a good thing. The recoil of a 600-grain bullet at 1,000 fps, in an "M4gery" of less than eight pounds (and no pad on the buttstock) can bring tears to your eyes. When you go to build your .458, you will be a bit disappointed at the weight of the barrel, when first you pull it out of the shipping box. It will seem "too heavy" if you are accustomed to handling M4 barrels and lightweight carbine barrels. Don't be, you'll love that weight later when you shoot. Also, don't let your friends make fun of the rubber-padded stock you select for your build. When you are done and step up to the line for your first shot, the idea of a nine-pound AR-15 will be a lot more attractive.

CMMG

I tested a CMMG MkW-15 chambered in .458 SOCOM. It came with a Lancer magazine marked for .458 SOCOM, and it was everything you'd want in a heavy thumper, and then some. The stock was a Magpul, and a thicker rubber pad would have been nice. The MkW-15 came with a muzzle brake, and for that I was also grateful. CMMG makes its ARs in a spectrum of sizes and features, and you can get yours built the way you want. Or get the bare bones setup and accessorize it the way you need to.

PISTONS

This is perhaps one instance where I might find a piston-system AR attractive. You see, you can save some serious coin if you reload your own ammo, and load plated or coated bullets. Acme Bullet makes coated bullets in a wide range of weights, for the .45-70 and the .458 SOCOM, that are relatively inexpensive. I mean, a .576-grain bullet (easily loaded subsonic) at 45 cents per shot? Or lighter ones, also subsonic, and easier on the shoulder, like a coated .405-grain flat point, for 28 cents per shot? That's a lot easier to take than a dollar a bullet, and the recoil of full-power ammo.

The Wilson Combat .458 HAM'R and its suppressor. Oh yes, there was fun that day.

SUPPRESSORS

In many other calibers, you will find it quite advantageous to be using a "too big" suppressor. It is not uncommon for shooters to invest in a .30 suppressor, and to use it on everything smaller. Yes, when shooting .223/5.56 through a .308 suppressor, you are giving up a few decibels because the center hole is too large. But two, three or four dB, compared to another $1,000 for a .223-specific suppressor, plus the wait and tax stamp, makes those "lost" decibels a whole lot less attractive.

You don't have that choice here, as there are few, if any, suppressors bigger than those meant for a .458. No problem, Wilson Combat makes a suppressor suited to the .458 HAM'R, and with it you can make shooting even more fun.

.458 HAM'R

It is a rare thing that comes into the world which cannot be improved upon. And so it was with the .458 SOCOM. Bill Wilson builds .458 SOCOM rifles, and they are good ones. But to up the .458 SOCOM game, Bill had to do more than work with an AR-15.

So that's what he did. First, he went with an AR-10 barrel extension and bolt face. This gave him more steel, and bigger locking lugs. That allowed him to up the chamber pressure to 46,000 PSI. I know what you're thinking. "That's more than the AR-15 can stand in a .458 SOCOM case." Correct. So, Bill moved the shoulder of the .458 HAM'R forward enough that it can't possibly chamber in a .458 SOCOM chamber. But it isn't so far forward that it decreases neck tension. No, you need lots of neck tension because you are upping the velocity of the bullets by a significant amount.

Wilson Combat does not keep you in the dark. You want to know what a rifle, or an upper, is chambered in? Look at the side and read it. And be prepared for recoil and fun.

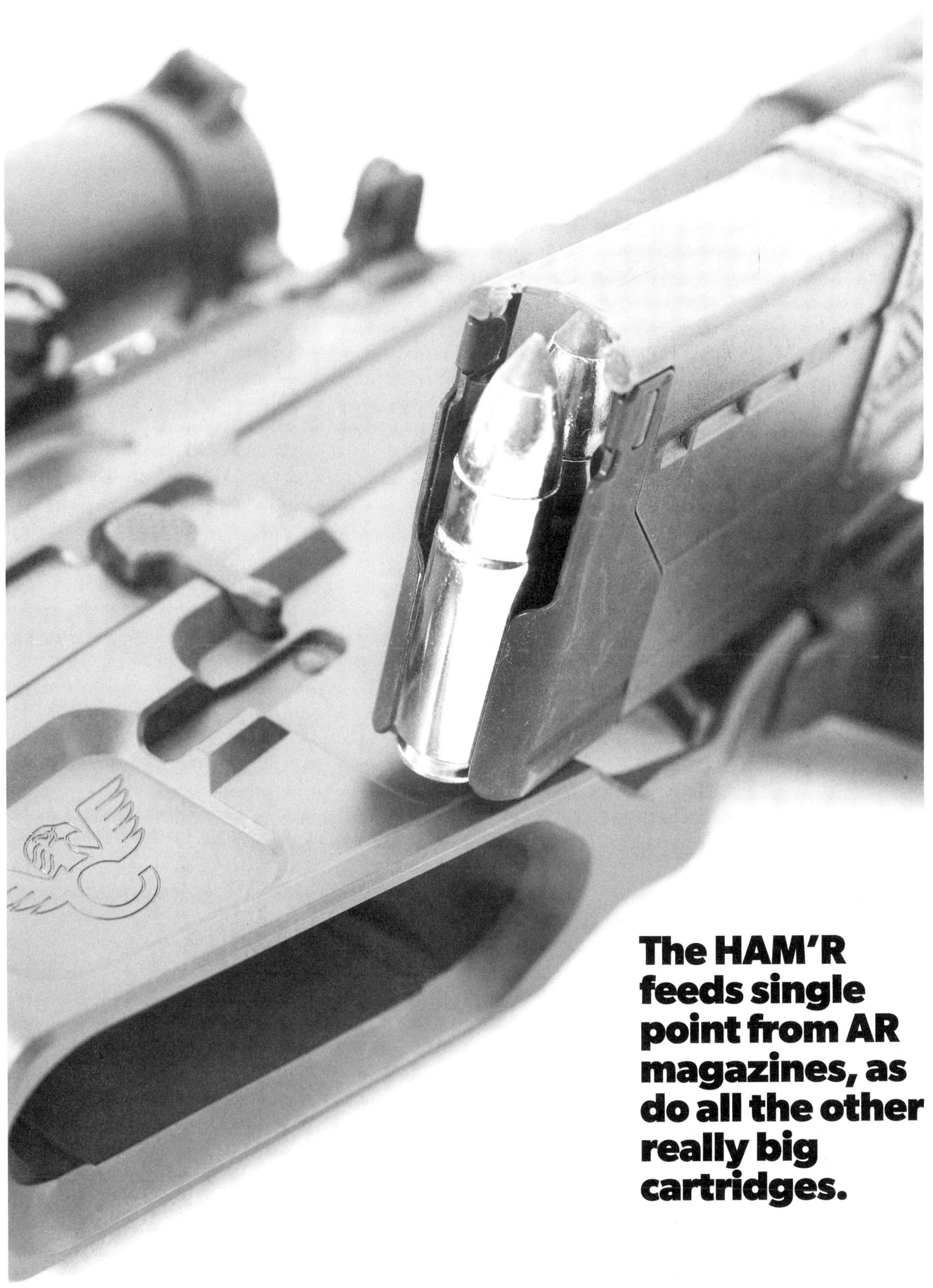

The HAM'R feeds single point from AR magazines, as do all the other really big cartridges.

Since he makes ARs, and the AR-10 barrel extension and bolt are not going to work on top of a pure AR-15 lower, Bill designed the rest of the rifle around the .458 HAM'R.

The results are impressive. A .458 SOCOM pushes a 300-grain bullet up to 1,900 fps, but a carbine-length barrel is going to be slower. A .458 HAM'R pushes the same weight to 2,100 fps even out of a carbine. And 200 fps might not seem like much, but remember, we're talking a .45-caliber bullet weighing

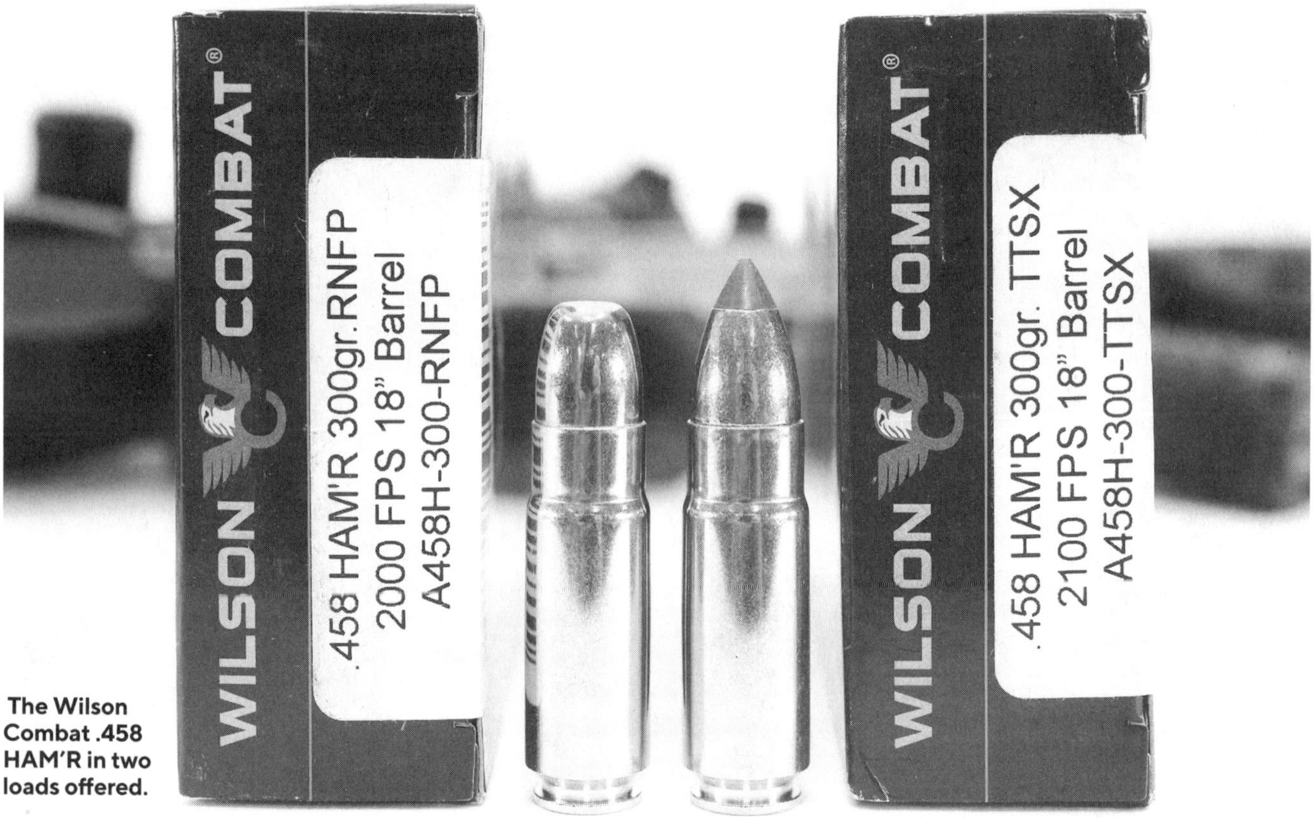

The Wilson Combat .458 HAM'R in two loads offered.

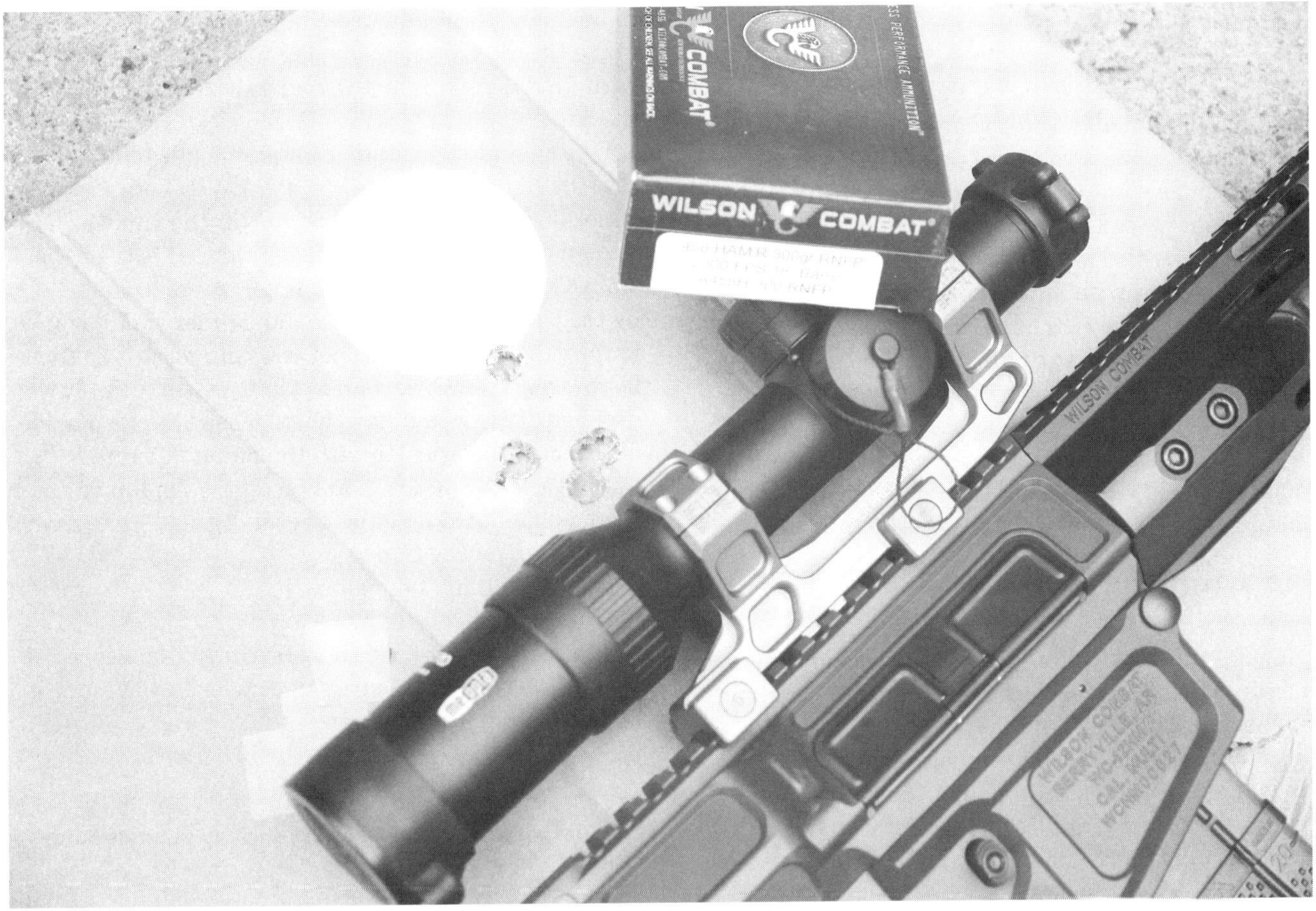

300 grains. It is going to leave a mark.

You can't convert your AR-15 to .458 HAM'R, you have to get a complete rifle from Bill Wilson. Which is not exactly a hardship, since you will be getting one of the best ARs to be had.

(above) Hang on tight, because the .458 HAM'R is going to come back at you. But if you do things right, you can have that power and this accuracy as well.

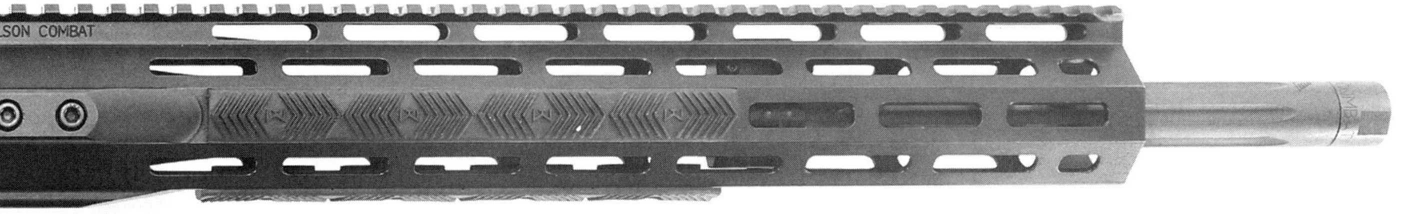

You want a rifle chambered in .458 HAM'R? Then contact Wilson Combat and explain what you want built. You can't build one yourself.

NEED

What do you need either of these for? To quote my brother Mike, "There you go again, confusing wants with needs." Now, if you were going to be hunting big game such as moose, elk or other critters in dense brush, heavy woods, or thickets, then a self-loading .45 rifle like either would be comforting. The .458 HAM'R, loaded with 300-grain, round-nose solids, is going to penetrate well. And the Lancer magazines Bill Wilson supplies with his HAM'R hold four, seven or nine rounds each.

A moose in the thickets can be a very dangerous thing. And the ability to deliver what horsepower you have, as quickly as possible (and much faster than a bolt-gun can) is a very good thing.

EVEN BIGGER BORE

Back in the early days of this wild ride of experimental ARs in the 21st century, .50 was the goal.

The .502 Thunder Sabre is a cartridge that pretty much only cartridge collectors will know of. The cartridge came to us from Robyn Church of Cloud Mountain Armory, and I wrote about it in my first AR-15 book. I don't know if Cloud Mountain is still in business, but there are other gunsmiths who can make the .502 for you, as it is another .50 AE case with an AK rim diameter, and it delivers as well as the rest.

One that got lots of ink, but pretty much never saw the light of day was the .499 LWR. Leitner-Wise Rifle. The parent case is the .50 AE, the rim was turned down to fit the bolt face of an AR bolt for the 7.62x39, meaning .443 of an inch. It was looked at by the Coast Guard. (Hey, a .50-caliber small arm, for putting engines into "not working" status so the boat can be boarded, sounded like a good idea.) It was dropped. This would have been before anyone outside of Illinois was familiar with the name "Obama."

I have seen ammunition listed for sale; I have not seen a rifle listed for sale. There's a great scene from the movie *The Big Short:*

"I'm not wrong, I'm just early."

"It's the same thing!"

Too early, or not enough R&D time or money, or who knows what. I'm sure someone does, but since it is now history, we move on.

The Alexander Arms .50 Beowulf, a scarily accurate hard-hitting carbine.

Trust me, you want the muzzle brake AA installs on the Beowulf.

.50 BEOWULF

Bill Alexander is an engineer. As I've said before, if you can keep up, an afternoon's discussion of things engineering with Bill should be worth a semester's credit at any good college.

So, he and the crew at Alexander Arms take the idea of a .50 rifle cartridge for the AR-15, and run with it. The .50 Beowulf uses the same parent .50 AE case as others.

Alexander Arms also uses the AK rim diameter for its bolts, with good reason: It is the same as the 6.5 Grendel case. (Yes, the Beowulf was introduced first.) With a solid bolt, and proper design and engineering of the rest, Alexander Arms produced a rifle that

The muzzle brake Alexander Arms installs on the end of a barrel chambered in .50 Beowulf.

(above) A partial lineup of loads you can buy or make for your .50 Beowulf. Yes, that puny little cartridge in the middle is a .223.

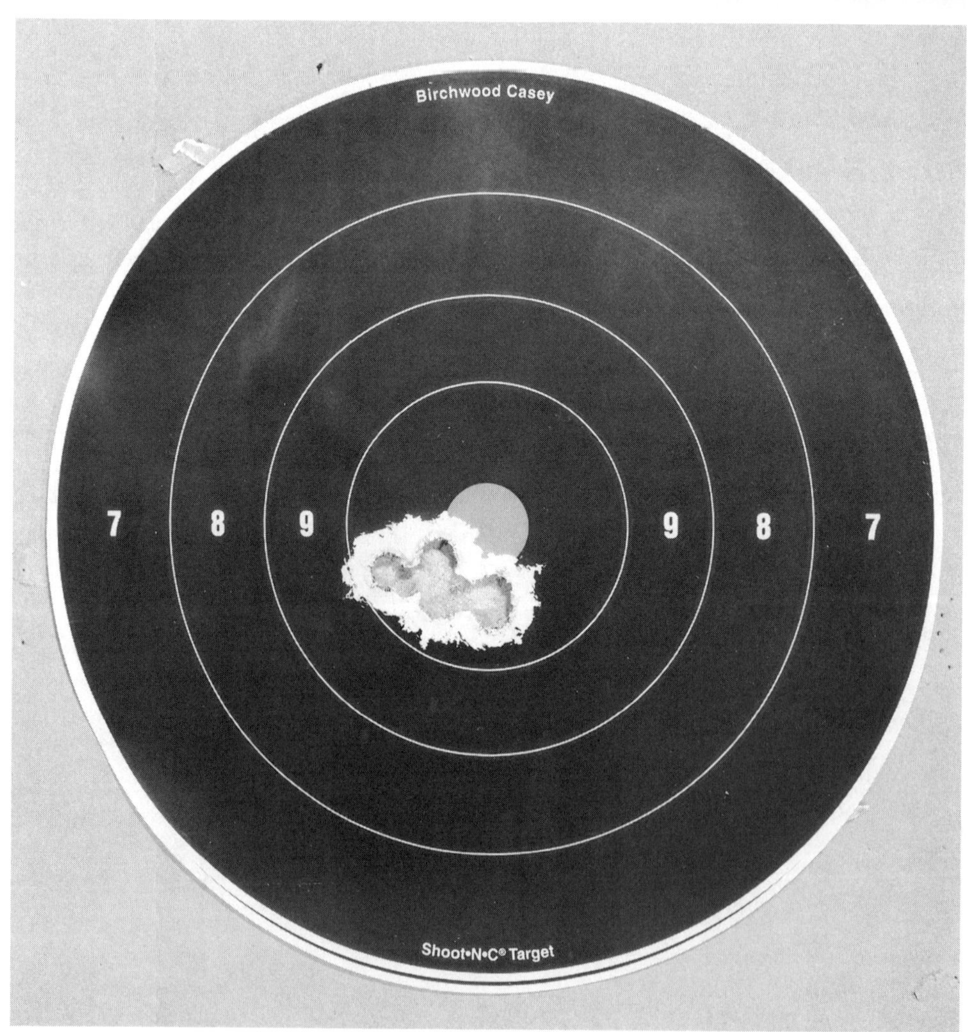

(right) Accuracy? You want accuracy? Provided you can hold on, this is what a .50 Beowulf can do for you at 100 yards.

performs the way you want a .50 rifle to. It hammers whatever you are shooting at.

Now, the name is trademarked, so it is not SAAMI approved. Other ammunition makers load the cartridge, but they have to call it something different. One such name is 12.7x42.

I tested one of Bill's carbines a few years back, and it was a tack-driver. The barrel seemed excessively large at first, but once you realize there's a half-inch hole down the middle, it becomes less of a tree-trunk of steel.

The .500 Auto Max cartridge feeds from an AR-15 magazine, but it has to be installed in an AR-10 rifle to handle the power. So Big Horn Armory just broaches the mag well of an AR-10 to AR-15 size. That's why it looks a little odd.

Despite the recoil (it delivered 325-grain bullets at over 1,800 fps, for a 585PF) it was a target vaporizer. Once I had done the obligatory accuracy work (I used a bag between my shoulder and the stock) and chrono work, I plinked at the 100-yard back berm. Whatever clod of earth I aimed at turned into dust. Any random target stick, or piece of wood, lying on the hill was shredded. It simply hit what I aimed at.

It isn't the AR-15 big-bore with the most horsepower (Bill Wilson claims that title), but it delivered plenty of muscle, and right on target.

.500 AUTO MAX

OK, we're going to make a big jump here, and go from the AR-15 to the AR-10. First, the cartridge. Big Horn Armory takes the .500 S&W Magnum, well, the case without the revolver rim, and makes it rimless. Then it stuffs a 400-grain bullet in it and use enough powder to get it up to over 2,000 fps. This is serious horsepower, and don't let anyone kid you otherwise. This is well in the range the .45-70 can deliver, except the AR500 is a self-loader, not a lever gun. This is 800-plus PF territory, something even a 3.5-inch 12-gauge slug gun is hard-pressed to deliver.

And, since it is a straight-wall cartridge, it is legal to hunt with in many locales. I shudder to think what a whitetail hit with one of these would look like, and there we perhaps do have too much of a good thing. But, if you want power, here you go.

Greg Buchel, of Big Horn Armory, having come up with this cartridge, then had to fit it into an AR of some kind. The problem he faced was this: He needed the AR-10 size and strength to handle the cartridge. But the cartridge would not feed from an AR-10 magazine. The wide case, at .526 diameter, was not going to stack properly in a magazine designed for cases with a .473 diameter. And it wasn't going to work as a single-point feed, as the gap between the feed lips is too wide for that diameter of a case.

But the .500 Auto Max would work out of an AR-15 magazine, with a few minor mods.

Simple solution: an AR-10 rifle with an AR-15 magazine well. Viola.

OK, time to back up. The .50 AE is actually a fatter case, at .547 of an inch, compared to the .500

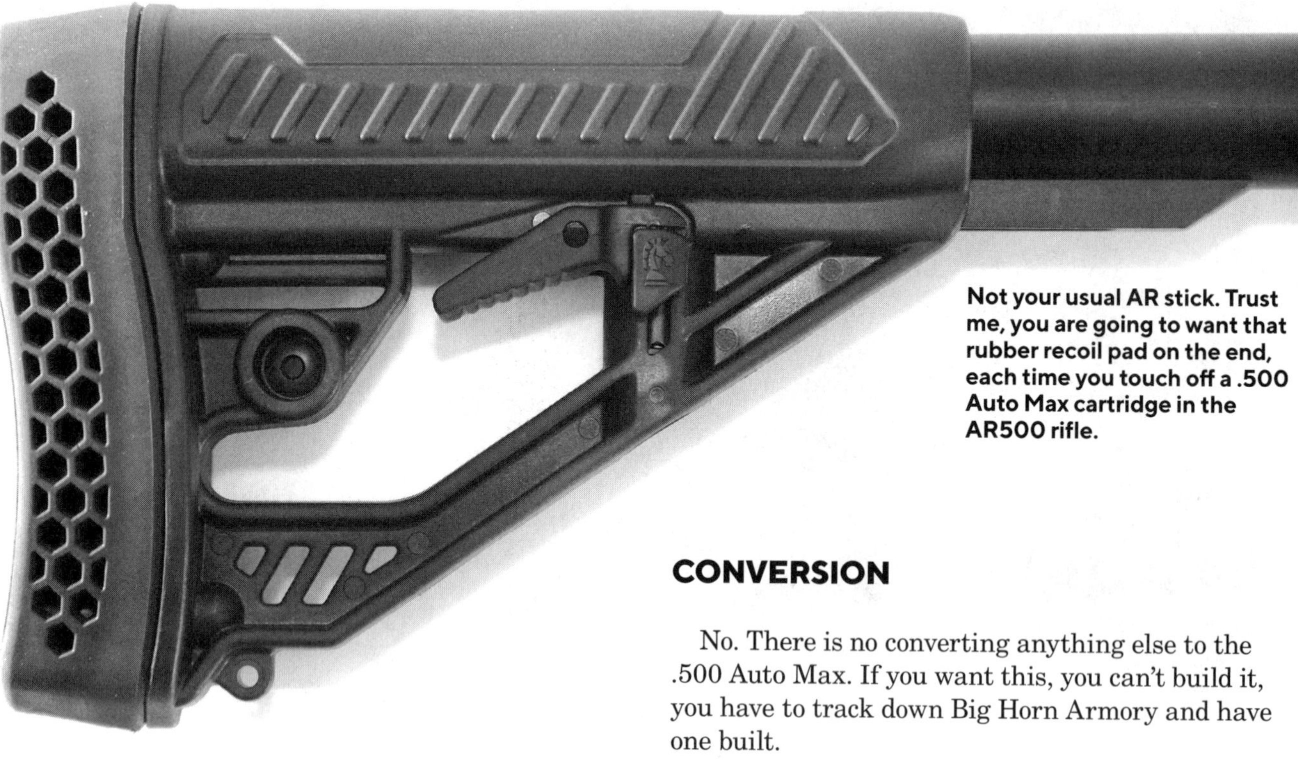

Not your usual AR stick. Trust me, you are going to want that rubber recoil pad on the end, each time you touch off a .500 Auto Max cartridge in the AR500 rifle.

CONVERSION

No. There is no converting anything else to the .500 Auto Max. If you want this, you can't build it, you have to track down Big Horn Armory and have one built.

Auto Max at .526. So, all the cartridges based on the .50 AE should be more powerful, right? Sorry, no. You see, the cartridges based on the .50 AE are fit into AR-15s, and thus have limited chamber pressures. Even Bill Wilson, with his .458 HAM'R, is limited in the chamber pressure he can use, as part of that rifle is of AR-15 proportion. Basically, the low to mid 30,000s are the AR-15 limit, and the Wilson limit is 46,000 PSI.

Since the .500 Auto Max goes into an AR-10 receiver set, bolt and so-on, it is limited to the pressures of the cartridges the AR-10 sees, so 55,000 PSI.

And boy does it deliver. The ballistics: a 400-grain bullet at 2,100 fps; a 350 at 2,300 fps; and, for the fans of hard-cast bullets (be prepared to scrub gas systems), a 440-grain, flat-point at 1,900 fps.

The recoil is not for the faint of heart, even with a muzzle brake installed.

The .500 Auto Max is basically the .500 S&W Magnum with the rim turned off to be flush with the case diameter.

The AR500 uses an AR-15 sized magazine in an AR-10 sized receiver set, and the end result is: It works just fine.

The AR500, firing the .500 Auto Max cartridge, is a handful, but once you are ready for it, it will be a whole lot of fun to shoot.

19

.300 AND .338 WIN MAGS

Holy cow. The Nemo.

Just when you thought it was safe to go into the water … they pull you back in again. OK, I mixed up two movies there, but we have two heavyweights here.

First up is the Nemo, chambered in .300 Winchester Magnum. Fit it into an AR-15? You have to be kidding. Even the AR-10 is a hopeless quest. The 5.56 loaded cartridge is 2.26-inches long, with a base/rim diameter of .378 of an inch. A .308/7.62 NATO is 2.80 inches in overall length, with a rim diameter of .473. The .300 Win Mag is 3.34 inches long, and the rim diameter is .532. You aren't going to make that fit into an AR, either a 15 or a 10, not with any amount of pushing.

The Nemo Omen is meant to be a long-range, hard-hitting and accurate rifle. Score on all three.

In order to fit a .300 Win Mag into an AR package, Nemo had to stretch everything. And it had to design new magazines, as well.

So, what Nemo did was make an AR that fit the cartridge. This entailed, well, everything. The lower, starting with the magazine well, is both longer and wider than standard. Known as the Omen, the Nemo .300 Win Mag is hefty. The length depends on what barrel you opt for, 18 inches or 24, or something in between. The base rifle tips the scales at just over 10 pounds, and by the time you load it up, install a scope and mount, attach a bipod and put a suppressor on the end (because, of course) you can easily be up to the weight of a lightweight belt-fed LMG in 5.56.

You get more reach and power per shot with the Omen than with a belt-fed 5.56, however, and at a lot lower price. Actually, just out of curiosity, I did a search for belt-fed 5.56 transferables. OMG. You could literally buy a nice, post-war ranch house in a nice little town, for the price any of them will go for. So, give up that little fantasy until after you have won the lottery.

Back to the Omen.

All the internals are first-rate, from a carrier (scaled up, of course, to handle the .300) made from 8620 steel, and then nickel-boron coated. The bolt is massively scaled up, and made of 9310 steel, the better-than-mil-spec new standard for AR bolts in the 21st century.

Magpul stock and pistol grip, and a free-float handguard with MLok slots on it all surround the Nemo magazine. You have a choice between 10-shot and 14-shot magazines. Obviously, magazines are proprietary, because no one, not even Magpul (and they make everything) is making AR magazines for the .300 Win Mag.

Which leads me to a thought, and one a bit impish. If the original was the AR-10, and the smaller became the AR-15, wouldn't that make the rifle chambered in .300 Win Mag an AR-5? There's one problem with that, the Armalite company, in the 1950s, developed an AR-5. It was a bolt-action survival rifle chambered in .22 Hornet. Armalite was a division of the Fairchild Engine and Airplane Corporation, and the Air Force needed survival rifles for the new XB-70 aircraft. Armalite developed the AR-5, but the XB-70 program was cancelled with only 12 prototype AR-5 rifles made.

So, the naming convention for the largest AR brings us back to the smallest centerfire Armalite made, and a cartridge that cannot be chambered in an AR-15. (Not that I haven't tried to figure a way.) But, I digress.

On top of the barrel, the gas system has an adjustable gas block, so you can tune it for a given load, or suppressed shooting. This is a good thing, as the .300 Win Mag has loadings in an impressive range of

This is the un-obtainium 5.56 belt-fed. There is rumored to be one and only one transferable M249 in existence. If you want a belt-fed 5.56, you have to go for something else. Even then, it will be expensive. A Nemo Omen is cheap compared to belt-fed anything.

bullet weights and velocities.

What does all this get you? Power.

A standard heavyweight long-range .300 Win Mag loading would be something like the Hornady 200-grain ELD-X bullet. Leaving the muzzle at a book velocity of 2,850 fps, with a BC of .597, the ELD-X does not go subsonic until it has passed 1,600 yards.

Now, this performance comes with a price. We've already discussed the weight, then there's the length. Full up, sans suppressor, the 24-inch-barrel version of the Omen is just under 46 inches long. Add a suppressor capable of handling the .300 Win Mag, and you have a rifle almost as long as the height of the shortest Oscar-winning actress, Mary Pickford. She was 4-feet, 10-inches tall. That's a lot of rifle to be hauling around, and it certainly isn't anyone's first choice for CQB.

But when you can tag someone a mile away (mystical wind-calling skills mandatory here) who needs CQB?

I have not had a chance to handle them, but I understand that you can get .300 Winchester Magnum ARs from Miller Precision, and from Noreen Firearms. Noreen also offers them, stepping up, in .338 Norma Magnum, and stepping down, in 7mm Remington Magnum.

The Omen delivers its .300 Win Mag power with this precision or more.

(above) The Rock River Arms .338 Win Mag rifle.

(below) Here you can see the quick-change barrel design of the RRA .338.

ROCK RIVER

If the .300 Win Mag is power, then the .338 is power on steroids. Where a standard .300 load is a 200-grain bullet at 2,850 fps, the .338 sends a 235-grain bullet, with a better BC, at the same velocity. This message to the unlucky does not go subsonic, due to its BC of .616, until it has passed the 1,700-yard marker. That's nearly a mile, folks. Now, adding 100 yards to the subsonic distance marker over the yardage of the .300 Win Mag may not seem like much, but remember, every step of the way, there's a heavier bullet arriving.

Rock River adds to the wonderfulness of this rifle by building it with a quick-change barrel system. Slide off the handguard, use the built-in lever/wrench to turn the barrel nut, and you can remove the old and then install a replacement.

It, too, is long and heavy, but that's the price you pay for this level of performance.

GUNSMITHING

Of course, with such beasts as these, you can also go up from there. We would be working in the extreme gunsmithing area first discussed in the book. It would require a gunsmith with lathe skills enough to fit a new barrel to a barrel extension, in the bore size you'd want. But it is theoretically possible to be making a Winchester magnum-based rifle that fired 8mm Remington magnum, .350 Magnum, .416 and even .458 Magnum.

Not that I would be in line to shoot such a beast, but for those who might want to, there is a clear path.

MILITARY?

The current en-vogue idea in the U.S. Army is "over-match." This involves having tools that can reach farther than the other guy's tools can reach. It assumes, of course, that our guys will be allowed the training and range time to actually be able to reach that far.

Since every time there's a budget crunch, or it seems like we don't need military force as much (Do I hear the strains of Kipling's "Tommy this, and Tommy that …" in the background?), training and range time get cut. Over-match is a reach. No pun intended.

To that end, the military is looking at making a squad-level belt-fed machine gun; something that shoots .338 Lapua. More reach than a mere 7.62.

Sig is all over it, of course, because it is always looking to get a leg up on the competition.

The Sig belt-fed over-match machine gun. It is so powerful you can't shoot it on steel targets inside the same zip code, or you'll damage them. (Small joke, but it will damage ranges if you aren't careful.)

20
FIRE
SAFE

.45-70 AUTO

I give up.

The quest for more power, the biggest gun, the artillery one can brag about the most, seems to be a trait inherent in mankind. On the bright side, that quest has brought us so many good things, and so many advances on all fronts, that it is a good thing we have it.

When I heard about this one, I just had to throw my hands in the air. Phoenix Weaponry did the obvious, but, boy, is it a studly piece. The rifle is an AR-10, mostly. Phoenix had to do some modifications to the basic platform, to get it to work with its brainstorm: the .45-70 Auto.

Not only can you have the .45-70 in an AR-10, but you can have it suppressed as well. Phoenix Weaponry can handle your desires on this subject.

Here you see the .45-70 AR cartridge, loaded with the most-excellent Hornady polymer-tipped bullets. These are 250 grains, but the Christine can shoot bullets up to 400 grains in weight.

Designers took the .45-70 cartridge, with its manly big rim, and turned the rim off. They added an extractor groove, and the rim they ended up with happens to be .473 of an inch in diameter. That should be familiar, because that is the diameter of the .30-06, and every American big-bore cartridge ever since. Well, most of them.

This leaves the case with a rebated rim, since the body of the .45-70 right above the (now gone) rim is .505 in diameter.

There is, of course, the matter of overall length. The AR-10 is based on the .308 Winchester, with its overall length of 2.800 inches. The standard .45-70 has an overall length of 2.550 inches, so that means there's no problem. But wait, there is.

You see, the .308 is pointed. No, yes, it is obvious, but no, the point means that it is a cone headed into a funnel. Easy feeding. Now, take a blunt cylinder, and try to feed it along the same path. As problems go, this is not one that is unsolvable. After all, handgun pistolsmiths who worked on and perfected the 1911 chambered in .38 special wadcutter handled this problem half a century ago. But still, this is the AR-10 we're talking about, and it requires some extra engineering. As a result of this minor problem, Phoenix has to use slightly modified M110 magazines. But, once the problem is solved, then feeding is no issue.

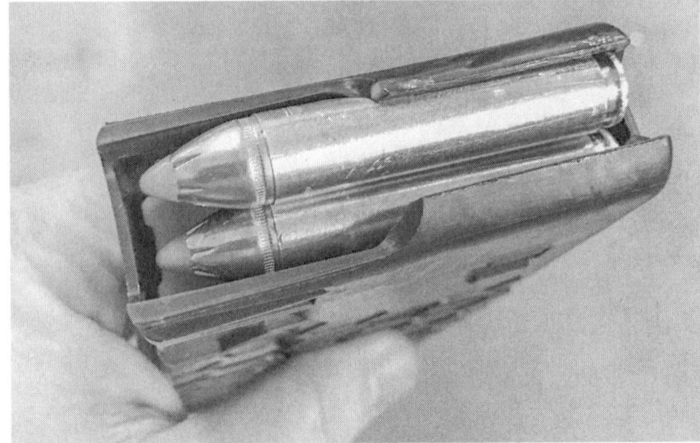

The modified magazines will feed the .45-70 Auto cartridges for as long as you can afford them, and stand the recoil.

Now, it might occur to some to call this the ".450 Bushmaster Supreme" or Bushmaster Super Magnum, but let's look at what you get. First of all, there's the matter of bullet weight. The Bushmaster (not to pick on it, but the Bushmaster is the first one that comes to mind as a comparison, so let's run with this) uses bullets of 250 or 260 grains. The .45-70 Auto uses standard .45-70 loading data, not just the old data for Trapdoor Springfields, but up to and including that reserved for the Ruger No. 1, the strongest action out there.

That means the .45-70 Auto can use bullets up to 400 grains, and push them in the direction of the

The Christine is a manly rifle, for sure. It is also a custom rifle, and Phoenix Weaponry can build it the way you want it, within reason.

target at just over 2,000 fps. Firing up the calculator, we realize that the .45-70 Auto generates an 800-plus Power Factor. Oh, my. That's going into the eye-watering level of felt recoil.

The rifle chambered for this is called the "Christine" by Phoenix Weaponry, and the list price starts at $4,800. That includes the muzzle brake that is a most desirable thing to have. One might even say an absolute must-have.

As a custom-built rifle, you can pretty much count on superb levels of accuracy. While this is the AR-10 (at least, in the starting point) engineers, gunsmiths and builders know how to make the Stoner system accurate these days. That problem was solved a long time ago.

To load ammo, you'll need .45-70 dies, a .30-06 shell plate or shell holder, and a ready supply of heavy bullets and cartridge-appropriate powder. As well as nerves of steel, to shoot it. Let us know how that goes.

The .45-70 Auto can be brilliantly accurate. Probably more accurate than most users, and when you add in the dollops of recoil, it takes practice and dedication to shoot this well. The rifle can do it. Can you?

Power? Plenty of power. Yes, hogs can need a lot, but I'm surprised there was enough left to identify, given the horsepower the Christine generates with its .45-70 Auto loading.

21

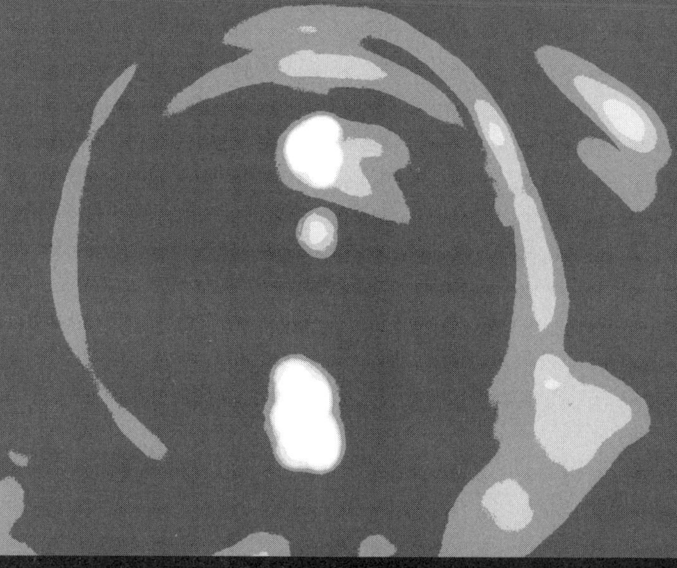

.50 BMG

The big 50 started life as an outgrowth of technology and the Great War. In 1914, warfare was much like it had been in previous generations. The great armies of the world still even had cavalry outfits, and fully expected to use them (and did, sometimes with horrifying results) in any conflict.

By 1917, when the United States entered the war, aircraft were fast, maneuverable, armed and common. Balloons were use for observation, filled with hydrogen, and tempting, if very dangerous, targets. Tanks had appeared in September 1916, and by the time our doughboys were shipping out, tanks had gone through a quick, violent and costly evolution.

A machine gun that could fire a round capable of quickly disabling an enemy airplane, one that could fire an incendiary round to ignite balloons, and punch holes into or through tanks would be very welcome.

John Browning, who by then had already been designing machine guns for two decades, took the obvious step: He scaled up his already in-production M1917 machine gun for one that used a .50-caliber bullet, in place of the .30 of the M1917. He delivered his prototype on Nov. 11, 1918.

With the pressure off, the War Department (they knew how to name organizations back then) took its time, and it was finally adopted as the M1921, a heavy machine gun. And heavy it was, as at that time all machine guns were water-cooled. The lighter ones were "automatic rifles" such as the BAR.

Compared to the .30-06, the .50 BMG is eye-opening. And, if you look closely, the .50 BMG is pretty much a scale model of the .30-06, just up-sized. The .30-06 fires a bullet of up to 180 grains, at velocities of 2,600 fps. To do this, it burns 45 to 50 grains of powder. The .50 BMG hurls a 750-grain bullet, and can do so at 2,800 fps, using 220 grains of powder. Recoil is, as you can imagine, also markedly greater. Just to give you an eye-opener, remember the Power Factor we've been discussing? A 165PF is handgun Major, a .308 rifle can deliver a 435PF, and the big-bore ARs can go as high as 600, 700, 800PF. Well, a .50 BMG, out of an M2HB, has a 2,100PF. Yes, a Power Factor of over 2,000. So much recoil that a rifle (not a machine gun) chambered in .50 BMG will come standard with a muzzle brake installed. If you ever find yourself wondering "What is the recoil like without it?" do not give it a try. I did, once. It was a Mauser 13mm anti-tank rifle that had been re-barreled to .50 BMG. I shot it once. Once.

In this regard, the .50 BMG has it all over even the big boys of the African dangerous game calibers. Something like the .458 Lott, which is the biggest cartridge I'd want to be putting into a bolt-action rifle, pales in comparison. The Lott is a .375 H&H magnum case that is left fully open, and accepts a .458-inch diameter bullet. (Big surprise there, eh?)

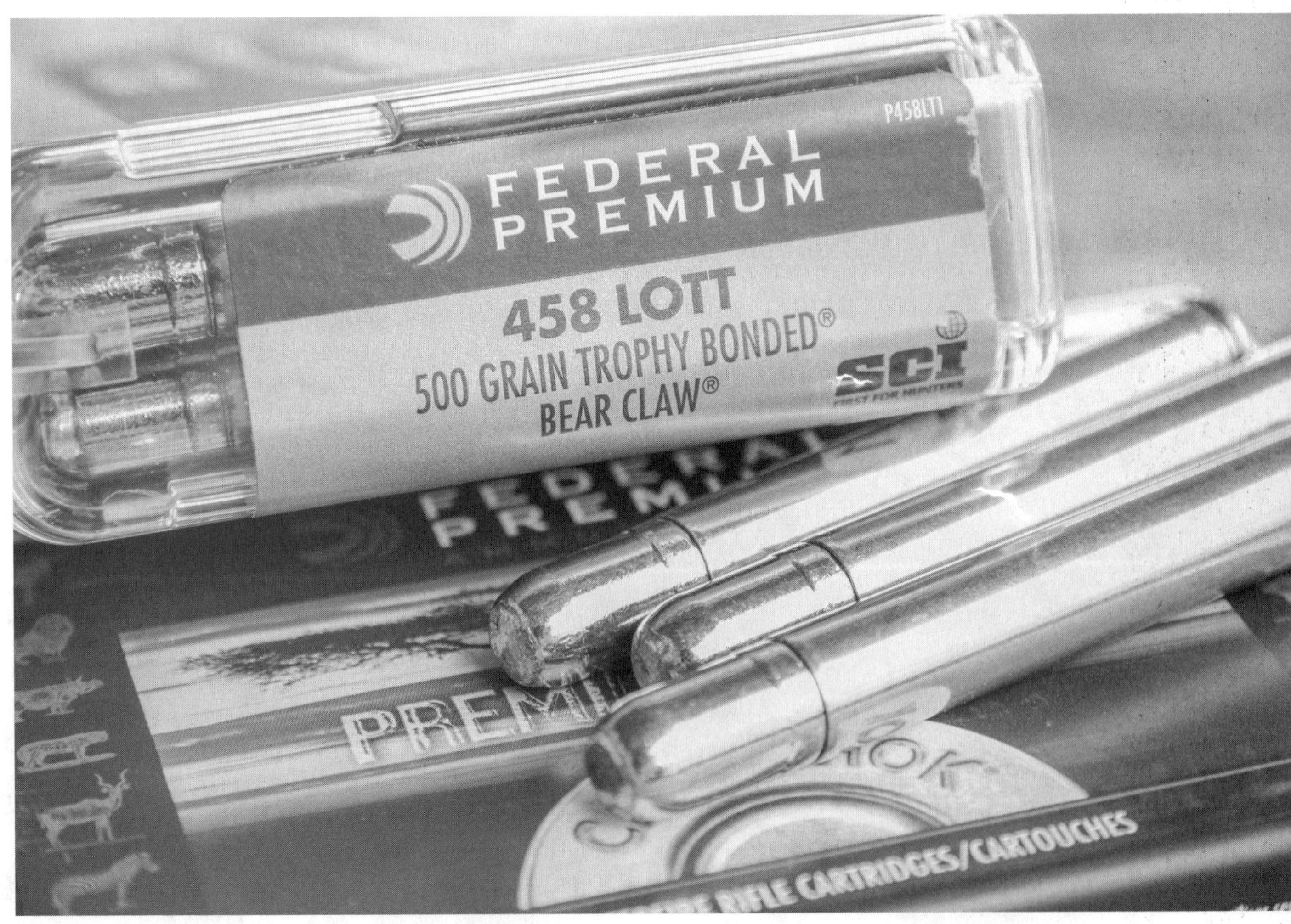

The .50 BMG has it all over even the biggest of the big-bore, dangerous-game cartridges like the .458 Lott.

It delivers a 500-grain bullet at 2,300 fps. That is a 1,150 PF.

In the past, .50 BMG (Browning Machine Gun) ammunition wasn't particularly accurate. Not because the makers weren't concerned with accuracy, or didn't know how. No, it was the nature of machine guns and their use. Let's say you want to give an abrupt surprise to an enemy unit, say, 1,000 yards out. Or you wanted to shellac an opposing artillery emplacement that you just turned the corner and saw, multiple football fields away. You do not want a firearm that will put each and every round through the same hole at those distances.

You want a slight spread, so you can aim for the center of the group, and count on the spread of the cone of fire covering the area, and awarding those unlucky enough to be in the path of a particular bullet a prize for their bad luck. That spread is called the "beaten zone." You want the spread to be just enough that you increase the probability of striking an enemy soldier, or vital piece of equipment, with your burst of fire, but not so large that the density of bullet strikes allows some to escape their portion of the bad luck being dished out.

Snipers want just the opposite. They want there to be no doubt about the exact location of each and every bullet impact.

As a result of the interest in long-range precision rifle marksmanship, ammunition makers now offer match-grade .50 BMG ammunition.

This puts the AR-15 owner in an interesting situation. The .50 BMG cartridge is absurdly long, compared to what an AR-15, or even an AR-10 can handle. One of the absolutes in the AR-15 world is that any new cartridge invented or designed has to be one that will still function in the autoloading cycle of the AR. This, the .50 BMG has no hope of accomplishing. Those of us in the AR-verse solve this conundrum in the usual manner we solve such problems: We jettison the hard-and-fast rule. As a result, the .50 BMG is the only chambering you'll find ARs made for, that is not a magazine-fed cartridge. Now that I write that, I realize there have to be others, but if so, they are uncommon. The self-loading feature is too great

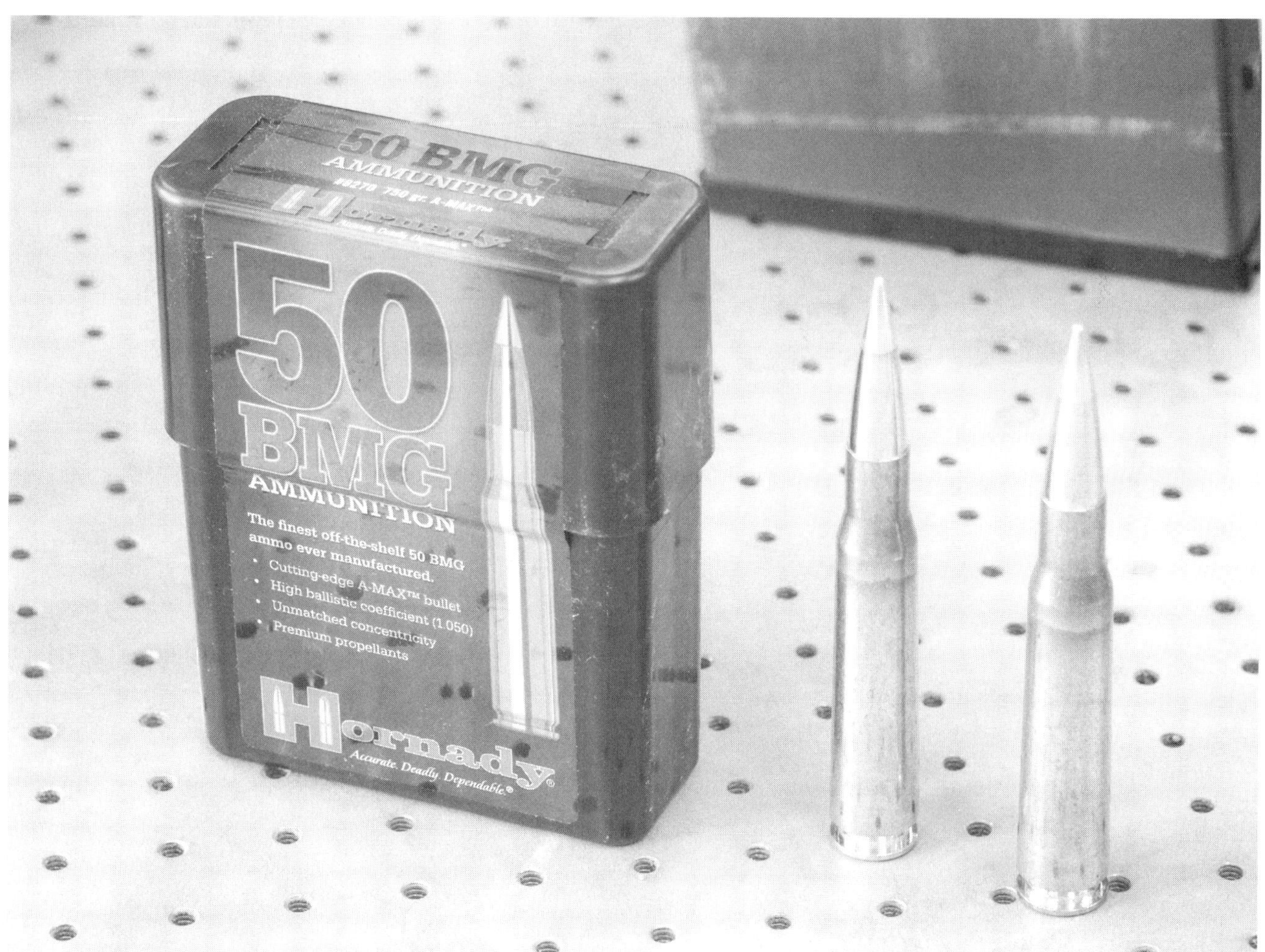

There is now sniper-grade .50 BMG ammo available, but you have to be willing to pay for it.

an identifier to give up, to get less than the power of the .50 BMG.

The usual approach to marrying the .50 BMG with the AR-15, as with the Safety Harbor conversion, is to make the .50 BMG part of it a self-contained unit. A single shot, bolt-action upper, with the bolt stout enough to handle the big 50. The AR-15 lower acts as the stock assembly and the fire-control part, where the hammer strikes the firing pin in the bolt of the upper. The .50 is a single-shot, and it is not unusual (indeed, sometimes necessary) for the bolt to come out of the receiver on each firing cycle, in order to chamber the next round.

The AR-15 lower, with a weight of three to four pounds, clearly is not the major part of this conversion, and its weight is not sufficient to deal with recoil. As a result, the upper half, the .50 half, will be all steel; stout, heavy and with a long barrel. And usually a muzzle brake.

How long? As long as you can handle, because the .50 BMG needs barrel length. The standard barrel on the M2HB, the air-cooled heavy barrel version of the Browning machine gun, uses a barrel that is 32 inches long. On a tripod-mounted, or vehicle-mounted heavy machine gun, 32 inches is not too long. For a rifle meant to be carried and shot by one person, 32 inches is a burden. Although, I have to say that someone who is using a suppressed, big-bore sniper rifle might be getting close. As an aside, a rifle chambered in, say, .338 Lapua, with a 24-inch barrel, and a suppressor on the end, might be getting close to 32 inches. After all, the suppressor only needs to add an additional eight inches of length, to end up matching the barrel of the M2HB.

But make no mistake: It will be a lengthy package, and not easy to handle.

One can go too short in barrel length. I have done a lot of chronographing of barrels; cutting them down an inch at a time, and when you get too short, things get really obnoxious. In regular rifle cartridges, "too short" and becoming obnoxious can happened when you go under 10 inches. On the .50 BMG, I'd say going under 20 inches is going to be too short. I recently had a conversation with a ballistician who works in areas I cannot discuss. He had been working with shorter-barreled .50 BMG rifles, for some people who thought they might be handy for CQB. Once he got barrel length down to the obnoxious level, not only did the

muzzle blast become oppressive, accuracy suffered.

So, 20 inches would be my limit for a "short" .50 BMG barrel. And then I'd only shoot it with both in-ear plugs, and external muffs, not ever under a covered firing line, and not for long periods of time.

The other aspect of the .50 BMG that needs to be addressed is cost. There's an adage in marinas around the world: "Owning a sailboat is like standing in a cold shower, tearing $100 bills into pieces." Boats are expensive. Ammunition for the .50 BMG is going to cost anywhere from $5 to $20 a shot. Reloading is an absolute must. However, you cannot use regular reloading presses for the .50, they are not big enough. Fortunately, the interest in .50 shooting has caused the press makers to construct presses large enough to handle the .50 BMG, and they make dies for it as well.

The costs will still be great, even reloading. Primers will be much the same in cost, but bullets will be heinously expensive, compared to typical calibers. Count on a bullet for the .50 BMG to cost you three to four times as much as bullets for, say, a .30-caliber rifle. And powder? At a nominal 220 grains per shot, a pound of powder is good for just under 32 rounds. If you are used to loading the .223, with 26 grains per shot, and 270 rounds per pound of powder, the .50 is going to be alarming.

One very good thing about reloading is that you can tailor your loads. As long as you are careful, and follow instructions properly, you can dial back the power. Instead of a 750-grain bullet at 2,800 fps, you can shoot a lighter-weight bullet as less velocity. This will save on powder costs, and on recoil costs.

Then again, given a pound of powder to load them, 270 rounds of .223 is a pleasant afternoon of plinking, drills and working on basics. The 32 rounds of .50 BMG is a full day's work to shoot, and if you aren't careful, you'll have a headache and a flinch by the time you are done.

Get into .50 BMG shooting slowly, with a plan, and with the full understanding that this is going to cost a lot of money.

A rifle chambered in .50 BMG is going to be long, because the barrel has to be long. Add a suppressor and you end up with four feet or more of hard-hitting (on both ends) rifle.

22

SHOTGUNS

The problem with shotguns is they fire shotgun shells. And those are not easy to fit into the AR-15, the AR-10, or any AR-like platform. The rim, in particular, wreaks havoc with magazine-lip design and dynamics.

The desire is to get the downrange performance of a shotgun, without the need for pumping an action, or the reloading hassle of tube magazines.

The military now uses the Mossberg 590, a pump-action shotgun. Great, but pumps are so 19th century, and this is the 21st. Photo By: Army Sgt. Timothy Hamlin

The shotgun is the poor man's .50 caliber. I mean, a one-ounce slug, at a listed 1,600 fps, that's going to leave a mark. For sheer horsepower, it is difficult to beat the shotgun. There's just one problem: The 12 gauge doesn't fit into an AR-15. Or an AR-10. There just isn't enough elbow room.

.410 BORE

However, all is not lost. If you really have to have a shotgun, and it has to be an AR-15, then you can get one in .410. I know, I know, the .410 isn't your first choice for alley sweepers, but you are the one who wants a shotgun that is an actual AR-15, or clone, or compatible.

So, you get an International Firearms Corporation .410. It is an AR-15 in .410, so much so that the magazines look like modified Magpuls. You can even put it onto a standard AR-15 lower, if all you want, or need, is the conversion upper.

Or, go on over to UniqueTek, a specialty supply outfit that offers many neat extras for reloaders and competition shooters, including a complete .410 upper, that simply slaps onto your AR-15 lower, and the magazines hold 10 rounds each.

Now, the .410 is not exactly a powerhouse. However, I can tell you from experience (and having won the bet that came about as a result of disbelief) that a .410 shotgun can clear pins off a table. And not just the 9mm pin set, with the pins six inches from the back. No, from the Main Event set, with the pins three feet from the back. Yes, I had to center-punch each of them, and they did go off slowly. But off they went. And that was with a standard birdshot load. With the modern loads available to shotguns now, with three OO buckshot pellets, or buckshot and birdshot, or even the buck and discs that are available, 10 shots of .410 are going to cause a bad guy or home intruder a serious amount of injury.

The IFC .410 shotgun, which might not seem like the hammer of Thor, but anyone who is the recipient of a magazine of .410 buckshot might disagree.

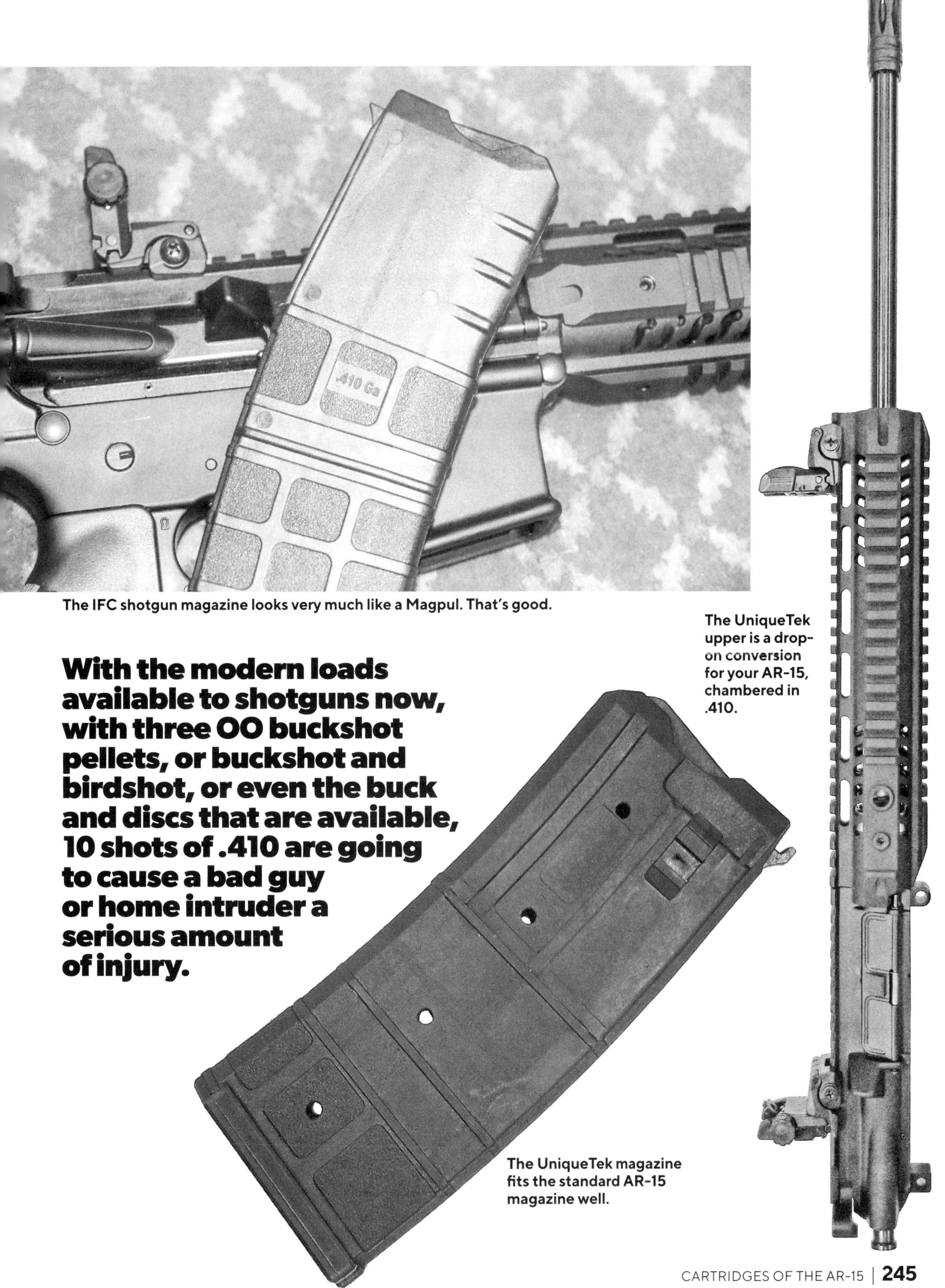

The IFC shotgun magazine looks very much like a Magpul. That's good.

The UniqueTek upper is a drop-on conversion for your AR-15, chambered in .410.

With the modern loads available to shotguns now, with three OO buckshot pellets, or buckshot and birdshot, or even the buck and discs that are available, 10 shots of .410 are going to cause a bad guy or home intruder a serious amount of injury.

The UniqueTek magazine fits the standard AR-15 magazine well.

12 GAUGE

If, however, you want 12 gauge, and you have to have at least kinda-sorta AR-15/AR-10 looks, then Rock Island Armory has just the thing for you. Its VR series are magazine-fed, 12-gauge shotguns that look like AR-10 rifles on steroids. Clearly bigger than a centerfire rifle, but not so big as to be bulky.

The one here at Gun Abuse Central is the VR80, and if you don't look with an eye toward proportion and scale, you'd mistake it for an AR-15/10 with a thumbhole stock. The upper and lower are 7075

The VR80 has typical AR-15 controls, and handles like a big AR-15 or AR-10.

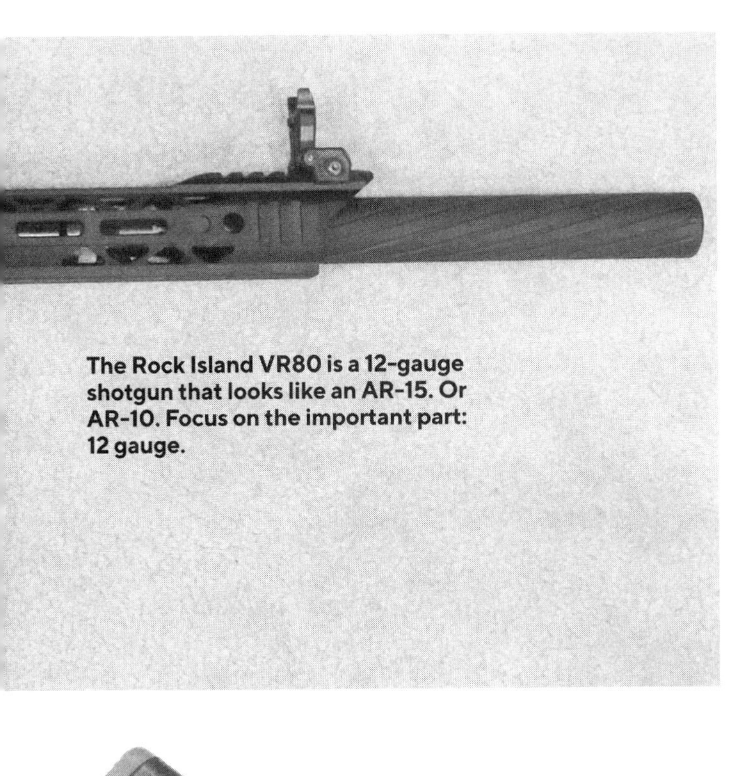

The Rock Island VR80 is a 12-gauge shotgun that looks like an AR-15. Or AR-10. Focus on the important part: 12 gauge.

aluminum alloy, the slim handguard is populated with MLok slots, and there is no worry about how to handle it. It handles like an AR-15, just bigger.

Oh, and the thumbhole stock? It covers a mil-spec buffer tube and connects to a standard AR-15 pistol grip socket. So, if you want, you can swap out the factory stock for whatever AR-15 stock and pistol grip you prefer. I would suggest you hold off on that for a bit. The recoil of a 12 gauge can be a bit stout, and taking some weight off and replacing the rubber recoil pad of the factory stock with a hard plastic GI stock might not be a lot of fun.

The VR80 comes with three choke tubes, and two pistons, one for light loads and one for heavy loads. So, if you use the VR80 for competition, and use light loads, use that piston and have fun. If you are using it for defense or hunting, and only feed it heavy loads, then use that piston and be safe. The chamber is reamed for three-inch shells, just in case you want to abuse your shoulder that way. The choke system is the Beretta MobilChoke, so you can order up whatever chokes you think you'll need or want.

There is a growing list of accessories for it, because of the competition use. And with the full-length top rail, you can swap out the factory folding iron sights for a scope, red dot, or other iron sights. Add a light, and you have a shotgun capable of dealing with most any problem short of incoming ICBMs.

Magazines? Capacity from some to a lot. And you can call Taylor Freelance and get plus-three magazine extensions, in case you need more than what's already there.

The VR80 has several magazine lengths, and you can add a replacement base pad to add a few more shells.

23

PISTOL CALIBER CARBINES

AR-15s chambered in pistol cartridges are not a new thing. In fact, anyone who makes an AR-15 seems to offer it now in a pistol caliber, and some offer only pistol calibers and no centerfire rifles. You have two choices of how you can go about it, and two avenues of approach. You also have a plethora of magazine choices.

Pistol-caliber long guns first saw the light of day with the Villar Perosa, a .380 machine gun fielded by Italian bicycle troops. Once their utility was discovered, pretty much everyone adopted something similar, from the German MP-40 to the American M3 "grease" gun and onward.

It all began, strangely enough, with Colt in the 1980s. I know, it surprises me, and I was a prolific shooter back then. The first article I recall on the new 9mm AR-15, was by Frank James, in the Vol 1 No. 1 of *SWAT AR-15/M-16 America's Assault Rifle*. That issue came out in 1986 (I bought a copy, and still have it) and Frank wrote up the new AR-15, one chambered in 9mm Parabellum.

We came late to the stamped-steel submachine gun (SMG) party, but when we did, we did it in that most American caliber, .45 ACP. My late father carried one like this through France and Germany.

The first, the Villar Perosa. In .380, and yes, first built as a paired-gun setup. Separate the two, add a stock, and you have an SMG.

The German MP40. The only thing Schmeisser about it are the magazines, and not all of them were so-marked.

The 9mm AR-15 was not exactly new, but it was new on the non-military market. Colt had been making them for a few years, beginning in 1982, for military and law-enforcement users. The original Colts had been SMGs, submachine guns, and they were intended to compete with the HK MP5. They did not succeed, for reasons we'll go into in a bit.

The SMG (the Model 633, 634 and 635, in Colt parlance) was a closed-bolt, blowback-system, select-fire firearm, with a 10.5-inch barrel, and except for the magazine sticking out of the bottom, looking like every other Colt of the time. Colt also offered the 635S, an integrally suppressed version, for the Drug Enforcement Administration (DEA) and others.

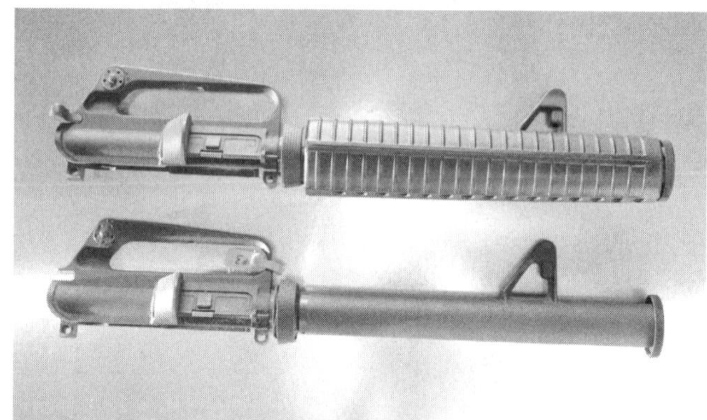

A pair of Colt 9mm uppers, the integrally suppressed one. The top one has the handguards installed, the bottom one shows the upper sans handguards.

You can see the three holes where Colt drilled the lower to drive in the pins holding the adapter blocks in place.

Oh, a brief aside here: The DEA wanted integrally suppressed 9mm SMGs not because the agents were looking to be sneaky. No, they were worried about flammability. They were doing a lot of busts of not just drug houses, but drug labs. The muzzle blast and residual powder heat could/might ignite the flammable vapors of drug production. I've never been able to find out if it was an actual thing that happened once or more, or if it was one of those "We keep running into rooms filled with flammable vapors, one of these days it will be a problem," sort of thing.

Colt made them, DEA bought them, and other departments as well. I've seen a few that were outside of the LE supply chain.

Select-fire ARs were not something Colt really wanted to be offering on the commercial market, and even if it had, the Firearm Owners Protection Act of 1986, with the Hughes Amendment, put the kibosh on that. So, Colt lengthened the barrel to 16 inches, and sold semi-auto-only versions of the 9mm SMG.

At the time Colt came out with this offering, my gun club was already deep into what we called Pistol-Caliber Carbines, or PCC competition. It is now one of the hottest Divisions in USPSA, but back then it was definitely looked at as odd. Even when talking to other USPSA/IPSC competitors at the time and after, it took some explaining to get the idea of PCCs across.

The Colt system started as a kludge, and never left it.

Since there are no locking lugs, the Colt 9mm barrel (right) is just the back end of the chamber. Colt still has to thread the barrel into a barrel extension, it is just one lacking locking lugs.

The magazines are modified Uzi mags. Colt modified them to incorporate a hold-open tab on the follower, and modified the feed lips to enhance feeding in the geometry of the Colt receivers. Unfortunately, the modified feed lips also had a slight "airsickness" problem. The wrong jolt on a loaded Colt magazine could see it spew a few, many or even all the rounds out of the magazine in a spontaneous unloading. There are a lot of magazines Colt could have used, but for some reason it used Uzis. (I have to point out that unmodified Uzi magazines do not have the "airsickness" problem.)

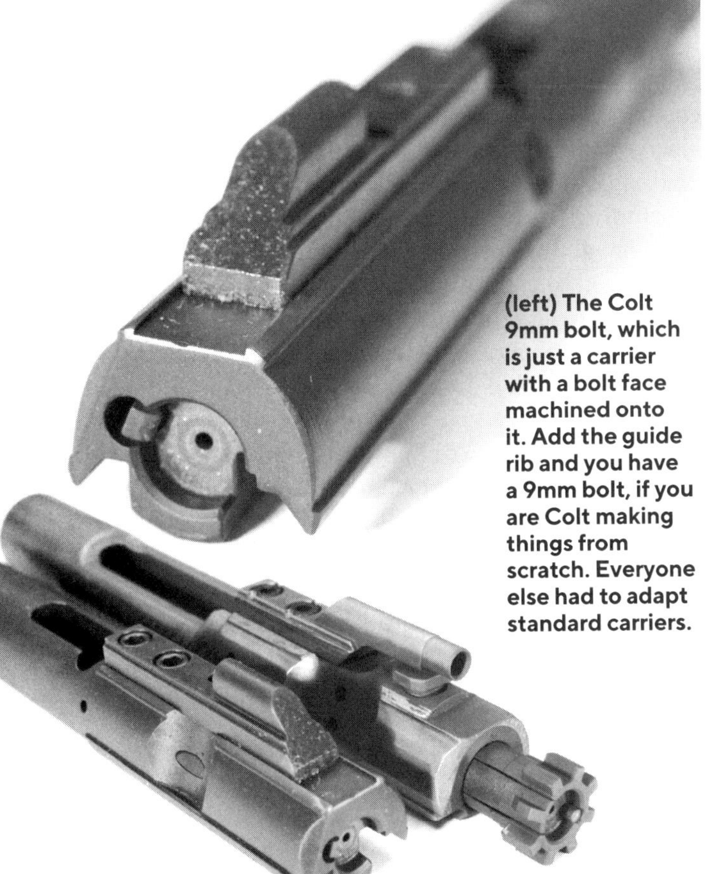

(left) The Colt 9mm bolt, which is just a carrier with a bolt face machined onto it. Add the guide rib and you have a 9mm bolt, if you are Colt making things from scratch. Everyone else had to adapt standard carriers.

Here you see the difference in length. The .223 bolt adds length to the carrier, the 9mm reduces it. This is how a 16-inch 9mm barrel can result in a shorter firearm than a .223 with a 16-inch barrel.

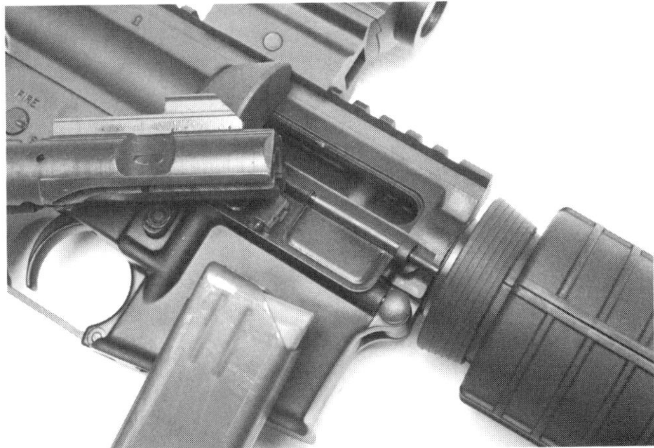

The Colt uses modified Uzi magazines (this one was made by CProducts) and they are prone to spontaneous unloading. Especially if dropped.

The second kludge is the lower receiver. The Uzi magazine is not nearly as long, front to back, as the AR-15 .223 magazine is. In order to do the R&D, the Colt engineers, I suspect, simply pinned in blocks to fill the dead space. I've seen Colt toolroom samples that had Delrin blocks in the magazine well. For an R&D project, pinned blocks, even Delrin ones, work fine.

However, Colt did that for production carbines and SMGs. No, I'm not kidding. If you haven't seen a Colt, the holes drilled through the receiver, and the pins in there holding the blocks, will come as a surprise. At least for the production versions, they used steel blocks.

A prototype Colt 9mm, showing the Delrin blocks pinned in place. For production, Colt used steel. Good choice.

For the longest time, Colt used 1960s-era "slickside" receivers in its 9mm builds. Now Colt offers M4 uppers.

Since the Colt 9mm is a blowback, there is no gas-tube hole in the upper receiver. The front sight does have the stub of a gas tube on it, but that is to keep the handguards from rotating. If the handguards turn, they can unscrew the barrel nut. No kidding. I've seen it happen.

Colt also always used a "slickside" A1 upper for its 9mms, with a big plastic case deflector as part of the ejection port door assembly. Colt continued to use the prehistoric A1 upper for decades, and only a decade or so into the 21st century did it start offering it with an M4-type flat-top receiver.

We didn't really care about Colt's new offering. For one thing it was far too expensive. The list price in 1986 was $695, about $1,650 in today's dollar. Those of us interested in PCC competition could build a suitable 9mm carbine for half that, and the difference represented a lot of practice ammo. The non-Colt carbines available back then weren't many, and some were definitely dodgy. One common one was the Marlin Camp Carbine. This was a 9mm carbine designed to look a lot like the M1 Carbine. In 9mm, it used S&W M-59 magazines, which were common and inexpensive, but held only 15 rounds.

The problem with the MCC wasn't magazine capacity, but everything else. The geometry of the ejector caused empties to be hurled nearly to the next zip code. Owners spent a lot of time gradually shortening the ejector until it kicked out the empties just enough, but not too much. Cut it to too short and they failed to eject, and then it was a trip back to Marlin. No, Marlin would not sell parts, and even if it did, one look at the mousetrap assembly of the trigger housing cooled even the most enthusiastic home gunsmith's ardor.

The Camps weren't happy with high round-count use, and needed regular cleaning. The trouble there was, they were a bear to take apart, and worse to get back together. And they were fragile. Once it broke, it was back to Marlin, where the service department would most likely also install a "proper" ejector, starting the trim-and-test process all over again.

Most everything else was worse. To give you an idea of the horror we could encounter, do a simple web search for Wilkinson Linda Carbine. The new ones are good, but the ones made back in the old days were Sisyphean endeavors. I took one in for repairs, once. It was years before I finally convinced the owner to give up on getting it to work. He was willing to pay to keep trying, but I wasn't willing to keep trying.

One approach was to go with Olympic Arms, which

had its own problems, but you could get the parts kit to build up a 9mm carbine on an existing AR-15. Since many of us were doing just that, building ARs that Colt didn't, we opted for Olympic.

The Olympics, however, had to kludge the one thing Colt did right.

Colt, to make a bolt for the 9mm AR, simply took the AR-15 carrier and turned it into a bolt. Instead of boring out the front and inserting a rotating bolt, engineers just machined a bolt face onto the front of it. They installed a spring-loaded firing pin inside, and bolted a guide rib, instead of a gas key, on top of the bolt/carrier.

Olympic couldn't do this. For one, it would have been too expensive, since it would have to made from bar stock. So, what Olympic did was make a new 9mm bolt, one that fit into the front of a standard AR carrier.

The bolt didn't have to rotate (nor could it have, since there was no gas system in existence for such a setup), but it did have to have a barrel to fit it. As a result, the rear of the Olympic 9mm barrel had a big cone shape, a cone leading to the chamber. Olympic touted this as a reliability-enhancing feature, but it was there because it had to be.

This had a curious effect on overall length. The Colt, with the face of the carrier as the bolt face, could be half an inch or more shorter than a 5.56 with a 16-inch barrel. The barrel length is measured from breechface to muzzle.

The Olympic, because the bolt extended forward of the carrier, had a longer barrel that was only a 16-inch barrel.

Also, the shape of the bolt/extension on the Olympic dictated magazine design.

The Uzi, like many second-generation SMGs, uses a double-feed magazine. Like the AR magazine, rounds feed alternatingly from one side then the other. The narrow bolt/extension of the Olympic required a single-point feeding magazine. It wasn't wide enough to reliably reach both case rims on a double-feed magazine like the Uzi. Luckily for Olympic (and I'd bet good money engineers looked into this before they got too deep into the project), Sten gun magazines would work just fine.

The Sten gun magazines required a magazine well block, as did the Colt/Uzi mags, but Olympic also took a shortcut and economy measure. Instead of blocks front and back, it simply used a single, rear block, and used the lower receiver magazine catch to hold it in.

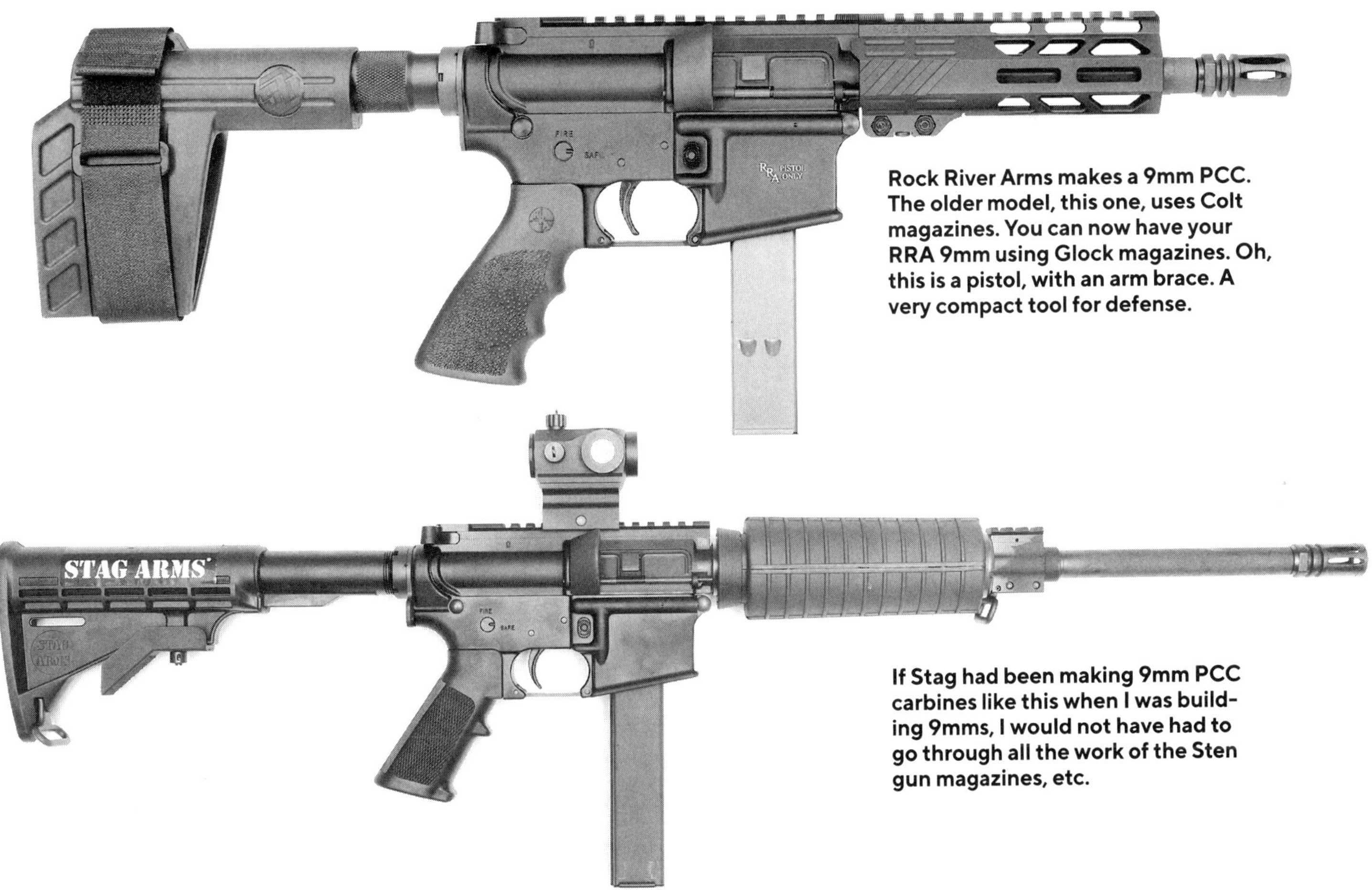

Rock River Arms makes a 9mm PCC. The older model, this one, uses Colt magazines. You can now have your RRA 9mm using Glock magazines. Oh, this is a pistol, with an arm brace. A very compact tool for defense.

If Stag had been making 9mm PCC carbines like this when I was building 9mms, I would not have had to go through all the work of the Sten gun magazines, etc.

The Sten magazines Olympic provided used a single small bolt installed on the rear spine of the tube, and a slot in the block. There was a lever, exactly like that on an AK, holding the magazine in place. If you forgot, and pressed the regular AR mag button, both block and magazine fell out.

I dedicated a lower receiver to be a 9mm receiver, and drilled a small hole for a locking screw to hold the block in place. Even if I pressed the mag button, the block would not come out.

Sten gun mags were cheap back then, even cheaper than M14 magazines. I stumbled on a source of them for a dollar each. They had been modified with internal brass rods, to constrict capacity from 32 rounds down to 20 rounds each. And they were caked, simply slathered, in cosmoline. For a buck, I was willing to do the work of extracting the brass rods (I used them later to reinforce cracked rifle stocks in customers' hunting rifles. How's that for salvaging?) and I scrubbed off the cosmoline. Then, located, drill and tap, and lock a bolt in place on each one, and viola, I had my own 9mm mags for my PCC.

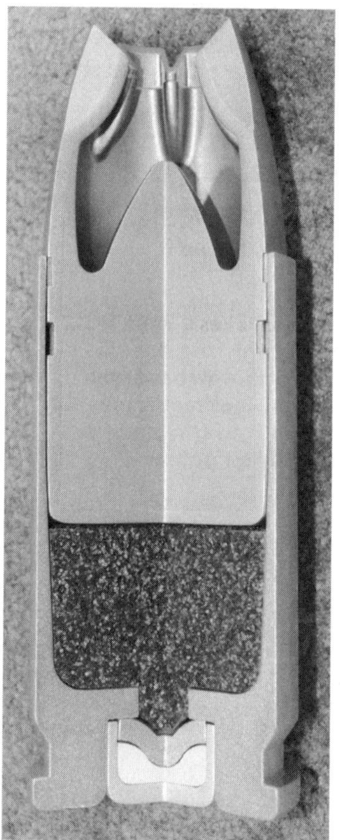

This cutaway demonstrator shows why the 9mm is so economical to load. The combustion chamber (the room in the case for the powder) is so small, it takes very little powder to get a 9mm bullet up to speed.

Oh, there was one other difference between the Colt and the Sten magazine PCCs. The Colt magazines were difficult to load. You could load them without a loading tool, but it took work. The Sten magazines, on the other hand, were absolutely impossible to load much past 10 or 12 rounds unless you had a tool. I had both, and I had several designs of loading tools for each. If you find yourself acquiring either, you too will have a supply of magazine loading tools in your gear bag. Trust me on this one.

Why go to all this trouble? Cost, practice and fun.

At the time, I could reload 9mm for a lot less hassle, and a lot less cost than .223. The 9mm brass empties only needed a quick rinse to get the mud off of them, and two hours of tumbling, to be ready for loading. No need to trim brass, or lube then clean the lube off as with .223 brass. The cost of components was a factor. If I bought in bulk (and I, and the others in my club, did) I could get the price of 9mm reloads down almost to $40 per 1,000 rounds. That compares to about $90 per 1,000 today. Which is half the cost of factory ammo, and about the same as in the old days, adjusted for inflation.

So, I could shoot more, and I could shoot indoors in the winter and not be subjected to the muzzle blast of .223.

And fun? We were shooting PCC on regular handgun USPSA courses. That meant we were shooting no farther than 25 to 50 yards, and we found we could do it at warp speed. The PCC was also a skills multiplier. A C-class handgun shooter could post A-class handgun scores with a PCC.

Today, the world is an entirely different place. You can hardly open a gun magazine without seeing an ad for an AR-15, and many manufacturers offer a pistol-caliber carbine as an option.

You have two paths for magazines, and two paths for a complete rifle or carbine.

The magazine paths are: SMG or pistol. The Colt magazine option is still there, simply because so many guns were made (despite Colt not liking making them, or so it seemed) and they still exist, and work. There is also the MP5 option. If the Colt 9mm carbine was not often seen back in the old days, the MP5 variants, aka HK94, were downright rare. And yet, they maintained a hold on the minds of shooters, and there are now a lot of MP5-derived semi-auto pistols and carbines being made in Turkey and imported to the U.S.

You can even get AR lowers built to accept MP5 magazines. No kidding.

The route to the Colt-type magazine AR gives you two options. One, you can find a Colt. The other is to take a regular AR-15 lower and install an adapter. One route is to use a two-piece Colt parts kit. Those will be rare, and you're probably better off just tracking down a Colt. The other is to use a one-piece adapter. The Uzi magazine isn't quite as wide as the AR-15 magazine body, and there is enough room on the sides for an adapter to be one piece and still fit the Colt magazine.

Brownells offers these, made by Pro Mag and Hahn. You can have the top-insertion type, or the bottom-insertion type. You simply install the adapter, swap out the buffer and spring (the 9mm requires a special, extra-heavy carbine buffer weight) and slap a 9mm upper on top, and you are ready to go.

Here is a Circle 10 PCC, in 9mm, built to use HK MP5 magazines. With the import of MP5 pistols and carbines built by Turkey, all of a sudden there are people making MP5 magazines new. You need not use the gold-wrapped HK mags from the 1990s.

This approach is so convenient that, miracle of miracles, Colt even started offering such an adapter.

Now, the whole idea of making a standard AR-15 lower, then pinning in blocks is so clumsy, you have to wonder why Colt stuck with it. The method of making the magazine well is an industrial process called broaching. Basically, Colt would drill a big hole down the center of the forging, where the magazine well would be. Then, they'd set the receiver in a fixture, and stick the end of what looks like a four-foot long file through the hole. Hydraulic power then pulls the broach through the hole. Along the four sides of the broach are cutting teeth, each row a fraction of an inch wider than the previous ones. In one pass, the hole is cut to shape.

So, why didn't Colt simply broach the lower to accept the 9mm magazine? I have no idea. But that approach was adopted later, in particular by Rock River, which makes a regular-contour AR-15 lower with the magazine well broached for the Colt/Uzi magazine. Stag Arms also did the same thing, and the end result was fabulous.

The uppers for the 9mm lowers are standard uppers, with a few differences, at least from Colt. The Colts lack the hole for the gas tube, and they also lack the clearance inside for the 5.56 cam pin head to cam over. So, a Colt 9mm upper can only ever be a 9mm upper. You can, however, install the 9mm upper parts into an otherwise .223/5.56 upper receiver, and they will work just fine. A 9mm Colt lower can be rebuilt to be a 5.56 lower, which might be why Colt did it that way. You'll have to drive out the cross pins that hold the adapter blocks in place. You'll also have to replace the 9mm bolt catch with a standard .223 catch, as the 9mm catch extends over the top of the rear block. You may or may not get away with using the 9mm-specific hammer if you rebuild your 9 to .223. And why are you doing this, anyway? Most people want to build a .223 into a 9mm, not the other way around.

But you can have both.

So, if you have an AR-15 lower built for .223/5.56, you can also have it as a 9mm PCC. You need the correct buffer and spring, an adapter block and magazines. And you need a complete 9mm upper. But you can have one rifle and two uppers easily with the AR-15.

There might be some disagreement in the trigger system you are using, as the 9mm can be a bit particular about what it will run with. Essentially, the 9mm has a different bolt speed and timing, and some triggers don't play well with 9mm, but that is a minor detail.

The Stag Arms 9mm PCC, with the lower broached to accept Colt 9mm magazines. Rock River did the same thing, and when it was the only choice, it was the best way to build a PCC.

THE 21ST CENTURY PCC

The other option is to go with a pistol magazine. Back when we were starting the PCC experiment (my gun club was the first to do it, as far as I've been able to determine) the largest-capacity pistol magazines you could get were 15 rounds. Yes, the Glocks held 17, but it was new. There were rumored 20-round Browning Hi Power magazines to be had, but no one ever saw one back then.

Then the Assault Weapons Ban hit the firearms

market in 1994. For 10 years, 10-round magazines were it. We used the Colt/Uzi and Sten mags because they were available, and even rather common.

Once the ban ended, suddenly hi-cap magazines were all over the place. And everyone wanted more, regardless of how many a given magazine held. Companies sprang up offering magazine extensions, to increase capacity.

In a few years, a 30-round pistol magazine was a common item seen at gun shops. The stage was set. Heck, ETS makes Glock-compatible magazines in 9mm that hold 40 rounds without the need for a basepad extension.

The first step was to make Glock-specific adapters. Like the Colt ones, they fit into the regular lower, and allowed the use of Glock magazines. But this didn't last long. You see, the making of AR receivers had changed a great deal in the time of the ban. The original method was to take forgings and machine their interiors. The new process was to use CNC machining stations and carve complete receivers from blocks of pre-hardened aluminum.

If you were going to do that, why mess around with adapter blocks? Just machine the lower for the Glock magazines. And if you were going to do that, why make the exterior of the lower big enough to hold a .223 magazine? Suddenly, lowers got changed in shape. They changed to be machined just for pistol magazines, mostly Glocks.

However, you can get them to accept other magazines, such as S&W, Beretta and Sig. Wilson Combat makes models that do that, as do others. And Wilson Combat is proud of its PCCs (and other rifles as well) based on the prices it charges. But what you get for that price is a superlative example of the gun builder's craft.

And to come complete circle, Stern Defense makes adapters that use pistol magazines, again, such as Glock, Sig, S&W and Beretta.

(above) CMMG, as do many others, provides an AR-located magazine release for its PCCs that use Glock magazines.

Stern Defense makes adapters that can utilize a bunch of different pistol magazines. This one is for Glocks, but you can also adapt others.

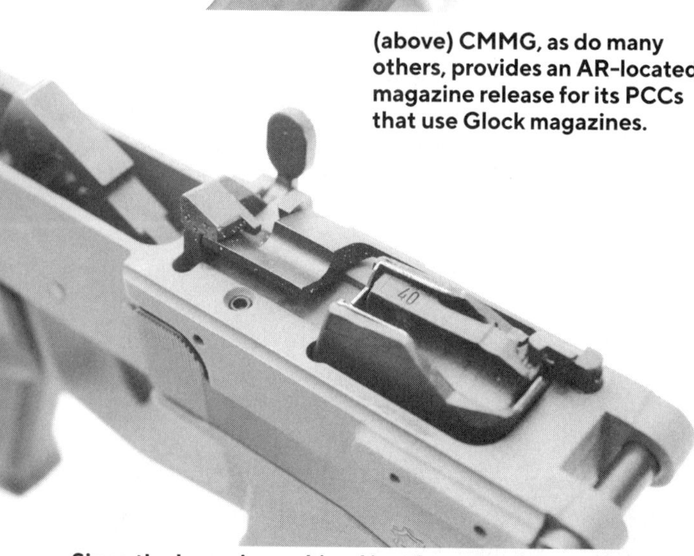

Since the lower is machined just for a pistol magazine, no adapter blocks, the feed geometry is much better than the Colt kludge.

Now, there are some problems. The width of the bottom of the bolt that feeds, called the stripper rail, is proportioned for the magazine it feeds from. A bolt for a Colt, wide enough to feed a staggered-column of 9mm rounds, is too wide to pass through the feed lips of a single-feed pistol magazine.

So, if you are walking through a gun show, and see a 9mm AR bolt lying on the table at a good price, take a look at the bottom front edge of the bolt face. The part of the bolt that feeds is called the stripper rail, and it is either wide enough to feed reliably from a double-feed magazine, or narrow, to feed from the single-point magazine.

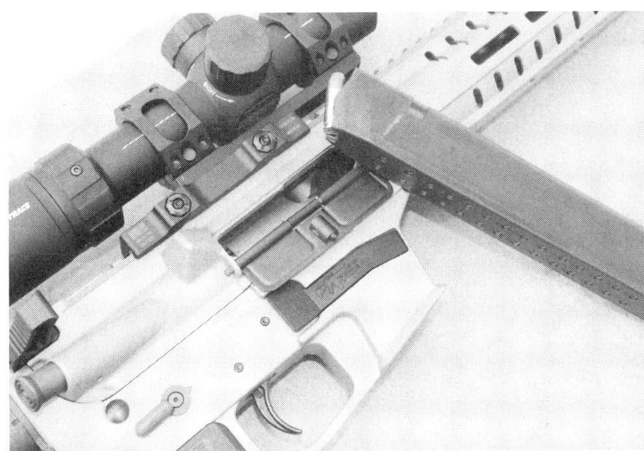

With billet-cut receivers, a product of CNC machining, we can have pistol-magazine-specific lowers, and life is not just good, it is great.

You have to be aware of the difference between the two types of 9mm bolts for the AR-15. On the left is the single-point magazine bolt, and on the right is the double-feed. The left one is for pistol magazines (and Sten mags) and the right is for Colt/Uzi magazines.

MAXIM DEFENSE

The Maxim Defense bolt, part of its 9mm PCC.

In addition to making very cool, very compact ARs in rifle calibers, Maxim Defense makes 9mm-specific PCCs, not adapted 5.56 firearms. The heart of these is the company's own bolt. Making bolts is a big deal.

SOME IS GOOD, MORE IS BETTER

If you want more than what the factory offers, then you need extended-capacity basepads. One option is to go to Taylor Freelance, and just add more. Robin Taylor machines Delrin and aluminum extensions, and they can add one, two, five and even 10-plus rounds to a magazine.

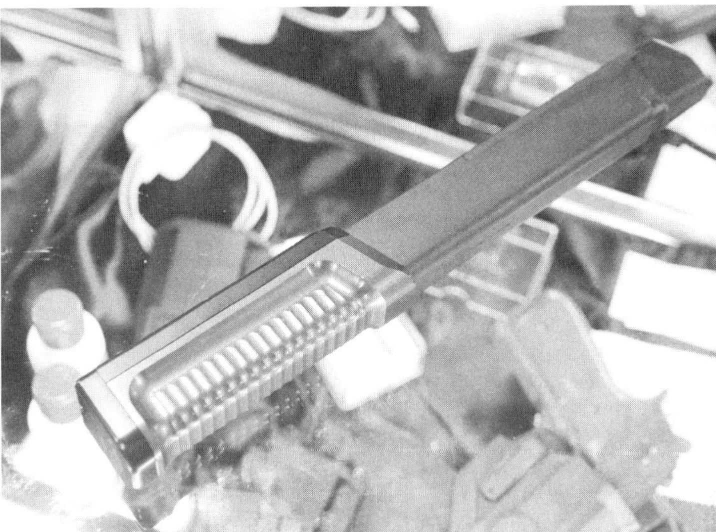

The Taylor Freelance mega-extension Glock mag, which gobbles up an entire box of ammo.

One I call the mega-extension adds more than 10 rounds to a Glock 9mm magazine. You end up with a magazine that holds an entire box of ammo.

You can also hunt down and install magazine extensions from Taran Butler at Taran Tactical, Arredondo and ZR Tactical.

CMMG

OK, just when it seems like everyone has things all figured out, CMMG comes along and does something different. It has approached the PCC magazine problem from an entirely different angle. Why modify the lower receiver, when you can just use a regular AR magazine?

The method was to design and manufacture a new set of internals for the AR-15 magazine, but the new internals hold and feed 9mm. Yes, why block the magazine well when you can block the inside of the magazine? Also available as complete magazines, the CMMG 9mm magazines are the same size as regular

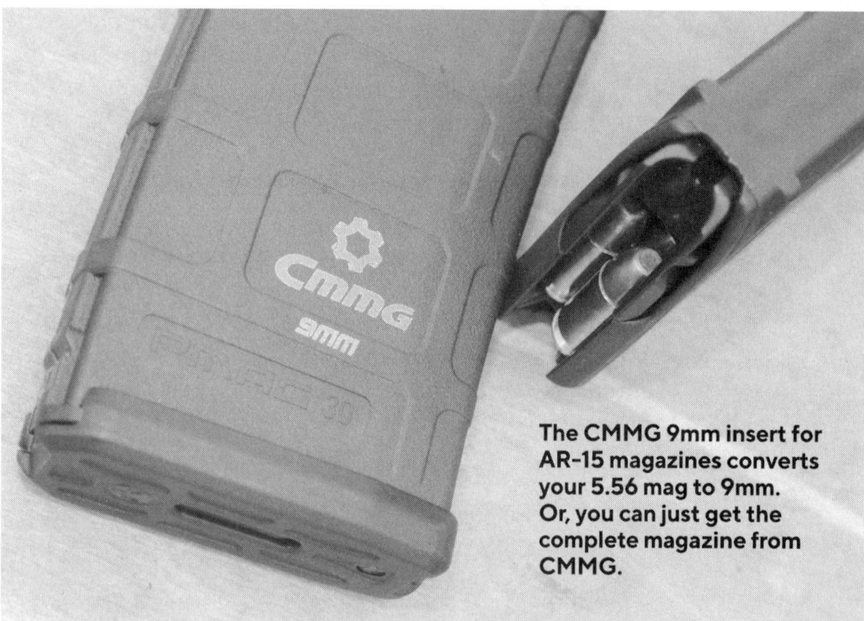

The CMMG 9mm insert for AR-15 magazines converts your 5.56 mag to 9mm. Or, you can just get the complete magazine from CMMG.

AR mags because the external tube is an AR magazine. As a result, they will fit your mag pouches or web-gear mag storage.

This raises the same problem that some of the other calibers have: keeping magazines organized. Just as you want to keep your 6.5 and 6.8 magazines straight, and separate from your 5.56 magazines, now you'll have to do the same with your 9mm mags. It would really be a bummer to get to the range and find the mags you have aren't the right ones for the rifle you brought.

This potential problem was solved just over a century ago, by the Imperial German Army, which was buying as many Mauser C96 pistols as Mauser could make. (And anyone else who made pistols, for that matter.) The problem was, the customary C96 chambering was 7.63x25 Mauser. The Army wanted 9mm pistols. It had enough problems as it was, and didn't want to have the headache of two different pistol cartridges to supply to the trenches.

So, the C96 pistols provided for the army had a large numeral 9 routed into the grips, and the 9 was painted red. And so, they were called "Red Nine" Mausers.

Paint your CMMG magazines with a big red "9" and you can use the same terminology.

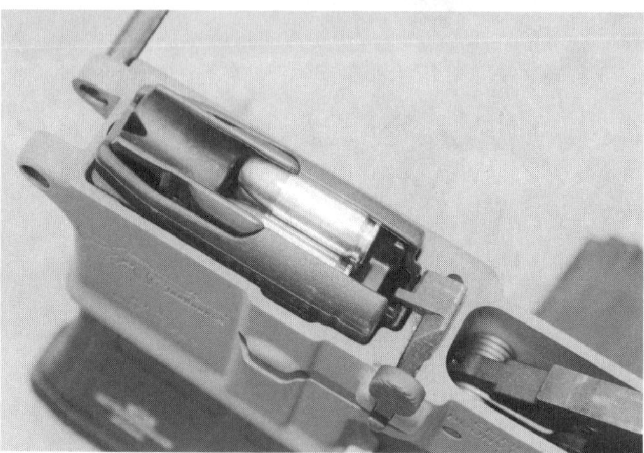
Here you see how the CMMG insert fits in the magazine and provides a feed ramp for the cartridge.

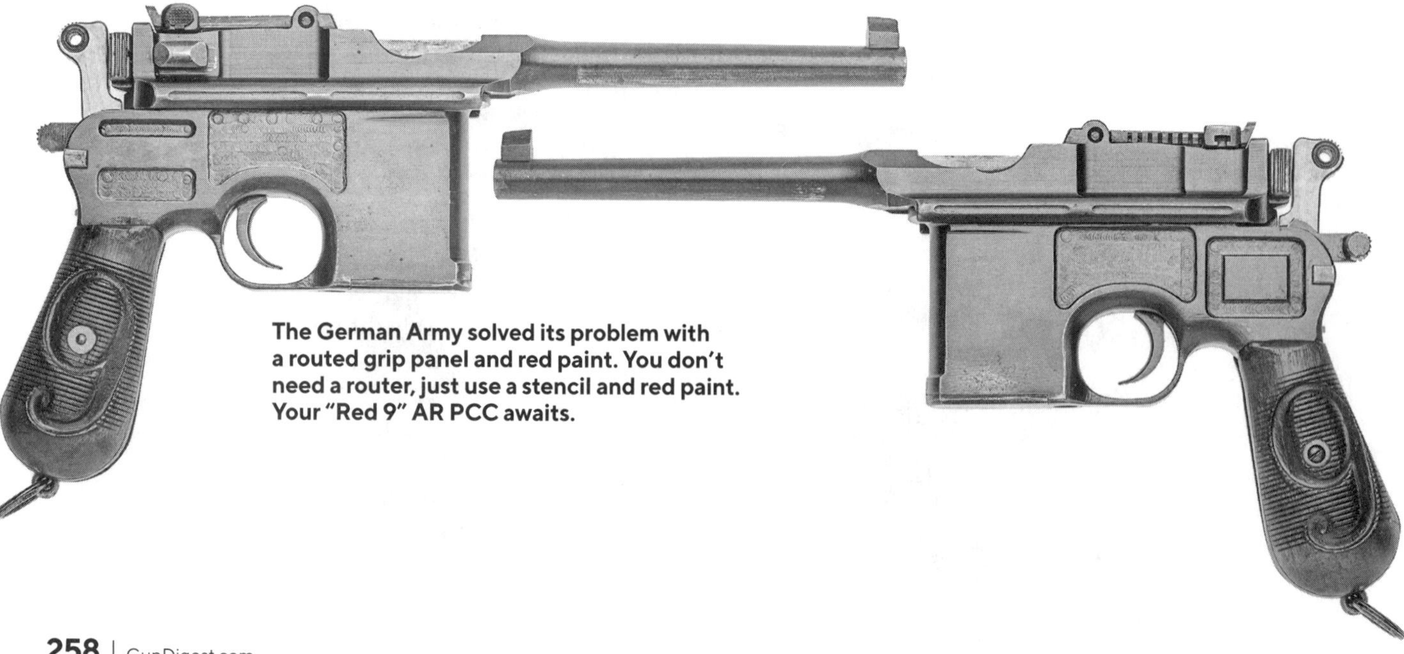
The German Army solved its problem with a routed grip panel and red paint. You don't need a router, just use a stencil and red paint. Your "Red 9" AR PCC awaits.

MR. DIFFERENT

There always has to be someone different. And that someone here is the designers at Sig. Their MPX, the pistol-caliber version of their line, is a 9mm. They promised a .40 as the second one, but soon after the MPX was announced, and while Sig was doing the engineering work on a conversion design, the FBI essentially killed any .40 development. The Sig plan was to have a lower that could use any 9mm, .40 or .357 Sig MPX upper, and use the same magazines as well, and you could swap uppers, or even just barrel assemblies. Clever engineering, a cool idea, and now dead because the FBI can't teach the troops to shoot "hard kicking" .40-caliber pistols. What a shame.

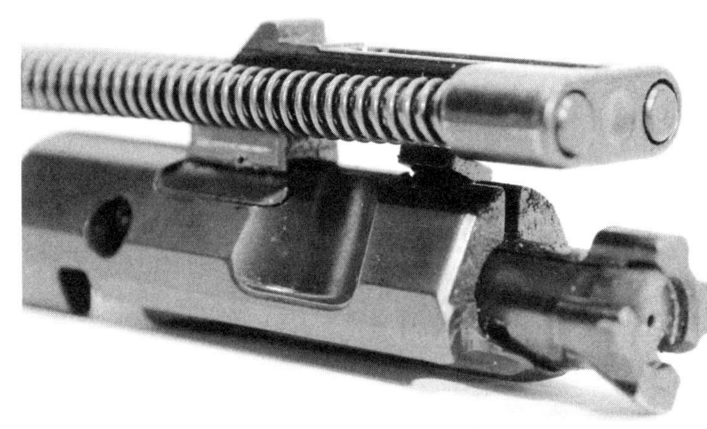

(above) The MPX is a locked-breech, gas-piston system, which explains why it is so soft in recoil compared to other PCCs.

The Sig MPX offers a really soft-recoiling 9mm, with magazine options, and while it isn't an AR, it looks close enough that we'll call it one for this book. The middle magazine has a Taylor Freelance magazine extension on it.

The MPX isn't really an AR-15, since nothing, and I mean nothing, will interchange with an AR-15 of any stripe. But the design is based on the AR-15, it looks kinda like one, and for all intents and purposes, it is one.

Oh, and it isn't a blowback system. The MPX is a piston-driven, locked-breech, pistol-caliber carbine. What that does is soften the bouncy recoil of the 9mm blowback system since there isn't nearly as much mass cycling back and forth on each and every shot.

And even more interesting, the piston system shrugs off the use of lead bullets, at least properly lubricated, hard-cast bullets.

It is too bad the .40 conversion never happened, because a .357 Sig, piston-driven PCC would be a marvelous thing.

And if the MPX is just a big too big for you, Sig offers the Copperhead. This is a pistol that is listed (curiously enough) in the Sig rifle section of its catalog. But with an arm brace on it, it is still a pistol, and it is the most compact braced 9mm pistol to be had. It is far enough appearing from the AR that it is hard to call it an AR, but it uses the same magazines as the MPX. Since the MPX is an AR for this book, so is the Copperhead.

The smallest AR-like 9mm PCC you can lay hands on, the Sig Copperhead is almost cute.

CLEVERLY DIFFERENT

CMMG came up with a way to have a locked breech and a blowback system in the same firearm. Its radial bolt operates in a clever way. The locking lugs are not square across the back of the lugs. The bolt has the back of each lug machined at an angle. When the CMMG bolt closes, it rotates just like a regular AR-15 does. But the lug angles do not provide an immovable lockup.

When you fire the CMMG, the thrust of the case on the bolt has the effect of camming the angled face of the lugs off of the locking lugs in the barrel extension. The camming movement has to push the carrier back, and push the hammer, which is resting against the carrier.

The camming and movement soak up enough of the energy of the case thrust that recoil is reduced, compared to a straight blowback system. There's still enough energy to cycle the bolt and carrier, and strip off the next round being fed. But the jolt of the cycling parts bottoming out in the buffer tube isn't there, as it often is in the 9mm blowbacks.

While it does call for a carrier and bolt design, like the .223 AR, it does not require a gas tube, piston or gas system.

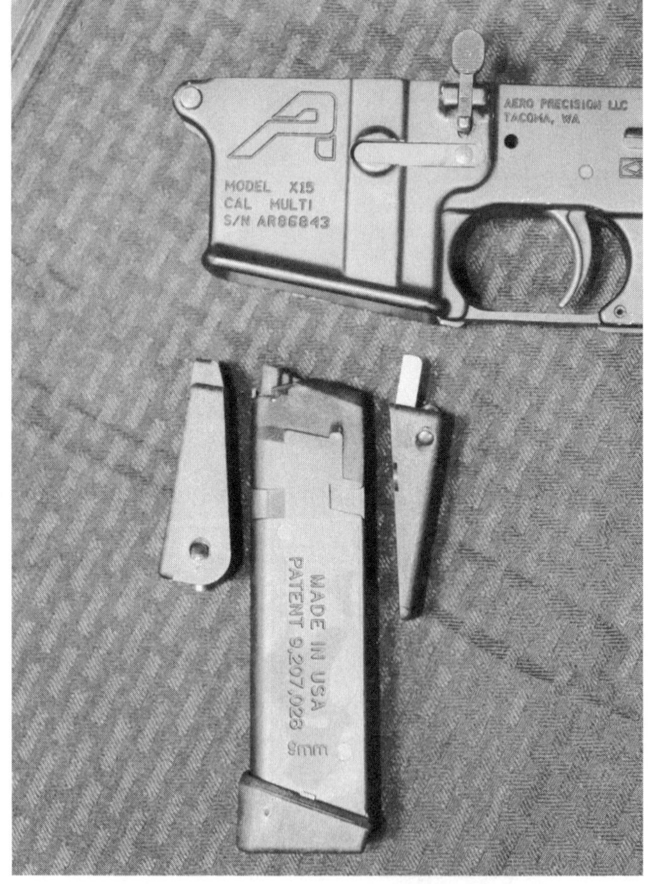

Here are the parts of the TorkMag conversion, ready to go into an AR lower.

TORKMAG

TorkMag makes adapters that fit a regular AR lower, but accommodate pistol magazines. The original was the Magdapt, a system that lets you use Glock 9mm (and .40) magazines, with the appropriate upper. Well, the company has gone a step further, now offering the Magdapt 1911, which fits 1911 magazines to your AR-15 lower, and you can thus feed it .45 or 10mm. And, to make sure no one is left behind, TorkMag offers it with a 10mm barrel should you choose. You can build with the TorkMag barrel, or acquire a complete upper.

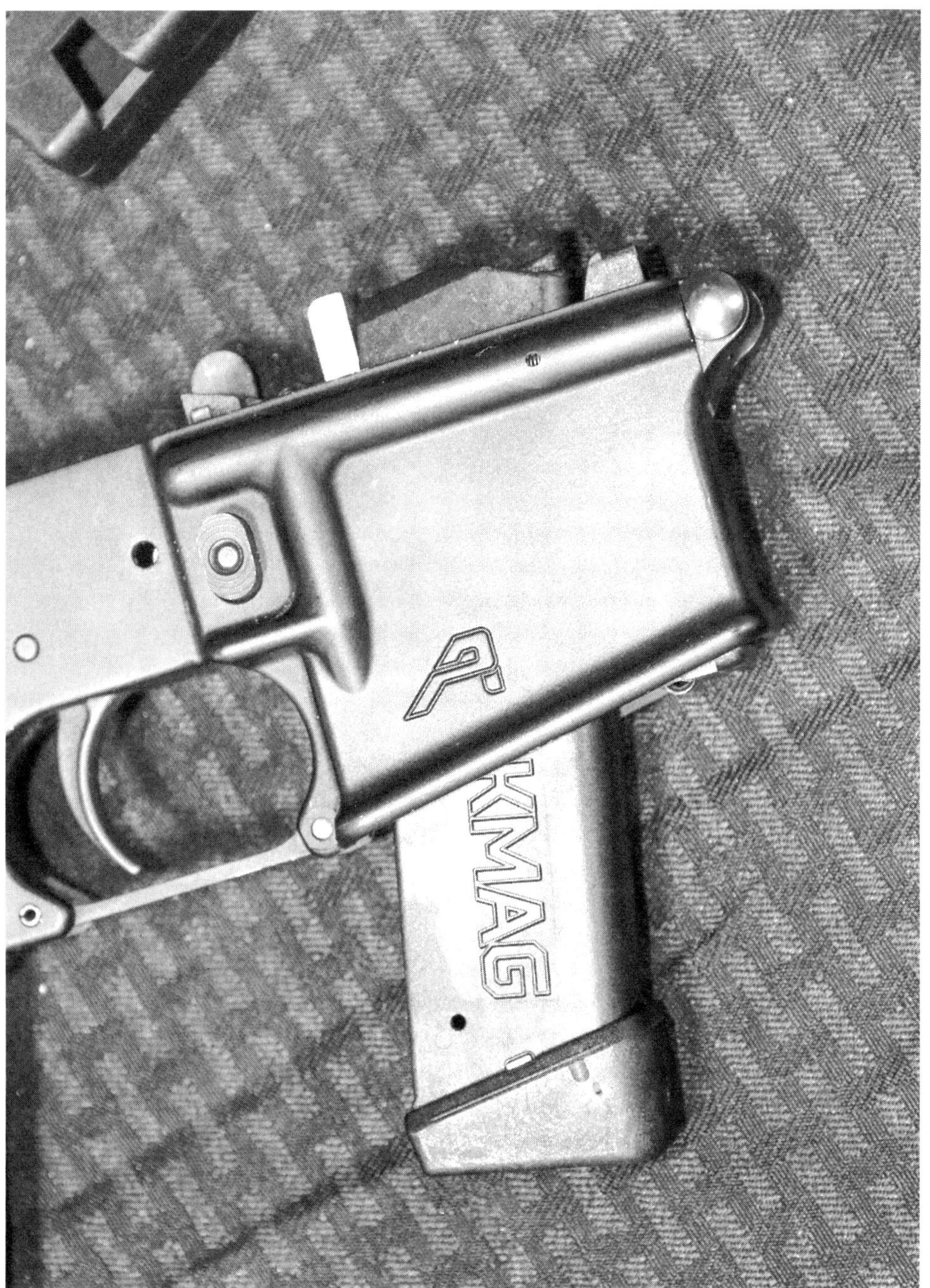

The TorkMag installed, and now available for 1911, in .45 and 10mm.

CALIBERS

The big one in number of users is the 9mm. The reasons should be obvious: Low recoil, low cost, low noise and the easiest mechanics to work out. Also, the head start of having SMG magazines to use to build the earliest PCCs with.

The blowback system of the AR-15 in 9mm means you can't do a lot to boost velocities, but the barrel length will do some of that for you. Also, the combustion chamber, the volume of the case under the bullet, is so small in the 9mm that you can't get much more powder in there than what it uses for pistol-like velocities.

Back when I was first working on the PCC, with Olympic conversions and Sten magazines, I noticed an interesting thing: Sten magazines are longer internally than the 9mm Parabellum cartridge needs. One could even fit a .38 Super in there. Alas, the dynamics of a blowback PCC in .38 Super, at anything more than the velocities of a 9mm, just didn't work out. I'm almost afraid to compare the internals of the Sig MPX magazine, just in case a Super would fit. That would be an R&D rabbit hole, I'm sure.

For use in competition, shooters follow one of two paths. They find the cheapest 9mm ammo in bulk, that runs reliably and accurately in their PCC, and just buy it. The cost between buying and loading is not as great as it used to be. A quick search for ammunition turns up $180 for 1,000 rounds for factory 9mm.

Doing the same for components to reload, I come up with $90 to $100 for 1,000 jacketed bullets, and $75 for hard-cast. Of the loaded-ammo cost, powder runs you $10 to $11 for the amount needed to load 9mm. Primers cost $27 per 1,000.

These are all calculated on large-volume purchases: 5,000 bullets, 5,000 primers, eight-pound kegs of powder. Smaller units will drive up the per-thousand cost.

So, the components cost (we are assuming you are using free brass, because there is no lack of empty 9mm at most gun ranges and clubs) your reloaded ammo costs you $113 per 1,000 rounds. Now, the price difference between $180 and $113 is not nothing. But, you have to invest in reloading equipment to get that price break, and it takes a year or so to get the investment back.

There's also time. At 500 rounds per hour loading rate, 1,000 rounds takes two hours. You are paying yourself $33 an hour to load ammo. But, that might be time away from your family. And an hour spent working overtime could make up the $33 and then some, depending on what work is. That's why some people do not reload, but buy new ammo.

However, the reason competition shooters reload ammo isn't just cost. (But it does add up. If you shoot 10,000 rounds a year in practice and

This CMMG chambered in .40 caliber is a great little pistol. And with the longer barrel an AR pistol provides, the .40 is a lot more robust. Too bad the FBI is killing the .40 just when it has found a home.

competition, you have saved $670 from the cost of new ammo.) No, they do it to tune the ammo to their PCC. To develop a load that just barely, with a margin of comfort, exceeds the required power factor, shoots tight groups, and offers the softest possible recoil. They reload for competitive advantage.

.40 S&W

The .40 caliber had its day in the sun. In pistols, it over-promised and under-delivered. I find it ironic that just when we find the best platform for the .40, the PCC, the .40 is shoved off the stage for the 9mm. The heavier bullet of the .40 gets a bit of a boost in longer PCC barrels, and the added recoil is not excessive for that gain.

An AR pistol, in .40, with an eight-inch barrel, offers more bullet weight than a 9mm, and more velocity than a .40 pistol. Combine that with the CMMG rotating bolt (or the Sig piston, had it ever offered it) and you have an increase in power without oppressive recoil.

10MM

If the PCC boosts the .40, it turbo-boosts the 10mm. The longer case of the 10mm allows for not just more powder, but slower-burning powder, and the 10mm in a PCC can show an impressive boost in velocity. Now, in a straight blowback system, the 10mm is going to be a thumper. As in, thump your shoulder and face. However, in the CMMG system, and (I hope they are listening) a Sig-like system, with a piston and metered gas flow, the 10mm would thump harder on the front end than on the back end.

As a brief aside, I had a day at the range with one of the fabled FBI 10mm MP5/10 subguns. Those who know of the MP5 might not know how it works. When the bolt is closed, two roller bearings are pressed out by the bolt carrier, and rest in recesses in the receiver. When you shoot one, the bolt thrust, by means of an angled, arrow-shaped cam called the locking piece, pushes the carrier back, allows the roller bearings to roll into the bolt assembly, and the assembly then slides (actually, is blown) back, cycling the firearm.

The angle of the cam determines how quickly the action opens and cycles.

The urban legend has it that the MP5/10 was received with a cool disdain because it wasn't reliable with all 10mm loadings. I don't know about the FBI and its attitude, but I can tell you from experience that having the wrong-angled locking piece in the bolt assembly was a problem. With the low-recoil locking piece and full-power ammo, brass disappeared over the side berm. With the full-power locking piece and low recoil ammo, the MP5/10 would not always reliably cycle.

Such is the burden of high-tech engineering.

Since the FBI could not settle on one particular 10mm power level, it was faced with a problem: SMG-specific ammo, or 10mm ammo that worked in everything. It "settled" the matter by dropping the 10mm pistols. The 10mm HKs languished in inventory for some time before being destroyed.

That's right, we taxpayers paid to buy them, and then paid to have them destroyed.

.45 ACP

Oh, how everyone wanted a .45 PCC back in the old days. Just as we were fixated on the .308 as *the* rifle caliber, the .45 was the one and only paragon of PCC desire. There was only one problem: It didn't play well with the AR-15. The most common .45 magazine of capacity was the one used in the M3 "Grease" gun, the American SMG. Unfortunately, the M3 magazine was too wide for the AR-15 receiver magazine well. There was a polymer lower made a couple of decades back, from Cavalry Arms. It was a one-piece affair, with stock and pistol grip all one piece. It had the magazine well molded with expansion slots, room for an M3 magazine.

The other novel feature of the CAV-15 lower was the manufacturing method. The shell was made by molding two halves, and then Cavalry Arms welded the two together via a linear vibration welding process, to create a finished receiver.

That was during the great "in-between" time. By then we were done with the idea of .45 PCCs, but not yet ready for the idea of polymer AR lowers.

I did build up one .45 ACP AR-15 that worked, but it was picky about functioning. This was offered for a short while by Olympic, and it utilized the .45 ACP Uzi magazines. Where 9mm Uzi magazines were relatively common (more than the Colt magazines, actually) the .45 Uzi magazines were as rare as hen's teeth. They were also single-point feed magazines, which isn't a problem feeding, but is a problem loading. And last, the magazines were short, internally. Not all factory 230 FMJ ammunition would even fit into the magazine, let alone feed.

It was definitely a reload-or-bust proposition. I bought the parts to build one, built it, tested it, lost my ardor for it, and yet cannot remember selling it.

Usually, those of us who are into firearms can remember to whom, and even when, we sold any firearm we ever owned. And hold grudges for those

CMMG offers its radial-lock PCC in .45, and if you have always wanted a .45 carbine, then now's your chance.

This JP Enterprises PCC is the apex competition tool. You won't see many of them this clean, because competition shooters will do anything to gain an advantage.

JP Enterprises firearms come in bright colors. This one is Robin's-Egg Blue, and shoots like a house afire.

that didn't hold up their end of the bargain. I cannot remember selling that AR. I suspect I sold it to a particular gun-club member, but he is now long dead, so I can't ask him.

Anyway, it was not what we expected, nor what we desired.

CMMG is offering its radial-lock PCC in .45 ACP, using Glock magazines. That's the stuff of wishes and desires.

The current AR-like .45 PCC is actually a subgun, made by LWRC. As a select-fire firearm, it is beyond any of us ever owning one. However, if LWRC ever offers a semi-auto-only version, either pistol or carbine, we will finally have the .45 PCC we wished for back in the good old days.

COMPETITION AND DEFENSE

As mentioned, my club was one of the first, if not the very first, to do PCC as an entry in USPSA matches. It proved to be so much fun we had to get organized. Shooters would sign up for both, but they had to shoot their handgun first. No way was anyone going to compromise club standings, competition for Nationals slots, or payback, by letting someone practice-run the stage with a PCC.

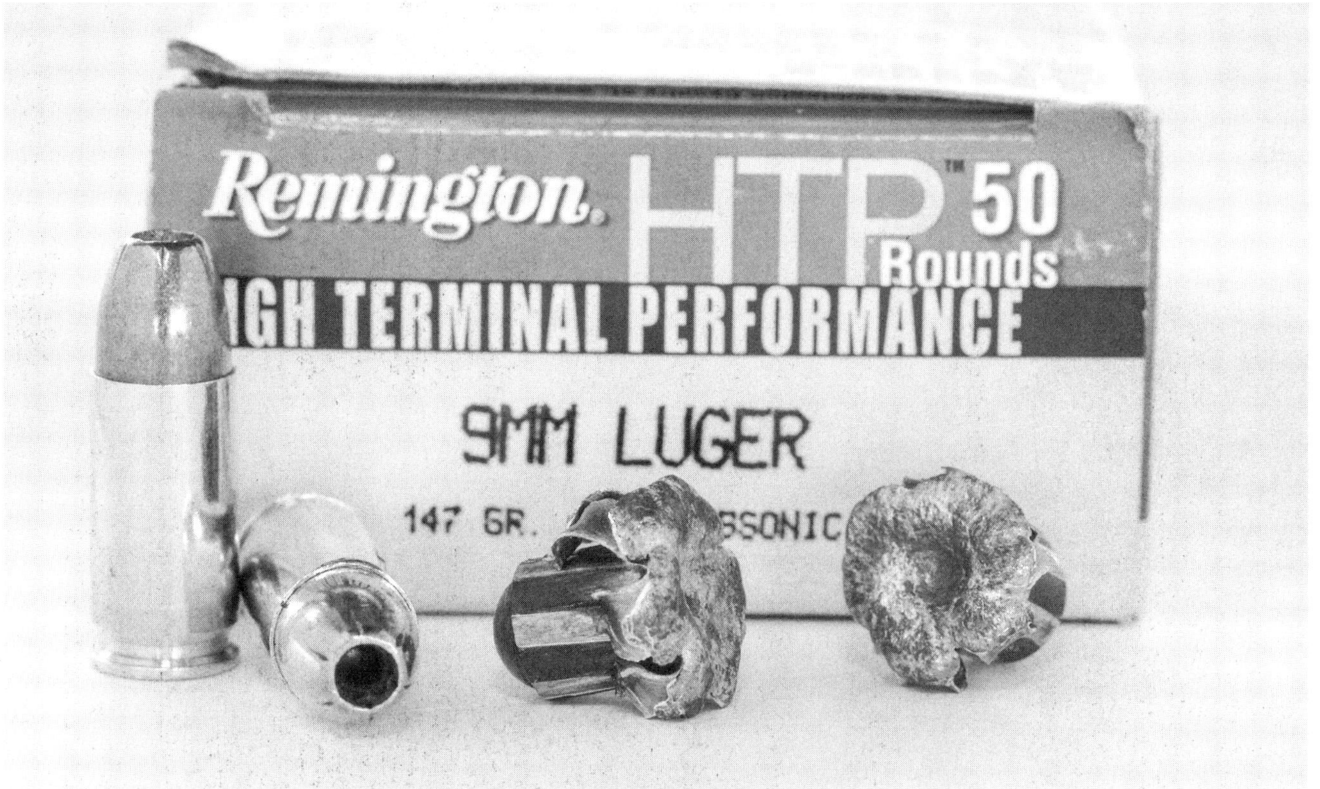

A 9mm PCC offers this kind of terminal performance, but with less recoil and muzzle blast than a rifle.

So, each of us worked up a belt arrangement that allowed us to wear a holster and spare mag pouches for our handgun, and also have a spare mag for the PCC some place.

You'd sign up twice, handgun and PCC. You'd gear up, and then arrange handgun and handgun mags. You'd shoot the stage as you would normally. Then, the PCC entrants would divest themselves of handguns and handgun mags, put a PCC mag on their belts, and shoot the stage. This was faster than shooting the whole match with handgun, then going back and doing it again with the PCC.

It could get unwieldy, however, since each such shooter took twice as much time in the squad. If you had a squad of ten shooters, but four were also PCC, that meant you really had a 14-shooter squad. The match director had to be a tyrant in keeping squads balanced, or else eight guys who were buddies would all want to be on the same squad, and all shoot handgun and PCC. The rest of the squads would stack up behind that slow-going squad.

Now that it is its own division, clubs have to work out if shooters can double-enter. Based on my experience of our growth back then, a small club can. Once your club matches get to be a certain size, you have to draw the line: pick one.

The advantages of the PCC in defense are many. It offers less recoil, noise, blast and flash, compared to a .223 AR. It is also absurdly easy to suppress. That makes it easier to handle for a new shooter, or one who isn't a dedicated shooter. The one drawback is penetration. Not of people, there the various 9mms are fine. No, it is structures.

A friend of mine who ran a multi-jurisdictional SWAT team, once had an opportunity to test everything on structures. A neighborhood was going to be razed, and they had time enough to test everything on walls. His summary: "If it is a handgun bullet, of any kind, it is leaving the building unless there is a brick veneer."

Keep that in mind.

COMPETITION LOOKS

Now, you will read the catalogs, and see many very tricked-out PCCs. When you go to your local USPSA match, to see about shooting in a match with a PCC, you will be shocked. Few competitors will

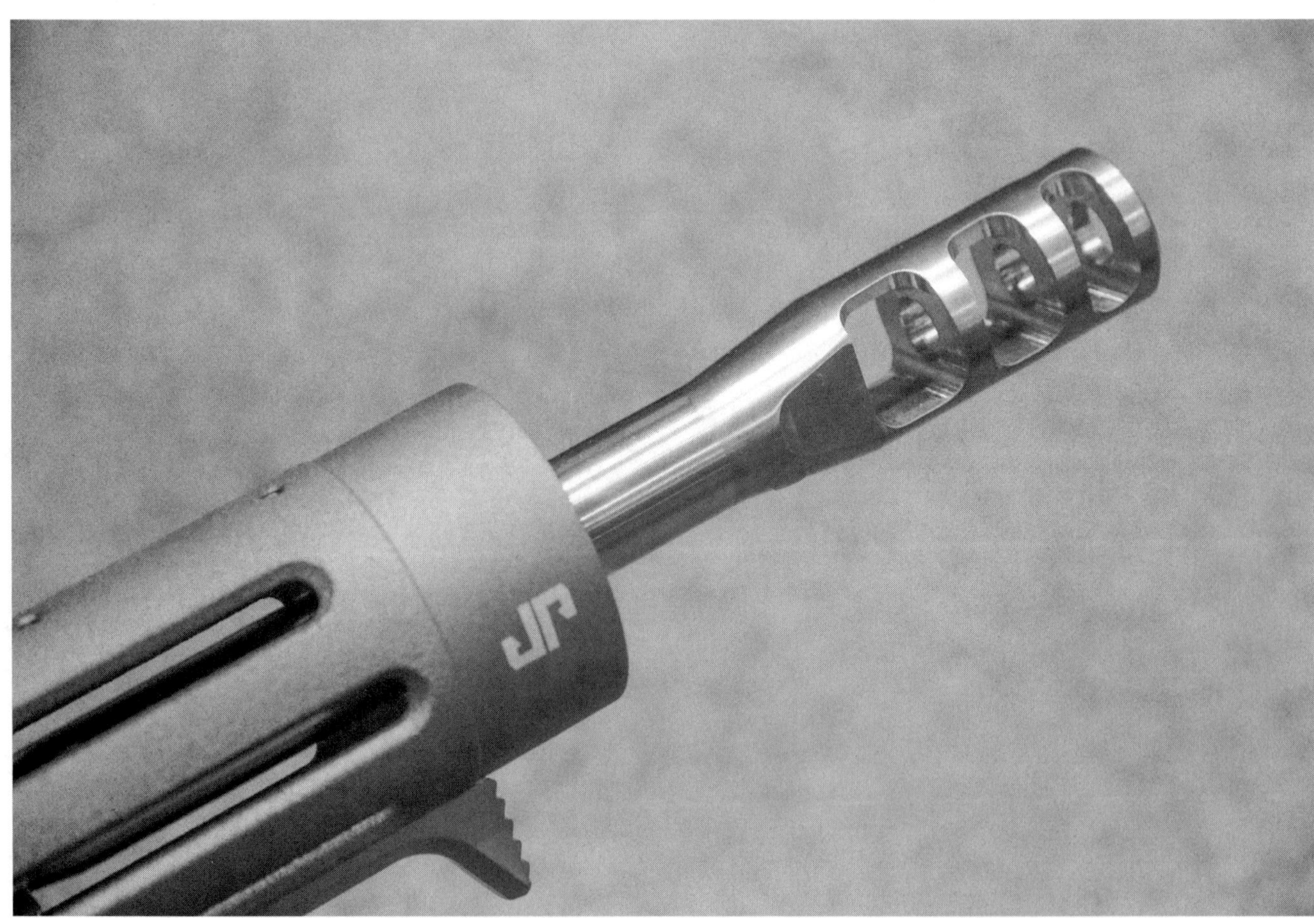

If you want a brake on your PCC, install a brake on your PCC. Just don't kid yourself that it makes much of a difference, if any.

have blinged-out, tricked-out, pristine PCCs like in the catalogs. That is because they are competitors. Competition shooters, if the match winner showed up with a PCC that he was dragging behind his car, would start doing the same. OK, an exaggeration. But, competition shooters are more than willing to pull a perfectly good part off and replace it with something that will give them even the smallest extra advantage.

That's why many of them use PCCs that look like they were built from parts bought at garage sales. Mismatched by brand, color, texture? Who cares? Does it help you win? Then go for it.

BRAKES

It is common now to offer AR-15s with muzzle brakes on them. On the rifle calibers, it can be anywhere from useful to a very good idea. In 9mm, not so much. The "uncorking" pressure, the residual pressure left in the bore just as the bullet exits the barrel, in a 5.56 can be substantial. As much as 17,000 PSI in a 5.56 carbine shooting real-deal 5.56 ammo.

In a 9mm, it can be so small it is only good for making noise. A little quick arithmetic will show this. The Ideal Gas law tells us that pressure is directly inverse to volume. Double the volume, you get half the pressure. So, we take (just as an estimate) the volume of a 9mm case, and we expand that to the volume of the bore of a 16-inch barrel. We come up with 1,710 PSI, if the 9mm load is the pressure max of 36,000 PSI. So, one-tenth that of a 5.56 carbine.

There just isn't much gas there to make a difference.

So why do competition PCCs often have muzzle brakes on them? As above, it is the attitude "every advantage, real or imagined" that drives many competition shooters. If you think it helps, it probably does. And if you take it off, it won't make any difference.

COULDA-BEENS

OK, back almost two decades ago, it looked like we were going to have the East Coast sagging from the volume of ex-Warsaw Pact materiel being imported. Gun shows were stacked with AK ammo. Well, 7.62x39 ammo. The 5.45x39 was just starting

When it looked like there was going to be shiploads of 7.63x25 surplus ammo, the idea of an AR chambered in that was really attractive. Now, we can only dream.

The KelTec Sub-2000 was an approach to building a 9mm (and .40) PCC that didn't involve an AR-15 receiver set. And it folds in half, right ahead of the trigger guard.

to come in. But it promised to be another tsunami of ammo.

And then there was the 7.63x25. The Tokarev ammo. We had visions of shiploads of that coming over. After all, the Soviets had kept the TT-33, the Tokarev pistols, in storage, along with their various submachine guns, because, well, that's what you do when you think the whole world is out to get you.

It was going to be glorious.

And then it wasn't. The first shiploads of 7.63x25 came in, and we snapped it up. And then it trickled in, and then it was done. You see, the Soviets hadn't really been keeping the 7.63x25 arsenals in production, not as soon as they got the AK and Makarov production spooled up. There was some, but nothing like the AK ammo supply. As their need for 7.63x25 ammo slacked off, they switched arsenal production over to 7.62x39.

But in the early heady days, when it looked like things were going to be great, Marty ter Weeme of Teppo Jutsu made an AR PCC in 7.63x25. Just when he had all the bugs worked out (he even had heavy-bullet, subsonic loads ready) we found out that there wasn't going to be a tidal wave of commie pistol ammo coming. Rats.

OTHER OPTIONS

The Marlin Camp Carbine fell by the wayside, in part because of its operational problems, but also because Marlin just didn't know what to do with it.

Right in the middle of the Assault Weapons Ban, KelTec came out with the Sub-2000. This isn't an AR by any means, but it is a PCC. And it uses pistol magazines. The big trick is, it folds in the middle, and cannot be fired when folded. That means it avoids the too-short problem most folders have. Too short as in not legal length to be a rifle.

Another approach is the Mech Tech conversion. This is a complete upper assembly that has a stock attached. You take your pistol and remove the upper assembly from it, and plug the receiver of your handgun into the Mech Tech. They offer three models, the XD/XDM, the Glock and the 1911. The 1911 also works with the wide-body 1911 clones like the STI, as well as classic single-stack frames. You have a choice of calibers (obviously you'll have to get a Mech Tech upper in the caliber of your pistol, so the magazines will work) and build options.

This is not an AR, so why do it? If you already have a pistol in the caliber you want, then you can keep using the same magazines and ammunition. You have the same trigger that you are used to on your pistol. And you can get into PCC competition for less than the cost of an AR-15 in 9mm.

The KelTec uses pistol magazines. This one is in 9mm, and uses Glock magazines. You have choices of other pistol magazines and other calibers.

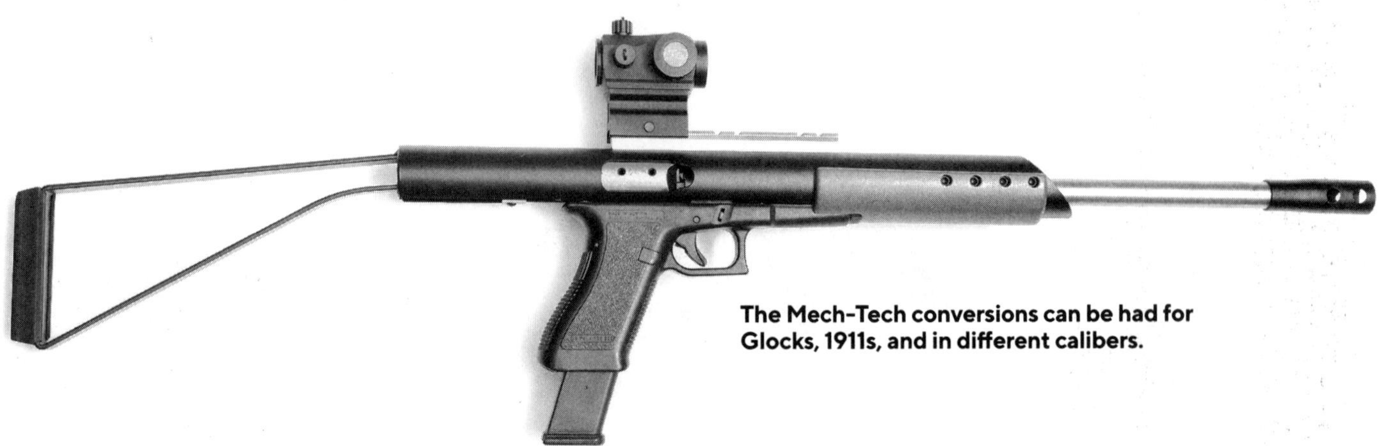

The Mech-Tech conversions can be had for Glocks, 1911s, and in different calibers.

A last option is the Hi Point. A fellow gun writer summed up the Hi Point line thusly: "They work right out of the box. The handguns work until they break, and the company will fix them. The carbines never break." Snicker if you will, but there's a mom in Detroit who swears by the Hi Point. Three men kicked in her door one cold winter night. She drove them off in a hail of Hi Point carbine fire, and even drove off one of them again, one who foolhardily came back for more.

PCCs get the job done.

In 1986, when I read that article on the Colt 9mm, I had no idea of the future. I didn't know that I would be a gunsmith for more than another decade, a competition shooter who rubbed elbows with the match winners. That I would be building, experimenting, designing, modifying and developing the AR-15. That I would be soaking up all the firearms knowledge I could, and have it stashed in my head. I hadn't a clue that I would become a writer, meet Frank James and call him a friend. And I had no idea of the sadness I'd feel, at hearing of his passing in the fall of 2015.

Often, when I peruse an AR PCC in the rack, I recall Frank and his willingness, nay even sometimes eagerness, to speak the truth as he saw it. Truth is, PCCs rock. And if you don't have one, you are really missing out on some fun.

A last option is the Hi Point. A fellow gun writer summed up the Hi Point line thusly: "They work right out of the box. The handguns work until they break, and the company will fix them. The carbines never break."

No, it isn't an AR-15. But not everyone gets a PCC for competition, or wants to spend a mortgage payment or two for protection. Hi Point carbines work, and work and work.

SUPPLIERS

AAC
1816 Remington Circle SW
North Dock Bay F
Huntsville, AL 35824
www.advancedarmament.com

Alexander Arms
U.S. Army, Radford Arsenal
P.O. Box 1
Radford, VA 24143
www.alexanderarms.com

AR57
www.57center.com

Armalite
525 E. Pinnacle Peak Road, STE 100
Phoenix, AZ 85024
www.armalite.com

Bear Creek Arsenal
310 McNeill Road
Sanford, NC 27330
www.bearcreekarsenal.com

Big Horn Armory
774 Road 2AB
Cody, WY 82414
www.bighornarmory.com

Black Dog Machine
9986 Cherry Lane
Nampa, ID 83687
www.blackdogmachine.net

Black Hills Ammunition
P.O. Box 3090
Rapid City, SD 57709
www.black-hills.com

Brownells
3006 Brownells Parkway
Grinnell, IA 50112
www.brownells.com

Circle 10
www.circle10ak.com

CMMG
P.O. Box 68
Boonville, MO 65233
www.cmmginc.com

Colt Manufacturing
P.O. Box 1868
Hartford, CT 06144
www.colt.com

Daniel Defense
101 Warfighter Way
Black Creek, GA 31308
www.danieldefense.com

Dillon Precision
8009 E. Dillon's Way
Scottsdale, AZ 85260
www.dillonprecision.com

DPMS
www.dpmsinc.com

Federal
www.federalpremium.com

FN
P.O. Box 9424
McLean, VA 22102
www.fnamerica.com

Garrow Firearms Development
www.garrowdev.com

Hornady
3625 West Old Potash Hwy.
Grand Island, NE 68803
www.hornady.com

International Firearms Corp.
www.internationalfirearmscorporation.com

JP Enterprises
P.O. Box 378
Hugo, MN 55038
www.jprifles.com

Knight's Armament
www.knightarmco.com

LaRue
850 CR 177
Leander, TX 78641
www.larue.com

KelTec
1505 Cox Road
Cocoa, FL 32926
www.keltecweapons.com

Les Baer Custom
1804 Iowa Drive
LeClaire, IA 52753
www.lesbaer.com

LMT
1600 E. Leonard Court
Eldridge, IA 52748
www.lmtdefense.com

LWRCI
www.lwrci.com

Lyman Products
475 Smith St.
Middletown, CT 06457
www.lymanproducts.com

Magpul
www.magpul.com

Maxim Defense
1265 Kuhn Drive STE 100
St. Cloud, MN 56301
www.maximdefense.com

Mech-Tech
P.O. Box 43815
Phoenix, AZ 85080
www.firearmsystems.net

Michiguns Ltd.
www.m-guns.com

Nemo Arms
2820 Brandt Ave.
Nampa, ID 83687
www.nemoarms.com

Nosler
107 SW Columbia St.
Bend, OR 97702
www.nosler.com

Olympic Arms
www.olyarms.com

Phoenix Weaponry
504 North 2nd Ave.
P.O. Box 1828
Berthoud, CO 80513
www.phoenixweaponry.com

POF
www.pof-usa.com

Remington
www.remington.com

Rise Armament
1605 E. Iola St.
Broken Arrow, OK 74012
www.risearmament.com

Rock Island Armory
150 North Smart Way
Pahrump, NV 89060
www.armscor.com

Rock River Arms
1042 Cleveland Road
Colona, IL 61241
www.rockriverarms.com

SAAMI
www.saami.org

Safety Harbor Firearms
www.safetyharborfirearms.com

SBR Ammunition
140 Indigo Drive
Brunswick, GA 31525
www.458socomammo.com

Sharps Rifle Co.
1195 U.S. Highway 20-26-87
Glenrock, WY 82637
www.srcarms.com

Sig Sauer
72 Pease Blvd.
Newington, NH 03801
www.sigsauer.com

Smith & Wesson
2100 Roosevelt Ave.
Springfield, MA 01104
www.smith-wesson.com

Springfield Armory
420 West Main St.
Geneseo, IL 61254
www.springfield-armory.com

SSK Industries
590 Woodvue Lane
Wintersville, OH 43953
www.sskindustries.com

Stern Defense
20780 Suite A, State Route JJ
Summersville, MO 65571
www.getstern.com

Sturm, Ruger Co.
www.ruger.com

Taylor Freelance
2559 Woodbine Place
Bellingham, WA 98229
www.taylorfreelance.com

Torkmag
www.torkmag.com

Wilson Combat
2452 CR 719
Berryville, AR 72616
www.wilsoncombat.com

Winchester
www.winchester.com

Wolf Ammunition
P.O. Box 757
Placentia, CA 92871
www.wolfammo.com